THE ENCYCLOPEDIA OF SIKHISM

THE ENCYCLOPEDIA OF SIKHISM

(Over 1000 entries)

by
Dr. H.S. SINGHA

Hemkunt

© Hemkunt Publishers (P) Ltd.

First Published 2000
Second Edition 2005

ISBN 81-7010-301-0

Published by :

Hemkunt Publishers (P) Ltd.
A-78 Naraina Industrial Area Phase-I, New Delhi-110 028
Tel.   : 2579-2083, 2579-5079, 2579-0032
Fax   : 91-11-2611-3705
E-mail   : hemkunt@ndf.vsnl.net.in
Website : www.hemkuntpublishers.com

Some Hemkunt Books on Sikhism

For Children
Illustrated in four colours and black and white
The Story of Guru Nanak
Life Story of Guru Gobind Singh
Life Story of Guru Nanak
The Story of Maharaja Ranjit Singh
Stories from Sikh History I-VII
Sikh Studies I-VIII

For Adults
Japji
Hymns from Guru Granth Sahib
Hymns from the Dasam Granth
(In above three books text in Gurmukhi and Roman scripts and meanings in English)
Introduction to Sikhism
Encyclopedia of Sikhism
Bhagat Bani in Guru Granth Sahib
The Holy Granth - Sri Guru Granth Sahib Vol. I-IV

Printed at Hindustan Offset Press, N.I.A., Phase-II, New Delhi-110028

PREFACE

It is a complete encyclopedia but at the same time keeping it handy for everyday use. It has over one thousand entries about Sikh Gurus, martyrs, heroes, places of worship, religious centres, practices, traditions, theological concepts, ethical principles and a whole lot of terms and facts with which a person culturally literate about Sikhism must be familiar.

The format is user-friendly. Entries are alphabetically arranged with cross-references given wherever needed. There are extensive quotations from the Adi Granth abbreviated as AG in the text and some from the Dasam Granth, abbreviated as DG in the text. Authenticity has been ensured by cross-checking the information with that given in the monumental work : *Mahan Kosh* by Bhai Kahn Singh and the *Encyclopaedia* of *Sikhism* brought out by the Punjabi University, Patiala. Other works which have been widely consulted in the preparation of this book include among others : *The Sikh Religion* (Vol. I-VI) by Max Arthur Macaulife and the *History of the Sikhs* (Vol. I-VII) by Hari Ram Gupta.

It is hoped that the *Encyclopedia of Sikhism* in its present form will be a popular reference book for students of Sikhism. Comments and suggestions for further improvement will be most welcome.

New Delhi   Dr. H.S. Singha

A

ABCHAL NAGAR : Abchal Nagar is the name given by Sikh tradition to the place near Nanded in Maharashtra on the River Godavari where Guru Gobind Singh passed away in 1708 AD. The name has its origin in the Sikh scripture. In popular parlance it is called Hazur Sahib. For more details see under Hazur Sahib.

ABDULLA, KHWAJA : Khwaja Abdulla was the keeper of the jail at *Kotwali* in Delhi at the time Guru Tegh Bahadur was imprisoned there. He was a pious man and tried to mitigate the rigour of the Guru's incarceration as much as his official position permitted.

Khwaja Abdulla was a native of Mani Majra near Chandigarh. After the execution of Guru Tegh Bahadur in 1675 AD he resigned his post at the *Kotwali* and went to live at Anandpur and served Guru Gobind Singh as a physician. His son, Ghulam Abbas, later served under Nawab Kapur Singh as a physician.

ABDUS SAMAD KHAN : Abdus Samad Khan was in the service of Aurangzeb and served him for many years in the Deccan without attracting much attention. However when Farrukh Siyar came to power he made him Governor of Lahore in February 1713 AD with the specific responsibility of destroying Banda Singh Bahadur's influence. In 1715 AD as Banda Singh Bahadur came down from his mountain retreat, Abdus Samad Khan marched from Lahore at the head of twelve thousand *sowars* and an equal number of foot soldiers besides a big *topkhana* (artillery). He besieged him at Gurudas Nangal, about 6 km from Gurdaspur in a *haveli*. After a rigorous siege of 8 months in which not a blade of grass or a grain of corn could go in, he succeeded in capturing alive Banda Singh Bahadur in December 1715.

Abdus Samad Khan was transferred in 1726 AD to Multan and his son Zakariya Khan was appointed as the Governor of Lahore. He died on July 26, 1737 AD.

ABLUTION : Ablution is ceremonial washing of body or hands as a part of some religious practice. Aryans had brought with them to India a strong love for rivers. This gradually grew into river worship among the Hindus along with its ritualism like pilgrimages to *tirathas* on the river banks and cyclical bathing as for example the *Kumbh* fair. Many of the notable rivers became holy, the Ganges being the holiest having the largest number of *tirathas* on its banks.

Since Sikhism is against rituals, its stand on ablution has been to reject ritualism but to accept bathing as a part of cleaning the body. According to it: "True ablution lies in adoring God constantly".

(*Sacha nawana tan thee-ai jan ahnese lage bhao*—AG 358)

By way of weaning the followers from the river cult, Sikhism has set up *sarovars* in important gurdwaras, the main at the Golden Temple. It explains : "Followers, the *sarovar* of Guru Ramdas is beautiful. One who takes a dip in it gets salvation for himself and his family" (*Santo! Ramdas sarovar neeka. Jo nawe so kul tarawe udhar hoa hai jee ka* —AG 623.) It further emphasizes: "If you bathe in the *sarovar* of Guru Ramdas, you wash of your sins" (*Ramdas sarovar nate, sabh lathe paap kamate*—AG 624).

Sikhism has tried to shift the emphasis from rituals to cleanliness. It has prescribed that one should get up early in the morning and do Nitnem after taking bath. The importance of cleanliness in Sikhism can be judged from the fact that bathing constitutes a part of the core principles enshrined in the trinity "Worship, Charity, Bathing" (*Nam, Dan, Snan*).

ACHAL SAHIB, GURDWARA : Gurdwara Achal Sahib is situated at about 6 km from Batala in Punjab close to the ancient Hindu temple dedicated to Kartikeya, son of Lord Shiva and known as Achal Vatala. Guru Nanak visited the temple from Kartarpur (Pakistan) at the time of Shivratri Fair and held a long discourse with the *Nath-Yogis* led by Bhangar Nath

The gurdwara commemorates the Guru's visit to the place.

A small gurdwara had initially been raised at the place where Guru Nanak had halted. It was managed by a succession of *mahants* till April 1926 AD when the management was officially handed over to the Shiromani Gurdwara Parabandhak Committee after the passing of the Sikh Gurdwara Act, 1925 AD.

The foundation of the present gurdwara was laid in October 1935 AD and the complex was completed in 1946 AD. The main celebration organized by the gurdwara is the annual fair which takes place from the ninth to the eleventh day after Diwali.

ADI GRANTH : It is the holy book of the Sikhs—a scripture that takes its place alongside the world's greatest scriptures: the *Vedas*, the *Bible*, the *Quran* and the *Zend Avesta*. The first edition of the Adi Granth was scribed by Bhai Gurdas on the dictation of Guru Arjan. He developed it from a Bani Pothi—a nucleus of the writings of the first four Gurus and some *bhagats* by adding a considerable material of his own. It was completed in 1661 BS (AD 1604) and was formally installed in the Golden Temple in the same year. Baba Buddha was appointed the first *granthi*. The second edition was transcribed by Bhai Banno and the third and the last edition was prepared by Bhai Mani Singh under the supervision of Guru Gobind Singh in 1762-63 BS (AD 1705). The final version which is the authorized version in use at present includes the hymns of Guru Tegh Bahadur as well.

Adi Granth is a collection of devotional hymns and prayers to the Supreme. It throws light on the path leading to the highest goal of spirituality. In it philosophy is propounded through the songs of love and devotion. The message of love, truth, contentment, humility, fatherhood of God, brotherhood of man, restraint of passions, mercy on living beings, purity of mind and body, search for the self and Higher Soul, equality of man and woman, service, liberalism in the matter of food and clothing constitute the main contents of the Adi Granth.

ADI GRANTH : BHAGATS : Besides the seven Sikh Gurus, the Adi Granth has in it also the compositions of *bhagats* or saints and *bhatts* or bards. Basic facts about the *bhagats* are given in the Table below.

Table

S.No	Name	Caste	Period (century)	Home	Shabads/verses
1.	Beni	x	12	x	3
2.	Bhikan	x	16	Oudh	2
3.	Dhanna	Jat	16	Rajasthan	4
4.	Farid	Afghan	12-13	Pakistan	123
5.	Jaidev	Brahmin	12-13	Bengal	2
6.	Kabir	Weaver	15-16	Varanasi	534
7.	Namdev	Tailor	13	Maharashtra	62
8.	Parmanand	x	14-15	Varanasi	1
9.	Pipa	x	15	Rajasthan	1
10.	Ramanand	Brahmin	14-15	Varanasi	1
11.	Ravidas	Chamar	15	Varanasi	40
12.	Sadhna	Butcher	13	Sindh	1
13.	Sain	Barber	14-15	Madhya Pradesh	1
14.	Surdas	Brahmin	16	Haryana	2
15.	Trilochan	Vaish	13-14	Maharashtra	5

ADI GRANTH : CONTRIBUTORS : The Adi Granth is the only scripture of the kind which contains within its sacred covers the songs and utterances of a wide variety of saints, savants and bards. There are compositions of seven Sikh Gurus, and other saints who had their origin as high-born Brahmins, proud Kshatriyas, lowly Sudras and unlettered Jats. The number of *Shabads* and other compositions contributed by them is as follows:

1. Guru Nanak 947
2. Guru Angad 63

3.	Guru Amardas	869
4.	Guru Ramdas	638
5.	Guru Arjan	2312
6.	Guru Tegh Bahadur	115
7.	Guru Gobind Singh	1
8.	Kabir	534
9.	Farid	123
10.	Namdev	62
11.	Ravidas	40
12.	Trilochan	5
13.	Beni	3
14.	Dhanna	4
15.	Jaidev	2
16.	Bhikhan	2
17.	Sain	1
18.	Pipa	1
19.	Sadhna	1
20.	Ramanand	1
21.	Parmanand	1
22.	Surdas	2
23.	Sunder	6
24.	Mardana	3
25.	Satta	8
26.	Bhatts	123

Although Guru Gobind Singh did not include his writings in the Adi Granth, one *sloka: Bal hoa bandhan chhute...* on page 1429 is sometimes attributed to him. The copy of the Adi Granth kept at Takhat Patna Sahib mentions Mahala Ten (Tenth Master) against it.

ADI GRANTH : GURU GRANTH :

The Adi Granth has been given the status of the eternal Guru of the Sikhs by the declaration of Guru Gobind Singh in 1708 AD just before his passing away. He terminated the human succession to the office of the Guru and established instead the dominion of the Adi Granth. The Sikhs remind themselves of it generally after the *ardaas* by the congregational singing of the following :

"Command came from the Timeless One,
And the Khalsa Panth was established.
All Sikhs are commanded,
To recognise the Granth as the Guru.
It is the visible body of the Masters
Those who wish to meet the Lord,
May seek him therein."

*Agya bhai Akal ki, tabai chalayo Panth
Sabh Sikhan ko hukam hai Guru maanio Granth
Guru Granth ji maanio, pargat Guran ki deh
Jo Prabh ko milbo chahe, khoj shabad main leh*
(Dasam Granth, p. 248).

Ever since then, the Adi Granth is the reigning Guru of the Sikhs. It is kept in every gurdwara in a *palki* in the congregational hall which is arranged as an oriental throne room. It is present on all occasions when Sikhs meet for prayers, deliberations or important religious functions. It is wrapped and dressed in brocade silk and other precious clothes symbolic of royalty. Every devotee who enters its presence generally presents a *nazar*—offering of money—before the *palki* in accordance with the ancient oriental custom and behaves with utmost decorum.

To understand that the respect shown by the Sikhs to the Adi Granth is not book worship or idolatory. One must understand the concept of the Guru in Sikhism. The most critical aspect of this is the importance of *Shabad*, the Word which represents the essence of things

"The *Shabad* as revealed by the Gurus is the only authentic portrait of the Guru". The Word is contained in the Adi Granth and, therefore, it is the Guru. By the above-mentioned declaration, Guru Gobind Singh passed on the spiritual leadership of the Sikhs to the Adi Granth thereby giving Sikhism constancy and absolute permanency.

ADI GRANTH : THE LANGUAGE :

The Adi Granth represents devotional poetry of the highest order. It is written in Gurmukhi script. The language principally employed is the language of the saints, evolved during the medieval period. It is a language which allowing for variations, enjoyed wide currency in Northern India during the days of Bhakti Movement. Its appeal lay in its directness, energy and resilience. This *Sant bhasha* contains words not only from Sanskrit, Prakrit and Apabhramsha but also from Persian and Arabic. Besides *Sant bhasha* we find writings in the Adi Granth in Eastern Punjabi and Western Punjabi (Lehndi). For example Baba Farid, Satta and Balvand are essentially poets of Western Punjabi but Guru Nanak and Guru Arjan have also written some hymns in that dialect in addition to other dialects.

ADI GRANTH : ORGANISATION AND RAAGS :
The complete musicalization of thought in the Adi Granth in a scientific and studied manner is its important distinguishing feature. The printed version which in its current form comes to 1430 pages is divided into 33 sections. Whilst the first section comprises the soulful and inspiring song of Guru Nanak called Japji and also a few selected *Paudis*, the final section is a collection of assorted verses including the *slokas* and the *swayyas* of *bhatts*. The remaining 31 sections are named after the well-known classical *raags* and are supposed to be sung in those *raags*. These are: 1. Sri raag 2. Majh 3. Gauri 4. Asa 5. Gujari 6. Devgandhari 7. Bihagra 8. Wadhans 9. Sorath 10, Dhanasari 11. Jaitsari 12. Todi 13. Bairari 14. Tilang 15. Suhi 16. Bilawal 17. Gaund 18. Ramkali 19. Nat 20. Maligaura 21. Maru 22. Tukhari 23. Kedara 24. Bhairo 25. Basant 26. Sarang 27. Malar 28. Kanara 29. Kalian 30. Prabhati 31. Jaijawanti.

The order of hymns under each *raag* is generally as follows : Shabads, Ashtpadis, Chhand, Var and hymns contributed by the *bhaktas*. The shabads of Guru Nanak are given first and are followed by those of other Gurus in chronological order. The Gurus are referred to as Mahalas in the text, thus Mahala 1 meaning Guru Nanak. Generally there is an indication regarding the main tune—*ghar*—to be used in the singing of the shabad. If no *ghar* is indi- cated, the shabad should be sung in pure form.

ADINA BEG :
Adina Beg had humble beginning being the son of an ordinary agriculturist of Shakarpur near Lahore, now in Sheikhupura District of Pakistan. By his diligence and manoeuvring he rose to become the administrator of Jalandhar and ultimately the governor of Punjab for a short period in 1758 AD. His original name was Bahram Jang but being born on a Friday (*Adina*), he had become known as Adina Beg.

Adina Beg played a game of love and hate with the Sikhs. He took Sikhs as allies with a view to expelling the Afghans from Punjab. Jassa Singh Ramgarhia joined him when he was the administrator of Jalandhar. But on directions from the governor of Punjab, in March 1753, he fell upon the Sikh pilgrims at Anandpur on the occasion of Hola Mohalla killing a large number of them. He hired a thousand woodcutters to clear up the forest in which the Sikhs were wont to seek shelter. He laid siege to the Sikh fort Ram Rauni at Amritsar in 1758 AD.

Adina Beg died of an attack of colic at Batala on September 10, 1758 AD. Honouring his will, his dead body was buried at Khanpur, 2 km northwest of Hoshiarpur.

ADULTERY :
Marriage is a very important institution in Sikhism. The man-woman relationship sanctified in Sikh wedding ceremony is unalterable unlike the contractual marriages in some religions. Consistent with the importance of this relationship, adultery has been forbidden.

Being questioned on the subject of marriage relations, Guru Gobind Singh had explained : 'When I received understanding, my father Guru Tegh Bahadur, gave me this instruction, "O son, as long as there is life in thy body make this thy sacred duty ever to love thine own wife more and more. Approach not another woman's couch either by mistake or even in a dream. Know that the love of another's wife is a sharp dagger. Believe me, death enterth the body by making love to another's wife. They who think it great cleverness to enjoy another's wife, shall in the end die the death of dogs".

AGAUL :
Agaul is a village 10 km from Nabha in Punjab. Guru Tegh Bahadur visited the village and sat under a *pipal* tree on the bank of a pond. The pond believed to have medicinal properties has been converted into a small *sarovar* and a historical shrine called Gurdwara Sri Guru Tegh Bahadur Sahib whose

construction started in 1919 AD and was completed in 1935 AD exists there.

The gurdwara has a lithographed copy of the Adi Granth printed in 1893 AD. It has 2134 pages and the volume ends with the *Raagmala* with which composition copies of the scripture as a rule conclude.

AGHAR SINGH : Aghar Singh belonging to Longowal in Sangrur District in Punjab was a nephew of the famous Sikh martyr Bhai Mani Singh. He had received *amrit* from Bhai Mani Singh himself when he was the high priest of the Golden Temple.

Aghar Singh, along with his brother Tharaj Singh, fought against the Mughals in Amritsar and avenged the execution of Bhai Mani Singh by slaying his tormentors. He also killed Mir Momin Khan of Kasur who after the death of Mir Mannu the governor of Lahore in 1753 AD had launched a renewed campaign of prosecution of Sikhs. He died in January 1764 AD at Sirhind fighting against the provincial governor Zain Khan.

AGRA : Situated on the banks of River Yamuna, Agra is a town in Uttar Pradesh and is an important tourist centre because of the Taj Mahal which is a cenotaph built by Shahjahan in memory of his wife Mumtaz. Agra was made the capital for the first time by Sikandar Lodhi. It remained an important seat of the Mughal emperors during the pontificate of the first six Sikh Gurus till Shahjahan shifted the capital to Delhi.

Guru Nanak visited Agra as a part of his first missionary travels (*udasis*) and set up a *sangat* there. Guru Ramdas, before his annointment, had attended Akbar's court on behalf of Guru Amardas. According to *Gurpartap Surya* Guru Hargobind came to the city with Jehangir. Guru Tegh Bahadur passed through it on his way to the eastern parts in 1665-66 AD. Guru Gobind Singh visited Agra in 1707-08 to meet Emperor Bahadur Shah.

There is only one historical Sikh shrine in Agra called Gurdwara Mai Than. Guru Tegh Bahadur during his second visit to the city had visited the house of a devout old lady Mai Jassi to receive a hand-spun yarn which she had longed to present to the Guru. Her house has been converted into a gurdwara.

The Radhaswami sect originated in Agra and has its headquarters in Dyalbagh, Agra.

AHANKAR : *Ahankar* is the Punjabi word for pride. It is also some times written as *hankar*. For details see under Pride.

AHIMSA : The term *ahimsa* is formed by adding the negative pre-fix 'a' to the word *himsa* which means to kill, to harm or to injure. *Ahimsa*, therefore, implies not-killing, not-harming or not-injuring. Although inadequate the commonly used English equivalent is non-violence. For more details see Violence.

AJIT GILL : See Gurusar.

AJIT SINGH PALIT : Ajit Singh Palit was the adopted son of Mata Sundri, mother of *sahibzada* Ajit Singh. He belonged to a Delhi goldsmith family and was adopted because of his striking resemblance with her son who had been killed in the battle of Chamkaur. She treated him with great affection and got him married to a girl of Burhanpur.

Emperor Bahadur Shah treated Ajit Singh Palit as a heir to Guru Gobind Singh after his death. At one point he even tried to use him as a counterweight against Banda Singh Bahadur who was then leading a general uprising of the Sikhs. He gave him a *jagir* and showed other favours as well. After Bahadur Shah's death in 1712 AD, Ajit Singh continued to live in style as a courtier and became arrogant and haughty even towards Mata Sundri who had to disown him ultimately

For the offence of getting a Muslim mendicant killed by his followers Ajit Singh Palit was ordered to be tortured to death by Emperor Muhammad Shah on January 18, 1725 AD.

AJIT SINGH SAHIBZADA : *Sahibzada* Ajit Singh was the eldest son of Guru Gobind Singh. He was born to Mata Sundri at Paonta on

January 26, 1687 AD. The following year, Guru Gobind Singh returned to Anandpur with family where Ajit Singh was brought up in the approved Sikh style. He grew up to be a handsome young man and a natural leader of men. From the age of 12 he started leading small expeditions as for example against Rangars of Nuh who had looted the *sangat* from Pothohar on way to Anandpur, and against the Pathan chieftain of Bassi near Hoshiarpur to rescue a young Brahmin bride. In the latter expedition he visited Harian Velan.

In the prolonged siege of Anandpur in 1705 AD *sahibzada* Ajit Singh displayed qualities of courage and steadfastness. When Anandpur was at last vacated in December 1705, he was incharge of the rearguard. He crossed Sarsa, then in spate, alongwith his father, his younger brother Jujhar Singh and some fifty Sikhs. The column was, however, besieged by the enemy in the *haveli* of a *zamindar* at Chamkaur. There was a grim battle and *sahibzada* Ajit Singh was killed while leading a sally on December 7, 1705 AD. Gurdwara Qatalgarh at Chamkaur marks the spot where he fell.

AJMER CHAND, RAJA : Raja Ajmer Chand was the ruler of Kahlur (Bilaspur) in the Shivalik Hills. Anandpur fell in his territory.

Before Ajmer Chand took over from his father Bhim Chand, the latter had led battles against Guru Gobind Singh. Ajmer Chand continued the hostility. He formed a league with the neighbouring hill rajas and also sought help from the Mughal Emperor Aurangzeb to evict Guru Gobind Singh from Anandpur. Their attacks in 1700 AD and 1703 AD were successfully repulsed by the Guru's followers but Guru Gobind Singh had to ultimately evacuate Anandpur in December 1705 AD after a prolonged siege. Ajmer Chand joined the imperial troops in their pursuit of the Guru upto Chamkaur where a grim battle took place in which the Guru lost two of his elder sons : Ajit Singh and Jujhar Singh.

AKAL : *Akal* is a Sanskrit word which literally means timeless as it has been formed by adding the negative prefix 'a' to *kal* which means time. The term has become very expressive in Sikhism in which timelessness is a pivotal attribute of God and therefore often stands for the timeless one for which a more complete expression is *Akal Purakh*. It is also a part of many other important expressions and names like *Akali Bani, Akal Takhat, Sat Sri Akal, Shiromani Akali Dal* etc. It occurs at a number of places in the Adi Granth but the Dasam Granth is the real respository of concepts and terms relating to time.

According to Sikhism, the cosmic drama, the wondrous show of the world is all a creation of Time. All are subject to Time." *Sabh jag kale was hai badha* (AG, p. 162). The power of time controls worldly events; the only entity independent of time is Time itself, and that is *Akal*, the Timeless one. That is how according to the Dasam Granth, God is both Time and Timeless. In other words *Kal* itself is a dimension of *Akal*, the only difference being the process that characterizes temporal events, and the eternality of *Akal*.

AKAL BUNGA, AMRITSAR : Some writers use Akal Bunga interchangeably with the Akal Takhat Amritsar while others make a distinction between the Akal Takhat as an institution and the building that houses it in the Golden Temple Complex in Amritsar, the latter being called Akal Bunga — something like the parliament and the parliament house. Also see Akal Takhat for more details.

AKAL BUNGA, ANANDPUR : The place at Anandpur where the severed head of Guru Tegh Bahadur was cremated when it was brought from Delhi by one of his devotees Jaita after his martyrdom. From Akal Bunga, Guru Gobind Singh had consoled his mother, grandmother and thousands of devotees who had gathered there.

AKALI : *Akali* literally means someone who is devoted to the *Akal*, the Timeless one. Since Nihangs used to say *Akal! Akal!* in their worship, during the latter half of the eighteenth century they came to be known as Akalis. The term was revived during the agitation leading to the Sikh Gurdwara Act of 1925, when it was used for these who struggled for the Sikh control of gurdwaras. Now-a-days it is used for the members of the political party in Punjab or elsewhere called Shiromani Akali Dal.

Originally Akalis formed a purely religious body in Sikhism. They took upon themselves the duties of Censors in order to maintain the purity of Sikh religion and unity in the Panth. They adopted an aggressive attitude and acknowleged no mundane authority. They decided any point of religious conflict by passing a *gurmata* before the Akal Takht.

AKALI MOVEMENT : The period after the martyrdom of Banda Singh Bahadur is the most turbulent in Sikh history. Many Sikhs retired to the hills and forests to avoid persecution. Some lived in low profile. Under those circumstances, *udasis* who were not being persecuted, looked after the gurdwaras. The negative aspect of this is that as time passed, they started mismanaging them and diluting the Sikh traditions. A typical example of this is that General Dyer who was responsible for Jallianwala Bagh massacre managed to present himself at the Golden Temple and received a *saropa*. Triggered by such happenings, the Sikhs started a movement popularly called the Akali Movement to liberate the gurdwaras from the hereditary control of *mahants* or government apponited managers. Initiative was first of all taken by local Akali *jathas* as for example for the liberation of Babe-di-Sarai at Sialkot in 1920. But soon two representative bodies : Shiromani Akali Dal and Shiromani Gurdwara Parbandhak Committee (SGPC) were set up. The former was to handle political affairs and the latter was responsible for religious and cultural affairs. Some gurdwaras were easily handed over to SGPC while in some others, there was a confrontation. The most tragic confrontation occurred at Nankana Sahib in February 1921 AD when an Akali *jatha* of 150 was most brutally massacred. This led to further eruptions at Guru-ka-Bagh, Amritsar in 1922 AD and at Gangsar (Jaito) in 1923 AD. The Jaito *morcha* in which even Jawahar Lal Nehru was arrested lasted upto 1925 when the Government of India finally yielded, released all the prisoners and passed the Gurdwara Act 1925. With this the control and management of gurdwaras was officially transferred to SGPC with well defined composition through general elections.

AKAL PURAKH : The Adi Granth uses various names for God many of them derived from Hindu and Muslim theologies to be consistent with the vocabulary to the followers of the Gurus who used to be Hindus or Muslims. According to one scholar who has counted the number of times various terms have been used for God, Hari is the most common term occurring 8344 times in the Adi Granth followed by Rama which occurs 2533 times. One should not read any other meaning in this except that such terms have been used for easy communication with the followers.

Akal Purakh is the main term used for God in Sikh theology. It means the Timeless One who is beyond time. It lends constancy and permanency to God and in a way denies the concept of *avtar* in Hinduism. However, in popular devotion, common terms used for God are *Sat-guru* (the true Guru) and *Waheguru* (the Wonderous Guru).

Akal Purakh as a single composite term appears only once in the Adi Granth (p. 1038). But the Dasam Granth uses the term very often as a substitute for God, the External Being.

AKAL TAKHAT : The Akal Takhat (Eternal Throne) is the oldest of the five *takhats* and is the primary seat of temporal power in which capacity it may issue directions to the Sikh community providing guidance or clarification on any point of Sikh doctrine or practice and may prescribe *tankha* (punishment) for Sikhs violating religious discipline or working against the interests of the community.

The origin of the Akal Takhat lies in the concept of *meeri* and *peeri* synthesis of the spiritual and the worldly—introduced by Guru

Hargobind. It started as just a platfrom. The Guru laid the corner stone and Baba Buddha and Bhai Gurdas completed the construction with no third person being allowed to lend a helping hand. The platform was used for the annointment ceremony of the Guru in June 1606 AD. Later on the Guru conducted the secular affairs of the community from here. A building subsequently raised over the *Takhat* was called Akal Bunga which is now used interchangeably with Akal Takhat.

The building of the Akal Takhat is situated in the Golden Temple Complex just opposite the sanctum to which it acts as a complementary shrine. As such the history of the Akal Takhat is inseparably linked with the chequered history of the Golden Temple itself. It was razed by Ahmad Shah Abdali in 1762 AD. It was later on reconstructed with the ground floor completed in 1774 AD and rest of the five-storeyed domed edifice during the reign of Maharaja Ranjit Singh. The gilded dome atop the building was built by Hari Singh Nalwa at his own expense. It was again destroyed in the army action called Operation Blue Star in June 1984. The Government of India got the building reconstructed in order to assuage the injured feelings of the Sikhs but this was not acceptable to them. The reconstructed building was demolished in 1986 AD and again brought up through *Kar Sewa*.

Traditionally all Sikh warriors sought blessings at the Akal Takhat before going to battle. During the 18th century when Sikhs had spread out to the forests and hills after the martyrdom of Banda Singh Bahadur, the Akal Takhat continued to provide them a rallying point. They used to hold meetings of the *Sarbat Khalsa* on every Diwali and Baisakhi to discuss matters of policy and strategy. Most of the recent political agitations of Shiromani Akali Dal have been directed from here. The status of the Akal Takhat can be gauged from the fact that its *Jathedar* (Head) Akali Phula Singh awarded punishment twice to Maharaja Ranjit Singh; once for marrying a Muslim woman according to Muslim rites and second time for presenting a used *chandni*.

AKAL USTATI : It is one of the major writings of Guru Gobind Singh included in the Dasam Granth. It is a collection of many subjects which were composed at different times and then compiled together. Its language is a mixture of Sanskrit, Braj Bhasha, Persian and Arabic. It contains 271½ verses in praise of God, the Timeless, the Formless One. It highlights the term *Akal Purakh* for God which is now commonly used in Sikh theology. About a third of *Akal Ustati* is a satire on false methods of worship; but it is a satire with the kindly purpose of showing that true praise is an inner state consisting of heart felt devotion to the One Supreme Creator.

AKAR : Akar is a village in Patiala district where a historical shrine called Gurdwara Nim Sahib is situated. Guru Tegh Bahadur during one of his travels to the region had visited the village. He had put up under a *nim* (margosa) tree and used its twig as *datun* (tooth brush) to cleanse his teeth. The *nim* tree still exists. A spacious gurdwara complex which was completed in 1972 AD has come up at the place.

AKBAR, THE GREAT : Akbar, the great was the second Mughal Emperor of India. After the death of his father Humayun, he was crowned king at Kalanur in Punjab on February 14, 1556 during the pontificate of Guru Amardas. Besides being a capable administrator he is famous for his policy of religious toleration and liberalism. Akbar died at Agra on October 16, 1605 during the pontificate of Guru Arjan.

Akbar, the Great had amicable relations with the Sikh Gurus during his reign. He is believed to have visited Goindwal and participated in the *langar* like any other pilgrim before having an audience with Guru Amardas. He called upon Guru Arjan also at Goindwal in November 1598 and at the Guru's instance remitted the annual revenue of the peasants of the district who had been hit hard by the failure of monsoon. When complaints were made to him that the Adi Granth contained material derogatory to Islam, he had it read at random while camping at Batala. He was pleased at the interpretation of the hymns and made an offering of fifty-one *mohars* (gold coins). He also gave presents to Baba Buddha and Bhai Gurdas who had brought the Adi Granth to Batala from Amritsar.

AKBARPUR KHUDAL: Akbarpur Khudal is a village in Mansa district of Punjab. Guru Gobind Singh visited the village in November 1706 to rescue a Sikh Gulab Singh from the captivity of the village chief. The house of the chief where the Sikh was kept was acquired and Gurdwara Bhora Sahib Patshahi 10 was constructed at the site in February 1951 AD. It was handed over to the SGPC in 1977 AD.

AKHAND PATH : *Akhand Path* means uninterrupted recital of the Adi Granth from beginning to end. Such a recital must be completed within 48 hours. The entire Adi Granth, 1430 large pages, is read through in a continuous ceremony. The reading must go on day and night without a moment's intermission. The relay of reciters who take turns at reading the Scripture must ensure that no break occurs. As they change places at given intervals, one picks the line from his predecessor's lips and continues. According to the Sikh *Rahit Maryada*, no fixed number of reciters is specified for the *Akhand Path*.

When and how the custom of *Akhand Path* began is not known. Conjecture traces it to the turbulent days of the 18th century AD when persecution scattered the Sikhs to far-off places. This practice must have originated in those exilic uncertain times as a means of unification.

Akhand Path is consistent with the Hindu tradition of reading the scriptures and epics, which must have influenced the Sikh practice.

AKOI: Akoi is a village near Sangrur in Punjab. According to local tradition Guru Nanak had visited this village. Later Guru Hargobind came here during his travels in the Malwa region in 1616 AD. A gurdwara which is managed by a local committee under the auspices of the SGPC has come up at the place where Guru Hargobind had stayed.

ALAMGIR: Alamgir is a village in Ludhiana district. Guru Gobind Singh halted here after the battle of Chamkaur in December 1705 AD. Here the Guru discarded the palanquin which he had used for part of the journey and took a horse presented by an old disciple Bhai Naudha. A very spacious gurdwara managed by a local committee under the auspices of the SGPC has come up at the village. It is called Gurdwara Manji Sahib Patshahi 10. It has a 63 metre square holy tank called Tir Sar attached to it. An annual fair is held in December every year.

ALCOHOL : See Intoxicants.

ALA SINGH, BABA : Baba Ala Singh was the grandson of Baba Phul a devotee of the house of the Gurus. He was born in 1691 AD at Phul in Bhatinda district. Baba Ala Singh became active soon after the execution of Banda Singh Bahadur in 1716 AD when central Punjab lay in utter confusion. He set up his *misl* known as Phulkian Misl with sovereignty extending over the area popularly called Phulkian States (Patiala, Nabha and Jind). This *misl* did not join the Dal Khalsa in 1748 AD but instead sometimes worked against its interests. Nevertheless he had been administered *amrit* by Nawab Kapur Singh in 1732 AD. He was an ally of Jassa Singh Ahluwalia in the attack on Sirhind in 1764 AD. He had a vacillating approach towards Ahmad Shah Abdali, remained neutral at the time of Wada Ghallughara in 1762 AD and accepted the title of Raja from him. Baba Ala Singh founded the city of Patiala in 1763 AD and made it his headquarters. He passed away there in August 1765 AD and was cremated in the Fort, now inside the city.

ALIF KHAN : See Sayyid Beg.

ALI SHER : Ali Sher is a village near Mansa which had the honour of being visited by Guru

Tegh Bahadur during his travels in the Malwa region A large gurdwara having 12 acres of land developed there during the nineteenth century under the patronage of the rulers of Patiala.

ALO HARAKH : Alo Harakh is a village in Sangrur District. Guru Tegh Bahadur halted here under a banyan tree. A historical shrine constructed in 1909 AD called Manji Sahib marks the site. The gurdwara is administered by the SGPC through a local committee.

AMARDAS, GURU : Guru Amardas, the third Nanak, was born in 1479 AD at village Baserke in Amritsar district. The name of his father was Tej Bhan (of Bhalla sub-caste). He was married to Mata Mansa Devi in 1502 AD from whom he had four children : two sons, Mohan and Mohri; and two daughters, Dani and Bhani. Bhani was married to Guru Ramdas, who was earlier known as Bhai Jetha. Guru Amardas had become a disciple of Guru Angad in 1540 AD and served him with such dedication that he installed him as the third Guru in 1552 AD.

Guru Amardas paid serious attention to the propagation of Sikhism. He appointed a devout Sikh incharge of each region. The total number of such dioceses was 22. The Guru also trained a number of travelling missionaries who spread the message of Sikhism in different parts of India. In order to bring the Sikhs closer to one another, he ordained that they must assemble on the occasion of Diwali, Baisakhi and Maghi.

The Guru started a new centre of worship at Goindwal where he got a well dug for the benefit of the people (See Baoli Sahib). He also perpetuated the concept of *langar*. He located the site for Amritsar and directed Guru Ramdas to construct the Holy Tank there.

The Guru was very friendly with Emperor Akbar who came to pay respects to him at Goindwal and according to the custom took meals at the *langar*.

Guru Amardas collected the compositions of his predecessors and some of the *bhaktas* of that time. When he had recorded these in *pothis*—two of them preserved by the descendant families to this day—an important step towards the codification of the canon had been taken. The Guru himself wrote verse in simple Punjabi. 869 of his verses are included in the Adi Granth. Best known among his compositions is the *Anandu*.

Guru Amardas died on September 1, 1574 after choosing Bhai Jetha, his son-in-law, as his spiritual successor as Guru Ramdas.

AMAVAS : According to Hindu tradition, which has been following a lunar calendar certain days of the month more especially *puranmashi* (full moon) last day of the waxing of the moon and *amavas* (no moon) last day of the wanning of the moon have assumed special significance. Certain religious performances and observances have come to lie associated with them.

The considered view of Sikhism is that no single day is more auspicious than others. That day alone is auspicious and well-spent which is spent in meditating on the Divine Name. Thus there is no ritualistic or formal observance prescribed in Sikhism either for *amavas* or *puranmashi*. Nevertheless perhaps because of the influence of Hinduism, *amavas* is marked by special congregations in gurdwaras. Devotees gather for ablutions in *sarovars*, the holy tanks of gurdwaras as Hindus would go to rivers for a dip. The shrines at Tarn Taran and Muktsar especially attract pilgrims from long distances on the occasion.

Amavas is called *massia* and *puranmashi*, *punnia* in Punjabi.

AMRIT : In Vedic literature *amrit* means anything sweet, commonly a liquid or drink, consuming which one attains immortality. According to Hindu mythology, *amrit* was extracted by the gods by churning the ocean with the assistance of demons and it was by drinking it that gods became immortal. Similar concepts exist in Greek and Semitic mythologies as well.

In Sikh speech and writings *amrit* is used both as a noun and an adjective. As a noun it generally refers to the baptismal water prepared by dissolving sugar (*patasas*) in water by means of a *khanda* reciting Japji, Japu Sahib, Ten Sawayyas, Benti Chaupai and abbreviated form of Anandu in the presence of the Guru Granth Sahib. The practice of taking *amrit* as a part of baptism was started by Guru Gobind Singh. Earlier Gurus took *Nam* to be the real *amrit* "There is but one *amrit* i.e. *Nam*; There is no other." *Nanak amrit eko hai, duja amrit nahi.* (AG, p. 1238). As an adjective, *amrit* means sweet, delicious, good, sweet-sounding as for example in *amrit vaila, amrit katha, amrit bani* etc.

AMRITDHARI : A Sikh who has undergone baptism according to the *Rahit Maryada*. At the time of baptism, he is asked to affirm to the transformation: "Today you take a new birth in the House of the Guru. You have become a knight of the Order of the Khalsa. Guru Gobind Singh is the Father, and holy Sahib Kaur the Mother of the Order of the Khalsa. Your birth place is the Blessed Fort of Keshgarh and you are a citizen of Anandpur. Your previous race, name, geneology, country, religion, customs and beliefs, your subconscious pulls and tensions, *sanskars* and your personality have today been burnt up, annihilated and transmuted. You have become the Khalsa, a sovereign man today owing allegiance to no earthly person or powers". He is also asked to observe the code of conduct, say his five prayers and avoid four grave breaches of discipline : (1) To trim body hair; (2) To eat kosher meat; (3) To have unnatural sex gratification or sexual relationship outside marriage; and (4) To use tobacco.

It may be mentioned that every *Amritdhari* is also a *Keshadhari* Sikh but every *Keshadhari* may not be an *Amritdhari*.

AMRITSAR : Amritsar is the principal holy city of the Sikhs and is intimately linked with the history and development of Sikhism. It is the largest city in Punjab and perhaps the most fascinating of all cities in northern India. It is also a centre for education, commerce and industry.

Amritsar had modest beginnings. According to Sikh tradition Guru Amardas is said to have found a magical herb on the edge of a pool of nectar which cured Guru Angad of a skin disease. But the real foundation of the town was laid in 1577 AD by Guru Ramdas when he inaugurated the digging of the holy tank on a piece of land gifted by Emperor Akbar to Bibi Bhani, daughter of Guru Amardas and wife of Guru Ramdas. Gradually a habitation grew around the holy tank for the craftsmen and workers from the towns of Patti, Kasur and Kalanur. In those days it came to be known as Chakk Guru, Chakk Ramdas or Ramdaspur. Soon a market also grew which was then called Guru-ka-Bazar and is still known by that name.

As Guru Ramdas had shifted his residence to the new town, his young son (Guru) Arjan got an opportunity to supervise the construction work right from the beginning. During his pontificate he took considerable interest in its development. He completed and lined the holy tank. In 1588 AD he had the foundation stone of the Golden Temple laid by the renowned Muslim Sufi Saint Mian Mir of Lahore at the centre of the holy tank. Guru Arjan also added two more tanks, Santokhsar and Ramsar.

When Guru Hargobind took over the leadership of the community after the martyrdom of his father Guru Arjan, he started a transformation in Sikhism. He emphasized the temporal aspects as much as the spiritual ones. As such in the Golden Temple Complex, Guru Hargobind added the Akal Takhat which as a seat of temporal authority became a complementary shrine to the Golden Temple. He also constructed the Lohgarh fortress on the western outskirts of the town. Guru Hargobind added two tanks Kaulsar and Bibeksar.

After 1635 AD when Guru Hargobind shifted his residence to Kiratpur, none of the later Gurus resided at Amritsar. In fact during the rest of the seventeenth century Amritsar was controlled by Guru Hargobind's cousin Miharban and the latter's son Harji who headed the Mina sect. Guru Tegh Bahadur when he visited Amritsar after his annointment was not allowed entry into the Golden Temple.

During the eighteenth century, Amritsar witnessed many vicissitudes. It however, remained a rallying point for the Sikhs in the troublesome days. Sarbat Khalsa used to meet here to take important decisions concerning strategy and policy. It was finally liberated in 1765 AD with the *misls* establishing sovereignty over Punjab. Different *misl* chiefs constructed their own *bungas* (halls of residence) around the holy tank.

In 1805 AD Amritsar was incorporated in the dominion of Maharaja Ranjit Singh. He took great interest in its development and almost treated it as his second capital. During his rule, Amritsar grew into a leading industrial and commercial city. It continued to enjoy its precedence as the holiest city of the Sikhs as well as the most important commercial and industrial centre in the north-west India even after the annexation of Punjab.

In the twentieth century Amritsar got highlighted on the political map of India because of the Jallianwala Bagh massacre in April 1919. More recently most of the political movements of Shiromani Akali Dal have been directed from here.

In terms of the percentage of population Hindus are in a majority and have their Durgiana Temple in Amritsar but it has retained the character of the holy city of Sikhs dotted with Sikh shrines honouring the memory of Gurus, martyrs and heroes which are covered at appropriate places in the book.

AMRIT VAILA : According to the ancient Indian system, the time between two consecutive sun rises is divided into eight equal parts each of 3 hours called *pahars*. The *pahar* before sun rise is called *Amrit Vaila*. That this time is auspicious for meditation has been highlighted at a number of places in the Adi Granth as for example (i) One must utter the True Name in the early ambrosial morning and must ponder over His Greatness. *Amrit vaila such nao vadiyaee vichar* (p. 2) (ii) in the early morning, the conscious mind swells up with joy. *Chauthe pahar sadhar kai surtiya upjai chao* (p. 146) (iii) The true Guru's Sikh must meditate on the Lord's Name when he gets up at dawn. *Gur satgur ka jo Sikh akhayai bhalke uth Harinam dhiyaai.* (p. 305) and (iv) Utter the Lord's Name in the early morning and attain refuge both here and hereafter. *Pratakaal Harinam uchari eet oot mai ot swari* (p. 743).

AMRO, BIBI : Bibi Amro was the elder daughter of Guru Angad. She was born in 1526 AD at Khadur Sahib and was married to the nephew of (Guru) Amardas of Baserke near Amritsar. Amardas who had never met Guru Nanak was very impressed by Guru Nanak's compositions which Bibi Amro used to recite in the morning while churning milk. He desired to meet the living successor of Guru Nanak. Bibi Amro is remembered in Sikh tradition for introducing Amardas to her father Guru Angad whose devoted disciple and eventually successor he became.

Bibi Amro died at Baserke where a shrine built in her honour still exists.

ANAND KARAJ : See Marriage.

ANAND MARRIAGE ACT 1909 : With the consolidation of Sikhism, its followers had evolved their own form of wedding ceremony called *Anand Karaj*. There was a legal controversy in the nineteenth century after the annexation of Punjab by the British. The Sikhs began to react against the British legal requirement that they should be married according to Hindu rites because they were classified as Hindus under the Indian Civil Code. In 1909 AD, the Anand Marriage Act was passed which made the Sikh form of marriage legal. It states that all Sikh marriages conducted according to the marriage ceremony common among Sikhs called *Anand* should be recognised as valid from the day of their solemnization as also all marriages which may be conducted as such in future.

ANANDPUR : Anandpur—also reverentially called Anandpur Sahib–which literally means the City of Bliss occupies a unique place in Sikh history and tradition. It is situated on one of the lower spurs of the Shivalik range in Ropar district of Punjab. Having been the abode of the last two Sikh Gurus for a number of years, the town has witnessed many momentous events in Sikh history. One of the five takhats : Keshgarh Sahib is situated here.

Anandpur was founded by Guru Tegh Bahadur in June 1665 AD on a piece of land purchased from the Raja of Bilaspur. He named the new habitation Chakk Nanaki after his mother and shifted there with his family from Kiratpur.

Guru Gobind Singh constructed five forts at Anandpur after the battle of Bhangani in September 1688 AD : Anandgarh, Lohgarh, Fatehgarh, Keshgarh and Holgarh and renamed the town Anandpur after one of the forts. These forts have been converted into gurdwaras now.

It was at Anandpur that Guru Gobind Singh founded the Khalsa Panth on the Baisakhi Day of 1699 AD. The emergence of the Khalsa Panth caused panic among the hill rajas who conspired with the Mughal rulers to dislodge Guru Gobind Singh from Anandpur. After a long siege, the Guru vacated it in December 1705 AD. Years later, Gulab Rai son of a cousin of the Guru, purchased the town from the Raja of Bilaspur and pretending to be a successor of the Guru established his own religious sect. The administration of the shrines at Anandpur was handed over to the SGPC in 1923 AD.

Besides the five forts which have been converted ints gurdwaras, Anandpur has a number of other important shrines like Gurdwara Sis Ganj, Akal Bunga, Damdama Sahib, Bhora Sahib, Thara Sahib, Manji Sahib and Gurdwara Mata Jito.

Every year, the Hola Mohalla festival on the day following Holi, is held at Anandpur when lakhs of devotees converge on the town. *Diwans* are held and the festival reaches its climax with the taking out of a large procession.

ANANDPUR SAHIB RESOLUTION : A document adopted unanimously by the Working Committee of the Shiromani Akali Dal at Anandpur in October 1973 AD has become popular under the title Anandpur Sahib Resolution. It was endorsed in the form of a series of resolutions at the 18th All-India Akali Conference of the Shiromani Akali Dal at Ludhiana in October 1978 AD.

Anandpur Sahib Resolution is a religio-political document. In a way it is an expression of the aspirations of the Sikh community in the last quarter of the twentieth century. It is quite comprehensive asking for more autonomy for state governments to strengthen the federal character of Indian polity; transfer of Chandigarh and Punjabi speaking pockets in Haryana to Punjab; retaining the present ratio of Sikhs in the Army, making an international airport at Amritsar; giving Punjabi the status of the second language in states adjoining Punjab, installing a broadcasting station at the Golden Temple for the relay of *Gurbani Kirtan* amending the Hindu Succession Act to safeguard the interests of rural farmers; insuring equitable distribution of Ravi-Beas waters and in general removing discrimination against the Sikhs in India.

ANAND SAHIB : See Anandu.

ANANDU : It is called Anand Sahib in popular parlance *Anand Sahib*—the Song of Bliss—is the spiritual and musical masterpiece of Guru Amardas. It begins with the lines : "Joy, my mother, that I have founded the True Guru! I have founded Him so easily that my mind is full of the music of congratulations!"
*Anand bhaya meri maaey Satguru mai paaeya
Satgur ta paaeya sahaj seti man vajeeiya waadhaaiya*
(995 p. 917)

It is believed that it was composed by the Guru in 1554 AD when his son Mohri was blessed with a son who was also named Anand. It has to be sung in Rag Ramkali to get its full import on the mind. It is a part of the Adi Granth, and is as important and philosophical as Guru Nanak's Japji and Guru Arjan's Sukhmani.

Anand Sahib consists of 40 Paudis (stanzas). As a matter of convention it is recited in its abbreviated form—the first five *Paudis* and the last *Paudi*—in Sikh congregations. It is laid down in the Sikh *Rahit Maryada* that at the end of the reading of the Adi Granth (whether Akhand Path or Sahaj Path), Anand Sahib must be recited before the final *ardaas*. It is also recited while preparing *amrit* for Baptism. In fact it is a part of every religious service announcing its end just before *ardaas*.

ANANTI, MATA : Mata Ananti also referred to as Nati and Nihal Kaur by some chroniclers was the mother of Guru Har Rai and wife of Baba Gurditta. She was the daughter of Ram Sil, a Khatri of Batala. She was married to Baba Gurditta in 1624 AD. Baba Dhirmal was her elder son.

ANGAD, GURU : Guru Angad was the second Guru of the Sikhs. He was chosen by Guru Nanak from amongst his disciples to carry on his teachings.

Guru Angad was born in March, 1504 AD at Matte-di-Sarai Wanga now in Faridkot district to Pheru Mal and Mata Daya Kaur. He was earlier known as Lehna. He was married in January 1520 AD to Khivi and had two sons named Dasu and Datu and two daughters named Amro and Anokhi.

Guru Angad was a devout worshipper of the goddess Durga. Every year he used to lead a batch of devotees from Khadur Sahib where he had settled to the temple of Jwalamukhi in the Lower Himalayas. In 1532 AD he met Guru Nanak at Kartarpur (Pakistan) on his way to Jwalamukhi and became his disciple. He impressed Guru Nanak with his service and devotion so much that he installed him as the Guru in 1539 AD with the new name Angad.

Guru Angad made Khadur Sahib his headquarters. Humayun, the Mughal Emperor called on him here. He continued to preach the teachings of Guru Nanak. In 1541 AD he introduced the use of the improved Gurmukhi script and encouraged all people to learn Punjabi and to read religious literature. In 1544 AD he got a biography of Guru Nanak written, which in a modified form is known as Bala Janamsakhi. Guru Angad also extended the *langar* and personally looked after the arrangements for serving. Sixty-three of his *slokas* are included in the Adi Granth.

He died in March, 1552 AD at Khadur Sahib at the age of 48 years.

ANI RAI, BABA : Baba Ani Rai was the son of Guru Hargobind and was born to Mata Nanaki at Amritsar on November 14, 1618 AD. Not much is known about him except that he grew up to lead the life of a recluse. He never married and died at Kiratpur where a shrine honouring his memory still exists.

ANOKHI, BIBI : Bibi Anokhi was the daughter of Guru Angad and Mata Khivi. She was born in 1535 AD. In the absence of many details about her, some chroniclers leave her out of the list of children of Guru Angad.

ANTIM ARDAAS : See Funeral Rites.

ARDAAS : The common prayer of the Sikhs. The first part of it appears as a prologue to Chandi-di-Var written by Guru Gobind Singh invoking blessings of God and the Gurus. The bulk of the remaining *ardaas* was incorporated by Bhai Mani Singh. Further additions continue to be authorised by edicts issued by Akal Takhat whenever a major religious event happens affecting the Sikhs.

The *ardaas* is a concise history of the Sikhs enumerating supreme sacrifices made by them to uphold their faith besides adoring God and the Gurus. It sets out before them the life style of a true Sikh and ends with the prayer for imbibing the fundamental tenets of Sikhism.

It is prescribed that *ardaas* must be said at the time of recitation of *Banis* of the *Nitnem*. It is also recited at the time of undertaking or finishing important tasks or ceremonies. Although not compulsory, it is generally said in the presence of Guru Granth Sahib and the entire congregation is supposed to stand with folded hands.

The first part of *ardaas* reads as :
Ik Onkar Waheguru ji ki fateh

Sri Bhagauti ji sahaye, Var Sri Bhagauti ji ki Patshahi 10

Pritham Bhagauti simarke Guru Nanak laeen dhiyai. Phir Angad Gur te Amardas Ramdase hoeen sahay-e. Arjan, Hargobind noo, simro Sri Har Rai, Sri Harkrishan dhiaeyai jis dithe sabh dukh jaayai, Tegh Bahadur simreyai ghar nau nidh aawe dhaye sabh thaeen hoe sahaye; Daswen Patshah Sri Guru Gobind Singh ji Maharaj sabh thaeen hoe sahaye, Dassan Patshahian di jot, Sri Guru Granth Sahib ji de paath deedar da dhiyan dhar ke bolo ji Waheguru!

O formless one victory be to the wonderful Lord.

May the Divine Spirit help us.

We recite Var Sri Bhagauti ji ki by the Tenth Master.

To begin with we remember the Divine Spirit and we think of Guru Nanak.

Then we invoke the blessings of Guru Angad, Amardas and Ramdas.

We also remember Guru Arjan, Hargobind and Har Rai.

Let us think of Sri Harkrishan whose sight dispels all sorrows.

Let us remember Tegh Bahadur and the nine treasures will come to us.

May God and the Gurus help us everywhere.

May the Tenth Master Guru Gobind Singh help us everywhere.

Turn your thoughts to the teachings of the Guru Granth Sahib in which is enshrined the spirit of the Ten Masters and say : Waheguru!

ARISAR, GURDWARA : It is situated outside village Dhaula near Barnala. According to the local tradition, Guru Tegh Bahadur's horse had refused to move further at the spot when the Guru was on his way to Dhaula (*Ari* in Punjabi means an act of stubbornness). The gurdwara affiliated to the SGPC marks the historic spot.

ARJAN, GURU : Guru Arjan the fifth Guru was the youngest son of Guru Ramdas and Mata Bhani. He was born at Goindwal in April 1563 AD. He was married in 1579 AD to Ganga Devi daughter of Krishan Chand and had one son Guru Hargobind. Guru Arjan was installed as Guru in 1581 AD.

Guru Arjan was a talented musician and a charismatic religious leader. He founded cities, set up institutions and consolidated Sikhism. In 1588 AD he got the Santokhsar tank paved and in the same year got the foundation stone of the Golden Temple laid. In 1590 AD the tank at Tarn Taran was constructed. In 1594 AD he founded the city of Kartarpur (Jalandhar). In 1604 AD he compiled the Adi Granth and in the same year got it installed at the Golden Temple with Baba Buddha as the Head Granthi (priest). Guru Arjan also started the tradition of Daswandh—contributing one-tenth of one's income for the common good.

Guru Arjan was a man of the masses and wielded great influence. His growing power and prestige roused the jealousy of Emperor Jahangir. He asked the Guru to change the text of the Guru Granth Sahib to include the praise of Prophet Mohammed. The Guru refused to do so. He was arrested and was subjected to extreme physical torment. Overwhelmed by "the sufferings, torments and dishonours" the Guru passed away in 1606 AD on the banks of the river Ravi at Lahore where we now have the Gurdwara Dera Sahib.

Guru Arjan was an unusually gifted and prolific poet. Over one-third of the Adi Granth consists of his own compositions. They comprise more than two thousand verses. These are, in part, philosophical, enshrining his vision of the Absolute. The *Sukhmani*, the Psalm of peace is perhaps the most well-known of his compositions.

ARTI : It is a form of Hindu worship in which oil lamps numbering one to hundred are waved in a prescribed order in front of idols of gods and goddesses and sometimes even before important persons. It is done even during the day. As Sikhism is against idol worship, this type of *arti* has no place in it.

Since Sikhism is against all rituals, it has tried to replace *arti* by appropriate *shabads*. Guru Nanak responded to *arti* at the temple of Jagannath Puri by giving a cosmological interpretation to it in his hymn:

"The sun and the moon O Lord, are thy lamps.

The firmament thy slaves. The orbs of the stars the pearls enchased in it ...."

Gagan main thal; ravi chand deepak bane; Tarika mandal janak moti................... (995, p. 663)

This hymn is popularly called *Arti* in Sikh literature and forms a part of Sohila which every devout Sikh repeats at bed time. There are some other Arti hymns too in the Guru Granth Sahib.

ASA : An Indian classical *raag* usually sung at dawn. It is one of the thirty-one *raags* used in the organisation of hymns in the Guru Granth Sahib—the fourth in order from the beginning—covering pages 347-488. The sequence of basic notes in Asa is :

Arohi : sa, re, ma, pa, dha, ne, sa...................
Avrohi : re, sa, dha, pa, ma, ga, re.................

Asa di Var is the most important *Bani* sung in this raag. According to religious tradition, it is used even at the time of choir singing of *Sodar Bani* which is otherwise an evening *Bani*.

ASA-DI-VAR : *Var* originally meant a dirge for the brave slain in battle, then it came to mean a song of praise and in the Guru Granth Sahib it means a hymn in praise of God. Collection of such hymns occurring towards the end of the section entitled Raag Asa in the Guru Granth Sahib is called *Asa di Var*. It is sung by musicians at Sikh congregations as part of the early morning service.

It is divided into *slokas* (staves) and *paudis* (stanzas) following one another alternately as a statement and commentary thereon. Except for a few verses by Guru Angad, the work is entirely that of Guru Nanak.

In *Asa-di-Var*, as in other compositions, the Guru did not restrict himself to a single theme or a logical development of a particular thesis. Nevertheless the one idea that predominates in this work is how a man can elevate himself from his low state to a godly one and thus prepare himself for union with God. It is severely critical of the Hindu ambivalence, of his pretence of orthodoxy on the one hand and sycophantic imitations of Muslim customs to please the ruling class on the other.

ASCETICISM : Hinduism, Jainism and Buddhism have exalted the life of the recluse and the ascetic because of the belief that such acts devote the pure life of spiritual attainment. While Sikhism treats *kam* (lust) as a vice, it has at the same time unmistakably pointed out that man must share the moral responsibility by leading the life of a *grihasth* (house holder). "If one were to be saved by celibacy or asceticism, then why did not the eunuchs attain the highest state of bliss." *Bindo rakh jo tariye bhai, khusre kio na param gati pa-ee.* (AG, p. 324). What is important is to be God-centred "The household and the forest are alike for one who lives in poise."

Grih ban sansare sahej subha-ee (AG. p. 351)

According to Sikhism, ascetics are certainly not on the right path.

"Those who call themselves ascetics do not know the way. That is why they leave their homes."

Jati sadawahe jugat na janhi chhad bahe ghar bar.
(AG. p. 469)

Accordingly Sikhism repudiates even the beliefs and practices of *Yogis*. See *Yoga*.

ASHTAPADI : *Ashtapadi* is a special kind of poetic verse used in many compositions of the Guru Granth Sahib. It is commonly a stanza of eight distiches, the two parts of each distich rhyme together. A distich contains 48 or 50 *kalas* and may have one or two *rahau*. No specific rhyme scheme, measure or burden is prescribed for an *ashtapadi* but all the eight distiches must be in the same metre and measure.

In the Guru Granth Sahib *ashtapadis* occur under different *raags* with different metres. The famous composition of Guru Arjan, the *Sukhmani* consists of 24 *ashtapadis* in *chaupai* metre under *raag* Gauri.

ASMAN KHAN : Asman Khan was a Pathan who had misappropriated the robe of honour, a sword and a horse bestowed on his father-in-law Painde Khan by Guru Hargobind. When questioned Painde Khan denied that the articles had been taken by Asman Khan. Nevertheless, Bhai Bidhi Chand recovered them from the possession of Asman Khan. Both Painde Khan and Asman Khan enlisting the support of the *faujdar* of Jalandhar rose against the Guru. A clash occurred at Kartarpur (Jalandhar) in April 1635 AD in which Asman Khan was killed.

ATAL RAI, BABA : Baba Atal Rai was the son of Guru Hargobind and was born to Mata Nanaki at Amritsar on October 23, 1619 AD. He died at the tender age of nine years. According to Sikh tradition he was admonished by his father for performing a miracle in which he had revived his dead friend to life. Atal Rai took the admonition to heart and went to eternal repose on the bank of Kaulsar on September 13, 1628 AD. A gurdwara called Baba Atal stands at the place now.

ATAR SINGH, SANT : Sant Atar Singh was a charismatic leader of the Sikh community in the beginning of the twentieth century. He was born on March 13, 1866 AD in village Chima in a farmer's family. As he grew up he joined as a gunner in the artillery but later got himself transferred to the 54th Sikh Battalion. He remained unmarried.

As Atar Singh had a deeply religious bent of mind, he got himself relieved from the army and devoted his entire time and energy in rejuvenating the Sikh community. He travelled extensively preaching the tenets of Sikhism, converting people and administering baptismal rites. Master Tara Singh who later became famous as a political leader and Bhai Jodh Singh, eminent theologian and educationist had taken *amrit* from him. He took keen interest in reforming Sikh education and was associated with many institutions. He took part in the Delhi Darbar in 1911 AD. He actively supported in gurdwara reform movement of the twenties of the twentieth century.

Sant Atar Singh passed away on January 31, 1927 AD at Sangrur. His body was cremated at Mastuana where now a beautiful gurdwara perpetuates his memory.

ATMAN : See Soul.

ATTACHMENT : Attachment called *moh* in Punjabi is one of the five vices identified in Sikhism. In simple terms it means immoderate bond that human beings may develop for certain objects or persons and a consequent delusion created by it. It gives them a tendency to view things wrongly and to become narrow-minded and mean. It makes men cling to certain things with which they identify. This tendency curtails their capacity to view things in the right perspective.

According to Sikhism it is the ignorant and the egocentric who get affected by attachment. "The ignorant are infatuated with attachment (to things) and do not know when they pass off". *Maha moh mohio gwara. Pekhat pekhat ooth sidhara* (AG. p. 740). "All attachments are vain illusions which bind an egocentric."
Moh maya wai sabh kalkha, in manmukh moor sajutiya. (AG. p. 776)

Sikhism advises very clearly: "Why involve yourself in pleasures and attachments for naked do we come and go." *Ab kya rang layo moh rachayo, nange aawn jawna.* (AG. p. 455)

Furthermore : "None is a child or mother of any. All are deluded by a false sense of attachment." *Na kis ka put na kis ki mai, jhoothe moh bharam bhulaee.* (AG. p. 357)

As always Sikhism suggests a very simple remedy for ridding oneself of *moh* through becoming God-centred. "He who is imbued with Truth is ever detached."
Sach rate sada bairagi (AG. p. 117)

AVTAR : See Incarnation.

AURANGZEB : Aurangzeb was the last of the great Mughal Emperors of India. He had virtually waded through a river of blood to ascend the throne in July 1658 AD after imprisoning his father and killing his brothers. Har Rai was the Sikh Guru at the time. Right from the beginning his relations with the Sikh Gurus were based on misunderstanding. He was made to believe that the Guru had helped Dara Shikoh when he was in Punjab. Consequently he called the Guru to Delhi who preferred to send his elder son Ram Rai. Aurangzeb came closer to Ram Rai and decided to keep him at Delhi in the belief that with the future incumbent of the Guruship in his power he would become the arbiter of the destiny of the Sikhs.

While at Delhi, Ram Rai had misread a line from the Adi Granth in the court of Aurangzeb. This angered Guru Har Rai who disowned Ram Rai and chose his younger son Harkrishan as his successor. The investiture of Guru Harkrishan did not please Aurganzeb who called the young Guru to Delhi in 1664 AD. He came and stayed at what is now Gurdwara Bangla Sahib and was then the bungalow of Mirza Raja Jai Singh. According to Sikh chroniclers, the Guru did not see the Emperor. There was raging in Delhi at that time an epidemic of small pox and cholera. The Guru was stricken with small pox and passed away on March 30, 1664 AD.

Guru Tegh Bahadur became the ninth Master. By that time Aurangzeb had unleashed a fanatical religious policy. In 1669 AD he issued a directive to all provincial governors "to destroy with a willing hand the schools and temples of the infidels and put an entire stop to their religious practices and teachings." Forcible conversions became the order of the day. A group of Kashmiri *Pandits* met the Guru in May 1675 to complain about conversions. The Guru told them to convey to Delhi that if he was converted, they would all voluntarily accept Islam. Subsequently the Guru was taken into custody and on his refusal to renounce his faith was beheaded publicly in the *Kotwali* now Gurdwara Sis Ganj at Delhi in November 1675 AD. This martyrdom paved the way for a complete transformation of the Sikh community.

Guru Gobind Singh succeeded Guru Tegh Bahadur after his martyrdom. He had realized that time had come for the young Sikh community to be completely transformed into a community of saint soldiers combining the impeccable purity of saints and fierce bravery of soldiers. For this purpose he founded the Khalsa Panth on the Baisakhi Day of 1699 AD. The unification of the community into a new order was bound to send danger signals to the Mughals. Aurangzeb was occupied with his compaigns in the South but his feudal vassals, the hill rajas resented the Guru's increasing power. They plotted in collusion with the local Mughal officers and led armies against the Guru. The Guru was besieged at Anandpur which he had to vacate in 1705 AD. The Mughal forces continued the chase and the Guru had to make supreme sacrifices. Two of his elder sons died fighting in the battle of Chamkaur. The two younger ones were bricked alive at Fatehgarh under the orders of the governor of Sirhind. The Guru's mother, Mata Gujri died of shock. Then the Guru wrote his famous letter called *Zafarnama* to Aurangzeb recalling how he had been forced to use the sword. Aurangzeb immediately sent directions to the governor of Lahore to make peace with the Guru. He also invited the Guru for a personal meeting. But before the meeting could take place, Aurangzeb died on Feburary 20, 1707 AD.

B

BAAZ : See Falcon.

BABA : *Baba* is a Persian word meaning father or grandfather and was used as such in Punjab before 1947 AD and is still commonly used in Pakistan. Among the Sikhs it is used as a title of affection and reverence for old as well as pious men. This was one of Guru Nanak's honorific titles used during his life time. It assumed a hereditary character and all the physical descendants of the Gurus came to be addressed by this title.

The title of *Baba* is also used for exceptionally pious persons as for example Baba Buddha who was a contemporary of the first six Gurus and personally performed the *tilak* ceremony of five of them; or few persons combining piety and authority as for example Baba Ala Singh, the founder of Patiala city and the progenitor of its royal family.

BABA ATAL : Gurdwara Baba Atal is situated very near the Golden Temple in Amritsar. Originally a *samadhi* (cenotaph), enshrining the remains of Atal Rai, a son of Guru Hargobind, it was transformed with the passage of time into a gurdwara. Atal Rai carried a wise head over young shoulders. It is said that when he was nine years old, he brought back to life a playmate Mohan, who had died of snake-bite. Guru Hargobind did not like this type of miracles and reprimanded him. Atal Rai laid down his life to atone for his mistake.

Baba Atal is a nine-storeyed octagonal tower representing nine years of Atal Rai's life. It is 45m high and has a gilded dome. It has four doors. The foundation of the present building was laid in 1778 AD. The first floor of Baba Atal has earned much fame because of the frescoes that it contains representing episodes from the life of Guru Nanak. By the side of the tower is a large tank, named Kaulsar built to commemorate the devotion of a Muslim girl, Kaulan who became a disciple of Guru Hargobind.

BABA BAKALA : Baba Bakala is a small town about 40 km from Amritsar. Guru Tegh Bahadur lived here for a long time with his mother Nanaki who initially belonged to Baba Bakala. Guru Harkrishan had pointed to Baba Bakala as the likely place where his successor could be found. Makhan Shah was able to spot the Guru here after going to all the twenty-two other claimants. It was at Bakala that the ninth Guru was anointed.

Guru Hargobind had also stayed here with his mother Ganga who died here in 1628 AD.

Baba Bakala is now a place of pilgrimage for the Sikhs. Important gurdwaras here are : Bhora Sahib (the place where Guru Tegh Bahadur lived), Darbar Sahib (where Guru Tegh Bahadur was anointed) and Manji Sahib (the place where Dhirmal got an assassination attempt made on the Guru).

BABAR : Babar was the founder of the Mughal dynasty in India. He had conquered Kabul in 1504 AD. Then he invaded India in 1505 AD, 1519 AD, 1520 AD, 1524 AD and finally in 1526 AD. After his victory against Ibrahim Lodhi in the battle of Panipat he became the master of Delhi.

Guru Nanak was an eye-witness to the havoc created during these invasions. It is believed that in 1520 AD he was taken prisoner at Saidpur which is now known as Eminabad and is 15 km from Gujranwala in Pakistan. Guru Nanak refers to the invasions of Babar in some of his verses which are collectively called *Babar Vani*.

Babar died on December 26, 1530 AD at Agra. Several years later his remains were moved to his present grave in one of the gardens of Kabul. Babar was succeeded by his son Humayun.

BABAR VANI : There are four hymns of Guru Nanak in the Adi Granth on pages 360, 417-18 and 772-73 which seem to have a reference to

Babar's invasions of India between 1505 AD and 1526 AD. These hymns are collectively called *Babar Vani*. They have been quoted in some *Janam Sakhis*.

Guru Nanak particularly gives a detailed account of Babar's massacre of village Saidpur where the Guru was then present and was made a captive. Babar himself admits in his Memoirs that people of Saidpur were killed, their women and children were taken prisoners and their property was looted.

Babar Vani is neither a narrative of historical events nor unlike *Zafarnama* an indictment of Babar. In spite of his destructive role Babar is seen by Guru Nanak to have been an unwitting instrument of the divine Will. Since Lodhi's had violated God's laws, they had to pay the penalty. So Babar descended from Kabul as God's chosen agent.

BABBAR AKALIS : Babbar Akalis were a splinter group of the Akalis involved in the Akali Movement for the reform of gurdwaras during the twenties of the twentieth century. While the mainstream Akalis had vowed to agitate peacefully and non-violently, the incidents at Tarn Taran and Nankana Sahib in 1921 AD led to the emergence of a group that rejected non-violence as a method of achieving their objective.

In April 1923 AD, the Babbar Akali Jatha which had been formed in August 1922 was declared an unlawful association by the British Government. Many Babbar Akalis were arrested and tried with senior leaders among them hanged to death on February 27, 1926 AD.

BABOO : See Gurplah.

BACHHOANA : Bachhoana is a village near Budhlada Mandi and was sanctified by a week's visit by Guru Tegh Bahadur. A gurdwara, administered by the SGPC through a local committee, commemorates the Guru's stay in the village and is known as Gurdwara Patshahi IX.

BACHITRA NATAK : One of the important compositions of Guru Gobind Singh included in the Dasam Granth. It is an autobiography of the Guru and was written by him at Anandpur in 1692 AD when he was 26 years old. He describes his penance in an earlier life in the snowy mountains of Hemkunt, his present birth and his mission. He also discusses the nine Gurus and the sacrifices of his father, Guru Tegh Bahadur. It also gives an account of the battles fought by the Guru.

Bachitra Natak has 471 verses divided into 14 chapters. Its language is old Hindi with a large number of Sanskrit words.

It is a clear and strong statement of God's and Guru Gobind Singh's role in history. This is described through a series of vivid battle scenes created with forceful imagination. Here the Guru conceives God as the embodiment of the fighting spirit. It is a confident call to saints to put on arms in continuation and transformation of earlier Sikhism.

BADDON : Baddon is a village 10 km from Mahilpur in Hoshiarpur district. *Sahibzada* Ajit Singh, the eldest son of Guru Gobind Singh had visited the village in May 1703 AD on his way back from Bassi Kalan where he had gone on an expedition to rescue a young Brahmin bride from the clutches of the local Pathan chief. He had halted at the village to cremate one of his warriors who had been wounded in the skirmish at Bassi Kalan and had later succumbed to his injuries. Gurdwara Baba Ajit Singh in the village commemorates the *Sahibzada's* visit. It is affiliated to the SGPC and is maintained by the local committee.

BAGHAIL SINGH : Baghail Singh was a brave Sikh leader of Karor Singhian *misl*. A Dhaliwal Jat, Bhagail Singh arose from the village of Jhabal in Amritsar district to become a formidable force in the cis-Sutlej region. The Mughals, the Ruhilas, the Marathas and the British sought his friendship. In the wake of the decay of Mughal authority in Punjab Bhagail Singh took possession of the Jalandhar Doab and established himself at Hariana near Hoshiarpur. In February 1764 AD he captured Saharanpur. In March 1783 AD, Khalsa Dal captured the Red Fort. Shah Alam II, then emperor of Delhi made a settlement with their allowing Bhagail Singh to develop the historical gurdwaras in Delhi. The credit of developing seven of the present nine historical gurdwaras at Delhi goes to him which he did staying at Subzi Mandi with 4000 followers. Bhagail Singh died probably in 1802 AD at Hariana where his *samadh* (cenotaph) still stands.

BAHADURGARH FORT: It is a fort situated about 9 km from Patiala. It was earlier known as Saifabad Fort and used to be the residence of Nawab Saif-ud-Din who was an admirer of Guru Tegh Bahadur. The Guru during his visit to the Malwa region in June 1675 AD had stayed in the Nawab's garden which no longer exists. Gurdwara Sri Guru Tegh Bahadur about 200m from the Fort commemorates the Guru's visit. Maharaja Karam Singh of Patiala got even the Saifabad Fort renamed as Bahadurgarh Fort after the Guru. He constructed another gurdwara in memory of the Guru inside the Fort.

BAHADUR SHAH : After the death of Aurangzeb, one of his sons Muazzam ascended the throne at Delhi in June 1707 AD with the title of Bahadur Shah and after the usual war of succession with his brothers. Guru Gobind Singh who had helped him in the war of succession because of his religious liberalism came to Agra in July 1707 AD to pay him a formal visit. The meeting became the starting point of parleys between the Guru and the Emperor on the question of state's religious policy. But Bahadur Shah had to leave suddenly for the Deccan to quell a rebellion by his brother. Guru Gobind Singh also travelled south to continue the negotiations. Bahadur Shah's conciliatory attitude towards the Guru was not liked by Wazir Khan, the governor of Sirhind who got the Guru fatally stabbed by two hired Pathans in October 1708 AD. The negotiations remained inconclusive but Banda Singh Bahadur left for Punjab to avenge the murder of the Guru and other atrocities on the Sikhs.

So when Bahadur Shah returned after the successful campaign against his brother in 1710 AD he found himself confronted with a Sikh rebellion under the banner of Banda Singh Bahadur. He ordered general mobilization of all his forces against the Sikhs. Bahadur Shah, with a massive imperial force – sixty thousand soldiers on horses and on foot – stormed the Lohgarh fortress of Banda Singh Bahadur but failed to capture him. He reached Lahore in August 1711 AD and Banda Singh Bahadur retired to the hills.

Bahadur Shah became melancholic and died on February 27, 1712 AD.

BAIRARI : An Indian classical *raag* usually sung within three hours (one *pahar*) before noon. It is thirteenth of the thirty-one *raags* used in the organisation of hymns in the Guru Granth Sahib covering pages 719-720.

BAISAKHI : Baisakhi is a traditional seasonal festival of North India where it is treated as the New Year's Day by farmers and others. Falling as it does on 13th April (First day of the month of Baisakh) every year, it coincides with the harvesting of wheat and is thus a harbinger of wealth and prosperity.

Baisakhi is celebrated by all communities but it has come to acquire a special significance for Punjabis in general and Sikhs in particular.

Guru Amardas convened the first assembly of the Sikhs at Goindwal on the Baisakhi Day of 1567 AD by sending *Hukamnamas*. The pilgrims took bath in the Baoli Sahib and participated in the *langar* before going to the Guru. Later on it became customary for the Sikhs to assemble and to offer prayers at gurdwaras on Baisakhi.

On the Baisakhi Day of 1622 AD Guru Hargobind had declared at Amritsar that any five good Sikhs could also initiate the new aspirants into the fold of Sikhism.

It was on the Baisakhi in 1699 AD that Guru Gobind Singh created the order of the Khalsa. So Baisakhi stands for the birth-anniversary of the Khalsa.

On the Baisakhi Day of 1748 AD, Dal Khalsa was created for giving a fight to Ahmad Shah Abdali.

On the Baisakhi Day of 1765 AD the Sikhs captured Lahore.

On the Baisakhi Day of 1801 AD Maharaja Ranjit Singh was coronated.

More recently the Baisakhi of 1919 AD saw the Jallianwala Bagh Massacre in Amritsar where hundreds of people laid down their lives to pave the way for the country's freedom.

In 18th century AD, the meetings of the Sarbat Khalsa were held, among other important days, on each Baisakhi.

BAKHAT KAUR, MATA : Mata Bakhat Kaur also called Lakhmi or Lakho was the mother of Guru Amardas. Born in a Duggal Khatri family, she was married to Baba Tej Bhan of Baserke near Amritsar. Four sons were born to her, Guru Amardas being the eldest. The other three were Ishar Das, Khem Rai and Manak Chand.

BALA, BHAI : Bhai Bala, a resdent of Guru Nanak's home-town Talwandi, became his disciple and constant companion. He was son of Chandar Bhan Sandhu. Being elder to Guru Nanak by three years, he is believed to have been born in 1466 AD. He travelled far and wide with Guru Nanak. He died in 1544 AD and the last rites were performed by Guru Angad himself.

One of the sources of information about Guru Nanak is *Janam Sakhi* by Bhai Bala. It is said to be dictated by Bhai Bala and written by Paida Mokha.

There are, however, some historians who reject the authenticity of both Bhai Bala's existence and his *Janam Sakhi*. According to them Bhai Bala's name does not appear in the list of prominent persons prepared by either Bhai Gurdas or Bhai Mani Singh. They also argue that if Bhai Bala were a genuine person, he could not have included some of the stories which are clearly disparaging. But the general consensus appears to be that Bhai Bala was a genuine person but his *Janam Sakhi* has been corrupted by Minas, Handaliyas and others.

BALA SAHIB, GURDWARA : It is a historical gurdwara situated in South Delhi. Guru Harkrishan passed away at Delhi after contracting small pox which was raging in the town during his visit. He was cremated where now stands Gurdwara Bala Sahib. Later Mata Sundri and Mata Sahib kaur, wives of Guru Gobind Singh, were also cremated here. It is being managed by Delhi Sikh Gurdwara Management Committee.

BALAK SINGH, BABA : Baba Balak Singh is the founder of Namdhari Movement in Sikhism. Son of a goldsmith of North-West frontier province in Pakistan, he was born in 1785 AD. He was outraged by the prevalence of moral laxity in the Sikh community. He specifically preached against the use of drugs, meat eating (though not strictly prohibited), sexual immorality, extravagance at weddings and the practice of dowry. He supported inter-caste marriages and the right of widows to remarry. By the time he died in 1862 AD, at Hazro this had become a veritabe movement. The work of Baba Balak Singh was sustained by his disciple Baba Ram Singh.

BALH, BHATT : Five *swayyas* composed by *Bhatt* Balh eulogizing Guru Ramdas are included in the Adi Granth. He highlights the unbroken continuity of the one unchanging spirit in all the Gurus. All those who surrender themselves to this spirit are delivered from passion, anger, sorrows and suffeings.

BALWAND, BHATT : A *rabab* (rebeck) player and a co-composer with his brother Satta in the time of Guru Arjan. A *var* composed by the two brothers is included in the Adi Granth. He was a Muslim *mirasi*. It is said that Balwand had become so proud of his art that he once refused Baba Buddha's request for reciting a *shabad*. Guru Arjan punished him and his brother by banishing them from his presence and the *sangat*. They were later pardoned on the intervention of Bhai Laddha of Lahore. See Laddha, Bhai.

Both Balwand and Satta are said to have passed away at Lahore in the time of Guru Hargobind and were burried on the bank of the River Ravi.

BAMBELI : Bambeli is a village about 12 km from Phagwara in Punjab. Guru Har Rai had visited it during one of his journeys between Kartarpur (Jalandhar) and Kiratpur. Gurdwara Chaunta Sahib (*Chaunta* in Punjabi means an earthen platform) commemorates the spot where the Guru had halted. The gurdwara is affiliated to the SGPC. Two Sikh penants close to the gurdwara mark the spots where four Babbar Akalis brought to bay by the police fell fighting in an encounter on september 1, 1923 AD.

BANDA SINGH BAHADUR : The famous Sikh hero who was sent to Punjab from the Deccan by Guru Gobind Singh to punish the enemies of the Khalsa. He attacked Samana in November 1709 AD and captured Sirhind in May 1710 AD killing Wazir Khan its Nawab in the battle of Chappar Chiri. Banda Singh Bahadur was crowned at Lohgarh and struck coins in the name of the Guru. He extended his sway up to Pathankot. Abdus Samad Khan, the governor of Lahore assembled a big army which besieged Banda Singh Bahadur for eight months before capturing him in December 1715 AD. He was brought to Delhi where he was tortured to death in June 1716 AD.

Banda was born in 1670 AD at Rajouri in Jammu State of Rajput parents and was named Lachhman Dev. He joined an order of *bairagis* (mendicants) at an early age and was given a new name, Madho Das. He went to south India and spent many years in Hindu monasteries. He had set up an establishment of his own at Nanded (Maharashtra), where he had lived for fifteen years before he met Guru Gobind Singh who gave him a new name *banda* (slave) to describe his relationship to the Guru. His name after baptism was changed to Gurbax Singh but he continues to be popularly known as Banda Singh Bahadur.

BANDA THAN : See Hazur Sahib.

BANDAI : This is the name given to the followers of Banda Singh Bahadur. Bandais regard him to be the spiritual successor to Guru Gobind Singh because of which they were expelled in 1721 AD from the mainstream by the Tatt Khalsa. Only a few Bandais survive now.

BANGLA SAHIB, GURDWARA : Gurdwara Bangla Sahib is one of the important historical gurdwaras of Delhi and is situated only at a stone's throw from Gurdwara Rakab Ganj. It is dedicated to the memory of Guru Harkrishan who had stayed at this place during his sojourn in Delhi. It used to be the bungalow of Mirza Raja Jai Singh. That is why it is called Bangla Sahib.

While Guru Harkrishan was staying here, smallpox and cholera broke out in the city and the Sikhs used to come to him for relief. He gave them water from a well in the bungalow. Now a *sarovar* (pool) stands there whose water is believed to have curative properties.

The dome of the gurdwara has recently been gilded.

BANGA : See Gurplah.

BANI : See Shabad.

BANI : *Bani* is a Punjabi word used for speech of any one but very often confined to the compositions included in the Adi Granth. See also Gurbani. The key concept was explained by Guru Ramdas when he sang: "The *Bani* is *Guru* and *Guru* is *Bani*." (AG. p. 982).

BANI POTHI : Bani Pothi which literally means a Book of Hymns is a collection of the compositions of the Gurus upto the third and some *bhagats*. It is a fore-runner of the Adi Granth. Indeed, it is the nucleus from which it was developed.

Guru Nanak had preserved his own compositions as well as those of some other *bhagats*. Following this example, Guru Angad and Guru Amardas added their own compositions to it. These hymns were arranged by Guru Amar-das' grandson, Sahansar Ram, son of Mohan, in two volumes of 300 and 224 leaves. At the time of Guru Arjan Bani Pothi was in the possession of Mohan at Goindwal. The Guru had to use lot of persuasion and inducement to get it from him at the time of compiling the Adi Granth. In fact, Guru Arjan went personally to Goindwal for the purpose and brought the two volumes to Amritsar in a palanquin.

BANNO, BHAI : Bhai Banno was the son of Bishan Chand Bhatia of village Mangat of district Gujarat in Pakistan. He became a faithful follower of Guru Arjan who involved him in the preparation of the Adi Granth. It was written on loose sheets and it was decided to get it bound in a beautiful hard cover at Lahore. Bhai Banno was entrusted with the task of taking the manuscript to Lahore for the purpose. He took Guru Arjan's permission to pass through his native village Mangat. It is said that on the way he prepared another copy with slight variations from the original. He extended the composition of Bhagat Surdas and included a stanza by Mira Bai. Guru Arjan crossed out these additions and declared that version as un-authentic. It is believed that this version is still in possession of the heirs to Bhai Banno. This un-authorized version of the Adi Granth is referred to in Sikh literature as *Khari Bir* or *Bhai Banno ki Bir*.

BAOLI SAHIB : *Baoli* is a Punjabi term for old type of masonry well with steps leading to the water level. Early Sikh Gurus constructed several *baolis* in villages and towns across Punjab. Some of them are :

  1. **Baolis at Anandpur :** There are two baolis at Guru-ka-Lahore near Anandpur.
  2. **Baoli Sahib, Bauran Kalan :** This is situated in village Bauran Kalan in Patiala district. It commemorates the visit by Guru Tegh Bahadur to the place.
  3. **Baoli Sahib at Dalla :** This is situated in village Dalla near Sultanpur. It was built by Guru Arjan in memory of the wedding of his son Guru Hargobind.
  4. **Baoli at Dhakoli :** This is located in village Dhakoli near Dera Bassi near Chandigarh. It is dedicated to Guru Gobind Singh.
  5. **Baoli Sahib, Goindwal :** This is the most famous of all Baoli Sahibs "This is the first great Sikh centre of pilgrimage which Guru Amardas himself got built in 1559 AD. He blessed that who ever, with a pure heart has the holy bath in the *baoli* and recites Japji 84 times will obtain release from the cycle of birth and rebirth."

The *baoli* has 84 steps and its entrance has been artistically decorated. Guru Amardas had himself put in manual labour at the time of its construction.

  6. **Baoli at Khahra :** This is located in village Khahra near Tarn Taran.

BAPTISM : The ceremony of baptism established by Guru Nanak for the initiation of his followers was called *charan pahul* and consisted in the drinking of water in which the feet of the Guru had been bathed. It continued up to Guru Tegh Bahadur. It still exists among the Nanak-Panthis.

The baptism of a Sikh now-a-days which was introduced by Guru Gobind Singh involves the administration of *amrit* by the *granthi* (preacher) in the presence of the Guru Granth Sahib. The neophyte should have washed his/her hair and should be wearing the five *Kakars*. Some *amrit* is sprinkled in his face and eyes and the remainder he drinks from the palms of hands, exclaiming "*Waheguru Ji Ka Khalsa Waheguru Ji Ki Fateh.*"

The *granthi* then instructs him in the articles of Sikhism. In addition to the *granthi* five *Amritdhari* Sikhs must be present to make initiation lawful. The ceremony is concluded by everybody present partaking of *karah prashad* which is distributed in equal proportion irrespective of caste.

Baptism includes *namkaran* as well. It is meant as complete transformation. Guru Gobind Singh had stated : "Since the time of Baba Nanak's *charan pahul* has been customary. Men drank the water in which the Gurus had washed their feet, a custom which led to great humility; but the Khalsa can now only be maintained as a nation by bravery and skill in arms. Therefore, I now institute the custom of baptism by water stirred with a dagger, and change my followers from 'Sikhs to Singhs or lions.' They who accept the nectar of the *pahul* shall be changed before your very eyes from jackals into lions, and shall obtain empire in this world and bliss hereafter." Here was a new revolutionary approach that provided social equality, moral sanctity, political legitimacy and vertical mobility for the lower castes and sections of society in their own right and with their own self identity. So baptism is not just a ritual, it has a sociological significance.

BARAH MAHA : *Barah Maha* is a form of folk poetry in which the emotions and yearnings of the human heart are expressed in terms of the changing moods of Nature over the twelve months of the year. Guru Nanak, Guru Arjan and Guru Gobind Singh have made use of this form of poetry.

1. Barah Maha by Guru Nanak : This is a part of the Adi Granth under *Raag* Tukhari. It stands out in Sikh literature for its poetic splendour and philosophical import. All the twelve months are important for it is in them that the interaction of the Timeless with time takes place— the young bride remaining in quest of her Timeless beloved.

2. Barah Maha by Guru Arjan : This is also a part of the Adi Granth under *Raag* Majh. It speaks of the separation of the human soul from the Divine Soul and its quest for union with Him. It artistically explains the existence of the Singular Reality and reiterates that there is none other beside Him. This *Barah Maha* is generally used at *Sangrand* congregation although sometimes the one by Guru Nanak is also used.

3. Barah Maha by Guru Gobind Singh : Guru Gobind Singh has used this poetic form in his composition Krishan Avtar which is a part of the Dasam Granth.

BARATH : Barath is a village 8 km from Pathankot. Baba Sri Chand, the elder son of Guru Nanak, who was a recluse, had established his hermitage here after the death of the Guru Barath, thus became the centre of the *Udasi* sect founded by Baba Sri Chand. Guru Arjan and later Guru Hargobind had visited the place to seek Baba Sri Chand's blessings.

Barath has the historical shrine Gurdwara Tap Asthan which is also sometimes called Gurdwara Barath Sahib. The shrine was maintained by the *Udasi* priests and was handed over to the SGPC during the Akali Movement.

BARGARI : Bargari is a village 15 km from Kotkapura in Faridkot district. Guru Gobind Singh visited it in December 1705 AD on his way from Dina to Kotkapura. Gurdwara Patshahi 10 commomerates the Guru's visit. During the Jaito Morcha, a *Shahidi Jatha* (band of martyrs) determined to reach Gurdwara Gangsar had made an overnight halt at the village in its march from Amritsar.

BARHE : Barhe is a village 6 km from Budhlada Mandi in Bhatinda distrcit. Guru Tegh Bahadur had spent a rainy season here while travelling in the Malwa region. Gurdwara Sri Tegh Bahadur commemorates the Guru's stay there. It is being administered by the SGPC.

BARNA : It is a village in Kurukshetra district of Haryana. Guru Tegh Bahadur once stopped here while journeying from Kaithal to Kurukshetra. Earlier a low platform was built at the spot where the Guru had set while visiting the home of a follower. Bhai Ude Singh the ruler of Kaithal later built a gurdwara over the memorial.

BASALI : It is a village 20 km from Kiratpur in Ropar district. Guru Gobind Singh had stayed here for several days after the battle of Nirmohgarh in October 1700 AD at the invitation of the chief of Basali. Gurdwara Guru Chaunki Jhira Sahib commemorates the

Guru's stay. The *chaunki* (low wooden platform) on which Guru Gobind Singh used to sit for meditation or while preaching still exists. The gurdwara is maintained by the local Sikh community.

BASANT : An Indian classical *raag* usually sung at night during the spring season. It is twenty-fifth of the thirty-one *raags* used in the organisation of hymns in the Guru Granth Sahib covering pages 1168-1196. The sequence of basic notes is :
   Arohi : sa, ga, ma, dha, re, sa ....
   Avrohi : re, na, dha, pa, ma ga, ma, ga, re, sa......

BASERKE : A village near Amritsar associated with Guru Amardas. The famous gurdwara Sanh Sahib is situated here. Guru Amardas is said to have gone into seclusion here on a disrespect shown by Guru Angad's son. The Guru had put up a notice on the door that anyone who enters the place will not be a Sikh. Baba Buddha had to break in through a hole in the opposite wall to have a glimpse of the Guru.

The *samadh* of Bibi Amro, the daughter of Guru Angad, is also situated near the village.

BEAS : See Radhasoamis.

BASSI KALAN : It is a village near Hoshiarpur. *Sahibzada* Ajit Singh, the eldest son of Guru Gobind Singh came here in March 1703 AD at the head of 100 horsemen to rescue a young Brahmin bride who had been forcibly taken away by the village chief : Jabbar Khan. Gurdwara Baba Ajit Singh constructed in 1980 AD commemorates the historic event. Earlier the memorial used to be just a mud hut.

BASSI PATHANA : Bassi Pathana is an old town near Sirhind. On Aurangzeb's orders, the governor of Lahore asked the *faujdar* of Sirhind to arrest Guru Tegh Bahadur in a manner not to raise any alarm. Accordingly he did not want to execute the order at Anandpur. The Guru moved out of Anandpur on July 11, 1675 AD accompanied by Bhai Mati Das, Bhai Sati Das and Bhai Dayala. After covering 40 km they halted for the night at Malikpur Ranghran where they were arrested next morning and whisked to Bassi Pathana where they were kept as under trial prisoners for nearly four months.

BATHU : Bathu is a village in Una district of Himachal Pradesh about 15 km from Nangal. Guru Gobind Singh visited the village in 1700 AD and held a discourse with Guru Nanak's direct descendant, Baba Kaladhari then living in Una. As the Guru has rested under a *plah* (Butia fondosa) tree, the commemorative gurdwara here is called Gurdwara Gurplah Patshahi 10.

BAURAN KALAN : See Baoli Sahib.

BAZIDPUR : It is a village 7 km from Ferozepur cantonment on Ferozepur Ludhiana highway. It has been sanctified by a visit by Guru Gobind Singh in 1706 AD after the battle at Muktsar. Gurdwara Gurusar which was earlier known as Tittarsar (*Tittar* is a Punjabi word for partridge) marks the site where Guru Gobind Singh had encamped.

BEGGING : See Kirat.

BENI : Beni was a great scholar who had made a deep study of the contemporary schools of thought. That is why he criticized not only the ritualistic Brahmanical religion of his time but also the *Yog Mat*. Little is known about Beni's date or place of birth. What emerges from his writings is the portrait of a great saint who dedicated himself, heart and soul, to the spiritual pursuits of life. Unperturbed by poverty, he enjoyed a life of calm contemplation and sweet serenity. Bhai Gurdas says that Beni always lived in solitude enriched by moments of spiritual edification.

Three verses of Beni have been incorporated in the Adi Granth under Sri Rag, Ramkali and Prabhati.

BENTI CHAUPAI : *Benti* in Punjabi means a

request, appeal or prayer. A prayer composed by Guru Gobind Singh in the poetic form of *chaupai* has been included in the Dasam Granth under the title Benti Chaupai. It starts :

"O God, give me Thy hand and protect me, And all my desires shall be fulfilled...............

Destroy all my enemies today, And all my hopes shall be fulfilled,"......................

BERAR : See Gurusar.

BER SAHIB : A number of *ber* (jujube) trees have been sanctified by their association with Sikh Gurus and personages. Some of the important ones are :

1. Ber Baba Buddha, Amritsar : It is an old *ber* tree standing in the *parikarma* (circumambulatory path) along the northern bank of the holy tank in the Golden Temple complex at Amritsar. Baba Buddha used to supervise the brick lining of the holy tank and later the construction of the Golden Temple itself sitting under this tree.

2. Beri Sahib, Seeloana : This is a gurdwara in village Seeloana in Ludhiana district. Guru Gobind Singh had stayed here under a *ber* tree.

3. Ber Sahib, Sultanpur Lodhi : This is a historical Sikh shrine at Sultanpur Lodhi. It marks the place where Guru Nanak during his stay at Sultanpur had planted a *ber* tree sapling on the banks of the *Bein* (rivulet) where he used to go for morning bath and meditation. The tree still exists.

According to Sikh tradition it was at this spot that Guru Nanak went into a trance for 72 hours. One day he dived into the *Bein* and was found only 72 hours later in a state of meditation across the *Bein*. When he was located, he had received the God's command to preach His gospel of universal brotherhood.

The shrine was constructed in the period 1938-42 and is all in marble and mosaic. At the back of the main hall of the shrine are the *ber* trees and the meditation spot.

BHADAUR : It is a small town about 25 km from Barnala in Sangrur district. Guru Gobind Singh came here from Dina in December 1705 AD when he was being chased by the Mughal forces. Guru Hargobind is also believed to have passed through the town. It has two important gurdwaras : (i) Gurdwara Andruni Patshahi X which is situated inside the town and has some relics of Guru Gobind Singh; and (2) Gurdwara Bairuni Patshahi VI which is outside the town and has been dedicated to Guru Hargobind. The latter used to be known as Samadh Bhai Charan Das until it was acquired by the SGPC during the seventies of the twentieth century and converted into a gurdwara.

BHAGAT RATNAVALI : It is an exposition in Punjabi prose of a *var* (no. 11) from Bhai Gurdas' *varan*. The *var* contains a roster of the names of some important Sikhs who lived during the times of the first six Gurus without giving many details about them. Bhagat Ratnavali attempts to give these details.

The authorship of Bhagat Ratnavali is generally attributed to Bhai Mani Singh although some historians treat it as doubtful. It is possible that the anecdotes might have been recorded by some one who had heard Bhai Mani Singh narrate them at congregations.

BHAGATS : See Adi Granth : Bhagats.

BHAGAUTI : Etymologically *bhagauti* is a Punjabi derivative of the Sanskrit word Bhagvati the name of a concort of Lord Vishnu, also known as Bhavani or Durga. However, in Sikh literature, the semantic evolution of the word *bhagauti* has led to a bifocal meaning.

Bhai Gurdas uses *bhagauti* as an equivalent of sword in English. "Iron when properly wrought becomes sword". *Nau bhagauti lohu gharaia* (Varan, XXII, 6) Guru Gobind Singh in his *Chandi di Var* where he describes the exploits of the Hindu goddess Durga does not restrict the use of *bhagauti* for Durga but extends its use for the Almighty the Divine Sword—the Power that brings about the evolution and devolution of the Universe. He uses the word *Sri* (For example *Sri bhagauti ji sahae*) to smoothen the gender distinction in the concept of God. Indeed remembering God through heroic symbols was the exclusive style of Guru Gobind Singh. Through his writings, the Guru has consecrated the sword—indeed, the whole spectrum of weaponry. He even made *kirpan* (sword) one of the five *kakars* to be always worn by the Sikhs.

BHAGO, MAI : Mai Bhago was a staunch Sikh by birth and upbringing and was the wife of Nidhan Singh Waraich of Patti. She was distressed to know in 1705 AD that some of the Sikhs of the neighbourhood who had gone to Anandpur to fight for Guru Gobind Singh had deserted him under adverse conditions. She rallied the deserters persuading them to meet the Guru when he was in the Malwa region being chased by the Mughal forces to seek apologies from him. They had hardly reached the Guru when the enemy forces overtook them. There ensued a battle at Khidrana (now Muktsar) on December 29, 1705 AD. All the 40 deserters died fighting the forces. Mai Bhago was the lone survivor of the battle, though wounded. Thereafter she joined Guru Gobind Singh as one of his bodyguards in male attire. After the death of the Guru at Nanded in 1708 AD, she settled down at Jinvara, 11 km from Bidar in Karnataka where she lived to attain a ripe old age. Her hut in Jinvara has now been converted into Gurdwara Tap Asthan Mai Bhago.

BHAGRANA : See Manji Sahib.

BHAI : *Bhai* is a Punjabi and Hindi word which means brother. But in Sikh literature it is seldom used with this connotation. In fact the word has been undergoing a semantic evolution. During the time of the Sikh Gurus it had an honorific connotation and was used with personages like Mardana, Gurdas and Mani Singh. In the twentieth century, it became a title for the few who earn substantial reputations for piety and religious learning as for example Jodh Singh, Vir Singh, Kahn Singh and Randhir Singh. No formal investiture is involved in such cases. It is simply conferred through repeated usage and thus reflects a general opinion rather than any conscious decision.

Bhai these days is also used to describe the vocational role of a person employed as manager, musician, or instructor in a gurdwara.

Since the days of Bhai Nand Lal, a contemporary of Guru Gobind Singh, the term has been appropriated by Sahajdhari Sikhs as a form of addressing each other.

BHAINI SAHIB : See Ram Singh, Baba.

BHAIRO : An Indian classical *raag* usually sung at dawn. It is twenty-fourth of the thirty-one *raags* used in the organisation of hymns in the Guru Granth Sahib covering pages 1125-1167. The sequence of basic notes is :
  Arohi : sa, re, ga, ma, pa, dha, ne, sa...................
  Avrohi : sa, ne, dha, pa, ma, ga, re, sa................

BHAKTI : *Bhakti* in general means a feeling of devotion or attachment particularly to God. In contrast to *shakti* (power), it represents a spirit of self-surrender. In certain Hindu sects as for example *Lingayats*, *bhakti* becomes an end rather than the means—a position unacceptable to Sikhism.

The Sanatana Dharma has thought of a threefold path for attaining *mukti*. The three paths are of *bhakti*, *gyan* and *karma* corresponding to the affective, cognitive and conative aspects of our psychological make-up. There are similar triads in other religions as well. For example Islam has : *shariat*, *tariquat*, and *haqiqat*.

Bhakti cult took strong roots in South India and gradually travelled to the North. In the words of Munshi Ram Sharma : The Dravid country is the birth place of *bhakti* school; *bhakti* became young in Karnataka, it grew old in Maharashtra and Gujarat, but when it arrived in Vrindravana, it became young again." (*Bhakti ka Vikas*; p. 353). Sikhism undoubtedy was considerably influenced by the Bhakti movement in North India.

BHAKTI MOVEMENT : *Bhakti* which in religious idiom means fervent devotion to God took roots as a cult in South India where generations of Alvar and Nayanar saints had sung their devotional lyrics and founded their respective schools of *bhakti* between 200-900 AD. From the south it gradually travelled upwards and in madieval times the cult had become a veritable movement there under the influence of scores of saints and savants. An important influence in north Indian *bhakti* was Ramanand whose many disciples including Kabir, Ravidas, Pipa, Sadhana and Sain radicalized the Bhakti movement. The reasons for this transformation are a matter of conjecture. Some find the influence of Islam as an important factor. Others trace it to Christianity.

It is believed that Bhakti movement reached Punjab through Nam Dev during the closing years of the thirteenth century. Sain Das set up a centre at Gujranwala. His successors established brancehs at a number of places in Punjab and Jammu regions. It is also asserted that Kabir's verses had become popular in north India, including Punjab.

Saints of Bhakti movement preached that God cannot be apprehended by the senses. He is beyond the ken of logic or argument, and is attained only through a whole-hearted devotion. They repudiated *avtarvad*, social ideology of caste, ritualistic formalism and idol worship.

Sikhism undoubtedly was influenced by Bhakti movement as well as Sufiism which was a similar movement in Islam. It is not, therefore, surprising that the compositions of some *Bhagats* and *Sufis* were included in the Adi Granth. See Adi Granth : Bhagats.

BHALH, BHATT : Only one *swayya* composed by *Bhatt* Bhalh in praise of Guru Amardas has been included in the Adi Granth. It testifies to his greatness as a poet with a flawless command of idiom and imagery. He sings of Guru's infinite virtues and imperishable greatness.

BHANA : Generally used interchangeably with *Hukam*. See God's will.

BHANA, BHAI : Bhai Bhana was the youngest son of Baba Buddha and was born in 1536 AD in village Kathu Nangal in Amritsar district. After the death of Baba Buddha in 1631 AD, Bhai Bhana succeeded him in the position of honour in Guru Hargobind's household. In that capacity, he had the honour of performing the last rites of Guru Hargobind and the installation ceremony of Guru Har Rai in March 1644 AD. He himself died the same year at village Jhanda Ramdas where his *samadh* (cenotaph) still exists by the side of his father's.

BHANG : See Intoxicants.

BHANGANI : Bhangani is a small village in Himachal Pradesh about 11 km from Paonta Sahib. Guru Gobind Singh fought his first battle here against the hill chieftains, in which he defeated them. This battle is mentioned in Bachitra Natak and was fought in 1688 AD.

Two gurdwaras exist at Bhangani commemorating the battle. Gurdwara Tirgarh stands on the mound where the Guru had stood to monitor the battle. Gurdwara Bhangani Sahib marks the site where the Guru had kept his munitions and provisions. Both the gurdwaras are locally managed.

BHANI, BIBI : Bibi Bhani who was the daughter of Guru Amardas, wife of Guru Ramdas and mother of Guru Arjan has been a unique Sikh personage. She was born to Mata Mansa Devi on January 19, 1535 at Baserke. She was married to Bhai Jetha (who later became Guru Ramdas) on February 18, 1554 AD and stayed on at Goindwal to be of service to her father. Sikh tradition speaks very highly of her devotion and service to Guru Amardas who had blessed her that her progeny would inherit the Guruship. It is also believed by some chroniclers that she was gifted a piece of land by Emperor Akbar when he visited Guru Amar- das at Goindwal and her husband was specially deputed to by the Guru to set up a habitation there. This habitation later on grew to become the beautiful city of Amritsar.

Three sons : Prithi Chand (1558 AD),

Mahadev (1560 AD) and Guru Arjan (1563 AD) were born to Bibi Bhani. She died at Goindwal on April 9, 1598 AD.

BHANO KHERI : It is a village in Ambala district. Guru Gobind Singh who was born at Patna in 1666 AD and spent his childhood there was being escorted to Anandpur in 1670-71 AD. On the way the party halted for some time at Lakhnaur. As he was playing with his friends one day, he hit the ball which landed near village Bhano Kheri. The Guru had come here to collect the ball. Gurdwara Gend Sahib outside Bhano Kheri commemorates the incident. *Gend* is a vernacular word for ball.

BHATTS : *Bhatt* is a term used for a bard or panegyrist who recites poetry landing the grandeur of a celebrity. According to Sikh tradition, they were poets with personal experience and vision of the spirituality of the Gurus whom they praise in their verses. The number of *bhatts* whose compositions are included in the Adi Granth is not yet finally settled, different scholars giving different numbers varying from 11 to 19 probably because of the fact that they used to sing in chorus. Most of the traditional scholars, however, believe that compositions of 17 *bhatts* are included in the Adi Granth. They have contributed 123 *sawayyas* as follows : Bhikha (2), Kalh (53), Jalap (4), Kirat (8), Mathura (12), Salh (3), Bhalh (1), Balh (5), Haribans (2), Nalh (5), Das (10), Sevak (4), Parmanand (5), Tal (1), Jalan (2), Jalh (1) and Gayanand (5).

BHIKHA, BHATT : *Bhatt* Bhikha was a Brahmin bard of Sultanpur Lodhi who was given initiation as a Sikh by Guru Amardas at Goindwal. He lived upto the time of Guru Arjan to whom he introduced sixteen other Brahmin minstrels from his community. They sang the praises of God and the Gurus. Some of their compositions are included in the Adi Granth. Two *swayyas* of *Bhatt* Bhikha are also included in the Adi Granth.

BHIKHAN : Bhikhan was a Muslim Sufi saint of Kakeri near Lucknow, who died in the early part of Akbar's reign. He was the most learned of the learned men of his time, abstemious and well-versed in the holy law. For many years he was engaged in teaching and instructing the people. It has been conjectured, with some show of probability, that Bhikhan was a follower of Kabir. He believed that only God's name can heal a diseased mind and body. Two of his hymns are included in the Adi Granth under Sorath Raag.

BHIM CHAND : Bhim Chand (1667-1712 AD) was the raja of Bilaspur in whose territory Anandpur fell. He was the most concerned because of the growing popularity of Guru Gobind Singh and the power of the Khalsa. Indeed he became the bitterest enemy of the Guru and conspired with other hill *Rajas* and Mughal forces to out the Guru from Anandpur. He led the first expedition against the Guru in 1682 AD when the Guru was just sixteen but he was beaten back. Later on there were many more skirmishes in and around Anandpur. See also Sayyid Beg. Finally Bhim Chand sought help from Emperor Aurangzeb. It was only when the Mughal forces joined those of the hill Rajas that Guru Gobind Singh had to evacuate Anandpur in December 1705 AD.

BHIRAI, MAI : Mai Bhirai or Virai was a pious lady who originally belonged to Matte di Sarai, the ancestral place of Guru Angad. She was married to Bhai Mahima of Khadur where Guru Angad's father Baba Pheru Mal had also settled. As she was like a sister to Baba Pheru Mal, Guru Angad respected her very much. According to Sikh tradition after Guru Angad was nominated as the spiritual successor to Guru Nanak and advised to return to Khadur from Kartarpur (Pakistan), he instead of going to his own home went to Mata Bhirai's and stayed there for some time in seclusion. Baba Buddha persuaded him to come out to assume leadership of the Sikh community. Gurdwara Mai Bhirai now marks the site where Mai Bhirai's house once stood.

BHOG : In Sanskrit *bhog* signifies delight or pleasure but in Sikh tradition it is used for a group of observances at the conclusion of the recitation (both *Akhand path* and *Sahaj path* of the Guru Granth Sahib.) The *bhog* must in all cases include the reading of the last five pages of the scripture beginning with the *slokas* of Guru Tegh Bahadur upto end of the Book. After the completion of the reading the *ardaas* is recited followed by *wak* (order of the day) and distribution of *karah parsad*.

BHORA SAHIB : General name for the basement of a building which has been sanctified by a Guru. Following Bhora Sahibs are important :

  1. Bhora Sahib Anandpur : It is a three-storeyed domed building close to Damdama Sahib at Anandpur. Here is a *bhora* (basement) Guru Tegh Bahadur used to retire for solitary meditation.

  2. Bhora Sahib, Baba Bakala : It is a nine-storeyed gurudwara with a gilded dome at Baba Bakala. Guru Tegh Bahadur used to sit in solitary meditation in the basement here. According to Sikh tradition, it was here that a wealthy trader Makhan Shah had discovered him absorbed in meditation and proclaimed publicly that he was the real Guru which settled the succession to Guru Harkrishan.

  3. Bhora Sahib, Fateh Garh : The basement of the main shrine at Fatehgarh where the two younger sons of Guru Gobind Singh were bricked alive.

BIBEKSAR : Bibeksar is a *sarovar* (tank) in the walled city of Amritsar between Chatiwind and Sultanwind gates. It was got dug by Guru Hargobind in 1628 AD for the convenience of such pilgrims as would prefer seclusion to the hustle and bustle of the Golden Temple. Gurdwara Bibeksar at the *sarovar* was raised by Maharaja Ranjit Singh in 1833 AD.

BIDAR : Bidar is a district town in Karnataka. Guru Nanak had halted here on his way to Sri Lanka during his travels. The Guru stayed next to a monastery of Muslim ascetics on the outskirts of the town. The *faqirs* and their head Pir Jalal-ud-Din, attracted by the holy *shabads* being sung to the accompaniment of Mardana's rebeck came and made obeisance to the Guru. The place came to be known as Nanak Jhira. Mai bhago who had settled at Jinvara in the south after the death of Guru Gobind Singh used to visit the place frequently. The shrine was initially looked after by Muslim priests. It gained prominence as a place of pilgrimage after the control was passed over to the Sikhs in 1948 AD which was confirmed by a judicial verdict in 1950 AD.

The local Sikh community has set up an engineering college and a charitable hospital at Bidar.

BIDHI CHAND : Bhai Bidhi Chand who was a resident of village Sur Singh of district Lahore started his career as a robber. Later on he became a devout disciple of Guru Arjan and also served Guru Hargobind. He showed tremendous bravery and cleverness in recovering Guru Hargobind's horses from the stables of the governor of Lahore. The horses had been forcibly taken away by the governor's men when they were being brought from Kabul. Some scholars call him the Robin Hood of Majha because of his dare-devilry.

  1. Bhai Bidhi chand was very close to Budhan Shah and his disciple Sunder Shah. In fact Bhai Bidhi Chand and Sunder Shah died on the same day at village Devnagar near Ayodhya on the banks of the river Gomti in September 1638 AD.

  2. Bidhi chand was the son of Hindal, a disciple of Guru Amardas for details, see Hindal.

BHIAGRA : An Indian classical *raag* usually sung at midnight. It is a variation of Bihag *raag* in which the basic notes occur in the following sequence.

  Arohi : sa, ga, ma, pa, ne, sa..............
  Avrohi : sa, na, dha, pa, ma, ga, re, sa,..............

Bihagra is the seventh of the thirty one *raags* used in the organisation of the Guru Granth Sahib covering pages 537-556.

BIKRAMI SAMWAT : Bikrami Samwat is the popular ancient Indian system of chronology, very commonly used in mentioning religious happening. It started 57 years before the beginning of the Christian era *i.e.* the birth of Christ. The Muslim era Hejira dating from the flight of Prophet Muhammad from Mecca to Medina began still later in 622 AD.

The origin of Bikrami Samwat is shrouded in mystery—various historians attributing it to various kings. The most commonly accepted view, however, is that it was started by Bikramaditya (Vikramaditya), a famous scholar king of Ujjain.

The first day of each month in Bikrami Samwat is called *Sangrand* when special congregations are held in gurdwaras.

BILAWAL : An Indian classical *raag* usually sung about two hours (beginning of the second *pahar*) before noon. It is sixteenth of the thirty-one *raags* used in the organisation of hymns in the Guru Granth Sahib covering pages 795-858.

BILGA : It is a village near Phillaur in Punjab. Guru Arjan passed through it in june 1589 AD, when he was going to Mau to get married. At Bilga, which was then a small habitation, the Guru changed his clothes. Gurdwara Pajvin Patshahi which is administered by the SGPC through a local committee commemorates the Guru's visit. Some of the discarded articles of apparel are preserved here as relics.

BINOD SINGH : Binod Singh was a direct descendant of Guru Angad and was a devoted disciple of Guru Gobind Singh whom he had accompanied to the Deccan in 1708 AD. When Banda Singh Bahadur was deputed by the Guru to go to Punjab to flight against the tyrannical forces, Binod Singh was sent with him as one of the *Panj Piaras*. In the ensuing expedition he was a constant ally of Banda Singh Bahadur. After the conquest of Sirhind, the frontier district of Karnal bordering Delhi was entrusted to him.

Binod Singh, however, parted company with Banda Singh Bahadur in October 1714 AD when the latter's followers got divided into Tatt Khalsa and Bandai Sikhs. The Mughal forces when they besieged Banda Singh Bahadur at Gurdas Nangal, had taken Binod Singh with him to fight on their side. There in 1716 AD he tried to retire without fighting and was killed by the Mughal forces along with a few thousand of his followers.

BIRK : See Manji Sahib

BIRO, BIBI : Bibi Biro was the daughter of Guru Hargobind and Mata Damodari. She was born at Amritsar in 1616 AD. She was married to Bhai Sadhu son of Khosla Khatri Bhai Dharma of village Jhabaal in 1630 AD. She gave birth to five brave sons: Sango Shah, Gulab Chand, Jit Mal, Ganga Ram and Mahri Chand. They were devoted followers of Guru Gobind Singh and fought valiantly in the battle at Bhangani. Sango Shah and Jit Mal were killed in the battle.

BIR SINGH, BABA : Baba Bir Singh was a devout Sikh preacher who was a contemporary of Maharaja Ranjit Singh and had initially worked for some time in his army. He was born in 1769 AD to Bhai Sewa Singh and Mai Dharam Kaur of village Gaggobooha near Tarn Taran. Under the persuasion of Baba Dasaundha Singh of Naurangabad he set up his headquarters there and influenced the spread and consolidation of Sikhism in Majha region. In 1845 AD Attar Singh Sandhawalia took shelter with Baba Bir Singh when he was camping at Hari-ke-Pattan. Raja Hira Singh Dogra asked Baba Bir Singh to hand over Attar Singh to his forces. On his refusal, Raja Hira Singh used force in which Baba Bir Singh was fatally wounded. His *samadh* exists at Naurangabad.

BOTA SINGH, BHAI : Bhai Bota Singh is a Sikh martyr of the eighteenth century. He belonged to village Bharana in Amritsar district and because of the persecution of Sikhs had sought the safety of forests. At nightfall, he would come out of his hiding and visit human habitations in search of food. Occasionally he would come to Amritsar by night to have a dip in the holy tank.

On one occasion, a party of *zamindars* met Bhai Bota Singh by chance. They were surprised to see a Khalsa around in those days when there was a price on the head of a Sikh. One of the party remarked that he could not be a Sikh for Sikhs being brave would not conceal themselves thus. This remark cut Bota Singh to the quick. He decided to come out of his hiding with his companion Garja Singh. Both of them stationed themselves in a dilapidated inn near Tarn Taran.

Zakriya Khan, the governor of Lahore, sent a contingent of one hundred horsemen under Jalal Din to capture Bhai Bota Singh and his companion. Both of them preferred dying after giving a valiant fight in 1739 AD to surrendering to Jalal Din.

BUDDHA, BABA : Baba Buddha is a unique personage in Sikhism. He was a contemporary of the first six Sikh Gurus and had personally performed the anointment ceremony for Gurus from second to sixth.

Baba Buddha was born in 1506 AD in village Kathu Nangal (District Amritsar). He met Guru Nanak for the first time in 1518 AD when the Guru had visited his village. He impressed the Guru as having an old head on young shoulders and won the appellate of "Buddha" (old).

In 1604 AD Baba Buddha became the first *granthi* (priest of the Golden Temple and in that capacity completed the first *path* (perusal) of the Adi Granth. He passed away in 1631 AD at village Ramdas (District Amritsar). The last rites were performed by Guru Hargobind. Two shrines stand at Ramdas in memory of Baba Buddha; Gurdwara Tap Asthan which was the residence for the family and Gurdwara Samadhan where he was cremated. So much respected was Baba Buddha among the Sikh masses that after the execution of Guru Arjan and when Guru Hargobind was in the prison in Gawalior, the affairs of the community were left, among others, in the hands of Baba Buddha and Bhai Gurdas.

Earlier he had played an important role in the development of Sikh institutions. He had devoted himself zealously to tasks such as the digging of the *baoli* at Goindwal under the instructions of Guru Amardas and the excavation of the sacred tank at Amritsar under Guru Ramdas and Guru Arjan. When Guru Hargobind raised the Akal Takhat, the first platform was built by Baba Buddha and Bhai Gurdas after the corner stone had been laid by the Guru and no third person was involved.

BUDDHA DAL : In 1734 AD Nawab Kapur Singh tried to organise various warrior groups of the Khalsa that had come up during the turbulent days in the post Banda Singh Bahadur period. He divided the Khalsa into two groups on the basis of age. The troops commanded by older leaders were called the Buddha Dal or the Veterans and the forces under the command of younger leaders were termed the Taruna Dal or the Verdants. Each group was further sub-divided into five units on the model of *misls* of Guru Gobind Singh's time. Nawab Kapur Singh retained the command of both as well as his own *misl*. Thus there were, indeed, eleven units as during the times of Guru Gobind Singh and Banda Singh Bahadur.

On the Baisakhi Day of 1748 AD, the Sarbat Khalsa, on a proposal by Nawab Kapur Singh, created the Dal Khalsa—the army of the Khalsa to face the expected invasions of Ahmad Shah Abdali. Jassa Singh Ahluwalia was made its Supreme Commander. The broad division into Buddha Dal and Taruna Dal was still retained. For better military organisation, they demarcated their respective areas of operation. After a great deal of discussion, the river Beas and the river Sutlaj after its influence with Beas at Hari-ke-Patan was accepted as the approximate dividing line. Buddha Dal was incharge of the area of its east and Taruna Dal was responsible for the area of its west.

The *misls* of the Buddha Dal continued cooperating in joint operations in Ruhila and Mughal territories in the Ganga-Yamuna Doab and in the country north and west of Delhi, Buddha Dal and Taruna Dal together defeated Ahmad Shah Abdali in Jalandhar Doab in

March 1765 AD. But such co-operations were becoming fewer. In fact as time passed, the two Dals entrenched in their respective spheres as separate *misls*. With this the term Buddha Dal as also Taruna Dal became redundant and went out of use.

BUDHMAR : Se Manji Sahib

BUDHU SHAH, PIR : *Pir* Budhu Shah was a Muslim sufi saint of Sadhaura near Ambala. He was a contemporary of Guru Gobind Singh and was known for his piety and holiness in the region. He had recommended 500 Pathans for being employed in the forces of Guru Gobind Singh. But when they deserted the Guru in the Battle of Bhangani, Pir Budhu Shah sent 700 of his disciples under the command of his four sons to assist the Guru. Two of his sons died fighting in the battle. After the victory, Guru Gobind Singh gave a *saropa* (robe of honour) to Pir Budhu Shah. Some of the articles are preserved as relics in the palace of the descendants of the Maharaja of Nabha.

Sixteen years later, he was tried for assisting Guru Gobind Singh by Wazir Khan, the governor of Sirhind. Pir Budhu Shah and his family were killed in cold blood in March, 1704 AD. He set up a noble example of being free from religious bigotry and of co-operation in the right cause. His descendants enjoyed a holy status in the area upto 1947 AD when they left for Pakistan. Their ancestral house in Sadhaura has since been converted into a gurdwara named after Pir Budhu Shah.

BUNGA : Bunga is a place about 5 km from Kiratpur. Guru Har Rai used to keep his horses here. It has a historical shrine called Gurdwara Bunga Sahib or Chubachcha Sahib. At the back of the gurdwara there is a row of rooms one of which has within it a square pit symbolizing the original trough (*chubachcha*) where the horse feed used to be mixed. The gurdwara is managed by the SGPC through a local committee.

BUNGAS : *Bunga* literally means a hospice or a dwelling place. In Sikh literature it is particularly used for the mansions that grew up around the Golden Temple and at other centres of Sikh pilgrimage. Amritsar has the largest number of such buildings. When Sikhs established their authority over Punjab, the chiefs of *misls* for whom Amritsar was a sort of political capital build their *bungas* on the periphery of the holy tank. Similarly other *bungas* also came up. They can be broadly classified into three categories: (1) those belonging to the different ruling clans; (2) those belonging to individual chiefs and (3) those belonging to different sects like *Udasis*, Nirmalas and Akalis. The third category had some *bungas* that were the centres of education and learning.

The *bungas* became the property of the SGPC after the passing of the Sikh Gurdwara Act 1925 AD. This was challenged upto to Punjab High Court by the owners but the court upheld the earlier decision.

Some of the old *bungas* had to be demolished at the time of widening the *parikarma*

BURHANPUR : Burhanpur is a town in Khandwa district of Madhya Pradesh. Guru Nanak visited it during his travels and left a *sangat* there. This has been converted into a small gurdwara known as Gurdwara Sangat Rajghat Patshahi I. Guru Gobind Singh encamped outside the town when he was travelling to Deccan with Emperor Bahadur Shah in 1708 AD. The site came to be designated as Gurdwara Bari Sangat. It has a copy of the Adi Granth with an inscription which is believed to be the signature of Guru Gobind Singh.

BURIA : See Manji Sahib

BURJ : *Burj* is a Punjabi word for tower. Some towers associated with famous Sikh personages have become historical.

1. Burj Akali Phula Singh, Amritsar : Akali Phula Singh had his head-quarters at Amritsar. A tower exists at the site which is known as Burj Akali Phula Singh.

2. Burj Mata Gujri : A gurdwara in Sirhind

built at a place where Guru Gobind Singh's mother Mata Gujri and his two younger sons: *Sahibzadas* Zorawar Singh and Fateh Singh were imprisoned in 1704 AD by Wazir Khan, the then governor of Sirhind. Mata Gujri had died here of shock on hearing of the execution of her grandsons.

   3. **Burj Baba Deep Singh, Talwandi Sabo :** This is a 20 m high tower with a dome at the top near Takht Damdama Sahib, Talwandi Sabo. This was got constructed by Baba Deep Singh, Chief of the Shahid *misl* who was camping at Talwandi Sabo during the middle of the eighteenth century.

BURJ SAHIB, GURDWARA : Gurdwara Burj Sahib is situated in village Fatte Nangal near Gurdaspur and is dedicated to Guru Arjan. The devotees raised an earthen tower at the place where the Guru had stayed which has now been converted into a gurdwara.

C

CASTE SYSTEM : The Sikhs are a casteless society. Guru Nanak did not like the caste system prevalent in his days. He advised : "Know people by the light illuminating them and do not ask their caste; for in the hereafter no one is differentiated by his caste.' *Janho joti na puchho jati; aage jati na hai* (AG. p. 349). "God does not mind our caste or birth. So let us learn the way of truthful living; for one's deeds proclaim one's caste and respect." (Ibid, p. 1330).

Taking the image of the potter's wheel Guru Arjan compared the different kinds of people to vessels of many types and patterns, but all made of clay. Guru Gobind Singh declared in unequivocal terms : "The caste of all mankind is one and the same." The Panj Piaras hailed from different castes and were unified by Sikh Baptism. The Adi Granth contains not only the compositions of the Sikh Gurus but also the hymns of Hindu and Muslim saints of all castes.

Bhai Gurdas has most beautifully expressed the position taken Sikhism on caste system. "All four castes have become one. All disciples of the Guru belong to the Gurmukh caste". *Char varan ik varan hoe; Gursikh waryam, Gurmukh gote.* (Var 29, Pauri 5).

It is unfortunate that in spite of the theological stipulations against caste system, some Sikhs are still carried away by it. Now there is a three tiered caste structure among Sikhs; Jats, Non-Jats and Mazahbis.

CELIBACY : See Asceticism.

CHABBA : It is a village about 10 km from Amritsar. Guru Hargobind is believed to have fought a battle here with the Mughal forces. Gurdwara Sangrana Sahib managed by the SGPC through a local committee is a reminder of the event. According to local tradition Guru Arjan had also halted here on his way to Amritsar from Goindwal while he was bringing the *pothis* of holy hymns borrowed from Baba Mohan.

CHAKAR : It is a village in Ludhiana district. Guru Hargobind passed through it in 1631-32 AD during his tour of Malwa region and Guru Gobind Singh did so in 1705 AD after the battle of Chamkaur. Chakar has an imposing Sikh shrine called Gurdwara Guru Sar patshahi VI & X managed by the SGPC through the village committee.

CHAK FATEH SINGH WALA : It is a village near Bhuchcho Mandi in Bhatinda district. Guru Gobind Singh had stayed here for a week in May 1706 AD on his way from Talwandi Sabo to Bhatinda. Gurdwara Sri Guru Gobind Singh in the village managed by the SGPC through a local committee commemorates the Guru's stay in the village.

CHALI MUKTE : *Chali Mukte* which literally means the Forty Immortals is the name given to a band of 40 brave Sikhs belonging to Majha all of whom laid down their lives fighting for Guru Gobind Singh in the battle at Khidrana (now Muktsar) on December 29, 1705 AD. Earlier they had deserted the Guru at Anandpur when they could not withstand the prolonged siege of Anandpur by the forces of hill chiefs and Mughal rulers. They did so by giving a written disclaimer to the Guru. A little later the Guru had to evacuate Anandpur after which he fought a battle at Chamkaur on December 6-7, 1705 AD and was still being chased by the enemy forces in the Malwa region. Mai Bhago persuaded the deserters to meet Guru Gobind Singh and seek his forgiveness. When they were coming to meet the Guru, under the leadership of Mai Bhago, the Guru had almost been overtaken by the enemy forces. There followed a fierce battle in which all the forty laid down their lives. Mai Bhago was the lone survivor. Guru Gobind Singh tore off the disclaimer and blessed these forty dead as. *Chalis Mukte*. Khidrana where the battle had taken place came to be known as Muktsar.

CHAMKAUR : Chamkaur also called Chamkaur Sahib is a small town, near Ropar, associated with Sikh history.

After a protracted struggle against the armies of the Mughal rulers and hill chieftains, Guru Gobind Singh was obliged to leave Anandpur. The next major engagement with the enemy took place at Chamkaur on December 6-7, 1705 AD. In this battle many Sikhs died fighting against heavy odds. The Guru's two elder sons, Ajit Singh 17 and Jujhar Singh 14 also laid down their lives in the battle of Chamkaur.

Chamkaur has a number of Sikh shrines : Damdama Sahib, Garhi Sahib, Qatalgarh Sahib, Tari Sahib etc. associated with the life and struggles of Guru Gobind Singh.

CHANDI CHARITRA : Two volumes of *Chandi Charitra* which were written by Guru Gobind Singh have been included in the Dasam Granth. The first contains 233 verses in 7 chapters. The second has 262 verses in 8 chapters. Both are based on *Markande Purana* and are written in Hindi.

The main point of these compositions along with their counterpart *Chandi-di-Var* lies in their virile temper evoked by a succession of powerful and eloquent similes and by a dignified echoic music of the richest timbre. They were designed by Guru Gobind Singh to create a spirit of chivalry and dignity among the Sikhs.

CHANDI-DI-VAR : A composition by Guru Gobind Singh included in the Dasam Granth. The general Sikh prayer called the *ardaas* begins with an extract from it, which is an invocation to the holy sword and the Sikh Gurus.

Chandi-di-Var is the story of Chandi or Durga who fought a holy war against cruel demons. It is based on a story from the Puranas. It consists of 55 verses in Punjabi which evoke a warlike temper through a succession of powerful and eloquent similes and a dignified echoic music of the richest timbre. Nihangs include it in their daily prayer to derive inspiration and spirit from its reciation.

CHAND KAUR, MAHARANI : Maharani Chand Kaur was the wife of Maharaja Kharak Singh, the eldest son and successor of Maharaja Ranjit Singh. She was the daughter of Sardar Jaimal Singh of the Kanhaiya *misl*. She was married to Kharak Singh in February 1812 AD at the age of 10.

After the death of Maharaja Kharak Singh and her son Kanwar Nau Nihal Singh in November 1840 AD, Maharani Chand Kaur staked her claim to the throne. However Sher Singh, the second son of Maharaja Ranjit Singh marched upon Lahore. A compromise was reached which did not last long. Sher Singh was proclaimed the sovereign and Maharani Chand Kaur was pensioned off in 1841 AD. Eventually she was got killed on June 11, 1842 through maid servants who smashed her head with wooden pikes at the instance of Dhian Singh Dogra who had come to wield considerable power in the court.

CHANDOA : Coloured silk canopy used in gurdwaras or elsewhere over the Guru Granth Sahib.

CHANDO RANI, MAI : Mother-in-law of Guru Nanak and mother of Mata Sulakhani. She was married to Mul Chand of Batala in Punjab.

CHANDRA SAIN SAINAPATI : Chandra Sain Sainapati who is sometimes referred to just as Sainapati was one of the 52 court poets of Guru Gobind Singh. Besides translation of some well known treatises into Hindi his work *Sri Gur Sobha*, completed in 1711 AD, a versified life-sketch of Guru Gobind Singh describing his major battles, the creation of the Khalsa and events following the evacuation of Anandpur, has much historical value.

CHANDU : Chandu was a *Khatri* of Lahore who was a revenue official in the Mughal court at Lahore. He was a contemporary of Guru Arjan.

Chandu was very keen to get his daughter married to Guru Hargobind the only son of Guru Arjan. But Guru Arjan had heard about his arrogance and therefore turned down the proposal. This made him a sworn enemy of the Guru. It is widely believed that he was instrumental in the Guru's arrest and torture to death.

Guru Hargobind later on explained to Jahangir the role played by Chandu in torturing his father to death. Jahangir, thereupon ordered Chandu to be handed over to Guru Hargobind to punish him in any manner. "Guru Hargobind took him to Amritsar and there had him dragged through the streets with a rope round his feet, and made him sit on heated pans and hot sand, as he had done with Guru Arjan. Thus he died (in 1613 AD) in the most excruciating pain."

CHANGA, BHAI : Changa Bhai of Sri Lanka had become a devotee of Guru Nanak during his visit to that country. He had converted his residence into a *dharamsala* and started preaching Sikhism. His name occurs in one of the compositions of the recension of the Adi Granth prepared by Bhai Banno.

CHAPPAR CHIRI : They are twin villages in Ropar district connected by Banda Singh Bahadur Road. A fierce battle took place in the area on May 12, 1710 AD between the Sikhs led by Banda Singh Bahadur and the forces led by Wazir Khan, the governor of Sirhind. In this battle the Sikhs got a decisive victory by killing Wazir Khan and capturing Sirhind. No memorial existed to commemorate this historic event till the fifties of the twentieth century when the two villages jointly established a gurdwara which is still managed by them.

CHARAN AMRIT : Literally *charan amrit* is water in which the Guru's feet have been bathed. It was used as a part of the Sikh initiation ceremony called *charan pahul* during the days of the first nine Gurus and till the time Guru Gobind Singh changed it to *khande-di-pahul*. For more details see Baptism.

CHARAN KAUL : Charan Kaul is a historic Sikh shrine in village Jindowal in Jalandhar district, Guru Hargobind had stayed here for a few days on his way from Phagwara to Kiratpur. The Guru's favourite horse had fallen sick here.

CHARAN PAHUL : See Charan amrit and Baptism.

CHARHDI KALA : *Charhdi Kala* is a composite expression representing a complex concept in Sikh thought. *Charhdi* in Punjabi implies rising, ascending or soaring. Bhai Kahn Singh gives about a dozen usages of the word *kala* in his *Mahan Kosh* but the most relevant in the present context of *Charhdi Kala* will be energy. So *Charhdi Kala* is an expression for an ever-rising state of the spirit of an individual or group.

The expression occurs most prominently in the general Sikh prayer—the *ardaas*. This is repeated every time a Sikh concludes his prayer by saying : *Nanak nam, charhdi kala, tere bhane sarbat da bhala*—"May Nam, the religion preached by Nanak, be always on the ascendancy. And by Thy Grace, may all prosper."

In popular Sikh tradition *Charhdi Kala* stands for high spirit or high morale. It has become a hallmark of Sikh character to be always in a perpetual state of certitude about one's success—never to be downcast even in the most adverse circumstances. This optimistic certitude is derived from a sense of self confidence based on the absolute faith in the Almighty that His Grace will be upon us. *Charhdi Kala* is also an attitude of mind of being ever ready to act without fear of adverse consequences but with a sense of discipline.

CHARITY : Charity which is called *daan* in Punjabi is a highly commendable act in Sikhism as in other religions. According to Hinduism, charity is a means of earning spiritual merit rather than a result of a feeling of compassion although the latter may not be completely ruled out. In terms of recipients, Brahmins get a preferential treatment, wandering ascetics come next and then ordinary beggars seeking alms. Buddhism and Jainism laid great stress on compassion and liberality and rejected the claims of Brahmins as special recipients. Nevertheless both Buddhist and Jain monks depend for their subsistence on alms and donations. In Sikh tradition, while the concept of charity is accepted, its mode is somewhat different. There are no special recipients. The offering is always in the name of the Guru and for common good usually through *golak* kept in a gurdwara.

Charity in Sikh tradition also refers to a kind and sympathetic attitude which one shows towards other people by being tolerant, helpful or generous to them. It is asserted that a person who gives charity himself becomes free from needs." *Daan datara, apar apaara.* Sikhism explains charity as an investment for the future—the life hereafter. "In the hereafter is received reward for what man gives in charity from his own earnings". *Nanak agge so mile, je khatte ghale dai-ee.* (AG. p. 472)

CHARNAULI : Charnauli is a village near Kiratpur on the other side of the River Sutlej. Guru Hargobind used to make a halt here on his way from Kiratpur to Jalandhar Doab region and back. A historic gurdwara has therefore, come up in the village.

CHAR SAHIBZADE : Literally *Char Sahibzade* means four scions. In Sikh writings and speech this term is reserved for the four sons of Guru Gobind Singh namely Ajit Singh, Jujhar Singh, Fateh Singh and Zorawar Singh. The first two died fighting in the battle of Chamkaur in December 1705 AD while the other two were bricked alive on the orders of the governor of Sirhind, Wazir Khan. Thus they symbolize supreme sacrifice which is invoked every time the *ardaas* general Sikh prayer, is said.

CHAUBIS AVTAR : A composition by Guru Gobind Singh included in the Dasam Granth. It was completed in 1698 AD on the banks of the river Sutlej near the foot of Naina Devi Hill.

Chaubis Avtar describes 24 incarnations of Brahma, mentioned in the *Puranas* in 1201 verses in Hindi. These *avtars* fought against the evil-doers to protect the good and the virtuous people.

CHAUNKI : *Chaunki* is a Punjabi word for a wooden platform with four legs used for various purposes including by the *raagis* for *shabad kirtan* in a congregation. In Sikh religious speech and writings *chaunki* has come to mean a session of *shabad kirtan* originally by four *raagis* but now usually by three. In all major gurdwaras at least four such *chaunkis* are held generally by professional *raagis* in the presence of the Guru Granth Sahib.

In addition to such *chaunkis* a tradition has been established at the Golden Temple according to which groups of devotees walk along the *parikarma* (path around the holy tank) chanting *shabads*. This operation is also called *chaunki*. Traditionally there are four such *chaunkis* introduced by important Sikh personages.

So strong is the veneration for the tradition of *chaunkis* in Sikh psyche that Sikhs pray for their perpetuation in the *ardaas* : *Chaunkian, jhande bunge, jug-o-jug atal.* "May the tradition of Sikh choirs, banners and mansions abide forever and ever."

It may be mentioned that in addition to the daily *chaunkis*, there are other monthly and annual *chaunkis* as well : for example the monthly *chaunkis* starting from the Akal Takhat for Tarn Taran and Goindwal.

CHAUPADA : *Chaupada* is a special kind of poetry very commonly used in the Adi Granth. It generally contains four tetrastiches of two distiches of 32 *matras*. One or two pauses (*Rahau*) are usually found in the stanza.

CHAUPAI : It is a Punjabi word for a four-line stanza used in many compositions in the Adi

Granth. There are different kinds of *chaupais* depending on the metre used. *Benti Chaupai* in the Dasam Granth is a well-known composition in this verse form.

CHAUR OR CHAURI : A bunch of hair with a wooden, silver or golden handle used as a fly-whisk for fanning the Guru Granth Sahib. This is done as a matter of respect. At the time of the first installation of Guru Granth Sahib in the Golden Temple, Guru Arjan waved the *Chaur* himself.

CHEEKA : Cheeka is a village in Karnal district of Hissar. It has a gurdwara dedicated to Guru Nanak and Guru Tegh Bahadur. Galaura who was appointed a *masand* belonged to this village.

CHHAINE : *Chhaine* is the Punjabi name for small cymbals. They are used for accompaniment in devotional music.

CHHAND : All verse originated in song, chant, and invocation and its basic patterns are rhythmical. This rhythmical pattern is called metre in poetry. *Chhand* is the Punjabi word for it. Since the Adi Granth is all in verse, we come across various kinds of *chhand* or metres used in different compositions.

The word *chhand* is also used for a special type of verse. It is generally a stanza of three couplets, each of which has its own rhyme and 56 *moras*—28 in each line.

CHHEHARTA : Chheharta which literally means six Persian wheels is a small town on the outskirts of Amritsar. It has a well got dug by Guru Arjan. The well was so wide that six Persian wheels could operate simultaneously on it. Hence the name of the town. The site of the well which is now covered has been converted into Gurdwara Chheharta Sahib. Earlier it was a part of village Wadali where Guru Arjan had stayed.

CHHATTIANA : Chhattiana is a village near Giddarbaha in Faridkot district. Guru Gobind Singh had visited it in 1706 AD after the battle at Muktsar and distributed money to the warriors of the Brar clan for the services rendered by them to the Guru. It has a historical shrine called Gurdwara Guptsar to commemorate the Guru's visit.

CHIEF KHALSA DIWAN : Singh Sabha Movement started and picked up quick momentum in the last quarter of the nineteenth century. The two main centres spearheading the movement were located at Amritsar and Lahore. Gradually they adopted the names— Khalsa Diwan Lahore and Khalsa Diwan Amritsar.

At the turn of the century, a need was felt to avoid duplication of work of the Khalsa Diwan Lahore and Khalsa Diwan Amritsar. So in October 1902 AD a new Panthic organisation known as the Chief Khalsa Diwan was set up with Sunder Singh Majithia as its secretary. It had as its objectives :

1. To uplift the Sikh cause in all spheres– political, social, moral and economic;
2. To propagate the teachings of the Gurus;
3. To remove illiteracy by giving education to all irrespective of caste and creed; and
4. To protect the political rights of Sikhs and seek appropriate redressal through constitutional means.

In pursuance of these objectives, the Chief Khalsa Diwan founded a number of institutions including orphnages and various types of schools including one for the training of *granthis* and *raagis*. It launched a weekly newspaper, the *Khalsa Advocate*. It tried to codify the Sikh rituals and rules of conduct and published the document entitled *Gurmat Prakash : Bhag Sanskar* which is in a way the fore-runner of the *Sikh Rahit Maryada* issued by the SGPC in 1950 AD.

In brief the Chief Khalsa Diwan helped in institutionalizing the Singh Sabha view of Sikhism as a separate religion with distinct rituals and traditions devoid of Hindu influence; it provided a unifying force for the then existing Sikh organizations linking them through an effective communication system and gave a survival kit to the Sikh

Community through the use of negotiation and compromise as a strategy for the resolution of internal conflicts and external relations as a minority community. By convening Sikh Educational Conferences, the Chief Khalsa Diwan did much to promote Western style education among the Sikhs—an activity which has continued upto the modern times and is reflected in the chain of educational institutions run by it.

CHIMTA : *Chimta* is tong-shaped percussion instrument. It has five pairs of metal discs on each arm. They rattle as the instrument is shaken. It is used for accompaniment at the time of devotional music.

CHOHLA : It is a village near Sirhali Kalan in Amritsar district. It has three historical shrines associated with Guru Arjan and Guru Hargobind who had visited it

1. **Gurdwara Chohla Sahib :** This is the spot where Guru Arjan sat and preached during his visit to the village.

2. **Gurdwara Guru ki Kothari :** This was the house inside the village where Guru Arjan and his wife Mata Ganga had stayed.

3. **Gurdwara Baba Adali :** This shrine commemorates Bhai Adali, a pious Sikh who was a contemporary of Guru Ramdas and Guru Arjan. He had brought Bhai Bidhi Chand into the Sikh fold.

All the three gurdwaras are affiliated with the SGPC.

CHOLA SAHIB : *Chola* is a Punjabi word for apparel. A gurdwara which has a Guru's apparel as a relic is generally known as Chola Sahib. The relic if it is kept elsewhere is also reverentially called Chola Sahib. The most famous Chola Sahib is at Dera Baba Nanak where a cloak presented to Guru Nanak by a Muslim devotee of Baghdad during his visit is kept there.

There are a number of Chola Sahibs associated with Guru Gobind Singh.

CHUBARA SAHIB : Chubara Sahib is a famous Sikh shrine at Goindwal. It is a two-storeyed building with an enclosed courtyard. It served as the residence of Guru Amardas. In this house Guru Ramdas was ceremoniously installed as the fourth Guru. In another room in the building Guru Arjan was born. Guru Amardas and Guru Ramdas both breathed their last in this very house.

On the first floor at the gurdwara is a room which used to be occupied by Baba Mohan, son of Guru Amardas. He had with him the compositions of the first three Gurus called Bani Pothi. When Guru Arjan was compiling the Granth Sahib, he came here from Amritsar to obtain the Bani Pothi from him. The palanquin in which he carried it is also preserved in the shrine.

CODE OF CONDUCT : Guru Gobind Singh had laid down a strict code of conduct for Sikhs in 1699 AD at the time of setting up of the Khalsa Panth. Its precise form had however been debated and various extant codes dating from the eighteenth century contained sometimes different interpretations. The Sharomani Gurdwara Parbandhak Committee worked on it and in February 1945 AD was able to produce an acceptable code of conduct called *Rahit Maryada* in Punjabi. It lays down norms for a Sikh. Also see Rahitnamas.

COMB : See Kangha.

COMPASSION : Compassion is a feeling of pity and sympathy for someone who is suffering and a desire to help him. It is called *daya* in Punjabi and Sikhism, like all other religions, treats it as a divine quality and a highly prized moral virtue. "The merit of pilgrimage to sixty-eight holy places and even all other virtues do not equal to the compassion for living beings."
Athsathi tirath sagal punnu, jia daya parvanu
(AG. p. 136).

In fact, Sikhism treats compassion as truth in action. "Truth dawns upon a person when he accepts truthful counsel, shows compassion for others and gives away virtuous charity."
Sachu ta paru jani-ai, ja sikh sachi lai

Daya jani-ai jia ki, kichhu punnu daan karai
(AG. p. 468)

Sikhism gives a clear advice :
"Keep your heart content and cherish compassion for all beings; this way alone can your holy vow be fulfilled."

Man santokh sarb jia daya; Inn bidhi bartu sampuran bhaiya (AG. p. 299).

CONGREGATION : Hinduism was based on individualism. As a reform, the saints of the Bhakti Movement insisted on congregational system. Sikhism further institutionalized the congregation.

The origin of congregation called *sangat* in Punjabi can be traced to the days of Guru Nanak. Wherever he went, he left an assembly of men and women called *sangat* who were asked to build a shrine where they could hold *diwans* and sing hymns together. Every Sikh– man, woman or child—was a member of one *sangat* or the other. These *sangats* served as a link between the common people and the Guru.

Guru Angad maintained the purity of the *sangat* by declining to associate *Udasis* with them. Guru Amardas organised them into twenty-two dioceses under *sangatias*. Their status was raised to *masands* by Guru Arjan, Guru Hargobind reinforced congregational prayer.

With the passage of time, *sangats* were sanctified until Guru Gobind Singh transferred the entire spiritual authority to them. With the creation of the Khalsa, congregation assumed the personality of the Guru. Even the Guru himself asked the Sikh congregation to pray for him. According to Guru Nanak : "Good *sangat* is superior; in its company sins are washed."

CONTENTMENT : Contentment is called *santokh* in Punjabi and is recommended as an ethical value in Sikhism. In its broadest sense it encompasses temperance, patience, detachment and surrender to the Will of God. Application of contentment will therefore, imply restrictions on a person's passions, furies, and infatuations. It demands of him a check on his tendencies for worldly pursuits, it prohibits self-indulgence, greed, lust, over-eating and over-sleeping etc. It recommends non-attachment with worldly affairs and further implies a control over egoistic and self-centred pursuits. "Without contentment no one is content."

Bina santokh nahi ko-oo raje (AG p. 279).

Contentment is a recognized way in Sikhism for God-realization. "To achieve God, wear the ear-rings of contentment, make modesty your begging bowl and smear yourself with His meditation, treating it as ashes."

Mundaa santokh saramu pat jholee, dhiyan ki kare bibhut. (AG. p. 6)

Sikhism also suggests an easy way for acquiring contentment." It comes through Nam, attuned to the Lord's feet".

Nanak Nam santokhia rate Hari Charni.
(AG p. 421).

CREATION, THEORY OF : Creation of the universe has been a mystery and a challenge to man. Both scientists and theologians from all religions have tried to piece together plausible explanations. The views expressed by Sikhism, if we call them a theory, come very close to the consensus among modern astrophyscists and cosmologists which has come to be known as the 'big bang theory'.

According to Sikhism, before the creation of the universe, God existed by Himself in his abstract form–*Nirgun*. "For countless years, there was darkness all around. There was neither earth, nor sky; it was His Will. There was neither day nor night; neither sun nor moon. But there was God in deep meditation".

Arbad, narbad dhundhkara Dharmi na gagna Hukam apara Na din rain, na chand, na suraj sunn smadhi lagaeda. (AG p. 1035).

"First of all the Lord activized Himself and manifested His Nam. Then he created the universe and abiding in it revelled in His wonder. *Aapne aap sajio, aaipne rachio Nao Doo-ee kudrat saji-ai, kar aasan ditho cha-o.*

(AG. p. 463).

"He created night and day, seasons and occasions; so also air, water, fire and nether regions. Amidst these he fixed the earth as a place for righteous actions."

Raati ruti thiti war pawan, pani, agani pataal Tis which dharti thapi rakhi dharamsaal (AG. p. 7)

In the process of creation God became a part of everything and everybody in the universe. "From the True Lord came air; from air came water; from water he created the three worlds and infused in every heart His own light."

Sache te pawna bhaeea, pawne te jal hoe, Jal te tribhawan sajia, ghat ghat jot samoe. (AG. p. 19)

The timing of creation is an intractable issue. Sikhism has responded to it in its own way by saying: "None but the Creator knows when he created the universe."

Ja karta sirthi ko saaje aape jaane soee.
(AG. p. 4)

D

DAAN : See Charity.

DAGRU : Dagru is a village near Moga. Guru Har Rai stayed here in the course of his journey through the Malwa region. Gurdwara Tambu Sahib commemorates the Guru's visit to the village.

DAL KHALSA : See Buddha Dal.

DALLA : Dalla is a village near Sultanpur Lodhi and is one of the oldest centres of the Sikh faith. Guru Amardas is believed to have visited the village. Guru Arjan visited it in 1605 AD leading the marriage party of his son (Guru) Hargobind who was married to (Mata) Damodari of the family of Bhai Paro of this village.

Dalla has a number of Sikh shrines : There is Gurdwara Janjghar where the marriage party accompanying Guru Arjan had stayed. There is Gurdwara Mata Damodari where the wedding ceremony of (Guru) Hargobind and (Mata) Damodari was held. There is Gurdwara Baoli Sahib said to have been built under the directions of Guru Arjan. But the most prominent shrine is Gurdwara Prakash Asthan Bhai Laluji which has the *samadh* of one of the earliest Sikh devotees.

DALLA, BHAI : Bhai Dalla who later became Dall Singh was the *chaudhri* of Talwandi Sabo. When Guru Gobind Singh arrived there with his entourage in early 1706 AD, he diligently attended to the needs and comforts of the growing *sangat* there. He was initiated into the Khalsa by Guru Gobind Singh and received the name Dall Singh. A small domed shrine within the precincts of Takht Damdama Sahib honours his memory to this day.

DAMDAMA SAHIB : *Damdama* literally means a place of repose where the Guru had some respite. Since the Sikh Gurus were most of the time on their move, many places sanctified by their halts have been developed as gurdwaras known as Damdama Sahibs. The important ones are :

1. Damdama Sahib, Amritsar : It is situated at a place near Amritsar where Guru Tegh Bahadur had halted in 1664 AD on his way from Amritsar to Valla after being disallowed to enter the Golden Temple. His devotees at Amritsar had caught up with the Guru at the place and begged his forgiveness for what had happened.

2. Damdama Sahib, Anandpur : It is situated along with Thara Sahib and Bhora Sahib in the same compound as was formerly called Guru-ke-Mahal in Anandpur. Guru Tegh Bahadur used to sit here addressing visiting groups of followers. Istallation of Guru Gobind Singh also took place at the spot which is now a gurdwara constructed in the early decades of the twentieth century.

2 (a) Damdama Sahib, Chamkaur : This marks the spot where Guru Gobind Singh first alighted upon reaching Chamkaur late on December 6, 1705 AD. The site was then a garden belonging to Rai Jagat Singh, the local landlord.

2 (b) Damdama Sahib, Daroli : This is a shrine on the outskirts of village Daroli near Moga. Guru Hargobind during his visit to the village used to hold religious congregations here.

3. Damdama Sahib, Delhi : It is situatednear Humayun's tomb in New Delhi. Guru Gobind Singh met Bahadur Shah (then Prince Muazzam) in June 1707 AD and agreed to help the latter in his struggle for succession. The present building of the gurdwara was constructed during 1977-84 AD.

3 (a) Damdama Sahib, Doraha : It is situated in village Doraha on GT Road about 20 km from Ludhiana. Guru Hargobind halted here for the night when travelling to Amritsar from Gwalior after his release. The gurdwara is managed by the local *sangat*.

4. **Damdama Sahib, Dhubri :** Guru Tegh Bahadur visited Dhubri on March 1670 AD with Raja Ram Singh of Amber who had been sent by Aurangzeb on a punitive expedition against Raja Chakardhwaj of Assam. The Guru brought about peace between the warring armies to celebrate which he had a high mound constructed with the help of soldiers. A small gurdwara called Damdama Sahib was constructed on the top of the mound in 1966 AD.

5. **Damdama Sahib, Hargobindpur :** Guru Hargobind decided to develop Hargobindpur which had been founded by his father Guru Arjan in 1595 AD in memory of Hargobind's birth in that year. There was a dispute about land which was claimed by Bhagwan Das Khatri in which he was killed. His son Rattan Chand approached the *faujdar* of Jalandhar who dispatched a contingent of troops, who were repelled by the Guru's forces. Damdama Sahib has come up at the place where Guru Hargobind held a congregation after the battle.

6. **Damdama Sahib, Khadur :** This is a gurdwara in village Kawan near Khadur. Guru Amardas used to visit the village every morning to take the water of River Beas to Khadur for the morning abiutions of his master Guru Angad.

6 (a) **Damdama Sahib, Kila Raipur :** See Kila Raipur.

7. **Damdama Sahib, Kiratpur :** This is a gurdwara in Kiratpur associated with Guru Har Rai.

8. **Damdama Sahib, Rakba :** It is a gurdwara in village Rakba of Ludhiana district. It commemorates Guru Hargobind's stay in the village.

9. **Damdama Sahib, Talwandi Sabo :** After vacating Anandpur in December 1705 AD and undergoing tremendous suffering and sacrifices, Guru Gobind Singh reached Talwandi Sabo near Bhatinda. Here the Guru built a house for himself having a spacious compound and a strong wall around it. He was joined here by Mata Sundri and Mata Sahib Kaur who came here from Delhi with Bhai Mani Singh. The Guru stayed here for nearly ten months converting people who visited him in large numbers. Here he had the revised version of the Adi Granth which is now used as the Guru Granth Sahib prepared by Bhai Mani Singh. Gradually Talwandi Sabo itself came to be known as Damdama Sahib. This is now treated as one of the five Takhats. (since Nov. 1966).

In the earlier half of the eighteenth century, Talwandi Sabo became a sort of cantonment as well as a seat of learning for the Sikhs. Baba Deep Singh had started his march to liberate and rebuild the Golden Temple after it was blown up by Ahmad Shah Abdali in 1757 AD from Damdama Sahib.

10. **Damdama Sahib, Una :** This is a gurdwara near Una associated with Guru Hargobind.

11. **Damdama Sahib, Wadali :** This is a gurdwara in village Wadali in Amritsar district. Guru Hargobind had rested here after pig hunting.

DAMODARI, MATA : Mata Damodari was one of the wives of Guru Hargobind and was married to him on February 15, 1605 AD at village Dalla near Sultanpur Lodhi as her father Narain Das belonged to it. She gave birth to a son, Baba Gurditta in 1613 AD and a daughter Bibi Viro in 1615 AD.

Mata Damodari passed away at Daroli Bhai now in Faridkot district on July 13, 1631 AD. A small shrine on the outskirts of Daroli marks the site where the cremation took place.

DANCING : Sikhism has very clearly expressed itself against religious dancing or dancing as a part of worship or devotion. "One does not worship the Lord by dancing about" *Nachi-ai tapi-ai bhagti na hoe* (AG, p. 159). In fact its opposition to ritual dancing is so strong as to assert : "To exhibit devotion through ritual dancing leads one to suffering."

Pakhand bhagti nirat dukh hoe. (AG. p. 364).

Sikhs wish : "May my ritual dance be the dance of devotion by my mind through which. I subdue my ego by the grace of God."

Nirat karee aiho man nacha-ee Gurparsadee aap gawa-ee. (AG. p. 506)

Nevertheless Sikhism is not puritanical to the extent of disapproving all kinds of dancing as for example dancing to give expression to one's happiness and joy. Sikhs do relish folk dances like *bhangra* and *giddha*.

DANI, BIBI : Bibi Dani was the second daughter of Guru Amardas and Mata Mansa Devi, the other being Bibi Bhani who was married to Guru Ramdas. Biographical details of Bibi Dani need to be researched to get a clear picture.

DARA SHIKOH : Dara Shikoh was the eldest son of Shah Jahan. He was born at Ajmer on March 30, 1615 AD. He had a scholarly and philosophical bent of mind and was friendly with Guru Har Rai as with Mian Mir and Mulla Shah. He was a favourite son of Shah Jahan and therefore when the latter fell ill in September 1657 AD he made his last will appointing Dara Shikoh as his heir apparent. Aurangzeb, Dara's brother, rebelled against the decision and defeated Dara near Agra when he fled towards Punjab. Aurangzeb sent a strong army in his pursuit. Dara Shikoh called on Guru Har Rai who was at Goindwal in those days. Guru Har Rai helped him by deploying his followers along the River Beas thus blocking the ferry for Aurangzeb's forces for about six hours. Nevertheless Dara was eventually captured, brought to Delhi and put to death in August 1659 AD. Guru Har Rai's help to Dara Shikoh was not liked by Aurangzeb who then turned his ire on the Sikh Gurus. He summoned the Guru to his court who sent his son Ram Rai to Delhi in September 1661 AD. For more details see Ram Rai and Guru Harkrishan.

DARBARA SINGH, DIWAN : Diwan Darbara Singh was a devoted Sikh who got his initiation into the Khalsa on the Baisakhi day of 1699 AD when the Khalsa was created. He took part in the battles fought by Guru Gobind Singh at Anandpur. In the turbulent days following the martyrdom of Banda Singh Bahadur, he commanded much respect in the Sikh community. In 1733 AD when Zakariya Khan, governor of Lahore, offered the title of Nawab to any outstanding Sikh leader to be chosen by the Sarbat Khalsa, Diwan Darbara Singh was the first choice. It was only when he declined to accept it on matters of principle that it was bestowed on Nawab Kapur Singh. He, however, continued as controller of provision (*diwan*) till his death at Amritsar in 1734 AD.

DARBAR SAHIB : *Darbar* is a Persian word meaning court of a king or noble man where he grants audience to the common people or deliberates with his courtiers on matters of public importance. The term came to be used in Sikhism with the Gurus being called *sacha patshah* (True King) and their courts being called *Gurdarbar*. With the Guruship passing eternally to the Adi Granth, the gurdwara came to be popularly called Darbar or reverentially Darbar Sahib. Following historical gurdwaras are still known by this name :

1. Darbar Sahib, Amritsar : This is a popular name for the Golden Temple Complex in Amritsar.

2. Darbar Sahib, Baba Bakala : This is the spot in Baba Bakala where Guru Tegh Bahadur was installed as the ninth Guru in 1664 AD. He also used to hold congregations here.

3. Darbar Sahib, Dera Baba Nanak : This is a gurdwara complex at the centre of Dera Baba Nanak. It has three important shrines : (i) Sarji Sahib which is a well belonging to Bhai Ajita near which Guru Nanak had sat; (ii) Kirtan Asthan which is a rectangular hall marking the spot where Guru Arjan had sat rapt in *kirtan;* and (iii) Thara Sahib which marks the platform on which Guru Nanak had sat when he first came to Bhai Ajita's well. A handwritten copy of the Adi Granth having 1660 pages is preserved in the gurdwara.

4. Darbar Sahib, Khadur : This is a gurdwara at Khadur Sahib raised at the cremation site of Guru Angad.

5. Darbar Sahib, Talwandi Sabo : This is another name for Gurdwara Manji Sahib Sri Guru Tegh Bahadur at Talwandi Sabo

(Damdama Sahib). Guru Tegh Bahadur is believed to have stayed and preached here.

6. Darbar Sahib, Tarn Taran : It is the name of the gurdwara complex at Tarn Taran. The main shrine resembles the Golden Temple except that it is not built at the centre of the *sarovar*.

DAROLI : Daroli also known as Daroli Bhai or Bhai-ki-Daroli is a village about 14 km from Moga in Faridkot district. The elder sister of Mata Damodari, the wife of Guru Hargobind, whose name was Mai Ramo was married here. As such the Guru stayed here twice in 1613 AD and 1631 AD. The Guru's eldest son Baba Gurditta was born here in November 1613 AD. Mata Damodari passed away here in 1631 AD. The association of Guru Hargobind with the village has been commemorated by a number of shrines managed by the SGPC. Gurdwara Damdama Sahib marks the site where the Guru used to call religious congregations during his stay in the village. Janam Asthan Baba Gurditta marks the spot in the *haveli* where Baba Gurditta was born. Angitha Mata Damodari marks the spot where Mata Damodari was cremated.

DAS : One of the seventeen *Bhatts* 10 of whose *swayyas* have been included in the Adi Granth. See under Bhatts.

DASAM DUAR : *Dasam duar* which is used interchangeably with *dasam duara* literally means the tenth gate. The term has been described by Bhai Kahn Singh as brain (*Mahan Kosh*). However it has its own history and a very complex significance.

Dasam duar has been used at a number of places in the Adi Granth. It seems to have come from the tantric literature of Naths in medieval India. According to them there are nine holes in the body (two eyes, two ears, two nostrils, mouth, anus and uretha) which operate the physical mechanism of the body. They believed that there is a mystical spiritual tenth gate which opens out the spiritual communion. Although Sikhism does not accept *yoga*, this concept of the tenth gateway has found its way into Sikh writings. Sikhism accepts *dasam duar* as the tenth gateway which opens into the abode of God.

Dasam duara agam apara, param purakh ki ghati
(AG. p. 974).

Furthermore, *Nau ghar thape thapan harai dasvain wasa alakh aparai* (AG. p. 1036)

The nine doors and the tenth gateway are often mentioned together in the Adi Granth to show their differences. The unstruck melody (*anhad shabad*) is heard at the tenth gateway when it is freed from the shackles of the nine doors in the body.

Nau darwaje dasvain mukta anhad shabad vajavania. (AG. p. 110).

It is *haumai* (egotism) which keeps the tenth gateway shut and the key is with the Guru.

Occasionally the term *dasam duar* has also been used in the Adi Granth in the sense of sensory and motor ograns which should be kept under check.

DASAM GRANTH : The *Dasam Granth*—the Book of the Tenth Guru—is a collection of the compositions of Guru Gobind Singh. It does not enjoy the same status nor does it rank theologically as the Shabad-Guru as does the Adi Granth. Nevertheless it is treated as a holy book by the Sikhs.

Guru Gobind Singh was a prolific writer. He started writing at Anandpur in about 1684 AD at the age of eighteen. He wrote a good deal of poetry at Paonta Sahib from 1685-88 AD. He continued his writings on his return to Anandpur from 1689-98 AD. When the Guru had to vacate Anandpur in December 1705 AD after a long siege, the manuscripts perished in the flooded Sarsa rivulet when he was crossing it. A few copies of many of his works had, however, been made by some of his 52 court poets and scholars. Out of these materials the first recension was compiled by Bhai Mani Singh, one of the Guru's devoted followers, at Amritsar some two decades after the passing away of Guru Gobind Singh. A second recension was prepared by Baba Deep Singh at Damdama Sahib (Talwandi Sabo) with bulk of the contents being the same as in the first recension. Later on some other recensions also came up with some variations in the text. During the Singh Sabha Movement, Khalsa Diwan Amritsar got all the recensions examined with a view to standardizing the text. The result was the recension now in use was first published at Amritsar in October 1902 AD.

The Dasam Granth reveals the spirit of the Khalsa. The episodes mentioned in it recall the heroic deeds of our ancestors. The incarnations of the Puranic literature have been converted into great warriors. The spirit of self sacrifice pervades throughout the holy book.

DASAM GRANTH, CONTENTS : Various compositions included in the Dasam Granth are given in Table below. For details see respective entries.

Table
Compositions of the Dasam Granth

S.No.	Name	No. of Verses
1.	Akal Ustat	271½
2.	Bachitra Natak	471
3.	Chandi Charitra I	233
4.	Chandi Charitra II	262
5.	Chandi di Var	55
6.	Chaubis Avtar	1201
7.	Fateh Nama	23½
8.	Gian Prabodh	336
9.	Hikayat	756
10.	Japu Sahib	199
11.	Mir Mahndi	10
12.	Pakhian Charitra	7569
13.	Ram Avtar/Krishan Avtar	4370
14.	Shabad Hazare	10
15.	Sahstar Nam Mala	1323
16.	Swayyas	33
17.	Zafar Nama	111
18.	Miscellaneous	59
	Total	17,293

Source : Gursharan Singh : *The Epistle of Victory*, 13.

DASAM GRANTH, LANGUAGE : The compositions in the *Dasam Granth* are in Avadhi, Braj Bhasha, Hindi, Punjabi and Persian with Arabic words here and there. Some hymns are in pure Punjabi of Majha.

All compositions are written in Gurmukhi script except 'Fateh Nama', 'Zafar Nama' and 'Hikayat' which are in Persian script.

DASAM GRANTH, POETRY : Guru Gobind Singh's poetry is marked by a very vast range of metres he implied. In old Indian languages the metres were divided into two broad categories : (i) *matrik* in which syllabic instants are counted and (ii) *varnik* in which order and number of short and long vowels are taken into account. Both these kinds of metres have been used in the Dasam Granth but *varnik* metres have been used more frequently and with perfect ease. In addition to these, the *baint*, a metre of Persian poetry, has also been used. Guru Gobind Singh even invented new metres to describe sentiments in their sublimity. Chaupai metre has been used to the maximum followed by Dohara and Sawayya.

DASU, BABA : Baba Dasu was the elder son of Guru Angad, the younger one being Baba Datu. He was born at Khadur Sahib in August 1524 AD. He was not happy at Guru Amardas being declared the successor to his father. He kept quiet at that time but after the passing away of Guru Angad, when Guru Amardas shifted to Goindwal, he declared himself as the Guru at Khadur Sahib. Later he recanted and apologized to his mother who took him to Goindwal. Guru Amardas forgave him and accepted him as his disciple.

DASWANDH : *Daswandh* is a Punjabi word literally meaning one-tenth, but in Sikh thought it refers to the tradition among the Sikhs of contributing one-tenth of their earnings towards the common good of the community. This has the status of a religious obligation and is highly valued by the members of the community. It is similar to the Christian tithes requiring members of a church to pay one-tenth of the produce of their land or its equivalent in money to support it and the clergy; and to the Muslim *zakat* requiring

Muslims to assign 2.5% of their annual wealth for the welfare of the destitute and the needy.

Daswandh is basically the idea of sharing one's honest earnings for the common good and has been nurtured by the institutions of *sangat* and *langer*. In the time of Guru Amardas, a formal structure for collecting religious donations was evolved. He set up *manjis* for the purpose as also for spreading the teachings of Sikhism. But *daswandh* proper was enjoined upon the community by Guru Ramdas when he needed large amounts of money for the construction work at the newly founded city of Amritsar. The tradition was kept alive by other Gurus and it became a part of the Sikh way of life.

Daswandh is different from *daan* (charity). It essentially attends to the needs of the community while *daan* is generally meant to alleviate personal needs of an individual or a group.

There is no organised way of collecting *daswandh*. It comes in the form of free-will donations It certainly serves the dual purpose of helping the common cause of the community and giving an opportunity to the doner to partake in *seva* (service).

DATU, BABA : Baba Datu was the younger son of Guru Angad. He was born at Khadur Sahib in 1537 AD. His elder brother was Dasu. The two brothers did not like Guru Amardas to be a successor to their father. In order to avoid impending conflict with them, Guru Amardas shifted to Goindwal, not far away from Khadur Sahib. Even at Goindwal he was harassed by Datu. He went to Goindwal and is widely believed to have kicked Guru Amardas in the congregation. The Guru retired from Goindwal and hid himself in a house at Baserke, his home village. Datu set himself up as the Guru at Goindwal. Guru Amardas was persuaded by Baba Buddha to return. Datu, finding no following, returned to Khadur Sahib.

Guru Arjan is also said to have met him at Khadur Sahib on his way from Goindwal to Amritsar with the *Bani Pothi*. He collected some loose sheets containing hymns of Guru Nanak and Guru Angad which were lying in a corner of the room. These were used in compiling the Adi Granth.

DAULAT KHAN, LODHI : Nawab Daulat Khan Lodhi was the governor of Jalandhar Doab with its capital at Sultanpur Lodhi, a town near Kapurthala in the last quarter of the fifteenth century. Jai Ram, the husband of Guru Nanak's sister, Bebe Nanaki, was one of his officials. Through him Guru Nanak got the job of a storekeeper of Nawab's granaries at Sultanpur. There are a number of *sakhis* (anecdotes) about complaints against Guru Nanak made to Nawab Daulat Khan Lodhi. But the latter is said to dispose them off in a just and fair manner.

Nawab Daulat Khan later became the governor of the entire Punjab with capital at Lahore. He, however, fell out with Ibrahim Lodhi, the emperor of Delhi and invited Babar to invade India. But Babar did not spare him and defeated him in a battle. Babar stayed on to establish the Mughal rule in India whereas Daulat Khan Lodhi died in obscurity.

DAULATPUR : See Tahli Sahib.

DAULOWAL : It is a village near Kiratpur in Ropar district. Guru Har Rai used to camp here in summer. It was here that the Guru received the summons to see the emperor at Delhi. Gurdwara Patshahi VII marks the site of the Guru's camp and is managed by the local community.

DAYA : See Compassion.

DAY OF JUDGEMENT : See Mukti.

DAYA KAUR, MATA :

1. Mata Daya Kaur was the mother of Guru Angad and wife of Baba Pheru Mal of village Matte-di-Sarai, now known as Sarai Nanga about 16 km from Muktsar. Chroniclers also give her name as Mata Sabhirai, Ramo or Mansa Devi. Very few biographical details of Mata Daya Kaur are known.

2. Mata Daya Kaur who has also been referred to as Anup Devi by some chroniclers was the mother of Guru Ramdas and wife of Hari Das, a Khatri of Sodhi subcaste and a resident of Chuna Mandi Lahore. Like all mothers, she was very keen that his son should take to some worthwhile avocation. According, at the instance of a neighbour who used to peddle roasted gram, Mata Daya kaur prepared a bagful of roasted gram and gave it to Guru Ramdas, who was known as Jetha in those days, to go out and sell. But Guru Ramdas went to the bank of the river Ravi and fed the gram to a band of *yogis* who had eaten nothing that day.

DAYAL, BABA : Baba Dayal is the founder of the Nirankari sect of the Sikhs. He was born at Peshawar on May 17, 1783 AD. He lost his father Ram Sahai while he was still an infant. His mother, a devout Sikh, nurtured him in the best traditions of the faith and took him every morning to the local Gurdwara Bhai Joga Singh. After the death of his mother in 1802 AD, Baba Dayal shifted to Rawalpindi where he opened a grocer's shop and started preaching a message of simple living and criticism of wrong practices that had crept into Sikhism. He inspired an emphasis on the Guru Granth Sahib and preached that social rituals should centre around it. For his own wedding ceremony he insisted on *lawan* being recited which is now quoted as the first Anand Karaj in Sikh history. Since Baba Dayal used to utter frequently the word *Nirankar*–a term for God his followers came to be known as Nirankaris.

As Baba Dayal was debarred from preaching from Gurdwara Peshaurian, he acquired a plot of land at Rawalpindi in November 1851 AD and laid the foundation of the Nirankari Darbar which became the central religious seat of the new sect.

Maharaja Ranjit Singh once visited Baba Dayal at Rawalpindi in 1820 AD. He died on January 30, 1855 AD and was succeeded by his eldest son Darbara Singh.

DAYALA, BHAI : Bhai Dayala was a devout Sikh who was arrested by Aurangzeb along with Guru Tegh Bahadur and two of his other followers Bhai Mati Das and Bhai Sati Das in 1675 AD. Bhai Mati Das was sawed into pieces from head downwards on his refusal to accept Islam. Bhai Dayala abused the Emperor and his courtiers for this atrocious act. He was tied up like a bundle with an iron chain and was put into a huge cauldron of boiling oil. Then he was roasted into a block of charcoal on November 11, 1675 AD.

DAYA SINGH, BHAI : Bhai Daya Singh who was known as Daya Ram before his initiation into the Khalsa brotherhood was the first of the *Panj Piaras* (Five loved ones) to rise at Guru Gobind Singh's call on the Baisakhi day of 1699 AD to offer his head. He thus became the first *Singh* to be admitted into the fold of the new brotherhood founded by the Guru. He was a Khatri from Lahore and was a devout disciple of Guru Tegh Bahadur.

Although the *Panj Piaras* enjoyed equal status as the Guru's confidants, Bhai Daya Singh was always regarded as the first among equals. He took part in the battles at Anandpur and was one of the three Sikhs who followed Guru Gobind Singh out of Chamkaur in December, 1705 AD. Guru Gobind Singh also sent him as his emissary to Aurangzeb at Ahmadnagar to deliver his letter called *Zafarnama*. Bhai Daya Singh then rejoined the Guru and remained in attendance on him till his death in October, 1708 AD at Nanded. Bhai Daya Singh also died soon after at Nanded.

DEATH : Sikhism takes a pragmatic view of death. At the outset it recognises it as inevitable. "One who is born is bound to die for half-way house is this world."

Baba aaya hai uth chalna adh pandhai hai sansarona (AG. p. 581).

"All that is born must die one day. The Lord Creator alone is immortal."

Jo aaya so chalsi amar so Gur Kartar (AG. p. 63)

The concept of death in Sikhism revolves around the separation of the soul from the body—an antithesis of life which is the union of the body and the soul. God is responsible both for the union and the separation of the two. "The Lord has brought about the union of the soul with the body. He is also responsible for separation."

Kaya hans sanjog mail milaya Tin hi kiya wijog jin upaya. (AG. p. 139)

"When the True Lord so wills, He gives command to the soul. The soul is separated from the body; and the separated ones then He unites again."

Sadre aaye tina janiya Hukam sache Kartaro, Nari purakh wichhonia, wichhoria mailan haro
(AG. p. 580)

Thus occurance of death is the Will of God. "According to his Will alone do we come and go" *Agya aawe agya jaye* (AG. p. 294)

Accordingly there is an injuction against loud lamentation in Sikh *Rahit Maryada* although in everyday practice, bereavement is distressing and weeping becomes incontrollable at funerals.

Sikhism has lot of advice to offer on how to die or to prepare for death "Kabir! the world has ever been subject to death but few know how to die while living. Whoever dies thus, shall never die."

Kabira marta marta jag moya mar bhi na jane koe Aisi marni jo mare bahur na marna hoe.
(AG. p. 555)

"O people you will not dread death, if you know how to die. Serve your all-powerful Lord and the path in the yond will be easy to tread."

Maran na manda loka aakhiye je mar jane aisa koe Saveh sahib sanmarth aapna panth suhela aage hoe
(AG. p. 579)

So we must know how to die. According to Sikhism the formula is pretty simple. "All talk incessantly of death. But one dying in equipoise achieves immortality."

Marno maran kahe sabh koee Sahje mare amar hoe soee (AG. p. 327)

DEEP SINGH, BABA : Baba Deep Singh has been one of the most revered martyrs of Sikh history. Paintings show him fighting with his head on the left palm, still wielding his sword with the right. He lived his life in the true 'saint-soldierly' spirit and laid down his life to save the sanctity of the Golden Temple.

Baba Deep Singh was born in 1682 AD at village Pahuwind about 40 km from Amritsar. He stayed at Anandpur for some time to study the sacred texts under Bhai Mani Singh. He was with Guru Gobind Singh at Damdama Sahib (Talwandi Sabo) in 1706 AD but stayed on there after the Guru left for the Deccan. He participated in the campaign of Banda Singh Bahadur but left him in 1714 AD when Tatt Khalsa rose against him. He is the founder of the Shahid *misl* as well as of the Damdami *Taksal*. Shahid *misl* had its sphere of influence south of the river Sutlej with headquarters at Damdama Sahib.

During his fourth invasion of India in 1756-57 AD, Ahmad Shah Abdali annexed Punjab to his kingdom, appointed his son, Taimur, the viceroy at Lahore with the veteran general Jahan Khan as his deputy. Jahan Khan ravaged Amritsar in May 1757 AD razing the Sikh fortress Ram Rauni and filling up the holy tank. This sent a shock wave among the Sikhs. Baba Deep Singh felt that it was upto him to atone for the desecration of the Golden Temple. He emerged from his scholastic retirement at Damdama Sahib and proclaimed his intention of rebuilding the complex. As he went from hamlet to hamlet, many villagers joined him. By the time he reached Tarn Taran he had over 5000 followers. The first encounter with the forces of Jahan Khan took place at village Gohlvar about 8 km from Amritsar in which the Khalsa had some initial advantage. Jahan Khan got fresh reinforcements and a fierce battle took place near Ramsar. Baba Deep Singh was fatally wounded and was barely able to get to the Golden Temple to keep his tryst with death. Two shrines now commemorate the brave martyr : One on the *parikarma* of the Golden Temple where he finally fell and the other Shahidganj Baba Deep Singh near Gurdwara Ramsar where his body was cremated.

DEG, TEGH, FATEH : This triad of three Persian words conveys a very important theo-ethical concept in Sikhism. *Deg* means a large-sized kettle or cauldron but is ethically symbolic of charitable distribution of cooked food—an idea linked to the concept of *langar*. *Tegh* stands for sword but symbolically it represents freedom and sovereignty as also chastisement of evil and protection of the good. *Fateh* implies victory. Read together, *Deg, Tegh, Fateh* give expression to the Sikh belief that the ideal of *deg* (charitable feeding) steadfastly cherished and the use of *tegh* (sword) as a last resort as permitted by Guru Gobind Singh must lead to *fateh* (victory).

The ideals of *deg* and *tegh* occur frequently in the writings of Guru Gobind Singh. According to him *deg* and *tegh* both prevail in the world.

Deg Tegh Jag mai dou chalai

(DG, *Krishnavatar*)

They constitute a composite virtue that was the characteristic of the heroes of the yore. Banda Singh Bahadur after getting control of territories between the Yamuna and the Sutlej started his own official seal with the Persian inscription.

Deg-o-tegh-o-fateh, nusrat-i-bedirang yaft az Nanak-Guru Gobind Singh.

It means : "The kettle, the sword, the victory and unhesitating patronage are obtained from Nanak-Guru Gobind Singh." The same inscription was reproduced on the coins introduced by Jassa Singh Ahluwalia in 1765 AD. The practice continued during the reign of Maharaja Ranjit Singh. The official seal of the Akal Takht also carries the words *Deg, Tegh, Fateh*.

Over the centuries, the doctrine of *deg, tegh, fateh* has taken deep roots in the Sikh psyche. Everytime the *ardaas* (Sikh general prayer) is said, a prayer is made, among other things, to the Lord to grant the boon of *deg, tegh, fateh* to the Sikhs.

DELHI : Delhi which is at present the capital of India was also the capital during the later part of the Mughal period coinciding with the pontificate of the last few Sikh Gurus. As such it is intimately connected with Sikh history. It has been sanctified by the visits of five Sikh Gurus: Guru Nanak, Guru Hargobind, Guru Harkrishan, Guru Tegh Bahadur and Guru Gobind Singh. Guru Harkrishan passed away here after contracting small pox. Guru Tegh Bahadur was martyred here at the orders of Emperor Aurangzeb. Guru Gobind Singh's wives Mata Sundri and Mata Sahib Devan stayed at Delhi for a long period after the passing away of the Guru. Delhi, as such, has nine historical gurdwaras which are now being managed by the Delhi Sikh Gurdwara Management Committee under Delhi Sikh Gurdwaras Act 1971 AD. They are : Bala Sahib, Bangla Sahib, Damdama Sahib, Majnu ka Tilla, Mata Sundri Gurdwara, Moti Bagh Gurdwara, Nanak Piao, Rakabganj and Sisganj. Their details are given under individual entries.

After the downfall of the Mughal empire, the Sikh *misls* extended their power virtually upto the walls of Delhi. In fact Dal Khalsa ransacked Malkaganj and Subzi Mandi areas in March 1783 AD and even entred the Red Fort. The then Mughal emperor, Shah Alam II came to terms with the Sikhs who agreed to withdraw their forces to Punjab provided Bhagel Singh, chief of Karorsinghia *misl* was permitted to stay on with 4000 men till the construction of the historical shrines. He was also authorized to collect 37.5% of the octroi duties for the purpose. During his stay, Bhagel Singh constructed seven of the historical gurdwaras. Gurdwara Nanak Piao was already in existence. Gurdwara Damdama Sahib was added later.

After the partition of India in 1947 AD, a large number of Sikh migrants from Pakistan settled in Delhi changing its demographic composition. In fact Delhi now has the largest concentration of Sikhs in any town in India or abroad.

DELHI SIKH GURDWARAS ACT 1971 : See Delhi Sikh Gurdwaras Management Committee.

DELHI SIKH GURDWARAS MANAGEMENT COMMITTEE : Since 1923 AD, the Delhi gurdwaras had been managed by the SGPC through an 11-member local committee called the Delhi Gurdwara Parbandhak Committee (DGPC). There was an influx of Sikh migrants from Pakistan to Delhi after 1947 AD. With the change in the demographic composition of Delhi, the authority of DGPC began to be questioned leading to disputes and litigation. Ultimately the Government of India passed an act in 1971 AD called the Delhi Sikh Gurdwaras Act 1971 passing on the control of Delhi historical gurdwaras to the Delhi Sikh Gurdwaras Management Committee (DSGMC) to be elected by Sikh vote every four years. It consists of 55 members 46 of whom are elected by the Sikhs of Delhi and 9 are co-opted. The DSGMC operates through an Executive Board elected annually by its members and consisting of 5 office bearers and 10 executive members. The DSGMC also runs degree colleges, schools, a technical training institute and a hospital.

DERA BABA NANAK : It is a small town in Gurdaspur district on the left bank of the river Ravi just opposite Kartarpur (Pakistan) on the other side of the river where Guru Nanak had settled with his family and had spent last about 20 years of his life practising and preaching Sikhism. On the Guru's death on September 7, 1539 AD at Kartarpur, a *samadh* (cenotaph) was constructed on the right bank of the river Ravi. But the changing course of the river washed away the *samadh* in the course of time. Baba Sri Chand, Guru Nanak's elder son, got the urn containing the ashes salvaged and reburied it on the other side of the river. Later Dharam Das, the son of Guru Nanak's younger son Baba Lakhmi Das, founded a new habitation around the spot and named it Dera Baba Nanak.

Dera Baba Nanak has two historical gurdwaras. The first one Gurdwara Darbar Sahib consists of three separate memorials: Thara Sahib, Sarji Sahib and Kirtan Asthan. Initially a modest shrine, the present gurdwara was constructed by Maharaja Ranjit Singh in 1827 AD. The second shrine is called Chola Sahib. A *Chola* (cloak) said to have been presented to Guru Nanak by a Muslim devotee of Baghdad is kept here as a relic.

DERA DERHA SAHIB : *Dera* is a Punjabi word of Persian origin. The original Persian word *derha* means a tent, camp, abode, house or habitation. In Sikh literature and speech in medieval times it was used for army camps or cantonments. In the Adi Granth, *dera* has been used both to mean abode or living place, permanent rather than temporary (AG, p. 256) and in the sense of a camp or citadel (AG. p. 628).

A number of gurdwaras have been named as *Dera Sahibs*. Some important ones are :

1. Derha Sahib, Anandpur : This is the place where Guru Tegh Bahadur's head was cremated after his martyrdom in Delhi on November 1675 AD. It is now called Gurdwara Sis Ganj.

2. Derha Sahib, Batala : This marks the place where the wedding ceremony of Guru Nanak was solemnized. It is also known as Viah Asthan Sri Guru Nanak Dev Ji. Guru Hargobind is believed to have visited the spot at the time of the wedding of his son Baba Gurditta.

3. Derha Sahib, Hoshiarpur : It is located in village Bahadurpur near Hoshiarpur. It is the cenotaph of an *Udasi* saint named Phoal Shah. Maharaja Ranjit Singh had patronized it.

4. Derha Sahib, Kiratpur : This commemorates the place in Kiratpur where Baba Gurditta was cremated.

5. Derha Sahib, Lahore : The most famous Derha Sahib is at Lahore now in Pakistan. It commemorates the spot on the River Ravi where Guru Arjan after several days of physical torture by the governor of Lahore took a dip in the river and never came out. This happened during the summer of 1606 AD. Guru Gobind Singh got constructed at the holy spot a small building and appointed Bhai Langha as its caretaker. Maharaja Ranjit Singh later reconstructed the shrine with its heavily gilded dome. The Maharaja's own *samadh* (cenotaph) is only a few metres away.

Devotees from India still visit Derha Sahib at Lahore every year on the martyrdom day of Guru Arjan.

6. Derha Sahib, Lohar : It is situated in village Lohar in Amritsar district. Guru Nanak's ancestors lived in a habitation called Pathevind at the spot. The Guru himself often visited the place. The shrine was first set up by Guru Hargobind and is now managed by the SGPC through a local committee.

DESTINY : See Ethical Determinism.

DEV GANDHARI : An Indian classical *raag* usually sung during the first about two hours (four *gharis*) after sunrise in the morning. It is the sixth of the thirty-one *raags* used in the organisation of hymns of the Guru Granth Sahib covering pages 527-536. The sequence of basic notes in it is :
  Arohi : *sa, re, ma, pa, dha, sa*..........
  Avrohi : *sa, ne, dha, ma, ga, re, sa*........

DHADI : *Dhadh* is a small hand-held percussion instrument–small hand held *dholak*. It is held in the left hand and music is created by striking it with the fingers of the right hand. Singers who sing ballads to the accompaniment of *dhadh* are called *dhadis*. Singing by *dhadis* as a part of religious *diwans* is a well established tradition in rural Punjab. It has flourished since the days of Guru Hargobind who engaged some leading exponents of the art to recite heroic ballads in *diwans*. It continues to be popular upto the modern times.

DHAKOLI : See Baoli Sahib.

DHALEO : See Manji Sahib.

DHAMOT : It is a village in Ludhiana district which was visited by Guru Hargobind during his journey through the Malwa region. A gurdwara managed by the SGPC through a local committee commemorates the visit of the Guru.

DHAMTAN : See Manji Sahib.

DHANSARI : An Indian classical *raag* usually sung in the afternoon. It is the tenth of the thirty-one *raags* used in the organisation of hymns in the Guru Granth Sahib covering pages 660-695. The sequence of basic notes followed is :
  Arohi : *sa, re, ga, ma, pa, dha, ne, sa*..........
  Avrohi : *na, dha, pa, ma, ga, re, dha, na*..........

DHANNA, BHAGAT : Dhanna, popularly known as Dhanna Jat is said to have been born in 1415 AD. He lived in the village of Dhuan Nagar in Taank area in Rajasthan. From his very childhood, he was simple, diligent and straightforward with a deep rooted faith in God.

Though Dhanna began life as an idolater, he became in riper years a worshipper of the one God and renounced all superstitious practices. He was a disciple of Ramanand. Three verses of Dhanna are included in the Adi Granth under Asa and Dhanasari *Raags*.

DHARAM SINGH, BHAI : Bhai Dharam Singh who was known as Dharam Das before his initiation into the Khalsa was one of the *Panj Piare* who rose to offer their heads to Guru Gobind Singh on the Baisakhi day of 1699 AD at Anandpur. He belonged to a *Jat* family of Hastinapur and had left home at the age of thirty in quest of understanding Sikhism. He spent some time at Gurdwara Nanak Piao in Delhi from where he moved to Anandpur in 1698 AD. A few months later he became one of the *Panj Piare* by responding to the call of Guru Gobind Singh. Thereafter he was always at the beck and call of the Guru. He participated in the battles at Anandpur and Chamkaur. Along with Bhai Daya Singh, another *Panj Piara* he went as a courier to deleiver Guru Gobind Singh's letter *Zafarnama* to Aurangzeb who was in the Deccan. He accompanied the Guru to Nanded where he passed away soon after the death of Guru Gobind Singh in October 1708.

DHARMSALA : *Dharmsala* is the name by which Sikh places of worship were originally known. The common term used these days is gurdwara although in rural areas the old terminology is still used. Namdharis have also retained this term.

It is a place where the Guru Granth Sahib is kept and Sikhs meet for worship as also for social rites. It is also sometimes used for the purposes of religious instruction.

In common parlance in India *dharmsala*, however, means a sort of hostel for pilgrims.

DHAULA : It is a village about 11 km from Barnala. It was sanctified by the visit of Guru Tegh Bahadur. It has two historical shrines associated with the Guru's visit—Gurdwara Arisar and Sohiana Sahib. For details see respective entries.

DHAULSAR, GURDWARA : See Dod.

DHILWAN : It is a village 25 km from Barnala. According to the local tradition Guru Tegh Bahadur stayed here for several months in the course of his travels through the Malwa region. This resulted in the conversion of a large number of people of the area to Sikhism. Gurdwara Patshahi IX on the outskirts of the village commemorates the Guru's stay. It is managed by the SGPC.

DHILWAN KALAN : It is a village about 5 km from Kotkapura in Faridkot district. Guru Gobind Singh was displeased with Chaudhary Kapura for not warding off the imperial army that was chasing him. He left Kotkapura and came to Dhilwan Kalan where he was received by Sidhi Kaul, a descendant of Guru Arjan's elder brother Prithi Chand. Here the Guru discarded the blue apparel that he had put on at Machhiwara as a disguise. Gurdwara Godavarisar marks the site where the Guru had stayed.

DHIRMAL : Dhirmal was the elder son of Baba Gurditta i.e. elder brother of Guru Har Rai and grandson of Guru Hargobind. He was born at Kartarpur (Jalandhar) in January, 1627 AD. He is notorious for his un-Sikh like activities.

Since Baba Gurditta had died in 1638 AD, it came to choosing his successor in 1644 AD. Guru Hargobind preferred Guru Har Rai over his elder brother Dhirmal. This made Dhirmal infuriated. Some historians believe that he administered poison to the Guru in the evening meal and immediately disappeared from Kiratpur and went to Kartarpur (Jalandhar) with the original copy of the Adi Granth. He thought that the original copy of the Adi Granth will enable him to claim Guruship. Indeed he continued his opposition to Guru Harkrishan and Guru Tegh Bahadur as well and conspired with Mughals against them. He even made an unsuccessful assassination attempt on Guru Tegh Bahadur at Baba Bakala.

Predictably Dhirmal did not have a good end. He was arrested along with his son by Aurangzeb and got killed in 1677 AD. His descendants, the Sodhis of Kartarpur (Jalandhar), are still in possession of the Adi Granth prepared under the direction of Guru Arjan.

DHOLAK : *Dholak* is a wooden drum with sheep skin at each end. It produces sound when struck with a curved wooden stick. It is used for accompaniment in *bhangra* and other folk music.

DHOLAKI : A small *dholak* is called *dholaki*. Hands are used in place of wooden stick to produce sound.

DHUBRI : Dhubri, on the bank of the Brahmaputra in Assam, was visited by Guru Nanak in 1505 AD. Around 1666 AD Guru Tegh Bahadur went there along with Raja Ram Singh of Jaipur who was leading an expedition at the behest of Emperor Aurangzeb to subdue the people of Kamrup. The Raja had approached the Guru at Patna to seek his blessings for his mission. The Guru brought about an amicable settlement between the opposing sides and bloodshed was averted. At Dhubri, all the soldiers were requested to carry some earth to a point to raise a mound in remembrance of Guru Nanak. The entire army of the Raja joined in the work and the task was accomplished in a few hours. The Guru then got a shrine constructed at the top. This gurdwara is named as Damdama Sahib.

DHUNI : It is a Punjabi word derived from the Sanskrit *dhvani* for sound or tune. In the Adi Granth, the term appears at the head of 9 of the 22 *vars* under different *raags*. It indicates the tune in which these *vars* are meant to be sung. The classical system of Indian music had well-established tunes and corresponding prosodic forms; but the *var*, being basically a form of folk music, did not have any prescribed order. The Adi Granth has laid down tunes for at least the *vars* for which models existed. For example, Var Majh, Mahalla I on page 137 of the Adi Granth is meant to be sung in Malak Murid tatha Chandrahara Sohia ki Dhuni.

Some scholars believe that these *dhunis* were not a part of the original Adi Granth but were added later under the directions of Guru Hargobind. But this is contested by others.

DHYAN SINGH : See Kattu.

DIALPURA BHAI KA : It is a village about 38 km from Barnala. According to the local tradition, Guru Gobind Singh during his stay at Dina in December 1705 AD retired one day to a grove around a pool of water. Here he composed the *Zafarnama* the letter of victory, which he sent to Aurangzeb from Dina. The site has been converted into Gurdwara Zafarnama.

DIKKH : It is a village in Bhatinda district. Guru Tegh Bahadur visited it during his travels through the area. It has a historical shrine called Gurdwara Patshahi IX affiliated to the SGPC.

DINA : It is a village in Faridkot district. After evacuating Anandpur and the batttle at Chamkaur in December 1705 AD, Guru Gobind Singh spent some time at Dina. It was during his stay at Dina that he composed the *Zafarnama*—the epistle of victory—after retiring for a day to Dialpur-Bhai-ka. It was from Dina that the Guru dispatched *Zafarnama* to Aurangzeb who was in those days at Ahmadnagar through Bhai Daya Singh and Bhai Dharam Singh—two of the original *Panj Piare*. The commemorative shrine established here has been named Gurdwara Lohgarh which is managed by the SGPC.

DIRHBA : It is a town about 30 km from Sangrur. It was visited by Guru Tegh Bahadur during his journey through that area. He had encamped on the edge of a deep pond on the outskirts of the town. The spot has been converted into a historical shrine called Gurdwara Patshahi IX and is administered by the SGPC through a local committee.

DIWALI : Diwali is one of the important festivals of North India. It is celebrated by the Hindus as Luxmi worship. According to mythology Lord Rama had returned to Ayodhya after 14 years of exile on this day.

Diwali is also celebrated by the Sikhs, although for a different reason. By way of regulating the visitors, Guru Amardas had asked his followers to receive his blessings on Baisakhi and Diwali. It is also believed that the foundation stone of the Golden Temple was laid on Diwali. The illuminations at the Golden Temple were first put up to celebrate the return of Guru Hargobind to Amritsar after his release from Gwalior. This tradition was started by Baba Buddha. It is also believed that a few years earlier, he had completed the first perusal of the Adi Granth on Diwali.

In the post-Guru Gobind Singh era, Sarbat Khalsa used to meet on Diwali and Baisakhi to discuss important issues concerning the Sikhs.

DIWAN : *Diwan* is a Persian word meaning royal court. In Sikh tradition the Guru was addressed as *Sachcha Patshah* (True King) and therefore his audience came to be known as *diwan*. As the office of the Guru was vested in the Guru Granth Sahib, any congregation in the hall where the Holy Book is kept is called the *diwan*. Most of the gurdwaras hold two *diwans* everyday—one in the morning and the second in the evening. Special *diwans* are held on the occasions of *gurpurbs*.

The word *diwan* is also used for a low couch without back.

DOD : Dod is a village about 10 km from Jaito in Faridkot district. It was visited by Guru Gobind Singh in his journey in the Malwa region after Dina in December 1705 AD. According to the local tradition, Guru Hargobind had also visited the place. It has two historical gurdwaras one inside the village Gurdwara Har Sar and the other on the outskirts known as Gurdwara Dhaulsar. Both these shrines are managed by the SGPC through a local committee.

DOHA : *Doha* which may be translated as couplet is a verse form very commonly used in the Guru Granth Sahib particularly by Kabir and Guru Nanak. Each stanza in a *doha* consists of two rhymed lines. By and large, each line will be in two stages; the first stage having thirteen syllables and the second eleven after a pause. This however, is not rigid. With variations in metre, we get different kinds of *doha*.

DORAHA : See Damdama Sahib.

DOUBT : As the saying goes doubts among thoughts are like bats among birds; they fly ever by twilight. Certainly in religious beliefs they are to be repressed, or at least well guarded; for they cloud the mind. This theme occurs at a number of places in the Guru Granth Sahib. "He sheds doubt, knows the Truth."

Jis ka bharam gaya tin Sacho pachhana
(AG. p. 330)

A God centred person has to be without doubts. "When his doubts are shattered, then no rift is left between him and the Lord."

Jab is te sabh binse bharama bhed nahi hai par Brahma. (AG. p. 235)

Sikhism is quite clear about the inevitability of doubt in a man's life. "In doubt is the man born; in doubt he dies."

Bharme aawe, bharme jaye (AG. p. 161)

It is also clear that to reach the Lord, one has to shed all doubts. Therefore it advises: "Brother! remove all your doubts. All that happens is by His Will."

Baba tun aise bharam chukahi jo kichh karto hai soee koee hai re. (AG. p. 162)

DOWRY : Dowry is strictly prohibited among the Sikhs. Aberrations from this approved practice may, however, be found because of deeply entrenched social practices among some communities. Guru Gobind Singh was very clear that such people are hostile to the organizational purity of the Khalsa. He, therefore, disallowed social relationship, among others with "those who corrupt the institution of marriage by exclusively basing it on monetary, somatic considerations." A person who disregards this precept may be declared a *tankhaiya* (religious defaulter).

DRESS : According to Sikh *Rahit Maryada* "For a Sikh there is no restriction on dress except that he must wear *kachha* (drawers) and *dastar* (turban). A Sikh woman may or may not use *dastar*." Of course wearing of 5 ks is compulsory. These have given special features to the Sikh dress particularly the head gear which is turban for males (*patka* for younger boys) and *dupatta* for ladies. One can also recognize a Sikh by the iron bracelet that he or she wears on the right arm.

DRINKING : See Alcohol.

DRUGS : There is a strong prohibition against the use of non-medicinal drugs and intoxicants in Sikhism. To ensure the purity of the Khalsa Panth, Guru Gobind Singh had disallowed a Sikh to have any social relations with persons, among others, "those who use drugs or intoxicants to befog their minds with a view to running away from reality." Accordingly Sikh *Rahit Maryada* clearly lays down that: "Sikhs should not partake of alcohol, tobacco, drugs and other intoxicants."

DSGMC : Abbreviation for the Delhi Sikh

Gurdwaras Management Committee.

DUALITY : Duality as the opposite of unity—permitting the existence of a God other than one—is severely disapproved in Sikhism. It does not permit this universe to be presided over by more than one God even when conceived by different religions. Like Judaism and Islam Sikhism insists on the unity of God, even though known by different names. It clarifies: "There is but one God whom Hindus call Gosain and Muslims Allah. Thus I have settled the dispute between Hindus and Muslims".

Aiko Gosaaee Allah mera,
Hindu Turk dohan nabera   (AG. p. 1136)
"Whom shall I call the second Lord when none such is there".
Dooja kaono kaha nahi koee   (AG. p. 223)
Sikhism realizes that in this world there are people who believe in duality. "This world is born out of duality."
Eh jug janmaiya dooje bhai   (AG. p. 161)
But at the same time it asserts that "those who are led by duality forget the Lord."
Tin noo wisrai je dooje bha-ai   (AG. p. 160)
Furthermore, "one caught in duality cannot achieve enlightenment through study."
Dooje bha-ai parhe nahi boojhe   (AG. p. 127)

DUGGHRI : It is a village about 5 km from Chamkaur in Ropar district, Guru Gobind Singh passed through it on his way to Chamkaur after evacuating Anandpur in December 1705 AD. Guru Tegh Bahadur is also said to have visited the village. The villagers have raised a gurdwara to commemorate these visits.

DUKH BHANJANI BERI : It is an old *ber* (jujube) tree in the *parikarma* (circumambulatory path) of the Golden Temple along the eastern bank of the holy tank. The tree is associated with the legend of Bibi Rajani whose leper husband is said to have been cured by having a dip in the pond that existed here before the founding of Amritsar. It is because of this legend that the pond was developed by Guru Ramdas into a proper bathing tank. The name Dukh Bhanjani (eradicator of suffering) is also said to have been given by the Guru.

DUKH NIWARAN, GURDWARA : Gurdwara Dukh Niwaran is situated in Patiala. It has been built in memory of Guru Tegh Bahadur who rested at the place for some time while passing through the area in 1662-63 AD. What attracted him to the spot was its solitude conducive to meditation and a banyan tree and a pond. Patiala had not yet been built. The site of the gurdwara was a village called Lehal.

A *Hukamnama* of Guru Tegh Bahadur is kept here in a glass paned cabin underneath a tree.

DULEY : It is a village about 17 km from Ludhiana. Guru Gobind Singh halted here for some time under a *phalahi* tree while travelling from Alamgir to Jodhan in December 1705 AD. Gurdwara Phalahi Sahib commemorates the visit.

DUMELI : It is a village about 18 km from Phagwara. Guru Hargobind visited it in March 1638 AD. A wooden column (*thamm*) believed to have been installed by the Guru himself is treated as a relic and Gurdwara Thamm Sahib has been raised at the site. It is managed by the SGPC through a local committee.

DUNI CHAND : Duni Chand was a *masand* of Majha at the time of Guru Gobind Singh. He was the grandson of Bhai Salo, a distinguished Sikh who lived in the time of the fourth and fifth Gurus.

The hill chiefs became scared of the rising popularity of Guru Gobind Singh and consolidation of the Sikhs. Realizing that the Guru would neither make peace nor surrender, they waged a war against him at Anandpur. At that time Duni Chand came to assist the Guru with five hundred Sikhs from Majha. But when he was asked to tackle Raja Kesari Chand, Duni Chand deserted the Guru. In fact he succeeded in persuading his followers who had accompanied him to go over to Dhirmal at Kartarpur (Jalandhar). He, however, broke his leg while scaling the fort wall by a ladder which interfered with his plans to put his troops under Dhirmal's command. So he returned to Amritsar where he died of snake bite.

DURGAPUR : It is a village near Nawanshahr in Jalandhar district. Guru Hargobind visited it in 1635 AD. A gurdwara was established here in 1863 AD with the support of Baba Ram Singh Namdhari. It was renovated in 1950 AD. The gurdwara is managed by the SGPC through a local committee.

DUSANJH KHURD : It is a village near Banga in Jalandhar district. It has a historical shrine called Gurdwara Guru Har Rai dedicated to the seventh Sikh Guru. It is affiliated to the SGPC.

DVAPARA YUGA : See Yugas.

DYEING OF HAIR : The Sikh Gurus had developed a theory of aesthetics in which they tended, to identify the idea of beauty with the idea of the holy. For them there was a common base for both the aesthetic and religious experiences. As such Sikhism disapproves of the dyeing of hair or other make-up which makes a person look different from what he or she is.

E

EDUCATION, SIKH VIEW OF : Sikh view of education may be said to have taken roots at Kartarpur (Pakistan) where Guru Nanak had settled during the last 20 years of his life and had set up an ideal Sikh community. He introduced what may be called true community-centred education—a completely innovative and radical idea involving the whole community and pooling all its resources for complete education of the whole man. It sought to do away with all sorts of water-tight compartmentalization between education and the world of work, knowledge and wisdom, science and religion, morality and spirituality and between man as man and man as a social being. Besides reintegrating education with the original purpose of life and giving a definite model for a living philosophy, Kartarpur Academy, if we call it by that name, worked as a comprehensive institution for wholesome nurture of the community as a whole. As the Gurus went on shifting their headquarters, the models were, by and large, replicated at Khadur Sahib, Goindwal, Kiratpur and Anandpur.

The aims of Sikh education have always been determined by the formula : Truth is the highest; but higher still is truthful living"

Sachon ure sabh ko; upar sach achar.

Thus the aim of education is the understanding of Truth and abiding by it in all one's feeling, willing and doing. 'Living in Truth' embraces and enshrines the entire gamut of excellence, the total spectrum of truth, Goodness and Beauty in the Sikh educational thought.

According to Sikhism spiritual, moral and social perfection of man go simultaneously in the formation of a perfect society and in that man and society form an intractable link in the whole process of evolution. Thus Sikh education envisages the preparation of godly men and godly society where man develops all his potentialities by living in society and performing his duties with the full understanding of Sikh values. Although knowledge is given its due importance, it is not allowed to tilt the balance of Sikh education towards scholasticism. Accordingly it has been stressed that "Only he knows the way of truthful living who earns his bread by honest hard work and shares the fruits of his labour with others." Dignity of labour is, therefore, an inseparable part of Sikh education.

Since Sikh education is a free flowing highway for man's journey towards Truth, smoother the highway, the smoother and easier would be the journey. Therefore, the Guru's constant and consistent effort has been to seek and find a method by which the teacher may teach less but the learner may learn more. The desired highway and the most expedient method lies in the working of Nature where the Gurus see a divine order and correspondingly a divine pedagogy that leads straight to the goal of perfection in the universe. But considerable emphasis is also laid on thinking, understanding motivation and good deeds;

Vidya Vichari taan par upkari (AD. p. 356)

Concept of an educated person in Sikhism is very well summarized as : "He alone is educated who understands what he reads; and who is stamped with the mercy of the Lord."

Parhia boojhe so parwan, Jis sir dargah ka nisan
(AG. p. 662)

EDUCATIONAL INSTITUTIONS : The Sikh educational institutions had their foundations in the historical settings and had been undergoing evolutionary changes under the impact of history.

A typical school serving the Sikh community before the annexation of Punjab by the British in 1849 AD was a Gurmukhi school corresponding to *Maktab* or *Madrassa* for Muslims or *Pathshala* for Hindus. Such a school was, by and large, co-educational in character, was entered by the students at 5 years of age and not after 7, and had its curriculum based on 3 Rs supplemented by religious education.

Within 25 years of the annexation of Punjab, while both buildings and teachers for Gurmukhi schools throughout the province were still available, there was a great decline in the number of pupils as the parents preferred that they should learn nothing at all than the system in vogue in government schools.

The Singh Sabha Movement provided an answer to this deteriorating situation.

The foundation stone of Khalsa College, Amritsar was laid in 1892 AD and it became a forerunner of progressive Sikh institutions. The model of a Sikh institution combining new education with religious education and having Punjabi as the medium of instruction became almost universally accepted. Colleges, however, continued to use English as the medium of instruction.

In the post-Independence era although the growth of Sikh institutions has started declining, 'public' schools are on the ascendancy. Very few old type Khalsa schools and colleges are being opened these days. But this has been largely, compensated by the opening of Sikh 'public' schools.

EGOISM : Egoism is treated as a vice and a malady in Sikhism. "The world is lost in egoism and cometh and goeth in vain." (1) "Egoism is a great malady; one involved in it is not released from transmigration" (2) "The world suffers through the impurity of egoism. Duality imposes on it this impurity." (3) Egoism is, in fact, a denial of God, the Supreme Reality; it is the denial of the existence of a cosmic order; it is the denial of the oneness of human society; it is the denial of the path of love, knowledge, service and devotion; it is living in an imaginary world of one's own fancy; it is living in constant conflict with all else in the creation. "He is the bravest of the brave who has overcome his inner ego." (4) "By stilling the ego, you are united with the Lord." (5) "The distinctive nature of egoism is that we act in ego. Egoism also binds us to the cycle of birth-rebirth. How does egoism arise? How is it eliminated. It is the God's Will that in egoism that one follows the writ of habit. Egoism is a chronic malady; but within it is also its remedy." (AG, p. 466).

Simple solutions for remedying egoism have been suggested. "One sheds egoism in the society of saints" (6) "Egoism is shed through the Guru's Word."

1. *Haumai wich jag binsda, mar janme aawe jaye.* (AG. p. 33)
2. *Haumai wada rog hai mar janme aave jaye.* (AG. p. 592)
3. *Jag haumai mayel dukh paya, mal laagi dooje bhai* (AG. p. 39)
4. *Nanak so soora waryam jin wich dusht ahankarn marya.* (AG. p. 86)
5. *Haumai mar milawliya.* (AG. p. 117)
6. *Sant ke sang mitya ahankar.* (AG. p. 189)
7. *Haumai marta Gur shabad vichari.* (AG. p. 225)

EMINABAD : Eminabad is an ancient town in Gujranwala district of Pakistan and was known as Sayyidpur in Guru Nanak's times. The town was sacked by Babar in 1521 AD. Chroniclers mention of Guru Nanak being taken a prisoner during the attack. Eminabad came under the Sikh rule when Sukkarchakia *misl* occupied it in 1760s. It had a number of Sikh shrines which were managed by the SGPC upto 1947 AD.

EQUALITY : Equality is a striking feature of the social organisation of Sikhs. Historically it came as a reaction to the social inequalities institutionalized in Hinduism as caste system. Sikhism asserts : "From the same air and the same clay has all creation come forth. In all shines the same light."

Aiko pawan matti sabh aika, aika jot sabaya.
(AG. p. 96)

It does not, therefore, approve distinctions being made on the basis of caste or sex. Emancipation of women came as a natural corollary to this cardinal principle of equality coupled with a strong respect for justice.

EQUIPOISE : Equipoise means mental equilibrium—calmness of mind and temper. It is a positive value in Sikhism and is touched upon at a number of places in the Adi Granth. "Without attaining equipoise all is blindness and storms of *Maya*—delusion. Through equipoise comes realization by means of the immeasurable holy word." (1) "Equipoise is the bar-woman who serves the wine and I pass my days enraptured by bliss." (2) "Through Truth and equipoise one gets repute and makes the Lord's name one's mainstay." (3) There are enough hints in the Adi Granth for man to attain equipoise. "The whole creation craves for the state of equipoise but without the Guru one finds it not." (4) It is again asserted: "One does not get equipoise without the Guru." (5) "Meditating on the Lord, you attain equipoise." (6) "When a man loses the egoism, he reaches the state of equipoise."

1. *Bin sahaje sabh andh hai maya; Moh gubar sahaje hi sojhi paie Sache sabad apar* (AG. p. 68)
2. *Sahaj kalalini jao mil aaee, Anand mate anand jaee.* (AG. p. 328)
3. *Sache sahaj sobha ghani Harigun nam adhar.* (AG. p. 61)
4. *Sahaje no sabh lochde bin Gur payea na ja-ee.* (AG. p. 68)
5. *Bajh Gur ko sahaj na paye.* (AG. p. 125)
6. *Prabh ke simran sahaj samani.* (AG, p. 263)

ETHICAL DETERMINISM : Ethical determinism is a doctrine that human action is not free but determined by motives regarded as external forces acting on the will. In fact, the question whether man is, or is not, free to mould his own destiny is one which has exercised the minds of philosophers and religious thinkers since Greek mythology conceived of the Fates as wearing a web of destiny from which no man can free himself. In the early days of Christianity, Roman Catholics, however, believed that soul is free but once enmeshed in the body loses its freedom in the life of sense. Nevertheless, man is still free to turn away from sensuality and towards God who is perfect freedom; for even when incarnated in matter, the soul does not lose the ability to rescue itself. But later on the Protestants believed in the doctrine of predestination which states that God has unalterably destined some souls to salvation to whom efficacious grace is granted and others to eternal domination.

In the matter of determinism, Islam is very close to Protestants by viewing God as Omnipotent. God determines the destiny of man. "He will forgive whom He will and He will punish whom He Will. Allah is able to do all things."

The response of Hinduism to the doctrine of determinism is the Law of Karma. According to it, life is a cycle of lives (*samsara*) in which a man's destiny is determined by his deeds (*karma*) from which he may seek release (*moksha*) through ascetic practices or the discipline of *yoga*. Failure to achieve release means reincarnation—migration to a higher or lower form of life after death—until the ultimate goal of absorption in the Absolute is reached.

Sikhism accpets the premises of both Hinduism and Islam. Therefore, the question of ethical determinism becomes very complex. The Law of Karma operates in Sikhism but it is moderated by God's Grace. It believes in the absolute rulership of God. "Everything is under His sway; nothing is outside it."

Hukame under sabh ko; bahar Hukam na koe.
(AG. p. 5)

It, however, reconciles the omnipotence of God with the moral freedom of man in a characteristically Indian way—freedom through knowledge. The only unconditionally free Being is God. Everything else operates according to God's Grace. Man is free, that is to say, he is liberated not just because of his *karma* but to the degree he gets God's Grace. That comes by aligning oneself with God. The way to align oneself with God is to understand His law and ordainments.

In short, in Sikhism man's destiny is determined both by his own deeds and the Grace of God. Man has been given the free Will. He is free to choose and act to some extent, and to that extent alone is he morally responsible and subject to praise or blame. This gives him his own individuality and personality. But at the same time, there is no such entity—and no such entity is conceivable—which is wholly 'uncaused' or 'undetermined'. "It is God's Will that makes men do high and low deeds. And His Will works in myriad ways".

Hukame ooch neech beohar; Hukame anik rang parkar (AG. p. 277)

EVIL: There is a paradox in the existence of evil especially in monotheistic religions. Why should God who is all-powerful create evil or allow its existence. Thus whether God created evil or whether it is due to the misuse of free-will given to man are issues which theology in every religion has to sort out.

Semitic religions have more or less accepted the existence of evil. In Christianity it has taken the shape of the doctrine of Original Sin which is the evil which is born with us as a result of Adam's fall. Islam has embodied evil as Satan. The Quran states : "Verily Satan is an enemy to you; so treat him as an enemy. He only invites his adherents that they may become companions of the Blazing Fire." (Surah 35 : 6)

Oriental religions have been viewing evil somewhat differently. The main trend of Hindu thought on the subject is that since the world itself is unreal, the existence of evil in it cannot be of greater concern to the individual than the world itself. So Hinduism is not much concerned about the existence or creation of evil.

Sikhism has gone neither with Islam nor with Hinduism on the issue of evil. It takes the stand that although there is no such thing as independent evil, yet there are evil things or deeds which we call vices as there are good deeds which we call virtues. "God is all-good and nothing that proceeds from all-good can be really evil and there is naught which proceeds from any other source but God."

Is te hoe so nahi bura; urai kah kine kichh kara. (AG. p. 294)

In other words Sikhism denies evil an ultimate status in the structure of reality but it accepts the concrete existence of evil deeds and also of the agents of evil in human affairs. "The cannibals say ritual prayers of Islam and the assassins strut about as practising Hindus. All concern for human decencies and respect for ethical conduct has disappeared and the Evil rules supreme."

Manas khane karhi namaz; chhuri vagain tin gal tag; Saram dharam ka dera dur; Nanak koor rahia bharpur. (AG. p. 471)

Sikhism calls upon all men to moral perception to oppose the agents of evil and in this even seeks the benediction of God. "O God, this blessing, above all, we do ask of you : the Will and tenacity to tread the path of good, promoting actions and fearlessness in opposition to the agents of evil."

Deha Siva bar mohi ihai, subh karman te kabhun na taron, Na daron ari son jab jai laron, nischai kar aapni jit karon. (DG, p. 99)

F

FALCON : The order *Falconiformes* or Birds of Prey is represented by the families *Accipitridae* (hawks, eagles etc.) and the *Falconidae* (falcons). Both are characterized by a short and strongly hooked bill for tearing flesh and powerful hooked claws. The hawks (*Shikra*) are round-winged birds while falcons (*Baaz*) have narrow and pointed wings and more spindle-shaped bodies, streamlined for extreme speed in chasing prey. Hawks live chiefly in wooded countryside affording concealment, while falcons are more at home in open unobstructed terrain. Two of the most common types of falcons availbale in India are : Shaheen Falcon which is of the size of a Jungle Crow and Redheaded Merlin which is smaller in size. They can be seen perched on mounds or other places of eminence.

In ancient times, rich people used to keep falcons for hunting. A falcon has also been associated with Guru Gobind Singh in his popular image. This has led to many myths among the Sikhs about falcons.

FARID, SHEIKH : Sheikh Farid is one of those Sufi saints whose 116 hymns are included in the Adi Granth. He had a rich fund of love and kindness for his fellowmen, for which reason he came to be known as *Shakkarganj*.

Sheikh Farid was the son of Sheikh Jala-u-din Sulaiman who could trace his ancestory to the second Caliph Umar of Islam and Mata Maryam. He was born at village Kothiwal (now known as Chawali Mushaikh) in Multan district of Pakistan in 1173 AD. He became a disciple of Khwaja Kutubdin Bakhtiar Kaki of Multan where he did hard penance. He spent 15 to 20 years at Hansi and then stayed at Ajodhan which was later known as Pak Pattan. This place is the spiritual seat of Sheikh Farid. In recognition of his deep piety, sacrifices and spiritual ability, Khwaja Bakhtiar Kaki appointed him leader of the *Chisti* order. His life is an excellent example of patience, contentment and humility.

Sheikh Farid was married to Hazabra, the daughter of Nasir-ul-Din, the Emperor of Delhi. He had five sons and three daughters from her. He died on October 15, 1266 AD.

The town of Faridkot in Punjab is named after Sheikh Farid.

FARRUKHSIYAR : Farrukhsiyar was a grandson of Emperor Aurangzeb. After the death of Aurangzeb, his son Bahadur Shah became the king and made peace with Guru Gobind Singh but he died in February 1712 AD. In the mean time Banda Singh Bahadur had moved to Punjab in 1708 AD and got early victories because of the declining Mughal rule. In the war of succession between the sons of Bahadur Shah, Jahandar Shah came out victorious but was not destined to enjoy power for long. He was strangled to death in 1713 AD when Farrukhsiyar ascended the throne. He asked all the governors and *faujdars* in the Punjab region to crush Banda Singh Bahadur. Accordingly he was besieged and captured near Gurdaspur in December 1715 AD. It was at the orders of Farrukhsiyar that Banda Singh Bahadur was brought to Delhi, paraded in the streets and was finally cut up limb by limb in June 1716 AD. He also ordered a general persecution and elimination of Sikhs.

In the court conspiracies, Farrukhsiyar was imprisoned and killed in 1719 AD.

FASTING : Fasting has been made a part of the religious rigour in the Semitic religions. Christianity has its Lent—the period from Ash Wednesday to Easter Eve of which the 40 weekdays are devoted to fasting and penitence in commemoration of Christ's fasting in the wilderness. The Quran has prescribed for the Muslims. "Oye who believe! Fasting is prescribed to you as it was prescribed to those before you." (Surah 2, 183) And further "Ramadan is the month in which was sent down the Quran. So every one of you who is present (at his home) during that month should spend it in fasting" (Surah 2 : 185). Fasting is also commended in Hinduism and is indulged in on many occasions.

Sikhism however ploughs its lonely. It furrow does not regard fasting as meritorious. God has given us the human body—the temple of the soul—which has to be nourished and cared for. Fasting as an austerity, as a ritual, as a mortification of the body by means of wilful hunger is forbidden in Sikhism. "Penance, fasting, austerity, alms-giving are inferior to truth; right action is superior to all". It clearly stresses that : "Fasting does not provide spiritual backing to the mind."

Wrat tapan kar man nahi bhijai. (AG. p. 905)

Sikhism encourages temperance and moderation in food. Neither starve nor overeat: this is the Golden Mean. Guru Nanak has made it very clear : "Practising self-torture to subdue desires only wears off the body. The mind too is not subdued through fasting and penances. Nothing, indeed, equals God's Name (in its efficacy for obtaining the desired state)" (Ibid.).

FATE : See Ethical Determinism.

FATEH DARSHAN : *Fateh Darshan* was the war cry introduced by Banda Singh Bahadur after setting up his headquarters at Lohgarh. He had not intended it to replace the accepted salutation :

Waheguru ji ka Khalsa; Waheguru ji ki Fateh.

Nevertheless in practice *Fateh Darshan* started replacing it. This was condemned by the Khalsa and Banda Singh Bahadur took no time to withdraw it.

FATEH GARH SAHIB, GURDWARA : This is a historical gurdarwa about 5 km from Sirhind. It marks the site of the execution of the two younger sons of Guru Gobind Singh at the behest of Wazir Khan, the *faujdar* of Sirhind in 1705 AD. Banda Singh Bahadur who ran over Sirhind had the first memorial built in 1712 AD at the site. This was converted into a proper gurdwara in 1764 AD and was rebuilt by Maharaja Karam Singh of Patiala in 1814 AD. Renovation and development of the shrine were taken up in 1955-56 AD.

FATEH NAMA : *Fateh Nama* is a composition by Guru Gobind Singh included in the Dasam Granth. It is believed to have been addressed to Emperor Aurangzeb prior to his letter known as *Zafarnama* and sent to him from Jatpura near Jagraon after the battle at Chamkaur and before the Guru learnt of the martyrdom of his two younger sons. It is a short letter comprising 23½ couplets in Persian. The theme is similar to that of the *Zafarnama*, though the tone is severer.

FATEH SHAH : Fateh Shah who is also known as Fateh Chand was the Raja of Srinagar (Garhwal). He, along with other hill rajas fought a battle with Guru Gobind Singh at Bhangani near Paonta Sahib in 1690 AD and suffered a defeat.

FATEHPUR SINGHAN : See Manji Sahib.

FATEH SINGH, SAHIBZADA : The youngest son of Guru Gobind Singh. He was born to Mata Jito in February 1699 AD. After the death of his mother in December 1700 AD he was brought up under the care of his grandmother Mata Gujri. He was arrested along with *sahibzada* Zorawar Singh and Mata Gujri in December 1705 AD. The two *sahibzadas* were bricked alive at the behest of Wazir Khan, the *faujdar* of Sirhind at a place where now stands the famous historical gurdwara Fatehgarh Sahib.

FOOD AND DRINK : In the matter of food and drink, three injunctions come out as the strongest in the Sikh Community.

1. Thou shall not smoke.
2. Thou shall not take intoxicants.
3. Thou Shall not eat Kosher meat.

Also because of proximity and respect for Hindu culture, it has also become a universal prohibition among the Sikhs not to take beef.

Traditionally the food served at *langars* is

vegetarian but Sikhs are not required to be vegetarian. But Guru Gobind Singh had prescribed that if meat be taken, it must be *jhatka* meat i.e. the flesh of animals killed with one stroke of the sword.

FORCE, USE OF : The Sikh symbol of *kirpan* tends to create an impression on the superficially informed persons that use of force is the essence of Sikhism. This is a misleading notion. However, it can be conceded that *kirpan*, by direct implication, rejects uninterrupted peace as a natural state of human existence, and it repudiates *ahimsa* (non-violence) as a literally approved way of life. The Sikh view on force is also quite contrary to the Christian view : "Those who live by the sword, shall perish by the sword" or "The meek shall inherit the earth." Sikhism is a religion of the strong and the brave. It preaches physical annihilation in preference to moral compromises and apostacy from spiritual integrity. "When the alternative is good or evil with choice between life and death, I choose death in fight with evil."

Jab aaw ki audh nidhan bane at hi run main tab joojh maro. (DG. p. 99)

The basic position of Sikhism on the use of force was explicitly stated by Guru Gobind Singh in his Zafarnama—a letter written to Aurangzeb in 1706 AD : "When all methods of persuation fail, it is justified to unsheathe the sword."

Chu kar az hameh hilate darguzasht, Halal ast burdan b-shamshir dast. (Zafarnama; 22.1)

FORGIVENESS : Forgiveness, the quality of not being angry with persons who do something wrong has been universally acclaimed as a virtue by all religions including Sikhism. It is said : "True joy comes from forgiveness and truthful living".

Sabad mahali khara too khima sach sukh bhai (AG, p. 937)

Furthermore : "Whoever grasps forgiveness, vows of purity, the noble way of life and contentment is rendered immune from all maladies and the malice of death."

Khima gahi brat seel santokh Rog na biape na jam dokh (AG. p. 223)

Therefore Sikhism advises its followers to acquire forgiveness as a quality of the head and the heart. "Make forgiveness and patience thy milch-cow; thus will the calf of thy soul be fed with milk of spiritual bilss."

Khima dhiraj kar gaoo laveri sahaj bachhra khir pi-ai (AG. p. 1329)

FREE WILL : Belief in one God who is all-powerful has created a veritable paradox for man who wants to have freedom of choice or activity. As mankind progressed towards monotheism, philosophers and religious thinkers became more and more concerned with the contradictory doctrines of God's Will and man's Free-Will.

Spinoza, a 17th century philosopher did not believe in Free Will of man. According to him all the necessities of survival determine instinct, instinct determines desire, and desire determines thought and action. "There is in mind no absolute or free will but the mind is determined in willing this or that by a cause which is determined in its turn by another cause, and this by another, and so on to infinity." He explained: "Men think themselves free because they are conscious of their volitions and desires, but are ignorant of the causes by which they are led to wish and desire." Spinoza compares the feeling of free will to a stone's thinking as it travels through space, that it determines its own trajectory and selects the place and time of its fall.

Schopenhaver, an 18th century German philosopher argues more or less on the same lines. "Everyone believes himself *a priori* to be perfectly free even in his individual actions and thinks that at every moment he can commence another manner of life, which just means that he can become another person. But *a posteriori*, through experience he finds, to his astonishment, that he is not free, but subjected to necessity."

More modern philosophers, as for example. Dewey, tried to reconcile Free Will with Divine Will. According to Dewey, Free Will is no violation of causal sequences; it is the illumination of conduct by knowledge. "A physician or an engineer is free in his thoughts or in his actions in the degree in which he knows what he deals with perhaps we find here the key to any freedom."

Religions have also tried to seek a compromise between Free Will and Divine Will. Christianity believes man to be free yet holds that Adam's sin was transmitted to all mankind and only Divine Grace can bring salvation. Islam also does not deny the freedom of actions to man but tends to make everything subservient to God's Will. It is clearly stated in the Quran : "Message to whoever among you wills to go straight is : Ye shall not will except as Allah Wills." (Surah, 81 : 28-29). In Hinduism Free Will is only constrained by the Law of Karma which is not exactly identical with pre-destination of Christian theology. The *karma* is not fate because all the time we are making our own *karma* and determining the character of our further status and births. The Law of Karma merely teaches that our present limitations are traceable to our acts of autonomous choice in our past lives. Our *karma* is a source of rewards and punishments which we must enjoy and endure. Supremacy of God's Will is, however, not ignored. Gita asserts that : "God sits in the heart of every creature with the consequence that all revolve in their set courses, helplessly tied to the wheel of *Maya*" (XVIII : 61)

It is not a mere coincidence that Guru Nanak and the subsequent Gurus had the closest doctrinal relations with the Qadariya and Chisti schools of Sufis who believed in Free Will in opposition to Jabariya Sufis who believed, like the orthodox Muslims, in complete dependence on Divine Will. But Sikhism gives a pride of place to Hukam (God's Will). On the one hand it says: "A man reaps only that what he sows in the field of *karma*"

Jeha bijai so lunai karma sandra khet.

(AG. p. 134)

On the other hand it asserts : "Say, what precisely it is that an individual can do out of his free choice? He acteth as God willth."

Kahu manukh te kia hoe awai, jo tis bhave soee karvai.

(AG. p. 277)

Kapur Singh has summarized the position of Sikhism on the subject thus : "That man is free to choose and act to some extent, and to the extent he is so, to that extent alone he is morally responsible and subject to praise and blame, is a true statement. That there is no such entity, and no such entity is conceivable, which is wholly uncaused or 'undetermined', and further that in the ultimate analysis the whole area of individuality can be linked to a cause or causes which are supra-individual is also a true statement; and these two true statements are not self-contradictory or incompatible with each other. This constitutes the Sikh doctrine on the subject." (*Sikhism for Modern Man;* p. 120).

FUNERAL SERVICE : The dead bodies among the Sikhs are cremated. The funeral service is a solemn affair. The practice of weeping, wailing, crying and all other ways of boisterous expressions of grief are strictly forbidden. As soon as the soul has winged its flight, the body is bathed and clothed in clean clothes and removed in any convenient manner for cremation.

At the cremation ground, the body is placed on the top of a platform of firewood and more firewood is placed on top of it. Then Japji and the general *ardaas* are recited and blessings of God and Guru are invoked for the soul of the departed. After this the pyre is lit and mourners return home after *Shabad Kirtan* and recitation of Kirtan Sohila.

Since the ashes of Guru Har Rai and Guru Harkrishan were immersed in the river Sutlej at Patal Puri in Kiratpur, devout Sikhs have adopted the practice for the immersin of ashes of their dead. Nevertheless, some Sikhs do the same at Hardwar or other convenient rivers or canals.

As soon as it can be conveniently arranged, the reading of the Adi Granth is arranged by the heirs of the deceased which is completed on the 10th day when Antam *ardaas*—the last of the last rites—is performed. This marks the close of funeral ceremony.

G

GADIAL : See Manji Sahib

GAGA : Gaga is a village near Sunam. Guru Tegh Bahadur had halted here on the edge of a *dhaab* (large pond) during his travels through the Malwa region. A gurdwara marks the spot where the Guru had camped. It was patronized by the erstwhile Patiala and Nabha states.

GAGGOBOOHA (GAGGOBUA) : Gaggobooha is a village about 16 km from Tarn Taran. Guru Hargobind had rested under a *pipal* tree here once when he was on a hunting expedition. The village produced the famous Sikh preacher Baba Bir Singh who had also worked for some time in the army of Maharaja Ranjit Singh.

GAHAL : Gahal is a village about 22 km from Barnala. Guru Har Rai had visited the village on his way to Mehraj. A gurdwara has been dedicated to the Guru to commemorate his visit. During the Wadda Ghallughara in February 1762 AD, the badly mauled, yet unvanquished, Sikh column is said to have passed through the village on its way to Barnala.

GAJPATI SINGH, RAJA : Raja Gajpati Singh was one of the descendants of Baba Phul and the maternal grandfather of Maharaja Ranjit Singh. He was born in 1738 AD. His daughter Raj Kaur was married in a grand ceremony to Mahan Singh chief of Sukkarchakia *misl* in 1774 AD and gave birth to Maharaja Ranjit Singh in 1780 AD. Raja Gajpati Singh captured Jind in 1763 AD and issued coins in his name. He died in 1789 AD at Safaidon.

GALAURA : Galaura was a resident of village Cheeka in Karnal district. Guru Tegh Bahadur had appointed him a *masand* and sent him to Hansi and Hissar for missionary work. The Guru had also visited his house once and had presented him a quiver of arrows.

GAMBLING : Gambling as an act of betting money with the hope of making more money is against the tenets of Sikhism. Even Islam takes the same stand on it.

Theologically gambling contradicts the basic Sikh concept of *Hukam* (God's Will) as the gambler starts with the assumption that the world is governed by chance—a position that is unacceptable to Sikhism.

Ethically gambling is a vice as it afflicts a person with *lobh* (greed) and deprives him of the virtue of *Kirat Karni*—earning one's bread by honest labour.

Intrinsically gambling ensures the defeat of the gambler. "The defeat of the gambler is inbuilt in gambling". *Haar juwar jua bidhe* (AG. M5). In reality when one gambler wins many others suffer losses. But the winner also loses morally.

GANDHUAN : A village about 20 km from Sunam in Sangrur district. It has a gurdwara dedicated to Guru Tegh Bahadur who had visited it in the course of his travels in the Malwa region. According to the local tradition the Guru came here to give *darshan* to Bhai Muglu who was on his death bed to fulfil a promise given to him by Guru Hargobind whose devotee he was.

GANGA, MATA : Mata Ganga was the wife of Guru Arjan and mother of Guru Hargobind. She was the daughter of Kishan Chand, a Khatri of village Mau near Phillaur in Jalandhar district. The site in Mau where her wedding ceremony was solemnized in 1589 AD is now a historic shrine. She breathed her last at Baba Bakala in 1621 AD. Here dead body was immersed in the River Beas in deference to her wishes that it should be consigned to water, as had been her husband's.

GANGA RAM : One of the five sons of Bibi

Viro, daughter of Guru Hargobind. He fought valiantly for Guru Gobind Singh in the battle of Bhangani in September 1688 AD. In this battle two of his brothers Sangram Shah and Jat Mal were killed.

GANGSAR : 1. Gangsar Sahib is a famous Gurdwara in Kartarpur (Jalandhar). When Guru Arjan founded Kartarpur in 1596 AD he felt that the first and foremost need for the residents was the supply of water. A well was, therefore, got dug. It is called Gangsar. A beautiful shrine stands here today which holds great attraction for the devotees.

2. The tank near the gurdwara at Jaito is also called Gangsar.

GANGU : Gangu, a Brahmin belonging to village Kheri near Morinda, was a domestic servant in the household of Guru Gobind Singh. After escaping the long siege of Anandpur in December 1705 AD, the Guru's household was divided into two groups. One of the groups comprising Mata Gujri and two younger *Sahibzadas* : Fateh Singh and Zorawar Singh were taken by Gangu to his native village.

In the meantime, Guru's forces suffered a setback at Chamkaur where the Guru lost, among others, his two elder *Sahibzadas*. The news of this battle spread like wild fire in the neighbourhood. Gangu got concerned about his own safety. He stole the entire belongings of Mata Gujri and in the morning informed the government officials at Morinda. They were then arrested and sent to Sirhind. The two *Sahibzadas* were martyred by Wazir Khan by bricking them alive. Mata Gujri died of the shock on hearing the news.

Banda Singh Bahadur avenged the deceit by Gangu by completely devastating Kheri village and killing Gangu and his family in 1710 AD. A new village has now come up which is known as Saheri and has a gurdwara dedicated to the two younger *Sahibzadas*.

GANGU SHAH : Gangu Shah was a Khatri belonging to Garshankar who was sent as a *masand* to Sarmaur (or Nahan) area for spreading Sikhism. His headquarters were at "Daon" in Ambala district. One of his descendants Jawahar Singh became very popular and set up his *dera* at Khatkar Kalan in Jalandhar district. His followers call themselves Gangushatu.

GANNI KHAN : Ganni Khan was a Pathan belonging to Machhiwara. He along with his younger brother Nabi Khan had worked at Anandpur for Guru Gobind Singh. When the Guru came to Machhiwara after the battle at Chamkaur, the brothers offered their services to the Guru and according to Sikh tradition carried the Guru on a cot upto the village Hehar. Here the Guru bid them farewell by giving a *hukamnama* mentioning that Ganni Khan and Nabi Khan were dearer to him than his own sons. For that reason the Sikh states continued giving stipends to their descendants.

GARHI NAZIR : Garhi Nazir is a village in Karnal district of Haryana. The village was founded by a Pathan named Bhikhan Khan who invited Guru Tegh Bahadur to bless the village by his visit.

The imperial troops who were asked to arrest the Guru arrived at Garhi following the Guru's scent. But Bhikhan Khan, the Muslim noble of liberal views with whom the Guru was staying denied the Guru's presence in his house and sent them away. A gurdwara which was patronized by Maharaja Karam Singh of Patiala commemorates the Guru's visit.

GARHI SAHIB, GURDWARA : This marks the site of a double-storeyed house (*garhi*) which was occupied by Guru Gobind Singh on December 6, 1705 AD after vacating Anandpur and was surrounded by imperial forces. Two elder sons of the Guru were killed here while leading sallies from the house. While the Guru himself was persuaded by the Sikhs to escape in disguise so as to continue the struggle. Maharaja Karam Singh of Patiala had the gurdwara constructed here.

GARNA SAHIB : A gurdwara near village Bodal in Hoshiarpur district associated with Guru Hargobind. This area used to be covered with thick forests. The Guru had halted here during his hunting expedition from Kartarpur (Jalandhar).

GATKA : *Gatka* is a sort of Indian gladiatorship with a stick. It is a game of skill played with a stick covered with leather and having a hilt—the stick itself is also called *gatka*. There is a small shield to accompany the stick. The game is similar to the traditional oriental fighting with a *gad* and is sometimes believed to be a way of practising for the same. It certainly equips a person for self-defence when he has nothing other than a stick with him.

Gatka has been associated with Sikhism since the times of Guru Gobind Singh. He made it a part of the mock battles organized at Anandpur at the time of Hola Mohalla. It continues to be so upto the present times.

GAUD : An Indian classical *raag* usually sung at noon. It is seventeenth of the thirty-one *raags* used in the organisation of hymns in the Guru Granth Sahib covering pages 859-874. The sequence of basic notes in it is :
Arohi : sa, re, ma, ma, pa, dha, sa, dha,
Avrohi : ne, pa, ga, ma, re, sa,.....

GAURI : An Indian classical *raag* usually sung in the evening before sunset. It is the third from the beginning of the thirty-one *raags* used in the organisation of hymns in the Guru Granth Sahib covering pages 151-346. It uses the sequence of basic notes :
Arohi : sa, re, ma, pa, ne, sa,....
Avrohi : sa, ne, dha, pa, ma, re, sa....

The Guru Granth Sahib also mentions various variations of the *raag* like *Gauri Chiet*, *Gauri Bairagan*, *Gauri Mala*, etc.

GAYAND, BHATT : Gayanad is one of the *bhatts* (bards) ten of whose compositions have been included in the Adi Granth. He describes the greatness of the Guru Jyoti (Flame) and its history in the *swayyas* that he composed about Guru Ramdas.

GHAKKA KOTLI : See Tahli Sahib

GHALLUGHARA : *Ghallughara* is a Punjabi word meaning large scale massacre of people or carnage or holocaust. Two events in Sikh history are particularly known as *ghallugharas*.

1. Chhota Ghallughara : This took place in 1746 AD. Early in that year, Jaspat Rai, the *faujdar* of Eminabad was killed in an encounter with a band of roving Sikhs. His brother, Lakhpat Rai who was a *diwan* at Lahore vowed to eliminate the Sikhs. Yahya Khan, the governor of Lahore supported him. Accordingly he set out at the head of a large force and surrounded a large group of Sikhs in the forest of Kahnuwan near Gurdaspur. When they escaped from there towards Lakhi forest in the Malwa region, he chased them. In this operation, about 7000 Sikhs were killed and about 3000 captured. This episode in Sikh history from March-May 1746 AD has been known as *Chhota Ghallughara*. (minor holocaust)

2. Wadda Ghallughara : This took place in 1762 AD. Ahmad Shah Abdali had invaded India again in 1761 AD. This time his main aim was to teach the Sikhs a lesson for capturing Lahore and other important areas. The Sikhs evacuated Lahore which Abdali re-occupied without any resistance and then started chasing the Sikhs. On February 3, 1762 AD he caught up with the Sikh families at Kupp near Malerkotla comprising 35000 women and children. Despite the efforts of Jassa Singh Ahluwalia and other Sikh generals, Abdali was successful in killing every Sikh man, woman and child who was camping at Kupp on February 5, 1762 AD. This massacre has become known in Sikh history as *Wadda Ghallughara* (major holocaust).

GHANI KHAN : See Ganni Khan.

GHAR : Literally *Ghar* means house but in the Adi Granth which is set to music, it is to be interpreted in musical terms. In devotional music, *ghar* may be interpreted to have two meanings : first, *tal* (rhythm) to be used in a particular *raag* specified for a *Shabad*; second, *swar* (note) with which the musical composition should begin. The second meaning takes strength from the concept of "home note" in western music.

The Adi Granth mentions *Ghars* from 1 to 17. This may be because of the fact that at the time of its compilation harmonium had not been invented and 12-note scale was not then known. Bhai Mardana usually played *Rabab* (Rebeck) for accompaniment and its strings produced 17 notes. It may be noted that 17-note scale is still used in Arabia.

GHARI : A unit for measuring time in the ancient Indian system. One *ghari* is equal to twenty-four minutes.

GHULAL : An old village in Ludhiana district about 8 km from Samrala. It has a gurdwara dedicated to Guru Gobind Singh. According to the local tradition, the Guru stopped in the village for a while before proceeding to Lall after leaving Machhiwara.

GHUMAN : A village in Gurdaspur district about 10 km from Hargobindpur. Namdev, whose hymns are included in the Adi Granth lived here for a considerable time during his sojourn in Punjab.

GHURANI KALAN : An old village in Ludhiana district sacred to Guru Hargobind. Two shrines : Gurdwara Chola Sahib and Gurdwara Nimsar commemorate the Guru's visit.

GIAN : See Knowledge.

GIAN PRABODH : A composition by Guru Gobind Singh included in the Dasam Granth. It consists of 336 verses in Hindi in praise of God who is described as formless, colourless, casteless and creedless. *Na rangam, na rupam, na jatam, na patam.* (DG, 127)

GILL KALAN : Gill Kalan is an old village of Bhatinda district. Guru Hargobind had visited it during his travels. Maharaja Hira Singh of Nabha got a gurdwara constructed in the village dedicated to the Guru.

GIRDHARI LAL : Girdhari Lal was one of the 52 court poets of Guru Gobind Singh. He belonged to Agra and was with the Guru for a long time. He is known for his anthology of poems entitled *Pingalsar*. He had started writing it at Agra but completed it at Paonta in 1688 AD.

GOBINDGARH : 1. A fort near Kamlah Garh in Himachal Pradesh built in memory of Guru Gobind Singh. The Guru had stayed at Kamlah Garh for some time.
2. A fort in the name of Guru Gobind Singh built by Maharaja Ranjit Singh in 1805-9 AD on the outskirts of Amritsar.
3. A fort in Bhatinda constructed by the ruler of Patiala State.
4. A gurdwara in village Dodhar near Moga associated with Guru Nanak and Guru Hargobind.
5. A town in Punjab which is famous for its iron and steel market. Guru Hargobind visited this place.

GOBIND GHAT : It is a place on the banks of Ganges in Patna where Guru Gobind Singh spent his childhood. The place has been sanctified by the Guru's playful activities. There is also a place of the same name associated with the Guru's visit to Pushkar near Ajmer.

GOBIND GITA : See Krishan Lal.

GOBINDPURA : A village near Mansa where Guru Tegh Bahadur had stayed for a night. Guru Gobind Singh also visited this place.

GOBIND SINGH, GURU : Guru Gobind Singh, the Tenth Guru, was born to Mata Gujri at Patna in 1666 AD when his father Guru Tegh Bahadur was touring Bengal. Guru Gobind Singh lived at Patna until he was five when he was taken to Anandpur. He was nine when Guru Tegh Bahadur was martyred in Delhi. At that young age he inherited the responsibility of guiding the Sikh faith and fulfilling the teachings of Guru Nanak. In the midst of his engagements with the concerns of the community, he gave full attention to the mastery of physical skills and literary accomplishment. He had grown into a comely youth, spare, lithe of limp and energetic. As a result of assiduous training and practice, the Guru gained unique facility in the use of arms. He showed similar prowess at learning. Besides Punjabi, he gained proficiency in Sanskrit, Braj and Persian. He had a natural genius for poetic composition. He patronized poets, thinkers and scholars. In 1677 AD at the age of eleven, Guru Gobind Singh was married to Mata Jito from whom he had three sons : Jujhar Singh, Zorawar Singh, and Fateh Singh. The Guru had two other consorts: Mata Sundri who joined in matrimony in 1684 AD and Mata Sahib Kaur who was married in 1700 AD. The former was the mother of Sahibzada Ajit Singh.

The Guru was an example of a perfect saint-soldier. He had been cherishing the idea that an effective armoury should be developed. He had been able to build a small but well-trained army. At the age of thirty-three years on the Baisakhi Day of 1699 AD, he established the new order of the Khalsa and gave Sikhism the present form.

The event, however, generated animosity in the hill chieftains who contacted the Mughal forces to curb the Khalsa. The Guru had to fight many battles at Anandpur, Chamkaur and Muktsar. His two elder sons: Ajit Singh and Jujhar Singh died fighting at Chamkaur. The younger ones : Zorawar Singh and Fateh Singh were captured by the ruler of Sirhind and were bricked alive. The Guru sacrificed his entire family and underwent untold hardships for righteousness.

After the death of Aurangzeb in February 1707 AD his successor Bahadur Shah made peace with the Guru. The Guru also accompanied him on his expedition to Deccan. It was during this travel that the Guru discovered Banda Bahadur. He also decided to settle at Nanded. But he did not have a long earthly span left for him. One of the two Pathans who had been sent by Nawab Wazir Khan of Sirhind stabbed the Guru on his left near the heart. The Guru succumbed to the injuries in October 1708 AD after declaring the Adi Granth as the reigning Guru—as the Guru eternal.

Guru Gobind Singh's work is best understood as the fulfilment of Guru Nanak's revelation. The Sikh organization had taken on the semblance of a State during his days.

The Guru was a prolific writer. His writings are compiled in the form of the Dasam Granth.

GODAVARI SAR : See Dhilwan Kalan.

GOD IN SIKHISM : God has always been a mystery to man who has been trying to unravel Him through the ages. Primitive man started with animism according to which natural objects have no life but may be abode of dead people, spirits or gods who occasionally give them the appearance of life. A typical example of this is the belief that erupting volcano is an expression of anger of God. The miserable and resourceless man felt the inclemency and fury of the elements, and prayed and sacrificed to avert their wrath or to gain their favour. The gods as well as their votaries appear to have lived in friendly continuity both in India and in Greece.

Indeed, in the evolution of religious thought, man got the idea of gods before he got the idea of one God. Inspite of Vedantic monoism, there is an element of polytheism in Hinduism. For many centuries thinking men in India have, however, rejected gods and goddesses and made no secret of their faith in the sole primal Creator. This got expression among Hindus as Bhakti Movement in medieval India. There was a parallel reform movement among the Muslims known as Sufism. Both Bhakti Movement and Sufism propagated that there is only one Supreme God; that he is beyond the ken of logic or arguments; that He cannot be apprehended by the senses; and that he is attained only through whole-hearted devotion.

As Sikhism is a merger of the two movements, we find the same line of thinking continued in it. The most concise and complete statement about God has been made in the *Mul Mantra*—the opening lines of the Adi Granth "God is one. His name is Truth. He is the Creator. He is without fear. He is inimical to none. His existence is unlimited by time. He is unborn, self-existent and can be realized through the grace of the Guru". *Ik Onkar, Satnam, Kartapurakh, Nirbhau, Nirvair, Akal-murat, Ajuni, Saibhang, Gurparasad.* (AG. P.1)

The usual concepts of Space and Time are not applicable to Him. Therefore God being formless is emphasized again and again "God, the formless, exists without any danger" *Tu sada salamat Nirankar* (AG, p.4) "God is exempt from form, colour or feature. He has none of the father, mother, progeny or relation.

"He is neither subject to lust nor to relationship with women" *Na tis roop varn nahi rekhya sache sabad nisan/na tis mat pita sut bandhap na tis kam na nari* (AG, p. 597). Guru Gobind Singh has also explained this: "He is formless, colourless; markless; He is casteless, classless, creedless, His form, shape, hue and garb cannot be described by any one. He is the spirit of Eternity, Self-radiant; He shines in his own splendour".

As a natural corollary to this, it became important to explain to the followers that God is incomprehensible to ordinary human mind. "O dear, God is unknowable and vast". *Baba Alah agam apar* (AG, P. 53). "No one knows how vast is Your expanse" *Koee na jane tera keta kewad chira* (AG, P. 349). Inspite of this it is made clear that God is the Supreme Being—the ultimate Reality. "He is the sole Supreme Being, no other." *Sabhna data eko hai, dooja nahi koe* (AG, P45) "He is short of nothing". *Ja kai oon nahi kahu baat* (AG. p.238)

With a view to helping man to relate to the unknowable Sikhism has introduced the concept of *Nam* derived from the Sanskrit word *naman* or the Greek *numenon* which is the antonym of phenomenon. Phenomenon is that which appears as reality to the sensory-motor apprehension of man and can be investigated by sciences. *Nam* is the essence of things; it lies at the root of all phenomena these may not be discernible either through physical senses or even through speculative process. "Lord's Name is the essence of all faiths".

Sagal matant kewal Harinam (AG. p. 296).

"O, my body and mind, *Nam* is the only mainstay. Through contemplation on it, is revealed the essence of happiness to me."

Mere man tan prem Nam adhar
Nam japi namo sukh sar (AG, p. 366)

"Nam is the panacea of all ills".

Sarab rog ka aukhad Nam (AG, p. 274)

Since essence of things is the ultimate reality, God in Sikhism is equated with Truth. "It was Truth in the beginning; it has been Truth during all the ages; it is Truth even now; and Truth it shall ever be."

Aad Sach, jugad sach, hai bhi Sach, Nanak hosi bhi Sach (AG, p.1)

"Truth, Truth, Truth is He".

Satya, Satya, Satya, so-oo (AG, p. 251)

"He who in his heart believes in God as Truth knows the essence of the Creator, the cause of causes".

Satya sarup ridai jin mania
karan karawan tin mul pachhania (AG, p. 285).

It has been well summed up in : "O True King, Truth is Your nature."

Sachi teri kudrat, Sache Patshah (AG, p. 463).

That God is present everywhere and in everything is also a recurrent theme in Sikhism. It automatically leads to the conclusion that God resides in us. "All creation is Yours, O Lord and You pervade it"

Sabh teri sirasti toon aap reha samae
(AG, p. 164).

"I searched through all the woods and was tired of the long search. When I met the saint, I found the Lord within my mind."

Ban ban phirti khojti hari bah awgahe
Nanak bhaite sadh jab Har payia man mahe
(AG, p.455).

"As the fragrance abides in the flower and the reflection in the mirror; so does God abide within you. So search Him within your heart."

Puhap madh jio bas bast hai, mukar mahe jaise chhaye

taise hi Har *base nirantar ghat hi khojo bhai*
(AG, p. 684)

In conclusion, we may summarize the basic position of Sikhism on God in the words of Kapur Singh.

1. That the Ultimate Reality (God) is not comprehensible through the sensory-motor perception or pure speculation of thought;

2. That the Ultimate Reality is continuous with and partakes of the religious experience of the *Nam*—which experience is the matrix of other values of Truth, Beauty and Goodness and which experience is implicit in and inheres in the universal human religious consciousness.

3. That there is a way of cultivating and making explicit this consciousness of the *Nam* such as leads to the vision of God."

(*Sikhism for Modern Man*; p. 31)

GOD'S GRACE : Sikhism has bestowed God with Grace expressed by terms like *nadar, mehar, kirpa, karam* etc. God is visualized as the most merciful and compassionate. "The One Lord is the Spouse of us all and on whomever is His grace, she alone is His true Bride."

"*Bhant Nanak sabhna ka pir eko so-e*
Jisno nadar kare sa suhagun ho-e" (AG, p. 351)

Grace is indeed a favourable disposition on the part of God, usually without any reference to merit. It does not mean that man does not have to be good or to put in any effort. It only preaches that reward depends on God's grace—there is no formula for it. "He sees all, but gives only to whomever He wants"

Sabh nadri undir dekhda, jai bhawe te dai-e
(AG, p. 36)

"To give or not to give is His pleasure."

Bhawe dai-e na dai-ee so-e (AG, p. 25)

If the law of *karma*, which is the counterpart of the law of cause and effect in the moral domain is carried to its logical extreme, there will be no need for man to crave for God's grace. But in Sikhism the basic belief is : "It is grace that fills the man with Bliss".

Nanak nadri nadar nihaal (AG, p8).

Therefore in Sikhism the doctrine of *karma* is modified by the concept of God's grace. In a significant line in Japji, Guru Nanak contrasts *karma* with grace by saying: "The body takes its birth because of *karma*, but salvation is attained through grace." *Karmi aawe kapra; nadri mokh duaar. Karma* is important, in that it will produce a favourable or unfavourable birth, but it is through God's grace that final salvation is attained.

The concept of grace does not, however imply that there are certain chosen people upon whom only God showers. His grace "The grace of God is on those who have meditated on Him with a single mind and have found favour in His heart."

Khasam ki nadar dilhe pasande jini kar ik dhiya-ya (AG, p.24)

GOD'S NAME : See Akal Purakh.

GOD'S WILL : God's will is a key concept in Sikh theology as in other monotheistic religions. It is called *hukum*, an Arabic word meaning order and is sometimes used synonymously with *bhana*.

Hukum as an attribute of God gives Him an infinite consciousness and therefore makes Him an active God than just being a principle. Because of it He becomes the Presiding Officer of the universe—the Ultimate Reality—the Truth. Guru Nanak has introduced this concept of *hukum* at the end of Paudi one of Japji by raising the question: "How shall one be truthful? How to break the wall of falsehood?" *Kiv sachiara hoi-ai, kiu koorh-ai tuttai paal*. Guru Nanak has answered it himself: "Nanak, one can do it by abiding the will of God as it ordained by him." *Hukum raja-ee chalna, Nanak likhia naal*.

This is followed in Paudi Two by a comprehensive statement on God's Will. "By His Will the bodies are created;

His Will cannot be defined;

By His Will life comes into them;

By His Will people are honoured;

By His Will they are placed high and low

As He Ordains they receive pain or pleasure;

By His Will some attain His graceful audience;

Others are made to go on forever in transmigration

All are subject to His supreme will. Nothing is outside the sphere of His Will. Nanak, if His Will is realized. None shall ever have ego."

Hukumi hovan aakaar; Hukum na kahe-aja-ee
Hukumi hovan jee; Hukum milai vadia-ee
Hukumi uttam neech; Hukum likh dukh sukh pa-ee-eh
Ikna hukumi bakhsees; Ik hukumi sada bhava-ee-eh
Hukumai under sabh ko; Bahar hukum na ko-e
Nanak Hukumai je bujhai;
Ta haumai kahai na ko-e

God's Will is the key to the Divine Order or Divine Law which determines the cosmic movements, life and death, pleasure and pain etc. "All that happens is according to God's Will." *Hog tisai ka bhana* (AG. P. 155) "In God's Will we wander or find the way. It is according to His Will that we utter His praise. In His Will we are cast in a myriad wombs. All this is His Will."

Bhane ujhar bhane raha; bhane Harigun gurmukh gawaha. Bhane bharam bhawe banh joo-ni; sabh kichh tisai raja-ee jee-o (AG, p 98).

With this view of God's Will, Sikhism has a problem like other monotheistic religions of accommodating man's Free Will, lest he be reduced to an non-entity. See the entry on Free Will for details.

GOINDWAL : Goindwal, about 25 km from Tarn Taran, is a small place in a region rich in agriculture and richer still in Sikh history. The River Beas flows close by.

Guru Amardas, after his anointment as Guru in 1552 AD shifted from Khadur to Goindwal. In 1559 AD, he commenced the digging of the *baoli* which, when completed, attracted pilgrims from far and near. Goindwal also became the centre of an annual fair on the occasion of Baisakhi. Guru Ramdas also lived here before shifting to Amritsar. Guru Arjan was born here.

Goindwal has a number of shrines, important ones being Baoli Sahib, Chubara Sahib, and Damdama Sahib.

GOLAK : *Golak* is a Punjabi term for a receptacle kept in a gurdwara for the devotees to put in their offerings. Sikhism, like all other religions, glorifies charity (*daan*). It expects the offerings to be made in the name of the Guru and through *golak*. (Cash payments made against receipt are as good as offerings through *golak*). This is the most approved method of giving charity. Those who do not use *golak* only trade in cheating. *Golak rakhe nahi ji chhal ka kare vipar* (Tankhanama). The offerings in the *golak* are counted in the presence of chosen representatives and used for common good like *langar*, education and hospitals.

GOLDEN TEMPLE : The Golden Temple also popularly known as Harmandir Sahib (Temple of God) or Darbar Sahib (Divine Court) situated in Amritsar is a living symbol of the spiritual and historical traditions of the Sikhs. Ever since its foundation it has been a source of inspiration to the Sikhs and their chief place of pilgrimage. It is the largest gurdwara in the world.

The glistening temple stands in the midst of a square tank of each side about 1500 m with some 18 m *parkarma* (path) on all four sides. A causeway about 60 m long has to be covered to reach the temple which itself is 12 m square and it rests upon a 20 m square platform. The temple has four doors, one in each direction. The marble slabs used for the embellishment of the temple proper have artistic engravings on them.

Guru Amardas had desired Guru Ramdas before his pontification to build a central place for the Sikhs to congregate at. The present spot, believed to have been gifted by Emperor Akbar was decided upon. Guru Ramdas started the excavation work in 1577 AD but did not live to see the project through. His son, Guru Arjan got the excavation of the tank completed in 1588 AD. That year, Mian Mir, a Muslim saint, laid the foundation stone of the temple at the invitation of Guru Arjan. The temple was completed in 1601 AD and the Adi Granth was installed there in 1604 AD with Baba Buddha as the *granthi*. After Guru Hargobind, no other Sikh guru lived in Amritsar. Guru Tegh Bahadur who went there in 1664 AD to pay his respects was refused admission by the *masands*, the keepers of the place. He did his obeisance from outside the temple.

The Golden Temple has had a chequered history in line with that of the Sikh community. It was always been a major rallying point for the Sikhs. When they were facing severe persecution and were fighting for survival from their hideouts, it was captured by the Mughal rulers and razed to the ground. Around 1740 AD Massa Ranghar, the ruler of Amritsar desecrated it by using it as a dancing hall. He was killed by Mahtab Singh. In 1762 AD Ahmad Shah Abdali gunned down the temple and filled up the tank. Baba Deep Singh laid down his life to save the sanctity of the Golden Temple. The construction of the Golden Temple in its present shape was taken up in 1764 AD when Jassa Singh Ahluwalia laid the foundation stone. Many of the doors and domes were covered with gold plated copper sheets during the reign of Maharaja Ranjit Singh. The Golden Temple Complex got partly damaged in the army action in June 1984 AD.

GONDPUR : A village about 20 km from Hoshiarpur. It has a historical shrine called Gurdwara Tahli Sahib dedicated to Guru Hargobind who came here from Pur Hiran on his way to Kiratpur and stayed in a grove of *tahli* trees.

GORAKHNATH : Gorakhnath was one of the nine heads of the Nath Cult which was quite a force in north India before Bhakti movement. The cult was the product of the tantric history of Hinduism and Buddhism. At one point of time *Vajrayana* or the *Vajra* path to salvation became very popular among the Buddhists. It is believed that *Vajrayana* inspired *Nathism* among Hindus who accepted some of its tantric doctrines, deities, *mantras*, *sadhanas* etc. The *Naths* introduced many new theories in the sphere of *hathayoga* and other esoteric practices.

Gorakhnath is said to have been born in Gorakhpur. Many believe that he was the son and disciple of Matsayindranath. His period is uncertain since the latest date given for his death is the end of the 12th century, he could not have been a contemporary of Guru Nanak as some of the *Janam Sakhis* would have us believe. They describe encounters between the two when they could never have met. While the Adi Granth is severely critical of the teachings and esoteric practices of the Gorakh Panth, *Janam Sakhis* describe Gorakhnath to have recognized the greatness of Guru Nanak and even inspired him to choose his successor. The issue need to be researched carefully.

GRANTH SAHIB, GURU : The Guru Granth Sahib which is another name for the Adi Granth is the religious scripture of the Sikhs as well as the Guru eternal for them. For details see Adi Granth.

There are several documents which attest the fact of succession having been passed on by Guru Gobind Singh to the Guru Granth Sahib. For instance, *Rahitnama* by Bhai Nandlal, one of Guru's disciples who was at Nanded in the camp of Emperor Bahadur Shah as one of his ministers at the time of Guru's passing away, thus records his last words in his Punjabi verse:

He who would wish to see the Guru,
Let him come and see the Granth.
He who would wish to speak to Him,
Let him read and reflect upon what says the Granth.
He who would wish to hear His word,
He should with all his heart read the Granth.
Or listen to the Granth being read.

That Guru Granth Sahib is the Guru eternal has been the understanding and conviction of the Sikh community since the passing away of Guru Gobind Singh.

GRANTHI : *Granthi* is a term used for the Sikh officiant whose main duty is to read the Guru Granth Sahib in public. He is the custodian of the Holy Book in the gurdwara and performs the morning and evening services, leads the *ardaas* and may also perform or lead *kirtan*. Baba Buddha was the first *granthi* of the Golden

Temple. Large gurdwaras may have a team of *granthis* led by the Head *Granthi*.

GREED : Greed or avarice called *lobh* in Punjabi is according to Sikh tradition one of the five chief vices of mankind. It is a desire to possess what belongs to others. Sikhism recognises that greed affects everyone. "O Greed, you have swayed even the best men by your waves. And men's minds waver and run in all directions to gather more and more" (AG, p 1358). It is also asserted that this pursuit of "more and more" is wasteful. "In vain, I have wasted my life in greed."

Jhoothe lalach janam gawayia (AG, p. 175)
"O Man, you are oblivious that day and night your life is nearing its end and greed has made you worthless".
Ahnis audh ghate nahi jane bhayo lobh sang haura (AG, P. 220)

A greedy person is not trustworthy for he is not loyal to anything except wealth. Like christianity, Sikhsim stresses the social aspect of greed and advises Sikhs to shed their avarice and make believe—

Man karhla toon meet maira pakhand lobh taja-e (AG, p. 234)

GRIHSAT : See Asceticism.

GUJJARWAL : A village about 30 km from Ludhiana. It has a historical gurdwara called Gurusar dedicated to Guru Hargobind. According to the local tradition, the Guru halted here in 1631 AD during his tour of the Malwa region. The local chief, Chaudhari Phatuhi served the Guru with devotion but became proud of the service rendered by him. One day he came to the Guru with full retinue of servants and a falcon in hand asking the Guru if he could be of any further service to him. The Guru asked for the falcon but Chaudari Phatuhi started making excuses. It so happened that the bird fell ill and was cured by the Guru's blessings. Then Phatuhi offered the falcon to the Guru but the latter declined to accept it saying that if he had shed his pride there was no need to make any further offerings.

GUJRI : An Indian classical *raag* usually sung in the first about two hours (four *gharis*) after sunrise in the morning. It is fifth *raag* from the beginning out of the thirty-one *raags* used in the organisation of hymns in the Guru Granth Sahib covering page 489-526. It uses the sequence of basic notes :
Arohi : sa, re, ga, ma, dha, ne, sa,....
Avrohi : sa, ne, dha, ma, ga, re, sa...

GUJRI, MATA : Mata Gujri was the mother of Guru Gobind Singh and wife of Guru Tegh Bahadur. She was witness to the unique saga of Sikh struggle and sacrifice.

Mata Gujri was born at Kartarpur (Jalandhar) in 1626 AD. Her father was Bhai Lal Chand. As per the custom of those days, she was married to Guru Tegh Bahadur at a very early age in 1633 AD. The Guru was elder to her by 10 years.

Mata Gujri spent 21 years at Baba Bakala. While on a tour of the east (Bengal and Assam), Guru Tegh Bahadur had left her in a pregnant state at Patna where she gave birth to Guru Gobind Singh in December 1666 AD. After the martydom of Guru Tegh Bahadur, Mata Gujri remained with Guru Gobind Singh. During the Guru's escape from Anandpur Mata Gujri along with her two younger grandsons got separated from the Guru. They were treacherously handed over to Wazir Khan, *faujdar* of Sirhind who confined them in a tower, *sahibzadas* Fateh Singh and Zorawar Singh were bricked alive in December 1705 AD. Mata Gujri died at Sirhind when she heard the news.

At Fatehgarh Sahib near Sirhind is a shrine called Burj Mata Gujri. This is where she spent the last four days of her life. Gurdwara Joti Sarup marks the spot near Sirhind where she was cremated.

GULABA : Gulaba also referred to as Gulab Chand was a *Khatri* Sikh belonging to Machhiwara in Ludhiana district. After giving up his duties as a *masand*, he was leading the life of a householder. After leaving Chamkaur in December 1705 AD, Guru Gobind Singh has stayed with him. According to Sikh tradition the Guru had changed over to the blue cloak in his house to disguise as a *pir*. His garden outside Machhiwara where the Guru had come first has been converted into a historical shrine.

GULAB CHAND : Gulab Chand was the son of Bibi Viro, daughter of Guru Hargobind. He fought for Guru Gobind Singh in the battle at Bhangani in September 1688 AD in which two of his brothers Sangram Shah and Jit Mal were killed.

GULABOO : Gulaboo was a tobacco seller belonging to the *bania* caste during the reign of Emperor Bahadur Shah. After the death of Guru Gobind Singh when Banda Singh Bahadur marched into Punjab, Gulaboo was very much impressed by the bravery of the Sikhs and therefore joined his forces.

In 1710 AD, a massive imperial force drove the Sikhs from Sirhind and other places to take shelter in the Fort of Lohgarh. Here Banda Singh Bahadur was closely invested by sixty thousand troopers. On December 10, 1710 AD, Banda Singh Bahadur made a desperate bid to escape the imperial cordon. Gulaboo helped him in it by disguising as Banda Singh Bahadur and surrendering to the imperial forces. He was brought to Delhi where he remained in prison till the capture of Banda Singh Bahadur before whose eyes he was killed in 1716 AD.

GULAB SINGH : Gulab Singh was the name given to Gulab Rai after his baptism by Guru Gobind Singh. He was the great grandson of Guru Hargobind (grandson of Suraj Mal). Guru Gobind Singh while evacuating Anandpur in 1705 AD had directed Gurbakhash, to look after the local *sangat* and the shrines particularly Sisganj where Guru Tegh Bahadur's head had been cremated. Years later Gulab Singh purchased Anandpur from the Raja of Bilaspur and tried to establish his own religious seat there pretending to be the Guru. This was resisted by Gurbakhsh. Gulab Singh's four sons predeceased him and he himself died of grief.

GULZAR SINGH : Gulzar Singh is an 18th century Sikh martyr. He was administered *amrit* by Guru Gobind Singh himself and he was a companion of Bhai Mani Singh. He was martyred along with Bhai Mani Singh at Lahore at the orders of Zakriya Khan in 1738 AD. His *samadh* (cenotaph) in Lahore was very close to the Shahidganj dedicated to Bhai Mani Singh.

GUPTSAR, GURDWARA : It is a gurdwara in village Chhatiana near Giddarbaha. It marks the site where Guru Gobind Singh had distributed salary to his soldiers after the battle at Muktsar. The treasure that was left was buried here which none could later on find. Hence the name of the shrine Guptsar (Secret place).

GURBAKHSH : Gurbakhsh Das, in short known as Gurbakhsh, was a disciple of Mahadev, an *Udasi* saint. Before evacuating Anandpur in December 1705 AD, Guru Gobind Singh directed Gurbakhsh to stay behind to look after the local *sangat* and the shrines, particularly Sisganj where Guru Tegh Bahadur's head had been cremated. Years later Gulab Singh one of the sons of Guru Gobind Singh's first cousin Dip Chand purchased Anandpur from the Raja of Bilaspur and pretending to be a successor to the Guru and established his own religious seat much against the wishes of Gurbakhsh.

GURBAKHSH SINGH : Gurbakhsh Singh is one of the 18th century Sikh martyrs. He belonged to village Leel of Amritsar district and was initiated formally into the Khalsa Panth by Bhai Mani Singh. Soon he rose to become a *jathedar*. He was martyred in December 1764 AD while defending the Golden Temple against a huge army of Ahmad Shah Abdali with a contingent of just about thirty Sikhs. A Shahidganj was constructed to honour him at the back of the Akal Takht in Amritsar.

GURBANI : *Gurbani* sometimes shortened to

just *bani* is a Punjabi term used for the hymns in the Guru Granth Sahib. When *gurbani* is recited in the prescribed Indian classical *raag*, it is called *Kirtan*.

GURDAS, BHAI : Bhai Gurdas, the amanuensis who wrote the Adi Granth at the disctation of Guru Arjan is also the author of 39 *Vars* (ballads in the heroic metre) in Punjabi and 556 *Kabits* (couplets) in Braj, of which the former are of some historical and theological importance. They are the only really authentic references to the period of the 3rd, 4th, 5th and 6th Gurus by a Sikh.

Bhai Gurdas was born at Goindwal between 1540 AD and 1560 AD. He was the son of Datar Chand, the younger brother of Guru Amardas, who took the child's education into his own hands. He was quick to learn and soon became one of the chief exponents of the teachings of the Gurus. On the death of Guru Amardas, Guru Ramdas formally initiated Bhai Gurdas into the faith and sent him to Agra as a missionary. On the death of Guru Ramdas, he returned to Amritsar and presented himself before Guru Arjan. He became his scribe and completed the volume of the Adi Granth.

After the execution of Guru Arjan and during the years when Guru Hargobind was in prison in Gwalior, the affairs of the community were left in the hands of trusted followers among whom were Bhai Gurdas and Baba Buddha.

Bhai Gurdas remained celibate and died at Goindwal in 1629 AD. His funeral rites were performed by Guru Hargobind himself.

Bhai Gurdas is also said to have met Emperor Akbar to explain to him that the Adi Granth does not contain anything derogatory to Islam. He was presented a pair of expensive Kashmere shawls by Akbar.

GURDAS NANGAL : See Gurdaspur.

GURDASPUR : Gurdaspur is a district town in Punjab about 75 km from Amritsar. It was here that Banda Singh Bahadur was captured after a long siege in December 1715 AD by Abd-us-Samad Khan, governor of Lahore heading twenty-thousand troopers on the orders of Farrukhsiyar, the then Mughal Emperor at Delhi.

According to Ganda Singh the actual place of siege was "the old village of Gurdas Nangal now a heap of ruins, known as *Bande-wali Theh* lying about one kilometer to the west of the present village of Gurdas Nangal about 6 km to the west of Gurdaspur. It had no regular fort. The Sikhs had, therefore, to shelter themselves in the *ihata* (enclosure) of Bhai Duni Chand." (*Life of Banda Singh Bahadur*, Punjabi Univ Patiala; p. 166).

GURDITTA, BABA : Baba Gurditta was the eldest son of Guru Hargobind. He was born to Mata Damodari at Daroli Bhai near Moga on November 15, 1613 AD. A gurdwara called Janam Asthan Baba Gurditta exists there.

Baba Gurditta received his education from his father Guru Hargobind. He had become a disciple of Baba Sri Chand and organised his sect of *Udasis* for the spread of Sikhism in India. He was married to Mata Ananti in 1624 AD and had two sons Dhirmal and Guru Har Rai.

Baba Gurditta passed away in 1638 AD during the life time of Guru Hargobind at Kiratpur where a shrine has been dedicated to him.

GURDITTA, BHAI : Bhai Gurditta (1625-75) was the son of Bhai Jhanda, a descendant of Baba Buddha. He was one of those who, after the death of Guru Harkrishan at Delhi in 1664 AD, were especially summoned to Bakala for the anointment of Guru Tegh Bahadur as the privilege of performing this ceremony had by tradition belonged to Baba Buddha's house. In 1675 AD when the Guru decided to proceed to Delhi to court martyrdom, Bhai Gurditta was called upon to perform the accession ceremony for Guru Gobind Singh. He went to Delhi after the ceremony, was not arrested but witnessed the martyrdom of Guru Tegh Bahadur on November 11, 1765 AD and he passed away the following day. He was cremated at Bhogal in Delhi.

GURDWARA : Gurdwara is the name given to a Sikh temple. Literally it means the gateway to the Guru which implies the Adi Granth. An essential feature of a gurdwara is the presiding presence of the Sikh Holy Book. It is a centre of congregational worship of propagation of Sikhism. The pattern of worship can be divided into two categories : *katha*, the reading of the holy hymns followed by their explanations and *kirtan*, the singing of hymns, the latter being more common. Attached to every gurdwara is invariably a free kitchen called *langar*.

Gurdwara is not a place for idol worship—not even for individual worship. It is open to all regardless of age, sex, caste or creed.

Gurdwara also plays a socio-economic role in the Sikh community. Devotees who go to a gurdwara make offerings in money or victuals. These offerings are not the property of any one person but are used for the common good—for running the *langar*, schools, colleges and hospitals.

In early Sikhism, the place used for congregational prayers was called *dharamsala*—the abode of *dharma*. Guru Nanak, wherever he went called upon his followers to establish *dharamsalas* and congregate in them for *Nam Japna*.

It is believed that the first gurdwara was erected at Eminabad where Guru Nanak met Bhai Lalo. Now-a-days you find gurdwaras all over the world. A gurdwara is known from a distance by the *Nishan Sahib*—the Sikh Standard.

GURDWARA ACT 1925 : Gurdwara Act 1925 is an act passed by the government of India handing over the control and management of gurdwaras to an elected body of the representatives of the Sikhs called Sharomani Gurdwara Parbandhak Committee (SGPC). This was done after a long agitation led by Sharomani Akali Dal popularly called the Akali Movement. For more details see the entry under Akali Movement.

GURMAT : *Gurmat* is a Punjabi word meaning the religion or the creed founded by the Guru. Therefore in Punjabi speech and writings it is synonymous with Sikhism. It obviously covers both the scriptural teachings of Sikhism and its code of conduct.

GURMATA : *Gurmata* means 'counsel of the Guru' or a resolution passed in a council presided over by the Guru. It may also be taken to mean the advice of the Guru.

Gurmata as an instrument of decision taking became important in post Gobind Singh era.

The congregation of Sikhs, which used to take important decisions in the presence of Guru Granth Sahib came to be known as *Sarbat Khalsa*. The decisions of such congregations were called *Gurmatas*.

These *Gurmatas* were not *Hukamnamas* but were many times respected as such particularly when they were announced by the *jathedar* (Head) of the Akal Takht.

A *Gurmata* cannot be pronounced on fundamentals of Sikhism and is valid only if the congregation is representative of the entire Sikh people.

GURMUKH : The term *gurmukh* occurs frequently in Sikh theological writings. Literally it means a person who is God-oriented and God-filled in contrast to a *manmukh* who is self-centred. The term obviously covers a much wider spectrum than what is implied by a "devout Sikh" or an "ideal Sikh". *Gurmukh* connotes an element of spiritual leanings in a person steeped with Nam and invested with Truth.

"If you dwell on the True Name, through the Guru's word, you are a true *gurmukh*, adjudged true at the Lord's court :

Sach Nam gur sabad vichar; gurmukh sache sachai darbar (AG, p. 355)

"The *gurmukh* gathers Truth, self-discipline and wisdom and they are attuned to the True Lord"

Gurmukh sach sanjam tat gian; gurmukh sache lage dhian (AG, p. 559-60)

"The *gurmukhs* are blessed with the Name and they merge in Truth".

Nanak gurmukh Harinam paye-aa, sahje sach smah (AG, p. 591)

Using the popular analogy of the Lord, being the spouse, the relationship of a *gurmukh* to God is very well expressed in : "Gurmukh is like the wife enjoying wedded bliss".

Gurmukh sada sohagani pir rakhia urdhar. (AG, p. 31)

GURMUKHI : Gurmukhi is the script used for writing Punjabi. The Adi Granth is also written in this script.

Gurmukhi has evolved out of the characters of Lande Mahajni which was in use in the plains of Punjab during the time of Guru Nanak and can be traced back to the ancient Brahmi and Aramic scripts.

There was a danger that Guru Nanak's hymns written in Lande Mahajni might be misread and misinterpreted. Therefore Guru Angad introduced improvement in them. He beautified and standardized the Lande alphabet by giving them better shape like the Devanagri alphabet. He also modified the order of the 35 alphabet. The new script came to be called Gurmukhi meaning that it came from the mouth of the Guru. Guru Angad wrote the hymns of Guru Nanak in this script, also gave lessons himself to village children and penned down his own compositions in the same.

According to *Mahma Prakash*, the Gurmukhi sript was invented by Guru Angad at the suggestion of Guru Nanak during the latter's life time.

GURPARTAP : The name of a gurdwara in village Guru-ka-Chak in district Jalandhar. Guru Tegh Bahadur stayed here for about a month on his way from Baba Bakala to Kiratpur. The village was founded by Mata Gujri.

GURPARTAP SURYA : *Gurpartap Surya* is a well known poetic composition by the 18th century scholar Bhai Santokh Singh. It recounts the stories of nine Sikh Gurus—Guru Angad to Guru Gobind Singh. It is popularly known as *Surya Prakash*.

GURPLAH : *Plah* is the name of a wild tree in Punjab. Some of these trees have been sanctified by their association with the Sikh Gurus. They or the shrines constructed there are generally called *gurplah*. Some of them are :

1. Gurplah, Baboo : This is situated on the outskirts of village Baboo about 15 km from Jaijon. Guru Gobind Singh had rested here under a tree.

2. Gurplah, Banga : It is situated in village Sotar on the outskirts of Banga in Jalandhar district. Guru Hargobind had rested here for a while.

3. Gurplah, Khairabad : See Khairabad.

4. Gurplah, Phagwara : It is on the outskirts of Phagwara, an old town on G.T. Road between Jalandhar and Ludhiana. It is dedicated to Guru Har Rai.

5. Gurplah, Sarala : It is in village Sarala about 10 km from Phagwara and is dedicated to Guru Tegh Bahadur.

GURPURB : *Gurpurb* is a generic Punjabi term for an important day associated with the Sikh Gurus. Generally it is a celebration connected with the anniversary of birth or death of a Guru. But anniversaries like that of the installation of the Adi Granth, the martyrdom of the *Sahibzadas* are also included. *Gurpurbs* on the birth anniversaries of Guru Nanak and Guru Gobind Singh and the martyrdom day of Guru Arjan are universally celebrated. Others tend to be organized only locally unless it is a centennial of the event.

Except for the martyrdom day of Guru Arjan, when Sikh communities in different parts of towns set up kiosks to serve cold sweetened water with milk in it on the roadside for thirsty wayfarers, other *gurpurbs* tend to consist of some or all of the following :

1. *Akhand path* with *bhog* ceremony in the morning. Many times it is accompanied with *langar*.

2. *Nagar kirtan*—taking the Guru Granth Sahib in a procession with various groups singing *shabads*.

3. *Diwan*—a congregation in which *shabad kirtan* is organized interspersed with speeches

concerning the life and achievements of the Guru.

GURSIKH : *Gursikh* is a Punjabi term used with respect for someone who is deeply and sincerely devoted to the service of the Guru. According to Bhai Kahn Singh, Gursikh is a person who follows the religion and philosophy of Guru Nanak. In that sense the term is sometimes also used for Sahajdhari Sikhs who do not believe in Guru Gobind Singh's baptism. Guru Ramdas' advice in the Guru Granth Sahib "Oh Gursikh friends, follow the path of the Guru". *Gursikh meet chalh Gur chaali* (AG, p. 667) contains in it the most general meaning of the term *Gursikh*.

GURU IN SIKHISM : Guru is a pivotal concept in Sikhism. It is basic to the understanding and pursuit of the religion.

The concept of Guru is not new. It has been a part of the Indian tradition and culture since time immemorial. There may be disagreements about the etymology of the term but they all tend to resolve when one comes to the functions of a Guru. Down the ages he has been a spiritual preceptor. He is a man and sometimes a woman who has become spiritually enlightened and who believes that he has a responsibility to guide others helping them to attain *moksha*—through knowledge, techniques or a combination of the two. Thus a Guru is not an ordinary teacher; neither is he a prophet or an incarnation of God. He is much more than just a *bhagat* or a saint. He is a spiritual torch—with the *jyoti* (light) that illuminates the path to the Lord.

To understand the complex concept of Guru in Sikhism, it will be better to revert to the Adi Granth which mentions different aspects of the Guru at different places.

"To attain to His Name, the Guru is the ladder, Guru the boat, Guru the raft, Guru the ship, the place of pilgrimage and the river"
Gur paori beri, guru, gur tulha Harnao
Gur sar sagar bohtho gur tirath daryao
(AG, p. 17)
"Guru is the embodiment of peace, truth, wisdom, the philosopher's stone whose touch turns all into gold"
Gurdev shanti sat budhi murat
Gurdev paras paraspar (AG, p. 250)
"True Guru is the pool of nectar and fortunate ones bathe in it."
Satgur purakh amritsar wadbhagi nawai aae
(AG, p 40)
"True Guru is the fountainhead of all blessings. One meets him with good luck"
Satgur data sabhna wakhu ka purai bhag milawniya (AG, p. 116)
"Guru is the tree of contentment which flowers in faith and fruitions in wisdom"
Nanak gur santokh rukh dharmo phul, phul gyan (AG, p. 147)
"True Guru is the treasure of glory"
Satgur wich wadi wadiyaee (AG, p. 361)
"Guru is the sea of wisdom and embodiment of Truth"
Gur sayer Satgur sach soe (AG, p. 363)

That the Guru occupies a very exalted position in Sikhism becomes clear from his functions as hinted in the Adi Granth at a number of places. It brings out the spiritual dimensions of the Guru very clearly.

"No one hath attained to the Lord without the Guru; he wastes his life in vain"
Bin gur kinai na payo birtha janam gawayo
(AG. p. 33)
"One does not get the equipoise without the Guru"
Bajh guru ko sahaj na paye (AG p. 125)
"The nine treasures of Nam are received from the Guru"
Nam navnidhi gur to paye (AG. p 159)
"One fasts; practises religious observances and atonement; one visits the river banks and pilgrim centres all over the earth but he alone is saved who takes refuge with the Guru."
Wart nem kar thake punh charna
tatt tirath bhawe sabh dharna
se ubre je satgur ki sarna (AG. p. 394)

To clarify the concept of Guru in Sikhism Dr. Tarlochan Singh emphasizes the mystic side of a Guru's personality as compared to the historical side. "On account of the divine prerogatives and attributes, the Guru, though human in form, is godly in spirit. God speaks to humanity through him. God enlightens the seekers of truth through him and his word. No historical phenomena of the lives of the Sikh Gurus can be explained correctly unless it is done in relation to the mystic personality of the true Guru" (*Sikhism* : Punjabi univ, p. 63).

Explaining the mystic personality, Guru Gobind Singh said to his poet laureate Bhai Nand Lal : "Listen O Nand Lal, I, the Guru, have three personalities : (1) *Nirgun*, attributeless, the light which is eternally with God and represents God's being in pure form. It is because of this consummate perfection, God is in the Guru, and Guru is in God" (2) *Sargun*, manifest. The Guru manifested Himself in the form of the historical Guru, and He is now eternally here in the form of *Sadh Sangat* (congregation of enlightened people). "One initiate is a disciple of the Guru, a Sikh; two or more make *Sadh Sangat*; in five, God's light shines as perfectly as it does in the Guru." (This is the basic concept of *Panj Piaras* as a part of the Khalsa order) (3) The Word (Shabad) is the Guru and in the Guru, the divine light is *Shabad*.

Guru Gobind Singh thus completed the transition from personal Guruship to corporate Gurship and finally to the situation which exists today, that of Guruship invested in the scripture which he did in 1708 AD just before his passing away. He ordained : "The order of the Khalsa was established as was the command of God. This is now the commandment to all the Sikhs :

'Accept the Granth as the Guru; know Guru Granth ji as the visible body of the Guru'. To shed the doubt that Sikhs have reverted to Book worship if not idolatory one must remember that Guru is not just the human, historical body as explained above, it is the spirit which is the Shabad as now contained in the Guru Granth Sahib. The utmost respect which the Guru deserves to be shown finds expression in the form of current practices in gurdwaras. They are derived from the oriental traditions of showing respect to high dignitaries like the kings. In fact the central hall of every gurdwara is set up as an oriental throne room with all its embellishments and customs with the Guru Granth Sahib as the presiding figure.

GURU-KA-BAGH : A general name for a garden sanctified by the Guru. A number of places and gurdwaras have been named as such.

1. A gurdwara in Sultanpur. Guru Nanak lived here after his marriage. Both of his sons were born here. It is a small two-storeyed structure with a bit of a garden attached to it. The room on the ground floor where Guru Granth Sahib has been kept has its walls covered with ceramic tiles, with frescoes above, with Guru Nanak's life as the theme.

2. A garden in Amrtisar associated with Guru Arjan.

3. A place in Varanasi where Guru Tegh Bahadur has stayed.

4. A garden in Patna at about two kilometres from Harmandir Sahib associated with Guru Tegh Bahadur.

5. A gurdwara in village Ghukewali district Amritsar. It has a small garden attached to it. Guru Arjan had stayed here. The gurdwara was built by Maharaja Ranjit Singh.

GURU-KA-CHAK : Earlier name of Amritsar. Also the name of a village in district Jalandhar in which a famous gurdwara Gurpartap is situated.

GURU-KA-LAHORE : A town in Bilaspur district about 10 km from Anandpur. Wedding of Guru Gobind Singh to Mata Jito was solemnized here in June 1677 AD. Gurdwara Anand Karaj marks the site where the ceremony was held. It has two other shrines associated with the Guru.

GURU-KA-MAHAL : A general name given to the residential quarters of the Gurus. The following places are especially known by this name.

1. A gurdwara situated in the heart of Amritsar. Its building was constructed by Guru Ramdas for his residence when he started the construction of the town. Guru Arjan and Guru Hargobind continued to live here. It was here

that Guru Tegh Bahadur was born. Guru Hargobind stayed here for a long time.

2. The place in Amritsar where Guru Hargobind was married to Mata Nanaki.

3. A gurdwara in Kartarpur (Jalandhar) where Guru Arjan had lived.

4. A gurdwara at Hargobindpur in district Gurdaspur where Guru Hargobind had lived. The building was built by the Guru himself.

5. The palaces of Guru Tegh Bahadur at Kiratpur.

6. A sacred shrine at Anandpur associated with Guru Tegh Bahadur. This is the place where the Guru lived. The building was got constructed by him under his own supervision in 1665 AD. His grand children, sons of Guru Gobind Singh the four *sahibzadas*—were brought up here.

GURU-KI-TAHLIAN, GURDWARA : It is situated on the outskirts of village Gaundpur near Mahilpur. Guru Hargobind had halted here on his way to Kiratpur. The trees (one *kikar* and six *tahlis*) with which the Guru's horses were tied still exist there. The gurdwara derives its name from them.

For other similar gurdwaras see Tahli Sahib.

GURU NANAK PRAKASH : Guru Nanak Prakash is the biography of Guru Nanak written by Bhai Santokh Singh in 1823 AD. It is largely based on Bhai Bala's Janam Sakhi (See the relevant entry). It is used as a source material for *Sakhis* about Guru Nanak.

GURUS, CHRONOLOGY OF : The pontificate of various gurus is as follows :

Guru Nanak	.... to 1539 AD
Guru Angad	1539 to 1552 AD
Guru Amardas	1552 to 1574 AD
Guru Ramdas	1574 to 1581 AD
Guru Arjan	1581 to 1606 AD
Guru Hargobind	1606 to 1645 AD
Guru Har Rai	1645 to 1661 AD
Guru Harkrishan	1661 to 1664 AD
Guru Tegh Bahadur	1664 to 1675 AD
Guru Gobind Singh	1675 to 1708 AD
Guru Granth Sahib	1708 onwards.....

GURUS, CONTEMPORARY RULERS :

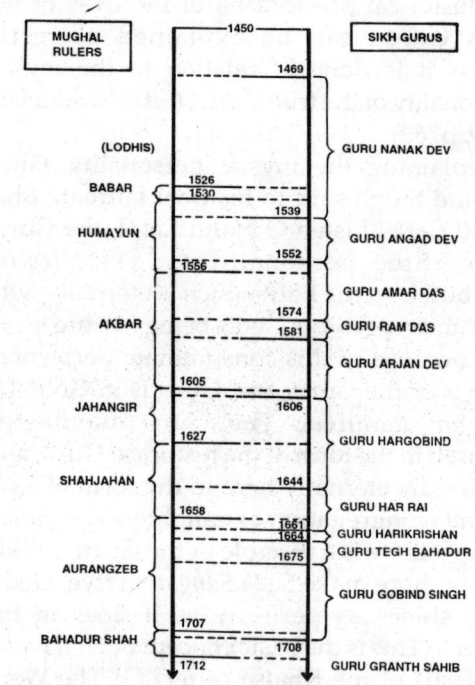

GURUS, FAMILY TREE :

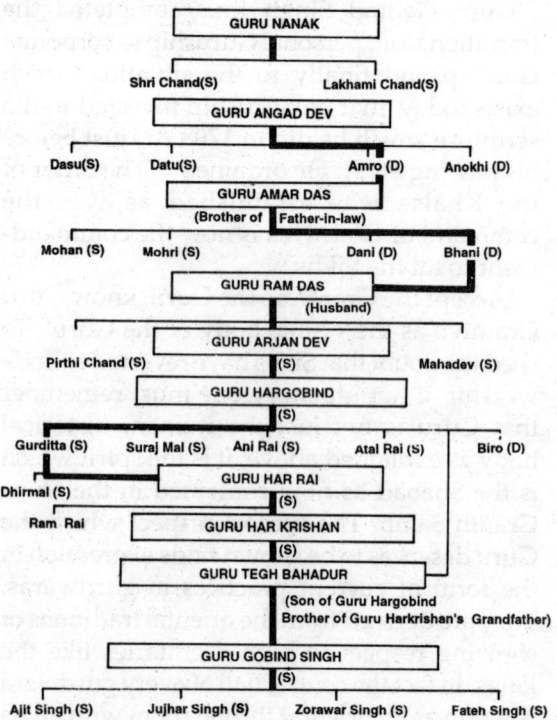

GURUS : PLACES ASSOCIATED :

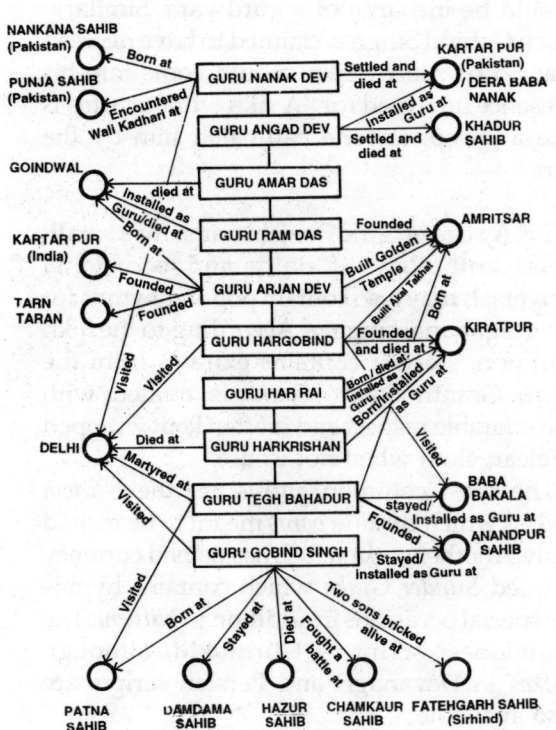

GURUS : PARENTS :

Guru	Father	Mother
Guru Nanak	Baba Kalu (Kalyan Rai)	Mata Tripta
Guru Angad	Baba Pheru Mal	Mata Ramo
Guru Amardas	Baba Tej Bhan	Mata Lakho
Guru Ramdas	Baba Hari Das	Mata Daya Kaur
Guru Arjan	Guru Ramdas	Bibi Bhani
Guru Hargobind	Guru Arjan	Mata Ganga
Guru Har Rai	Baba Gurditta	Mata Damodari
Guru Harkrishan	Guru Har Rai	Mata Krishan Kaur
Guru Tegh Bahadur	Guru Hargobind	Mata Nanaki
Guru Gobind Singh	Guru Tegh Bahadur	Mata Gujri

GURUS, WIVES :

Guru	Wife/Wives
Guru Nanak	Mata Tripta
Guru Angad	Mata Khivi
Guru Amardas	Mata Mansa Devi
Guru Ramdas	Bibi Bhani
Guru Arjan	Mata Ganga
Guru Hargobind	Mata Damodari
	Mata Nanaki
	Mata Mahadevi
Guru Har Rai	Mata Krishan Kaur
Guru Harkrishan	
Guru Tegh Bahadur	Mata Gujri
Guru Gobind Singh	Mata Jito
	Mata Sundri
	Mata Sahib Kaur

GURUSAR : *Sar* is a short form of *sarovar* (tank) in Punjabi. *Gurusar* therefore means a tank associated with a Sikh Guru. Some of the well-known *gurusars* are :

1. Gurusar, Ajit Gill : It is situated in village Ajit Gill near Kotkapura. Guru Gobind Singh had halted here to tie his turban.

2. Gurusar, Berar Medoke : This is in village Berar Medoke in Amritsar district. It is associated with Guru Hargobind.

3. Gurusar, Chakar : Chakar is a village in Ludhiana district. Both Guru Hargobind and Guru Gobind Singh had visited it.

4. Gurusar, Damdama Sahib : It is a bathing tank 130 x 90 m² with a 10 m wide *parikarma*. It was originally got dug by Guru Tegh Bahadur. Guru Gobind Singh got it desilted and deepened during his stay at Damdama Sahib. Lining and paving was done only recently.

5. Gurusar, Dhilwan Kalan : This is also known as Godavarisar and is situated in Dhilwan Kalan about 5 km from Kotkapura. Guru Gobind Singh came here in December 1705 AD from Kotkapura when he realized that Chaudhry Kapura was not prepared to ward off the imperial forces chasing the Guru. Here he discarded the blue attire he had put on at Machhiwara as a disguise.

6. Gurusar, Gujjarwal :
(a) Gurusar Jatpura : See Jatpura.

(b) Gurusar Kaonke : See Kaonke.
(c) Gurusar, Kattu : See Kattu.

7. Gurusar, Kotkapura : This is a village of the same name near Kotkapura. It has a gurdwara with a tank associated with Guru Gobind Singh.

8. Gurusar, Khemkaran : See Khemkaran.

9. Gurusar, Lall : It is a gurdwara dedicated to Guru Gobind Singh in village Lall near Machhiwara. The Guru was stopped and questioned here by Mughal forces after the battle at Chamkaur.

10. Gurusar, Lopo : It is dedicated to Guru Hargobind who had visited the village of Lopo near Moga during his travels in the Malwa region.

11. Gurusar, Mehraj : See Mehraj.

12. Gurusar, Mehron : This shrine commemorates the visit of Guru Gobind Singh to Mehron, a village near Moga.

13. Gurusar, Muktsar : This is a village of the same name near Muktsar. Guru Gobind Singh had halted here on the edge of a big pond.

14. Gurusar, Nabha : This is a village of the same name in the former Nabha state. Guru Gobind Singh came here for a walk from Dina. The village did not exist in those days. A gurdwara has been dedicated to the Guru.

15. Gurusar, Patto : Patto is a village near Moga. It was visited by Guru Nanak, Guru Hargobind and Guru Gobind Singh.

16. Gurusar, Sadhar : This is dedicated to the visit of Guru Hargobind to village Sadhar in Ludhiana district.

17. Gurusar, Sarawan : This is in village Sarawan near Kotkapura.

18. Gurusar Satlani : See Satlani.

GURWILAS : There are two writings of this name relating to the time of Guru Hargobind and Guru Gobind Singh respectively. The Gurwilas of Guru Hargobind dates from the period 1833-43 AD and its author has kept himself anonymous. The Gurwilas of Guru Gobind Singh was written in about 1795 AD by Bhai Sukha Singh of Anandpur.

The purpose of these writings was perhaps to remind the Sikhs of important teachings which the authors thought were being neglected or wanted otherwise to emphasize. For example, Guru Hargobind is claimed to have decreed that only a man knowledgeable in *gurbani* should be incharge of a gurdwara. Similarly Guru Gobind Singh is claimed to have decreed that no *keshadhari* Sikh should come into his presence unarmed for "A sikh without arms is like a sheep; anyone can catch him by the ears."

GUTKA : *Gutka* is the Punjabi name for a small-sized anthology of daily and occasional prayers. It may also contain popular hymns for congregational singing. According to the Sikh tradition, since it contains extracts from the Guru Granth Sahib, *Gutka* is treated with considerable respect and is often kept wrapped in clean cloth when not in use.

The most common *gutkas* are the *Nitnem Guktas* which contain *banis* meant to be recited daily. Another *gutka* which has gained currency is titled *Sunder Gutka* which contains hymns for special occasions in addition to *Nitnem*. The commonest script is Gurmukhi, although *gutkas* in Devanagri and Persian scripts are also available.

GYAN : See Knowledge.

GYANI : Derived from the word '*Gyan*' meaning knowledge. In general it means a person who had deeper knowledge. In Sikh literature it is used for a person or religious teacher who has knowledge and understanding of Sikh scriptures and is attached to a gurdwara. *Gyani* is also the name of an examination. A person who has passed that examination is also called *Gyani*.

GWALIOR FORT : Gwalior is an old town in Madhya Pradesh overlooked by the Fort. During the reign of Jahangir the fort was used as a jail (*Zindan-e-adal*) for political prisoners. Because of the conspiracy hatched by Chandu Shah, Jahangir summoned Guru Hargobind to Delhi and then put him under custody in the Gwalior Fort. In the absence of the Guru, the secular affairs of the Sikhs were looked after by Baba

Buddha while the spiritual affairs were with Bhai Gurdas, though Baba Buddha continued to work as the high priest of the Golden Temple.

Historians hold varying views about the period of incarceration of Guru Hargobind in the Gwalior Fort. Some are of the view that he was kept in prison for a short time. Giani Gian Singh says that he was in the fort for two months only. (*Panth Prakash*, p. 124). Teja Singh and Ganda Singh write : "The period of the Guru's stay there is stated by Mohsin Fani to be 12 years, which is impossible on the very face of it as during these very years several children were born to him. The Guru could not have spent more than two years at Gwalior and must have returned home in 1614 AD" (*A Short History of the Sikhs*, p.40 fn 1). Hari Ram Gupta seems to agree with Mohsin Fani. According to him the Guru was kept in prison for 12 years but being a political prisoner was allowed to live with his wives. The Guru was arrested early in 1609 AD and was released in October 1620 AD on the recommendation of Mian Mir. *History of the Sikhs* Vol. I p. 162)

The Sikhs celebrate Diwali to commemorate the Guru's return to Amritsar after his release from Gwalior Fort.

H

HADIABAD : Hadiabad is a village near Phagwara. A gurdwara on its outskirts is dedicated to Guru Hargobind who visited it on his way from Kartarpur (Jalandhar) to Kiratpur. According to some, even Guru Har Rai is believed to have visited it.

HADIAYA : A village about 5 km from Barnala in Sangrur district. Guru Tegh Bahadur visited it in 1665 AD and camped in a grove near a pond which has been developed into a *sarovar*. The water of the *sarovar* is believed to have curative properties. A gurdwara now commemorates the Guru's visit.

HAIDARI FLAG : Haidar is another name for Ali, son-in-law of Prophet Muhammad who was also the fourth Caliph after the Prophet's death. Haidari Flag, named after Ali, is therefore symbolic of the religious war (*jehad*) of Muslims. In Sikh history when Banda Singh Bahadur came to Punjab and won early victories and all the Sikhs of Majha joined him, there was consternation among the Muslims in Punjab. The Mughal rule was on the decline and Islam Khan, the governor of Lahore, was not prepared to face the Sikh forces. Under the circumstances, the Muslims organized their own private territorial army in 1710 AD under the Haidari Flag to wage a religious war against the Sikhs. Islam Khan also reluctantly joined the "War of the Haidari Flag." The Sikh forces retained an upper hand over them.

HAIR : See Kesh.

HAKIMPUR : See Nanaksar.

HALAL MEAT : *Halal* meat is the meat prepared by killing an animal according to the Muslim rites. It is also called kosher meat. With the coming of Islam into India and the Muslim political hegemony, it became a state policy not to permit slaughter of animals for food in any other manner except as laid down in the Quran–to make the slaughter a sacrifice to God and to expiate the sins of the slaughterer. Guru Gobind Singh took a rather serious view of this aspect of the whole matter. By way of repudiating the theory of expiatory sacrifice and the right of ruling Muslims to impose it on non-Muslims, he prohibited the Sikhs from taking kosher meat. He made *jhatka* meat (See corresponding entry) obligatory for those Sikhs who may be interested in taking meat as a part of their food. In fact, taking *halal* meat is one of the *kurahits* for Sikhs. An *amritdhari* Sikh who infringes it becomes *patit* (apostate).

HAMAYUN : Hamayun was the son of Babar and after his death became the second Mughal emperor in December 1530 AD. He was born in Kabul in March 1508 AD. He was defeated by Sher Shah Suri in 1540 AD. According to the Sikh tradition, while fleeing to Iran, Hamayun waited upon Guru Angad at Khadur and asked him to bless him with sovereignty. The Guru did not care for him at which Hamayun pulled out his sword. The Guru remarked that this sword should have been better used against his rival Sher Shah Suri. The Guru being an embodiment of forgiveness, did not attach any importance to this incident. After a number of years, with the help of Iranian army, Hamayun recaptured Delhi in June 1555 AD. Six months later in January 1556 AD he died after falling in the library. Hamayun's Tomb in Delhi is a memorial raised by his wife in 1565 AD.

HANDI SAHIB, GURDWARA : Gurdwara Handi Sahib—the Shrine of the Earthen Pot—is situated at Dinapore about 15 km from Patna. Guru Gobind Singh as a young lad of 7 years had stayed here in 1671 AD with his mother and other family members on his way to Anandpur from Patna. Here an old woman Mai Jamni had offered him gruel in an earthen pot (*Handi*) with love and devotion. Mai

Jamni and her earthen pot became immortalized. Her humble hut became a place of pilgrimage and now it is a gurdwara.

HANKAR : *See* Pride.

HANS RAM : Hans Ram was a reputed poet in the court of Guru Gobind Singh. Besides other compositions, he translated a part of Mahabharata into Hindi.

HAQIQAT RAI : The story of Haqiqat Rai, the young martyr of the 18th century is the story of extreme religious bigotry claiming the life of a virtuous young man.

Haqiqat Rai was born in 1724 AD in a well-to-do pious *Sahajdhari* Sikh family of Sialkot now in Pakistan. His father Diwan Bagh Mal was an offcial in the local kutchery. He had been married to the daughter of Kishan Singh of Batala.

While in school Haqiqat Rai one day had an argument with the Muslim boys who had made disrespectful references to Hindu gods. He dared to return the same language for Prophet Mohammad. For this the school *Maulvi* took him to the *Qazi* who sentenced him to be executed for showing disrespect to the Prophet. On appeal the case went to the Lahore Governor, Zakriya Khan who confirmed the *Qazi's* sentence with the proviso that if the boy embraced Islam, the sentence might be commuted or even set aside. As Haqiqat Rai refused to embrace Islam, he was executed at Lahore in 1741 AD and was cremated at a place where now stands his *samadh* (cenotaph).

It is believed that Kishan Singh, father-in-law of Haqiqat Rai, along with his brothers approached the Khalsa for avenging the martyrdom. Accordingly the Khalsa made a surprise attack on Sialkot and killed the *Maulvi* and the *Qazi*.

HARBANS, BHATT : Bhatt Harbans is one of the seventeen *bhatts* whose compositions (two *swayyas* in his case) are included in the *Adi Granth*. In his *swayyas* he brings out the spiritual excellence of Guru Arjan and the bestowal of Guruship on him.

HARBHAGAT : Harbhagat was a *Niranjania* of 18th century belonging to Jandiala near Amritsar. He, like other people of his sect was anti-Sikh and was rewarded by the Muslim rulers for helping them in the persecution of Sikhs. He was instrumental in getting Mehtab Singh arrested and martyred by Zakriya Khan, the governor of Lahore.

HARGOBIND, GURU : Guru Hargobind was the only son of Guru Arjan and Mata Ganga. He was born at village Wadali near Amritsar in June 1595 AD. He received his early education and training at the hands of the revered Sikhs of the time—Baba Buddha and Bhai Gurdas. He was barely eleven years of age when his father Guru Arjan was martyred in May 1606 AD and the responsibility of leading the nascent community fell on him. He responded to the situation by adding a new dimension to Sikhism. Right from the day of his installation, he started wearing two swords—one for *meeri* and the other for *peeri* to emphasize the complementary nature of the spiritual and the temporal. As a further step, he laid the foundation stone of the Akal Takht as the highest seat of temporal authority of the Sikh community opposite the Golden Temple which is the highest spiritual centre. Guru Hargobind started dispensing justice from the Akal Takht, a practice that has continued upto the present times.

Threatened by the increasing and improved organisation of the Sikhs, Emperor Jahangir had him detained in the Gwalior Fort for 12 years. But this only enhanced his reputation. During this period the affairs of the community were looked after by Baba Buddha and Bhai Gurdas.

When Shahjahan became the emperor in 1628 AD, he intensified the oppression of the Sikhs. As a result, the Guru had to fight four battles against the imperial forces. This represents a break from the *sant* traditions of the earlier Gurus. Guru Hargobind did not compose any hymns either.

The Guru founded Kiratpur in the Himalayan foothills and spent the last few years of his life there. He passed away in March 1644 AD at Kiratpur.

Guru Hargobind, like his predecessors, lived a married life. He had six children—five sons and a daughter. Gurditta, Ani Rai and Bibi Viro were born to Mata Damodari, Suraj Mal and Atal Rai to Mata Mahadevi and Tegh Bahadur to Mata Nanaki. Two of his sons, Baba Gurditta and Atal Rai died in his life time. The Guruship was passed on to Guru Har Rai, grandson of Guru Hargobind (son of Baba Gurditta) after the latter's death.

HARGOBIND PUR : See Shri Gobindpur.

HARIAN VELAN, GURDWARA : Gurdwara Harian Velan is a historical shrine about 10 km from Hoshiarpur. According to the local tradition, Guru Har Rai had visited the spot and the whithered creepers (*velan*) had become green again. Hence the name of the gurdwara. According to another tradition *Sahibzada* Ajit Singh visited the spot after his expedition against the Pathan chief of Bassi Kalan to rescue two young Brahmin girls. The soldiers who were killed in the expedition were cremated here. The *samadhs* (cenotaphs) of the two girls also exist close by.

HARI CHAND : 1. Name of the father-in-law of Guru Hargobind.

2. Also the name of a hill chieftain who helped Raja Bhim Chand against Guru Gobind Singh in the battle of Bhangani in 1689 AD in which he was killed. He was so brave that the Guru has mentioned his name in Vichitra Natak.

HARI DAS, BABA : Baba Haridas was the father of Guru Ramdas. He was a Sodhi *Khatri* residing in Chuna Mandi of Lahore. He was a God-fearing man and lived a simple life. He was blessed with a son in 1534 AD after twelve years of married life whom he named Jetha—the first born, who became the fourth Guru of the Sikhs.

HARI PUR : Haripur is a village about 15 km from Abohar. It was a gurdwara dedicated to Guru Nanak and Guru Gobind Singh. The latter had visited it on his way to the Deccan.

HARI SINGH NALWA : Hari Singh Nalwa, the Marshal of the Khalsa, was a brave general of Maharaja Ranjit Singh. As the governor of Peshawar, he was a terror in the area now called North Western Frontier Province in Pakistan. The tribals in the area were so scared of him that mothers used to silence their children by saying : *Haria ragle da* (Hari Singh has come).

Hari Singh Nalwa was born in 1791 AD at Gujranwala, now in Pakistan. His ancestors were originally the residents of Mijitha near Amritsar. His grandfather Hardas Singh was in the service of Sukarchakia *misl*. His father Gurdial Singh Uppal had followed the footsteps of his father and was the recipient of a *jagir*. He died when Hari Singh Nalwa was only seven years of age leaving him in the care of his maternal uncle. When he grew up he joined the services of Maharaja Ranjit Singh as a personal *khidmatgar* (attendant) and gradually rose to be his general. He fought almost all the formidable battles for Maharaja Ranjit Singh. Hari Singh Nalwa was not just a brave warrior, he was also a competent administrator in whom Maharaja Ranjit Singh reposed full confidence. He was governor of Kashmir in 1820-21 AD, of Multan in 1822 AD and Peshawar in 1834 AD. As governor of Peshawar he fought his last battle at Jamrud in which he was killed in the battlefield.

Hari Singh Nalwa was a versatile general and administrator possessed of strong qualities of head and heart. He was a God-fearing man, merciful in ordinary life but stern and obstinate in fulfilling his mission. He was a staunch follower of Sikh Gurus having full faith in their teachings.

HARKRISHAN, GURU : Guru Harkrishan was the eighth Guru of Sikhs. He was the younger son of Guru Har Rai. He was born to Krishan Kaur in July, 1656 AD. As Guru Har

Rai was not happy with his elder son Ram Rai because of his having changed the text of a line of the Adi Granth in Mughal Court at Delhi, he appointed Guru Harkrishan as his successor in October, 1661 AD at the tender age of five. That is why Guru Harkrishan is also known as Bal Guru (Child Guru).

On a complaint by Ram Rai, Aurangzeb called Guru Harkrishan to Delhi. He came to Delhi and stayed at the bungalow of Raja Jai Singh (now known as Gurdwara Bangla Sahib) but refused to meet the king. An epidemic was raging in Delhi at that time. The Guru provided a healing touch to the sick. He was himself taken ill and died of small pox in (March 1664 AD) and was cremated on the banks of Yamuna in Delhi where now stands Gurdwara Bala Sahib.

On his last day, the Guru called for five paise and a coconut. He took them and not being able to move his body waved his hand three times in the air by way of pointing out his successor and said "Baba Bakale" i.e. his successor will be found in the village of Bakala. The words were deeply significant as they helped in maintaining the line of succession.

The Guru's life, though short chronologically speaking, made the foundation of Sikhism much stronger by maintaining the hallowed traditions of self-sacrifice, truthfulness, care for others and fearless resolve and by providing continuity in the line of succession. His pontificate is marked by the revival of Mughal interference in Sikh affairs.

HARMALA : See Rosary.

HARMANDIR SAHIB :

1. Harmandir Sahib is the original name of the highest spiritual seat of the Sikhs popularly known as the Golden Temple. See Golden Temple.

2. There is a Harmandir Sahib in Kiratpur at the place where Guru Hargobind resided during the last few years of his life.

3. Harmandir Sahib is also a famous gurdwara in Patna built at a place where Guru Gobind Singh was born in 1666 AD and is regarded as one of the five Takhts.

According to tradition, the place, where the imposing Harmandir Sahib now stands, was originally the *haveli* (mansion) of Salis Rai Johri, who after becoming a disciple of Guru Nanak had transformed it into a *dharamsala*. The first building of the gurdwara came up in the 18th century AD. Early in the 19th century AD a devastating fire which broke out in the area caused considerable damage to it. Maharaja Ranjit Singh undertook its reconstruction in 1839 AD and the job was completed in two years. In the earthquake which hit Bihar in 1934 AD a portion of the gurdwara fell down. The construction of the present four-storeyed building, all made of marble, was started in 1954 AD and completed in 1960 AD.

Some articles used by Guru Gobind Singh are preserved at Harmandir Sahib. These include a small cradle, a small sword, four iron arrows, one pair of ivory sandals and copy of the Adi Granth bearing his signatures.

HAR RAI GURU : Guru Har Rai, the seventh Guru, was the grandson of Guru Hargobind, the sixth Guru. He was the son of Baba Gurdita, the eldest son of Guru Hargobind. Baba Gurditta had died during the life time of his father. Guru Har Rai was born in February, 1630 AD. His mother's name was Nihal Kaur.

Guru Har Rai was married in 1640 AD to the two daughters Kotkalyani and Krishan Kaur of Daya Ram a resident of Anup Shahr in Uttar Pradesh. He had two sons : Ram Rai from Kotkalyani and Guru Harkrishan from Krishan Kaur. He was anointed as the seventh Guru in March 1644 AD.

Guru Har Rai kept up the style Guru Hargobind had introduced. He was attended by armed followers, but no conflict occurred with the ruling power. The Sikh faith continued to gain strength. The Guru appointed disciples to preach in different regions of the country. He made Kiratpur his headquarters.

During the struggle for succession among the sons of Shahjahan, Dara Shikoh had met the Guru at Goindwal to seek his blessings.

This was misrepresented to Aurangzeb who called the Guru to Delhi after taking over. The Guru sent his elder son Ram Rai to the Mughal court. The latter performed miracles and even changed the text of a line of the Adi Granth to please the Emperor. The Guru was much displeased with Ram Rai on this account and resolved to have no connection with him. Because of this, the Guru chose his younger son Harkrishan as his successor. A day after Harkrishan was installed, Guru Har Rai passed away in Kiratpur in October, 1661 AD.

HAR RAIPUR : A village about 20 km from Bhatinda (which was earlier known as Bhokhri) named after Guru Har Rai who once stopped here during his travels in the Malwa region. Guru Gobind Singh is also said to have visited the place. A gurdwara with a *sarovar* named after Guru Har Rai stands on the outskirts of the village.

HARSAR, GURDWARA : See Dod.

HASSAN ABDAL : See Punja Sahib.

HASSAN KHAN : Hassan Khan was an agent sent by Commander Lalla Beg to Mehraj to spy on Guru Hargobind. He was so much impressed by the Guru's personality that he became his devoted disciple. Through the Guru's blessings he was later given a senior posting by Shahjahan.

HASSAN PUR : Hassan Pur—Kabool Pur near Rajpura has a gurdwara dedicated to Guru Tegh Bahadur and Guru Gobind Singh both of whom had stayed here. The *sheikh* of the village was a devotee of Guru Tegh Bahadur.

HATHA YOGA : See Yoga.

HATT SAHIB : Hatt Sahib is the site of the store where Guru Nanak was employed in Sultanpur Lodhi as the *modi* (storekeeper) entrusted with the supply of provisions to the palace, the army and others on state account. (Hatt means a big store). A gurdwara has been built at this site together with a tank adjoining it. Eleven stone weights, said to have been used by the Guru in the store are preserved in the shrine.

HAUMAI : *See* Egoism.

HAZARE, SHABAD : Hazare Shabad also called Shabad Hazare is the name given to seven shabads of the Guru Granth Sahib and ten of the Dasam Granth. This name has not been given by the Gurus nor was current in their times. The word hazare means prominent or selected. Some scholars link it to the Persian word *Hijr* meaning parting—Hazare Shabad implying those compositions dealing with separation or parting as for example : *Mitr piare noo haal muridan da kahena* from the Dasam Granth.

Hazare Shabad included in the Dasam Granth are believed to be ten of the remaining verses out of a much bigger collection of thousands of such compositions. They insist on the worship of one God only. "Worship none but the Creator, not the Creation."

HAZUR SAHIB : Hazur Sahib is a place on the banks of Godavari in Maharashtra where is situated one of the five Takhts. It is also called Abchal Nagar. Guru Gobind Singh breathed his last here in 1708 AD. It was here that Banda Bahadur had met the Guru who sent him to Punjab.

The most important shrine at Hazur Sahib is Sachkhand which has a two-storeyed building with its architecture and design resembling the Golden Temple. The inner room of this shrine is called Angitha Sahib—the place where the Guru was cremated. Sachkhand is treated as a Takht.

Other important gurdwaras are : *Shikar Ghat* where the Guru used to go for hunting; *Sangat Sahib* where he used to hold discourses; *Nagina Ghat* where the Guru had flung into the river a costly ring presented to him by a devotee to preach detachment from worldly wealth; *Hira Ghat* where he similarly disposed of a diamond ring presented by the emperor; Mata Sahib

Kaur Gurdwara where his wife used to stay; *Banda Than* the hut of Banda Bahadur and *Maltakery* which was the Guru's treasury.

HEAVEN AND HELL : The idea of heaven and hell is basically linked with the concept of life after death. At the time when Sikhism was taking roots in India, there were obviously two streams of thinking: Hindu and Muslim. Hinduism advocates reincarnation with the help of the Law of Karma. Salvation or *mukti* which is an escape from the cycle of birth-rebirth according to Hinduism, is the realization of one's identity with the Absolute. So heaven and hell do not exist as geographical localities in time and space as in Islam. The Quran depicts heaven and hell with concrete and even sensual imagery which must not be taken literally. Nevertheless they are interpreted as actual places by the mass of the faithful and perhaps this has been the consequence of the imagery itself : the gardens, the flowing rivers, fountains, the houris, the chaste mates, fruit and drink, the goblets of gold of heaven and in contrast the blazing fire, the boiling water, the roasting skins, the bitter food, the marching in chains of hell. There are innumerable references to the pleasures in heaven as reward for good deeds and to the tortures in hell as punishment for bad deeds.

While largely accepting the Hindu view, Sikhism at the same time has adopted an ambivalent attitude towards the Islamic view of heaven and hell. For example, Kabir at one place says in the Guru Granth Sahib : "What is heaven and hell—the wretched places? The saints have rejected them both" (Ramkali) He further asserts : "Do not seek an abode in heaven, nor be afraid of being cast into hell. Whatever is to be will be; so divert your mind of desire."
Suraj bass na bachhiai; dari-ai na narak niwas;
  Hona hai so ho-ee hai, man na keejai aas
(AG. p. 337)

Inspite of this obvious rejection, there is a mention about heaven and hell at a number of places in the Guru Granth Sahib. One view is that the Gurus used popular vocabulary about heaven and hell to communicate with their followers without fully developing the concept. At one place it is mentioned : "Millions dwell in heaven and hell."
Kaee koti narak surg niwasi (AG. p. 276)

At another place it is said : "The dark hell, with multiple suffering and reeking is the abode of those guilty of ingratitude to God."
Narak ghor bahu dukh ghane, akirtghana ka than
(AG. p. 315)

What can be called the prominent feature of the Sikh concept of heaven and hell is that they are states of mind. They are symbolically represented by joy and sorrow, bliss and agony, light and fire. There is no such thing in Sikhism as eternal damnation or an everlasting pit of fire created by a revengeful God. Therefore Sikhism lays great emphasis on the present without rejecting life after death. "Heaven is where abide the Lord's saints and where one enshrines in one's mind the Lord's lotus feet."
Baikunth nagar jeha sant wasa, Prabh charan kamal rid mahe niwasa. (AG. p. 742)

"Heaven is where the Lord's praises are sung and he brings faith to man."
Teha baikunth jeh kirtan tera, toon aape sardha lahi. (AG. p. 749)

Resembling the concept of reward and punishment in Islam, Sikhism advises its followers; make good actions the soil, put into it the seed of the holy word; from the stream of Truth ever irrigate it. Be such a cultivator; make firm thy faith. Thoughtless man! such is the way to heaven and hell."
Amal kar dharti, beej shabado sach ki aab nit deh pani; Hoye kirsan iman janmai lai bhist dojak moore aiw jani. (AG. p. 23-24)

HEHARAN : See Kirpal Das.

HEMKUNT : The gurdwara at Hemkunt is located in picturesque surroundings at a height of 4600 metres in the Garhwal hills of Uttar Pradesh. There is a mention about the Hemkunt mountain in the Mahabharata and also in Vichitra Natak by Guru Gobind Singh. The Guru describes himself as being in deep meditation there for a long time in his previous incarnation. God then commissioned him to go to the world to spread his religion and to restrain the world from senseless acts.

Though Guru Gobind Singh had given a description of the place, the spot was discovered only in the early thirties of the 20th century by Pandit Tara Singh Narotam. A small room was built there in 1936 AD and Guru Granth Sahib installed a year later. Since then the shrine has been growing in both size and popularity.

HIKAYATS : A composition by Guru Gobind Singh included in the Dasam Granth. *Hikayats* are eleven tales in Persian extending over 756 verses dealing with human weaknesses. When the Dasam Granth was compiled by Bhai Mani Singh, some devout Sikh scholars were against their inclusion in it. However, finally they were allowed to be retained as per the design of Bhai Mani Singh.

HIMMAT SINGH, BHAI : Bhai Himmat Singh whose original name was Himmat Rai was one of the first *Panj Piare* who had offered their heads to Guru Gobind Singh on the Baisakhi day of 1699 AD at Anandpur and were thus the first to be initiated into the Khalsa brotherhood. Very little is known about his biographical details. According to one version, he was the son of Gulzari of Puri belonging to the *Jhiwar* (water carrier) caste. He was born in 1661 AD. After his initiation into the Khalsa he remained in the devoted service of Guru Gobind Singh and died fighting in the battle at Chamkaur in December 1705 AD.

HINDAL : Hindal (1573-1648), a resident of Jandiala was a disciple of Guru Amardas. For quite some time, he was incharge of the *langar* run by the Guru and was finally sent as a missionary to be incharge of a *Manji*. Since he used to utter "*Niranjan-Niranjan*" his followers are called *Niranjanias*. His village is now known as Guru-ka-Jandiala.

Hindal had a son named Bidhi Chand who married a Muslim and became an apostate, apparently as a result of the criticism of his marriage by Sikhs. He has written a biography of Guru Nanak known as Hindaliya Janam Sakhi which contains episodes in which Guru Nanak is denigrated. He in fact set up an anti-Sikh movement which ironically assumed the name of Hindalis after his father who was a devout Sikh.

HINDALIS : See Hindal.

HIRA GHAT : See Hazur Sahib.

HOLA MOHALLA : A fair is held on a very large scale at Anandpur every year on the day following Holi. Thousands of devotees come from all parts of the country to pay their homage to Guru Gobind Singh. The fair reaches its climax with a large procession called *Hola Mohalla*. There is a great enthusiasm among the participants who chant devotional hymns and display feats of *gatka*, horsemanship and soldiery as they march.

The word *Hola* seems to have been derived from *Hamla* or *Halla* meaning attack. It is believed that on this day Guru Gobind Singh used to arrange a battle at Anandpur to train his army—a sort of military exercise in modern terms. The first *Hola Mohalla* was celebrated in 1700 AD a year after the birth of Khalsa, and it was ordained that while others celebrate Holi, the Sikhs shall celebrate *Hola Mohalla*. A large number of Nihangs participate in it.

Hola has no connection with Holi which is a Hindu festival except that if falls on a day next to Holi.

HOLGARH, GURDWARA : Gurdwara Holgarh Sahib has come up at the site of Holgarh Fort, one of the five fortresses constructed by Guru Gobind Singh. It is 1.5 km north of Anandpur across the Charan Ganga rivulet. It was here that Guru Gobind Singh introduced the tradition of celebrating the Sikh festival Hola Mohalla on the day following Holi. The present three-storeyed building was completed in 1970 AD.

HOLI : See Hola Mohalla.

HUKAM: See God's Will.

HUKAMNAMA: *Hukamnama* is a Persian word meaning a royal command. In Sikhism it refers to instructions which are regarded as the commands of the Guru and thus binding on the whole Panth.

As the Sikh community grew in size and complexity, *hukamnama* became a powerful tool of communication between the Guru or the Sikh personage and the community particularly in the times of *dharam yudh* or when the Guru led a peripatetic life.

Hukamnamas have been issued by the Sikh Gurus, the wives of Guru Gobind Singh, Sikh personages like Banda Singh Bahadur, the Akal Takht Amritsar and other *Takhts*. Among the available *hukamnamas* other than those issued by the *Takhts*, two are by Guru Hargobind, one by Baba Gurditta, one by Guru Harkrishan, twenty-two by Guru Tegh Bahadur, two by Mata Gujri, thirty-three by Guru Gobind Singh, two by Banda Singh Bahadur, nine by Mata Sundri and nine by Mata Sahib Kaur.

The *hukamnamas* of Guru Gobind Singh were addressed to congregations of various places and in some cases to individuals. They are orders for financial assistance or for arms, horses and young men of dash and daring to fight in his army, or an invitation to meet the Guru on a festival day or to warn the devotees not to hand over their offerings to *masands*. Guru Gobind Singh generally dictated the *hukamnamas* and put certain signs or formulas in his own handwriting at the top to establish their authenticity.

Hukamnamas are of great historical importance. They tell us of the condition of congregations and Sikh community in those days.

HUMILITY: Sikhism has recommended humility as an anti-dote to pride (*hankar*) which is one of the five vices. Using the analogy of a *simmal* tree, Guru Nanak explains it as the essence of virtue." The *simmal* tree is straight, tall and thick. Those who come to it with hope go away disappointed. Its fruit is tasteless; flowers brackish and leaves of no use. Says Nanak: In sweetness and humility lies the essence of merit and virtue."
Mithat niwi Nanaka gun changiayian tat.
(AG. p. 470)
He further explains: "Everyone bows to oneself, not to others for when weighed in a balance, the heavier pan dips lower."
Sabh ko niwai aap ko par kau niwai na koe,
Dhar trazoo toliai niwai so gaura hoe.
(AG. p. 470)
As a practical advice, Guru Nanak says: "If one wants one's good, one should be humble while himself doing good."
Je loria-ai changa apna kar pun neech sada-ee-ai
(AG. p. 465)
Humility is a saintly virtue. "Humility is the glory of saints."
Sadh ki sobha ati maskini. (AG. p. 676)
As such it becomes the hallmark of a *gurmukh*. "O my mind! do not be proud that you know even a thing for the *gurmukh* is always humble."
Man toon mat maan kar je how kichh janda;
Gurmukh namana ho. (AG. p. 441)
Sikhism also preaches that salvation or *mukti* is not possible without humility. Says Nanak: "The door of salvation is narrow and he who is humble passes through it. How can the mind that has grown gross with ego pass through it."
Nanak mukti dwar ati nika nana ho-ai so ja-ai
Haumai man asthool hai kio ke wichdai jai-ai.
(AG. pp. 509-10)
In sum : "He who is blest with humility by the God's grace, obtains deliverance here and peace hereafter."
Kar kirpa jis kai hirdai garibi basawe.
Nanak eeha mukt aage sukh pawe. (AG. p. 278)

HYAT KHAN: Hyat Khan was the chief of hundred horse men. Pir Budhu Shah had sent him to Paonta Sahib to serve Guru Gobind Singh. However he betrayed the trust of the Guru in the battle at Bhangani and joined the hill *rajas* against the Guru. He was killed by Kirpal Das in the battle.

I

IAALI KALAN : Iaali Kalan is a village in Ludhiana district. Guru Hargobind visited it during his journey through the Malwa region. A historical gurdwara commemorates the Guru's visit.

IBRAHIM LODHI : Ibrahim Lodhi was the son of Sikandar Lodhi and became the Emperor of India in 1517 AD when Guru Nanak was, spreading his message. Daulat Khan Lodhi with whom Guru Nanak had worked as a storekeeper at Sultanpur had become the governor of the entire Punjab with Lahore as its capital during the reign of Ibrahim Lodhi. But the former fell out with Ibrahim Lodhi and conspired to invite Babar, the ruler of Afghanistan to attack India. Babar came and defeated Ibrahim Lodhi and killed him on April 20, 1526 AD in the first battle of Panipat, thus ending the reign of Lodhi dynasty and establishing the Mughal rule in India.

IDOLATORY : Idolatory is the practice of worshipping statues or other objects believing them to be God. It is commonly associated with Hinduism, particularly the post-vedic Hinduism. Some Hindu scholars, however do not accept this view at least in the sense that God has a form. According to them, the Hindu who does not conceive a form for God cannot have an idol of God; to him a *vigraha* is not the image of God, but a symbolic representation of the formless Absolute, on whom qualities are superimposed in a well-defined and technical manner to suit the learnings of the worshipper, in order to enable him to conceive and meditate upon the Absolute.

In Islam, contempt for idolatory has been inbuilt in the concept of Allah. The attributes of Allah can not be ascribed to a created being. An idolator who worships an idol is a sinner if he regards the idol as the possessor of Allah's attributes. This contempt for idolatory was somewhat diluted by the Muslim Sufis who accepted it as a way of worshipping God.

Sikhism is, however, quite unequivocal in its disapproval of idolatory. In *Vars* under Raag Bihagra, Guru Nanak says in simple and direct language :

"The Hindus have forgotten God, and are going the wrong way; they worship according to the instruction of Narad. They are blind and dumb, blindest of the blind. The ignorant fools take stones and worship them. O Hindus, how shall the stone which itself sinketh carry you across."

O hi ja aap dube tum kaho tarnhaar (AG. p. 556)

He reinforces the same point by saying :

"My brethren, you worship goddesses and gods; what can you ask them? And what can they give you?"

Even if a stone be washed with water, it will still sink in it."

Devi deva puji-ai bhai kia mago kia deh,
Pahn nir pakhali-ai; bhai jal me doob teh.

(AG. p. 637)

According to a *Sakhi*, Guru Gobind Singh is said to have advised: "All worship is valueless without love. The worship of idols is unreal; the worship of God alone is real. Nothing can be obtained by idol worship. They who place idols before them and worship them are fools. Let my Sikhs ever meditate upon the Immortal One and worship none besides. Let them even practise arms, that they may be enabled to defend themselves against the enemies."

Bhai Gurdas while reflecting on the issue has summarized it in one of his *Kavits* which may be translated as follows:

"If a man looks at two mirrors, no distinct reflection will be formed;

If a man puts his feet in two boats, he cannot reach the shore;

If a man goes in two directions, his feet will be worn out;

If a man travels by two roads, he will be puzzled and not know where to put down his feet.

When there are two kings, the subject cannot be happy;

When a woman has two husbands, she cannot be chaste;

When a Sikh accepts the support of other gods;

Accursed is his life in this world, and hereafter punishment from Death awaits him."

IKLAHA : Iklaha is a village near Khanna in Ludhiana district. Guru Hargobind stayed here during his travels through the Malwa region. The stay has been commemorated by constructing a gurdwara initiative for which was taken by an NRI Bhai Ralla Singh of the village who was working in Africa way back in 1906-7 AD.

IK ONKAR : *Ik Onkar* is an important acclesiastical word symbol in Sikhism. It corresponds to and probably is derived from the Hindu symbol AUM (OM). One can find it on many Sikh religious objects, even worn as a part of the necklace by some devout Sikhs like the cross worn by Christians.

The term *Om* originally appears to have had only an affirmative sense; it is still used in that sense in certain religious and social ceremonies. But it is also a seed-letter (*bijaksara*). According to one interpretation, *Om* as *bijaksara* connotes the trinity of Brahma, Vishnu and Shiva, all three conceived together as one. According to *Manu Samhita*, the three letters, a, u, m constituting *Om* were milked out of three Vedas by Prajapati so that they represent the quintessence of the *trayi* (the three original Vedic canons). Buddhists and Jains also use *bijaksaras* including *Om* in their ritualistic formulae.

The Punjabi term *Onkar* is derived from the Sanskrit term *Om* representing all aspects and facets of God. By putting the word *Ik* (one) before *Onkar*, Sikhism has emphasized the oneness of God—one of the most important features of its concept of God. Thus *Ik Onkar* is the symbol for the Transcendental Absolute, the Supreme Being. It means that there is but one God. He is one without an equal. He is not the sum total of so many forces bundled together. This gives finality and constancy to God and puts an end to the theory of incarnation.

Quite appropriately *Ik Onkar* are the opening words of the Guru Granth Sahib—in fact the opening words of the *Mul Mantra* with which every section of it based on a *raag* begins. Every sub-section in each *raag* also begins with *Ik Onkar Satgur Parsad*. The Sikh general prayer called *ardaas* also begins with *Ik Onkar Waheguru ji ki Fateh* (Formless one victory be to the wonderful Lord).

ILLUSION : See Maya.

INCANTATIONS : Incantations or *mantras* form an inseparable part of the tantric lore of Hinduism.

The essence of Vedic religion is ritualism. Whatever might have been the nature of Vedic sacrifice in the early Vedic period, it developed into a highly mystical ritual in course of time. Its chief aim was attaining ascendancy over the forces of nature in order to guide them in the interest of the sacrificer. Correct recitation of *mantras* was the most important means of producing the desired effect.

Tantra is defined as a class of texts which promulgates profound matters concerning *tattava* and *mantra*. The words *tattava* and *mantra* are used in a technical sense : *tattava* means the science of cosmic principles while *mantra* means the science of the mystic sound. *Tantra*, therefore is the application of these sciences with a view to attaining spiritual ascendancy. The religious attitude in the *tantras* is fundamentally the same as in Vedic ritual. They in fact, emerged out of the Vedic religion and were then developed as a distinct type of esoteric knowledge. The Vedic ritualism continued side by side with *tantras*.

It appears quite probable that 'tantriacism' received impetus from Budhism and Jainism. Later on Nathism derived its inspiration from Buddhist *tantras*. It modified them and popularized *hathyoga*.

Sikhism rejects all forms of *tantras* and *yogas*. Kabir refers to peculiar incantations practised in his days. After the cremation of a corpse and before the bones were collected, strangers would go to the cremation ground at night and try to control through incantations the ghost of the departed as to be serviceable to them in their worldly objects. Kabir remonstrates against this:

"Kabir, the woman who ceasing to remember God goes at night to wake the dead through incantations shall be born as a serpent and eat her own offspring."

Kabira Har ka simran chhad ke raat jagawan jaa-ai
Sarpani ho-ai ke uttrai jaye apne khaa-ai
(AG. p. 1370)

To wean the followers away from Hindu system of incantations, Sikhism advised them to use 'Waheguru' as the only incantation. "*Waheguru* is the only incantation repeating which one sheds one's ego." *Waheguru gurmantar hai jap haumai kho-ai* (Vars of Gurdas). Sarbloh Granth also reinforces the same idea :
Sar mantar charon ka char Waheguru mantar nirdhar.

INCARNATION, THEORY OF : The theory of incarnation implies that God appears in this world with a mission assuming the form of a living being called *avtar*. This has been a basic thinking in Hinduism and Buddhism. The Bhagvad Gita clearly states : "Whenever there is a decay of *dharma* (righteousness) and outbreak of *adharma* (non-righteousness) I descend myself to protect good, to annihilate the wicked and to re-establish *dharma*. I am born from age to age." In keeping with this Lord Vishnu is said to have many *avtars*, the ten principal ones being: Matya (fish), Kurma (tortoise), Varaha (boar), Narasimha (man-lion), Vamana (dwarf), Parasurama (warrior with an axe), Rama, Krishna, Buddha and Kalki. The Kalki Avtar is yet to come which Hindus believe will be at the end of *pralaya*.

The theory of incarnation exists even in semitic religions in a somewhat modified form. For example Christians believe Jesus to be an incarnation of God—the Son of God. In Islam, the concept of *avtar* has been replaced by the concept of Prophet who is a human being to whom the message of God is revealed. There is a whole chain of prophets including Abraham, Adam, Moses, Jesus and ending with Prophet Mohammad.

Sikhism does not subscribe to the theory of incarnation or the concept of prophethood. But it has the pivotal concept of the Guru (See relavant entry). He is not an incarnation of God, not even a prophet. He is an illumined soul—a spiritual torch with the *jyoti* (light) that illuminates the path to the Lord. God is "timeless, formless, beyond life and death." The Guru, though human in form is godly in spirit and is thus a spiritual preceptor of humanity.

INFANTICIDE, FEMALE : Female infanticide had reached the proportion of a glaring social evil in medieval India. The lower caste Hindus killed their infant daughters to avoid dowry; the upper caste did so to avoid the necessity of giving them in marriage to men of inferior birth. There are many *sakhis* (anecdotes) to prove that the Sikh Gurus resolutely set themselves against this practice—including disallowing the followers who indulged in it from coming into their presence. The high point of the opposition was reached when Guru Gobind Singh laid down a vow against female infanticide in the prescribed baptism. At the time of the administration of *pahul*, one of the obligations imposed on neophytes is not to kill their daughters and to avoid all association with those who do.

INITIATION CEREMONY : See Baptism.

ISHNAN : See Ablution.

INTOXICANTS : Sikhism has expressed itself very clearly and forcefully against the use of all kinds of intoxicants. It is laid down in the Code of Conduct for Sikhs (*Rahit Maryada*) that: "Sikhs should not partake of alcohol, tobacco, drugs and other intoxicants." There is a clear injuction against taking alcohol even in the Guru Granth Sahib. "One man brings alcohol and another pours from it for himself; but it makes everyone crazy and senseless. One cannot distinguish between one's own and another's and is cursed by God. Taking alcohol, one forsakes one's Master and is punished in His court. Yes, drink not this vicious thing under any circumstances."

Jit peetai khasam wisrai, dargah milai saja.

(AG, p. 554)

Bhang finds also a special mention in the Guru Granth Sahib. "Whoever of the mortals partake of *bhang*, fish or alcohol; whatever pilgrimages, fasting and daily rituals they perform, they go to hell."

Kabir bhang macchli sura pani jo jo prani Khaa-ai;
Tirath brat naim kee-ai te sabhe rasatal jaa-ai.

(AG. p. 1377)

These injunctions are obviously meant to ensure good personal health along with family and social welfare.

J

JADO RAI : Jado Rai was an employee of Nawab Daulat Khan at Sultanpur Lodhi at the time when Guru Nanak was working as a storekeeper there. He used to balance the accounts of the store with the Guru.

JAGAT SETH : Jagat Seth was a sweet meat seller of Patna who became very rich and was therefore called *seth*. He served both Guru Tegh Bahadur and Guru Gobind Singh at Patna.

Some chroniclers identify him with Bhai Jaita who had carried the head of Guru Tegh Bahadur, after his martyrdom in 1675 AD, from Delhi to Kiratpur. He had been renamed Jiwan Singh after the administration of *amrit* by Guru Gobind Singh and died in the battle at Chamkaur.

JAGERA : Jagera is a village near Ahmadgarh in Ludhiana district. It has a gurdwara dedicated to Guru Hargobind.

JAHANDAR SHAH : Jahandar Shah was the eldest son of Bahadur Shah and grandson of Emperor Aurangzeb. He was born in April 1663 AD and ascended the throne in 1712 AD after the death of his father and being victorious in a war of succession with his brothers. But he was a cruel and frivolous king and was not destined to enjoy power for long. Farrukhsiyar took over from him in 1713 AD after getting him strangled to death. Though Bahadur Shah had pushed Banda Singh Bahadur to the hills, he came out again and became active during the reign of Jahandar Shah.

JAHANGIR : Jahangir became the third Mughal Emperor when he ascended the throne after the death of his father, Akbar the Great in October 1605 AD. There was a minor revolt by his own son Prince Khusrau whom some liberal courtiers were favouring. The Prince had visited Guru Arjan at Goindwal in the compnay of his grandfather Akbar and respected the Guru as a great sage. When he was chased by the royal forces he made for Punjab where he met the Guru at Tarn Taran and sought his benediction. The Guru received him warmly by applying a saffron *tilak* on his forehead and even gave him a few thousand rupees. The Prince was ultimately captured in April 1606 AD and was partially blinded but his meeting with the Guru became an excuse with Jahangir to turn against Sikhism. He summoned Guru Arjan to Lahore and fined him rupees two lakhs. The Guru's property was confiscated but it could not fetch that much amount. The Guru was arrested and chained to a post in an open place exposed to the hot May sun from morning to evening from which he died on May 30, 1606 AD. Thus the first martyrdom in Sikh history took place during Jahangir's reign.

Jahangir's hatred for the Sikh Gurus continued even during the pontificate of Guru Hargobind. But the martyrdom of Guru Arjan had prompted his son to transform the community. His king-like and war-like activities aroused Jahangir's anger still further. He ordered Guru Hargobind to pay the balance of the fine of two lakh rupees imposed on his father Guru Arjan after deducting the amounts already realized by auctioning his property. For non-compliance he confined the Guru in the Gwalior Fort which was then the jail reserved for political prisoners but did not specify the period of incarceration. There is a difference of opinion among historians about it but H.R. Gupta in his *History of the Sikhs* concludes that the Guru was arrested in early 1609 AD and was released in October 1620 AD on the recommendation of Mian Mir.

Jahangir fell seriously ill in 1627 AD. He went to Kashmir for a change of climate. While returning from there, he died at Rajauri on November 7, 1627 AD.

JAHAN KHAN : During his fourth invasion of India in 1756-57 AD, Ahmad Shah Abdali annexed Punjab to the Afghan dominions and appointed his son Taimur as the viceroy at Lahore. At that time, Jahan Khan, who was a veteran general, was made a deputy to Taimur with the specific objective of destroying the Khalsa. He invaded Amritsar in May 1757 AD, razed the Sikh fortress of Ram Rauni and filled up the sacred pool. Baba Deep Singh marched towards Amritsar to rebuild the Golden Temple. Jahan Khan's troops laid in wait for the *jatha* of Baba Deep Singh at Gohlvar (Golerval) village, 8 km from Amritsar. In the ensuing encounter Jahan Khan was killed at the hands of Dyal Singh.

JAHIRA JAHOOR, GURDWARA : Jahira Jahoor is the name of a gurdwara dedicated to Guru Hargobind. It is situated near village Pur Hiran about 3 km from Hoshiarpur. The Guru had stayed here on his way to Kiratpur from Garne Sahib.

JAIDEV : Jaidev was a medieval saint two of whose hymns are included in the Adi Granth. In these he brings out the attributes of God, moral injunctions and the futility of Hindu forms of worship.

Very little is known of Jaidev's early life except that his father was Bhoidev a Brahmin of Kanauj, and his mother Bamdevi. He was born at Kenduli about thirty kilometres from Suri near Birbhum. He was a diligent student of Sanskrit literature and developed rare poetical talents. Towards the end of 12th century AD he became the most famous of the five distinguished court poets of Lakshman Sen, king of Bengal.

Jaidev is famous for his poem the *Gitagovind* which is an elaborate religious allegory. His other well-known works are : *Rasana Raghava* a drama and *Chandarlok* an essay on the graces of style.

JAIDPRANA : Jaidprana was the chief of Bhokhari in Malwa region. He used to harass Chaudhry Mohan, grandfather of Baba Phul and did not give him land to settle inspite of the advice of Guru Hargobind. Finally Chaudhry Mohan had to fight against him with the help of the Guru. He was killed in the battle and Chaudhry Mohan founded Mehraj.

JAIJAWANTI : Jaijawanti is an Indian classical *raag* usually sung at dawn. It is the last of the thirty-one *raags* used in the organisation of hymns in the Guru Granth Sahib covering pages 1352-1353. The sequence of basic notes followed is:
Arohi : sa, re, ga, ma, pa, dha, ne, sa..........
Avrohi : sa, ne, dha, pa, ma, ga, re, sa..........

JAI SINGH, MIRZA/RAJA : Raja Jai Singh was the ruler of Amber in Rajasthan during the reign of Emperor Aurangzeb. He used to serve the emperor which prompted him to confer the title of Mirza on him. Aurangzeb also made him the governor of Deccan in 1634 AD.

Mirza Jai Singh was a scholar of Sanskrit, Arabic and Persian. He should not be confused with a later Raja of the same name who founded the city of Jaipur and set up observatories at a number of places including the Jantar Mantar in Delhi.

Mirza Jai Singh respected the Sikh Gurus and played an important role in Sikh history during the pontificate of Guru Harkrishan. In fact, the Guru had agreed to come to Delhi on his personal assurance and even stayed in his bungalow which is now Gurdwara Bangla Sahib near the Parliament House.

The forces of Mirza Jai Singh used to camp close to his residential quarters. Near the place a village called Jaisinghpura had also come up to provide services and provisions to the forces. This however vanished in the development of New Delhi.

Mirza Jai Singh died in 1666 AD.

JAI SINGH PURA : See Jai Singh, Mirza.

JAITA, BHAI : Bhai Jaita was a *Rangreta* Sikh of Delhi. Little is known about his earlier life but in November 1675 AD he was a witness to the martyrdom of Guru Tegh Bahadur and his companions in front of the *kotwali* in Delhi, now Gurdwara Sis Ganj. After Bhai Dyal Das.

Bhai Mati Das and Bhai Sati Das were done to death, he disguised himself as a sweeper with a broom and basket collected the remains of the three martyrs and consigned them to the river Yamuna flowing nearby. Next day Guru Tegh Bahadur was publicly beheaded at the same place. This had spread panic among the Delhi Sikhs but Bhai Jaita picked up the head of the Guru, tied it in a sheet and made straight for Azadpur on the road to Sonepat. (The headless body of the Guru was carried by another brave Sikh on his cart and was cremated at the place where now stands Gurdwara Rakab Ganj near the Parliament House). Escorted by his friends Nanu and Uda he reached Kiratpur after five days where Guru Gobind Singh formally received the Guru's head and later on cremated it the next day. Guru Gobind Singh had held Bhai Jaita in tight embrace declaring : *Rangrete Guru ke bete* (*Rangreta* Sikhs are the sons of the Guru). He bestowed the same affection and honour on Nanu and Uda as well.

According to some historians, when the Khalsa Brotherhood was created in 1699 AD, Bhai Jaita was baptised by Guru Gobind Singh and was named Jiwan Singh. He remained very close to the Guru and was killed in the battle of Chamkaur in 1704 AD fighting alongside *Sahibzada* Ajit Singh.

JAITO : Jaito is a village on the railway line between Bhatinda and Ferozepur which has a gurdwara associated with Guru Gobind Singh. The tank near the gurdwara is called Gangsar. The Akali Dal had started a *morcha* (agitation) at the historic place in 1923 AD which ended in July 1925 AD. Jawahar Lal Nehru who became the first Prime Minister of India in 1947 AD had also participated in the Jaito *morcha* and courted arrest.

JAITSIRI : Jaitsiri is an Indian classical *raag* usually sung within three hours (one *pahar*) from sunset. It is eleventh of the thirty-one *raags* used in the organisation of hymns in the Guru Granth Sahib covering pages 696-710. The sequence of basic notes is :

Arohi : sa, ga, ma, pa, ne, sa..........
Avrohi : sa, ne, dha, pa, ma, ga, re, sa..........

JALAN, BHATT : Jalan is one of the 17 *Bhatts* (Bards) whose compositions (two *sawayyas* in his case) are included in the Adi Granth. See under *Bhatts*.

JALAP, BHATT : Jalap composed four *sawayyas* as a mark of respect to Guru Amardas which are included in the Adi Granth. He stresses the point that Guru Amardas achieved Guruship only through *Nam Simran*. According to this belief many Indian saints have attained the height of spiritual glory through meditation on God's Name. See also *Bhatts*.

JALH, BHATT : Jalh is one of the 17 *Bhatts* (Bards) whose compositions (one *sawayya* in his case) have been included in the Adi Granth. See under *Bhatts*.

JANAM SAKHIS : *Janam Sakhi* literally means a biography. In Sikh literature the term is genrally used for the biography of a Sikh Guru and more especially that of Guru Nanak. *Janam Sakhis* strictly speaking, are not biographies but hagiographies that is literature about the lives and legends of saints. Guru Nanak did not dictate any *Janam Sakhi* of his own. His most devoted disciple and successor, Guru Angad, also did not compile any *Janam Sakhi*. Some of the *Janam Sakhis* were written by Guru Nanak's admirers in the last quarter of the sixteenth century or during the seventeenth and eighteenth centuries. About a dozen *Janam Sakhis* have been written. Some of the important ones are : Bhai Bala's *Janam Sakhi*; Bhai Mani Singh's *Janam Sakhi*; *Mehma Prakash*; Bhai Gurdas' Vars. They act as a resource about the life and achievements of Guru Nanak. They are full of parables which most aptly communicate the teachings of Sikhism. They are widely used by preachers even today.

JANAM SAKHI BY BHAI BALA : Some scholars doubt whether Guru Nanak had any companion having the name Bala. But the

Janam Sakhi attributed to him has been in great demand by the Sikh masses. Its earlier manuscript copies are available at many places. It was published in 1923 AD at Lahore. On the first page it is stated that it was dictated by Bhai Bala. It was written by Paida Mokha who orignially belonged to Sultanpur Lodhi. It is said to have been read out to Guru Angad.

According to Dr Trilochan Singh the *Janam Sakhi* by Bhai Bala is "authentic, but it was corrupted by Minas, or Meharban and his followers. Then during the lifetime of Guru Gobind Singh by the *Hindaliyas* and then by the printers who in their zeal to give simple, all inclusive and sensational *Janam Sakhis* changed the language and made whatever changes they liked." (Guru Nanak, p. 494).

JANAM SAKHI BY BHAI MANI SINGH : Bhai Mani Singh, a contemporary of Guru Gobind Singh and a great theologian rose to become the head priest of the Golden Temple in the post Banda Bahadur period. As desired by the Sikhs he expanded the first of the *Vars* of Bhai Gurdas into the life story of Guru Nanak called *Gian Ratnavali*. It is regarded as one of the most important *Janam Sakhis* of Guru Nanak also referred to as *Janam Sakhis* by Bhai Mani Singh. Dr Trilochan Singh is of the view that this was distorted by some malicious persons. He writes: "In no other *Janam Sakhi* it is easier to sift the matter interpolated and distorted than in this *Janam Sakhi*. Bhai Mani Singh follows the historical chronology of Bhai Gurdas' *Var* and the person who has distorted it, introduces new material by destroying that order." (Guru Nanak, p. 495).

JAND SAHIB : Jand (*Prosopis spicigera*) is a wild tree in Punjab. Some of such trees have been sanctified by their association with the Sikh Gurus during their itineraries. The shrines constructed at the sites are called Jand Sahibs. Some of the important ones are :

1. Jand Sar, Bhagi Bandar : Gurdwara Jand-Sar is located in village Bhagi Bandar near Talwandi Sabo. Guru Gobind Singh visited the site during his stay at Talwandi Sabo.

2. Jand Sahib, Near Chamkaur : Guru Gobind Singh had rested under a *Jand* tree about 5 km from Chamkaur after leaving Garhi. A Sikh shrine and a village also named Jand Sahib have come up at the spot.

3. Jand Sahib, Dehriwala Kalan : This is on the outskirts of village Dehriwala Kalan 25 km from Faridkot. Guru Gobind Singh had rested here under a *Jand* tree.

4. Jand Sahib, Gunmati : This marks the *Jand* tree near village Gunmati in Bhatinda district under which Bhai Rupa a devotee had offered cold water to Guru Hargobind out of a leather bag.

5. Jand Sahib, Lahili : This shrine commemorates the *Jand* tree on the outskirts of village Lahili Kalan in Hoshiarpur district. During one of his journeys Guru Har Rai had tethered his horse to the tree.

6. Jand Sahib, Theri : There is a gurdwara complex in village Theri near Muktsar. Some of the *Jand* trees used by Guru Gobind Singh for hanging weapons and dresses still exist there. The place thus sanctified by the Guru is now a historical shrine known as Jand Sahib as a part of the complex.

JANDALI : Jandali is a village near Payal. A gurdwara is dedicated to Guru Hargobind who had visited the village during his journey through the Malwa region.

JANDIALA : See Harbhagat and Hindal.

JANDU SINGHA : Jandu Singha is a large village near Jalandhar on Jalandhar-Hoshiarpur road. Guru Hargobind came here from Kartarpur (Jalandhar) to tackle Chaudhary Kapura who was harassing the people there. But he had left before the Guru arrived and according to the local tradition the Guru shot five arrows in the air creating five ponds of water. Gurdwara Panj Tirath Patshahi VI (probably a later formation from Panj Tir) on the outskirts of Jandu Singha commemorates the event. It is being administered by the SGPC through a local committee.

JANI KHAN : Gangu, the domestic servant of Guru Gobind Singh, had taken Mata Gujri and two younger *sahibzadas* : Zorawar Singh and Fateh Singh to his native village Kheri (now Saheri) after the Guru had evacuated Anandpur in December 1705 AD. When the news of the Guru's reverses in the battle at Chamkaur reached Gangu, he got panicky and informed about Mata Gujri and two *sahibzadas* the government officials at Morinda.

Jani Khan and Mani Khan were two Ranghars belonging to Morinda. They were responsible for taking Mata Gujri and two *sahibzadas* from Kheri to Sirhind to be handed over to the governor there. Buddha Dal took revenge in 1763 AD by destroying Morinda and killing Jani Khan and Mani Khan.

JAPJI : *Japji* is probably the first composition of Guru Nanak and is the most comprehensive statement on Sikh theology. As it contains the essence of Sikhism, it has the same status among the Sikhs as the *Gita* has among the Hindus.

The Guru Granth Sahib begins with *Japji* which acts as a sort of its preamble. For that reason perhaps it has been kept out of the metrical organization of the Guru Granth Sahib in accordance with 31 Indian classical *raags*. Besides the *Mul Mantra* and the *Sloka*, *Japji* consists of 38 *paudis* (stanzas).

Japji covers many theological concepts like the oneness of God, God's Will (*Hukum*), God's Grace (*Nadar*) *Nam* as the Ultimate Reality, creation of the universe etc. It is an answer to the basic question : "How shall one be truthful? How should the screen of falsehood be torn?"

Kiv sachiara hoi-ai; Kiv koorh-ai tuttai paal
(Paudi 1)

Sikhism has given importance to *Japji* by making it a part of the morning prayers of *Nitnem* (Daily meditation). A Sikh is expected to learn it by heart. *Guru Nanak Prakash* says : "If you learn *Japji* by heart, you are freed from the cycle of birth-rebirth."

Japji kanth nitaprati ratte; janam janam ke kalmal katte.

Japji is used as a part of the Sikh initiation ceremony as also at the time of funeral.

JAPMALA : See Rosary.

JAPU SAHIB : As the Adi Granth begins with *Japji* the Dasam Granth which is a compilation of the compositions of Guru Gobind Singh begins with *Japu Sahib*. It is believed that *Japu Sahib* is perhaps the first composition of Guru Gobind Singh and was written by him in 1684 AD at Anandpur.

Japu Sahib is a *stotra* or panegyric which is a well-established poetic form used in devotional literature in Sanskrit. It has 199 stanzas in which ten different metres have been used. The language is predominantly Hindi and Sanskrit with a smattering of Arabic words here and there. The text may be taken as an example of the blending of Indian and Semitic linguistic cultures.

Japu Sahib is a hymn lauding the Lord who is remembered by as many as 950 different names. God is described as the Supreme Power; the most beautiful; bountiful, merciful; unborn, changeless; wielder of arms and omnipresent. *Jale hai; thale hai.*

Japu Sahib is a part of the morning prayers in the *Nitnem* (daily meditation) for Sikhs. It is also used as a part of the Sikhs initiation ceremony.

JASPAL BHAIKE : Jaspal Bhaike is a village near Ludhiana. It has a historical gurdwara preserving a few articles given by Guru Har Rai to Sagar Mal, incharge of his *langar*.

JASPAT RAI : Jaspat Rai was for sometime (before Adina Beg) the *faujdar* of Jalandhar but was later on shifted to Eminabad by Zakriya Khan. Early in 1746 AD he was killed in an encounter with a roving band of Sikhs. His brother Lakhpat Rai who was a *diwan* (revenue minister) at Lahore vowed revenge declaring that he would not put on his head dress nor claim himself to be a *Khatri* until he had scourged the entire Sikh Panth out of existence. Yahya Khan, the then governor of Lahore helped him in the persecution of Sikhs. He led a large force and perpetrated the *Chhota Ghallughara* (minor holocaust) killing 7000

Sikhs and capturing another 3000 in a major operation in May 1746 AD.

JASSA SINGH AHLUWALIA : Jassa Singh Ahluwalia is a well-known Sikh hero of the post-Guru Gobind Singh era. He was born on May 3, 1718 AD in a small village Ahlu near Lahore. His father, Sardar Badr Singh died when he was just five. His mother brought young Jassa Singh to Delhi in 1723 AD to seek the blessings of Mata Sundri, wife of Guru Gobind Singh. Mata Sundri looked after Jassa Singh as her own son. He spent seven years in Delhi and grew into a promising lad well-versed in Persian and Arabic. He became proficient in the use of arms and also learned music to sing hymns from the Adi Granth.

In 1728 AD the then emerging leader of the nascent Sikh community, Kapur Singh, while visiting Delhi to pay homage to Mata Sundri, was deeply impressed by the deportment and piety of young Jassa Singh. Soon Jassa Singh and his mother were taken into his fold. Tradition has it that on Jassa Singh's departure from Delhi, young Jassa Singh was blessed by Mata Sundri, presented with weapons and a prophecy made that Jassa Singh would achieve fame among the Sikhs and that the symbols of royalty and honour would accompany him in the days ahead. In his youth, Jassa Singh worked with Nawab Kapur Singh but later on set up his own Ahluwalia *misl*.

In 1748 AD at a Sarbat Khalsa meeting Nawab Kapur Singh constituted the fighting body of Sikhs—the Dal Khalsa and appointed Jassa Singh Ahluwalia as its leader. A title *Sultan-ul-Quam* (King of the Community) was subsequently accorded to him by his followers.

It was Ahmed Shah Abdali's inroads into Punjab from 1748-1767 AD that exercised a very decisive influence in the history of the Sikh power under the stewardship of Jassa Singh. Among the exploits the important ones are : Liberation of Amritsar (1741), capture of Lahore (1761), Liberation of Captives (1761) (This act earned him the appellation of *"Bandi Chhor"*), rebuilding of the Golden Temple (1764), occupation of Kapurthala (1779) and capture of Red Fort in Delhi (1783).

Jassa Singh passed away in 1783 AD. As a rare gesture of the recognition of his services to the Panth, his mortal remains were cremated in the holy precints of Baba Atal Amtirsar where his *smadh* (cenotaph) exists this day.

JASSA SINGH RAMGARHIA : Jassa Singh Ramgarhia was the chief of Ramgarhia *misl* in the hey days of Dal Khalsa. Although the *misl* was a part of Dal Khalsa whose recognized commander was Jassa Singh Ahluwalia, Jassa Singh Ramgarhia was many times in conflict with him.

Jassa Singh Thoka (carpenter) as he was originally known because he belonged to the carpenter class was the son of Giani Bhagwan Singh. He was born at Lahore in 1723 AD. As he grew he became known for his bravery and weaponry skills.

Khalsa Panth had excommunicated Jassa Singh for killing his daughter. As a result he moved to Jalandhar with his four brothers and took employment with Adina Beg, the Administrator there who made him the chief of his Sikh forces. During the attack on Punjab by Taimur, Adina Beg fled to the hills. Jassa Singh returned to Amritsar and asked for pardon from the Panth.

In 1747 AD, Sarbat Khalsa passed a resolution to construct a fort at Amritsar which on completion was named as Ram Rauni. This was blown up along with the garrison under the orders of Mir Mannu in 1753 AD. Sikhs decided to rebuild the fort and the job was entrusted to Jassa Singh Thoka and his contingent. The new fort was named Ramgarh. Because of his association with it, Jassa Singh Thoka came to be known as Jassa Singh Ramgarhia and his *misl* became Ramgarhia *misl*.

As mentioned earlier, he did not see eye to eye with Jassa Singh Ahluwalia who forced him to the eastern side of river Satluj. He remained in that area for a long time with his ravages extending to Sirsa, Meerut and Delhi.

In March 1783 AD, when he came to know that Dal Khalsa under Jassa Singh Ahluwalia was advancing upon Delhi he joined them. However, when Dal Khalsa entered the Red Fort on March 11, 1783 AD and some Sikhs placed Jassa Singh Ahluwalia on the throne in *Diwan-e-Am,* he opposed it on which the former immediately vacated it.

Jassa Singh Ramgarhia died in 1803 AD at the ripe age of 80.

JASSI : Jassi is a village near Bhatinda which has a gurdwara associated with Guru Gobind Singh. There is a tank near the gurdwara which the Guru is believed to have crossed on his horse. According to the popular *sakhi* Guru's blue dress had turned white (*Bagga*) when he came out. That is why the tank is called Baggsar.

JASSI, MAI : See Agra.

JATA : *Jata* is a Punjabi word meaning matted hair as was the custom among the Hindu ascetics of a monastic order. In fact, *jata* came to symbolize renunciation of social citizenship which Sikhism does not approve of. Guru Gobind Singh institutionalized this disapproval by prescribing comb (*Kangha*) as one of the five *kakars* which every Sikh must wear. Keeping *kangha* in the hair implies that hair must be kept in an orderly un-matted condition as a symbol of active social citizenship.

JATHA : A Punjabi term for a herd, flock, multitude, troop, band that in Sikh tradition signifies a band of volunteers coming forth to carry out a specific task which may be an armed combat or a peaceful and non-violent agitation. The term is derived from the Sanskrit word *yutha*. After the execution of Banda Singh Bahadur in 1716 AD and subsequent persecution of Sikhs, the Khalsa dispersed to the hills and forests in small bands or *jathas* led by a leader called *jathedar*. The *misls* grew out of these *jathas*.

JATHEDAR : Literally it means some one who maintains or leads *jatha*. It regained respectability in the twentieth century because of the leadership provided and sacrifices made by persons leading *jathas* (groups) at the time of *morchas*. Now commonly used as an honorific for political leaders of social workers of all types among the Akalis. It is also used as a title for the head of a historic gurdwara.

JATPURA : A village adjacent to Lamman about 15 km from Raikot in Ludhiana district. Guru Hargobind is believed to have visited it during his travels in the Malwa region in 1631-32 AD. Some chroniclers and historians believe that Guru Gobind Singh composed his *Fatehnama* which is included in the Dasam Granth at Jatpura in 1705 AD. He had stayed in the village for a few days on his way from Chamkaur to Dina and Kangar while Rai Kalha had dispatched a fast messanger to Sirhind to bring news of Mata Gujri and two younger *sahibzadas* rumoured to have been taken into custody by the *faujdar* of Sirhind. It was here that he got the news of their martyrdom. There are two gurdwaras here to commemorate the visit of Guru Gobind Singh : Manji Sahib inside the village and Gurusar on its outskirts.

JAT-SIKHS : Although there is no caste-system among the Sikhs, they may be thought of as divided into four major groups : Jat-Sikhs, Khatri-Sikhs, Ramgarhia-Sikhs and Mazhabi-Sikhs.

Jats, in general, constitute a prominent community of North-Western India and is almost a branch of Rajputs. They were initiatlly the inhabitants of Central Asia. Some of them came down and settled on the banks of the river Indus whence they spread to the Jamuna and Chambal. Others went and settled in Western Europe (Sweden and Denmark). It is from them that Jutland gets its name. According to some historians, it is from Jutland that they moved to Kent and some other parts of England. Jats are famous as a martial community and are largely engaged in agriculture.

When Islam came to India, many Jats became Muslim. Later on there were massive conversions from the community into Sikhism especially during the days of Guru Hargobind and Guru Gobind Singh. This became an important factor in the transformation of Sikhism into a community of brave, self-sacrificing people fighting for justice and fair play.

JAUNPUR : Jaunpur is a district town in Uttar Pradesh on the banks of the river Gomti. Guru Tegh Bahadur had stayed here with a devotee and had offered a *mridang* (a percussion instrument) for *Shabad Kirtan*. A gurdwara called Sangat Mridangwali commemorates the Guru's visit. The *mridang* is preserved as a relic.

JETHA SINGH : Jetha Singh was a Sikh trader of Ahmadabad. Bhai Daya Singh when he was carrying Guru Gobind Singh's letter called the *Zafarnama* for Emperor Aurangzeb who was in the south from Dina had stayed with him.

JHABAAL KALAN : A historical village about 15 km from Tarn Taran. Guru Hargobind came here to perform the marriage of his daughter Bibi Viro in May 1629 AD. A gurdwara now marks the spot of the Guru's stay. The village has produced some eminent personalities in Sikh history as for example Mai Bhago and Sardar Baghel Singh chief of the Karorsinghia *misl*.

JHANDA, BHAI : Jhanda was a great grandson of Baba Buddha. He is often quoted as an example of the most devoted Sikh. Once Guru Hargobind while strolling in the garden casually asked him stay at a place. As it happened the Guru went out through the other gate but Jhanda kept standing at the place for three days till the Guru called him through a message.

JHANDA KALAN : A village about 7 km from Sardulgarh in Mansa district. Guru Gobind Singh stayed here for a night in 1706 AD while on his way from Talwandi Sabo to Sirsa. A gurdwara commemorates the Guru's stay.

JHANDA SAHIB : Same as Nishan Sahib.

JHAR SAHIB : A tree associated with any of the Gurus. Important Jhar Sahibs are :

1. A gurdwara associated with Guru Gobind Singh near village Chuharwal (near Machhiwara). The Guru had rested here under a tree while going to Machhiwara from Jand Sahib.

2. A gurdwara in Wan village near Tarn Taran. The tree with which Guru Arjan had tied his horse is still present.

JHATKA : Concerned mainly as they were with spiritual liberation, the Sikh Gurus were rather loath in pronouncing upon vegetarianism versus non-vegetarianism. The position is best demonstrated by what is stated in the Guru Granth Sahib : "Men, out of ignorance, quarrel over this matter. Do not bother to know what is flesh and what is non-flesh; which food is sinful which is not." (AG. p. 1289) Guru Gobind Singh while maintaining the same position stipulated that if Sikhs want to take meat, it must be *jhatka* meat i.e. meat prepared by killing the animal in a single stroke or shot in contrast to *halal* meat prepared by slow killing according to Muslim customs. By this he restored the ancient Aryan tradition according to which only such meat as is obtained from an animal which is killed with one stroke of the weapon, causing instantaneous death, is fit for human consumption. This was a reaction to the Muslim political hegemony which had made it a state policy not to permit slaughter of animals for food, in any other manner, except as laid down in the Quran as also repudiation of the theory of expiatory sacrifice as believed by Muslims.

JHIRA SAHIB : 1. A village about 6 km from Anandpur in which is situated a gurdwara associated with Guru Hargobind. The Guru used to go out hunting there.

2. A gurdwara in Kanjhle village near Dhuri associated with Guru Hargobind.

JIND KAUR : Jind Kaur was the wife of

Maharaja Ranjit Singh and mother of Dalip Singh. After the British took over Lahore, Jind Kaur was kept under detention first at Sheikhupura (Pakistan) and then at Chunar Fort in District Mirzapur (Uttar Pradesh) from where she escaped to Nepal disguised as a beggar. She went to England in 1861 AD to see her son and she died there on August 1, 1863 AD at the age of 46.

JINDOWAL : Jindowal is a village near Banga in Jalandhar district. It has a gurdwara named Charankaul dedicated to Guru Hargobind who had halted at the village while proceeding to Kiratpur from Phagwara. The Guru had to stay here for a few days as his favourite horse Suhela had fallen sick.

JINDWARI : A village about 15 km from Anandpur in Ropar district. According to the local tradition, Baba Gurditta, the eldest son of Guru Hargobind had inadvertently killed a cow here during the chase which had displeased the Guru. Guru Gobind Singh is also said to have visited the place. It has a historical shrine called Gurdwara Jindwari Sahib.

JINVARA : A place about 11 km from Bidar in Karnataka. Mai Bhago, a brave Sikh woman who had fought in the battle at Muktsar and constantly remained in the train of Guru Gobind Singh's followers after the battle had settled here after the Guru's death in 1708 AD. She lived to attain a ripe old age. Her hut was just outside the walls of the village fortress. The hut is now a shrine known as Gurdwara Tap Asthan Mai Bhago.

JIOWALA : Jiowala is a village near Tarn Taran. It has a gurdwara dedicated to Guru Hargobind who according to the local tradition is said to have come to the village from Jhabaal.

JITO, MATA : Jito or originally Ajito who became Ajit Kaur after baptism was one of the wives of Guru Gobind Singh. She was the daughter of Harjas, a Subhikhia Khatri of Lahore.

It is believed that once Harjas came to Anandpur to visit Guru Gobind Singh. Seeing him handsome and well-proportioned he thought he would be a suitable match for his daughter. Mata Gujri was pleased at the proposal and asked her brother Kirpal to advise the Guru to accept it. The Guru did so and the marriage was solemnized in 1677 AD at a place near Anandpur called Guru ka Lahore as the Guru, contrary to custom, was unwilling to go to Lahore with a marriage party. Mata Jito gave birth to three sons : Jujhar Singh, Fateh Singh and Zorawar Singh.

Mata Jito died in 1700 AD at Anandpur.

JIWAN SINGH : See Jaita, Bhai.

JOGA : A village about 200 km from Mansa. It was founded by Jugraj, the local chief at the request of Guru Tegh Bahadur who had camped at the site during his travels in the region. A historical shrine called Gurdwara Patshahi IX marks the spot where the Guru had camped.

JOGA SINGH, BHAI : Bhai Joga Singh was a devotee of Guru Gobind Singh. He was baptized by the Guru and used to be always at his service. It is said that when Bhai Joga Singh's marriage was being solemnized in Peshawar (Pakistan), the Guru sent him a *Hukamnama* to return to Anandpur immediately. This was done to test his dedication. He was indeed so obedient and devoted that he left his *Lawan* incomplete to return to Anandpur. The marriage was, however, solemnized in absentia. In forgetfulness of Guru's teachings, he on arriving at Hoshiarpur on his way to Anandpur thought of visiting a courtesan to drown in her company the regret of interrupting his wedding ceremony. It is believed the Guru came to his rescue when he was about to go astray.

JOHAR SAHIB : It is a gurdwara of Guru Nanak about 12 km from Dharampur in Himachal Pradesh. The Guru had stayed here during his travels. It is believed that the Guru brought out water at this place by lifting a rock, at the request of a villager named Mahiya. The tank that has been constructed there is called "Mahiya Johar".

JOTISAR : It is a big tank near Kurukshetra. According to the Mahabharata, Lord Krishna had preached the message of Gita to Arjun at this spot in the beginning of the war between the Kaurava and Pandva princes. A grand Gita Bhavan commemorates the event. Guru Amardas and Guru Gobind Singh had visited the place.

JUJHAR SINGH, SAHIBZADA : *Sahibzada* Jujhar Singh was the second son of Guru Gobind Singh. He was born to Mata Jito in 1690 AD. He died fighting in the battle at Chamkaur in December 1705.

JUSTICE : John Lacke rightly said in his *'An Essay Concerning Human Understanding'* "Justice and truth are the common ties of society; and therefore even outlaws and robbers, who break with all the world besides, must keep faith and rules of equity amongst themselves or else they cannot hold together" (p. 31) Sikhism has accorded a pride a place to truth. Infact, Truth is according to Sikhism is the name of God. Justice also has been a basic principle of social organization with Sikhs. Quite obviously it has been thought to operate at two levels.

At the individual plane, justice is taken as giving everyone his due or being fair to everyone "To deprive one of his due is like beef to the Hindu and pork to the Muslim."

Hak praya Nanaka us soor us gai (AG. p. 141)

Sikh Gurus forbade their followers even to plunder enemy property. They were indeed the protectors of the rights of man. Guru Tegh Bahadur and Guru Gobind Singh made supreme sacrifices to get justice. Guru Tegh Bahadur was trying to ensure justice for Kashmiri Pandits who were forcibly being converted to Islam. While describing Guru Har Rai as the protector of human rights and justice, Bhai Nand Lal writes :

"Hak parwar hak kesh, Guru karta Har Rai"
(Tausif-O-Sana)

Sikhism's concern for social justice found practical expression in the abolition of caste system in Sikh society, ethos of equality as for example through the concept of *langar*, injunctions against female infanticide, the emancipation of women as through widow remarriage and condemnation of *sati* etc. There is an undercurrent against exploitation of man by man in Sikhism.

JYOTI : *Jyoti* in Sikh theological writings and speech refers to Divine Light which illuminated the souls of all the Gurus and is now enshrined in the Guru Granth Sahib. It has gone deep into the Sikh psyche through writings as of Bhai Gurdas on Guru Nanak's birth: "When Guru Nanak was born there was light all round dispelling the mist. As the sun rose, darkness vanished and stars became invisible."

Satgur Nanak pargatia, miti dhund jag chanan hoaa. Jiokar Suraj niklia, tare chhupe andher paloaa. (Var 1, Paudi 27)

This *Jyoti* acts as a unifying force providing continuity to the teachings of all the Gurus.

There are a number of references to *Jyoti* in the Guru Granth Sahib. Kabir at one point describing the slow appearance of God says : "There was light and darkness disappeared."

Pargati jyoti, mitia andhiara (AG. p. 1349)

That this runs through all the Gurus has been explained by Bhatt Kalh: "From Guru Nanak was Angad; from Angad, Amardas received the sublime rank. From Guru Ramdas descended Guru Arjan, the great devotee of God" (AG. p. 1407). The concept of all the Gurus being one light, one voice has become a fundamental principle of the Sikh faith.

JYOTI SWARUP : It is a gurdwara in Sirhind about 1½ km from Fatehgarh Sahib. The mortal remains of Mata Gujri, *sahibzada* Zorawar Singh and *sahibzada* Fateh Singh were cremated here. Cremation under the circumstances then prevailing demanded much daring and courage. Braving the consequences, a Muslim *faqir* provided the land for the purpose, a Hindu gave the rulers a huge sum of money for permission to cremate the bodies, and several others joined hands in performing the ceremony.

K

KABIR : Kabir was the most celebrated revolutionary saint of the Bhakti Movement. He condemned social and religious abuses and emphasized the fundamental equality and fraternity of all mankind.

Kabir was born in 1398 AD of an unwed Brahmin mother who abandoned him on the bank of a lake called *Lahar Tara*, a short distance from Varanasi. He was found by a Muslim weaver Ali who adopted him and brought him up. When he grew up, he came under the influence of Ramanand's thinking and philosophy.

A staunch believer in the worth of constructive human endeavour, Kabir was opposed alike to ritualism and asceticism. He fought against all vicious influences and pulled up the Hindu pundits and Muslim *mullas* and inveighed against the *yogis* and *sadhus*. He was arrested by Emperor Sikandar Lodi on a complaint that he had been preaching what ran counter to the Islamic canon.

Once an attempt was made to drown him in the Ganges; and, on another occasion, he was thrown before a drunken elephant to be crushed to death. Kabir remained undaunted by these events and eventually became the leader of the *Bhakti* movement. He was a worshipper of the godly and an enemy of the wicked and it was his desire to spend all his time in communion with God.

Kabir's contribution to the Adi Granth, comprising 534 different verses arranged under 17 *raags* exceeds that of any other *Bhakt*. Besides this, there is a long list of works attributed to him, the most famous of which is *Kabir Bijak* which is the holy book for *Kabir Panthis*.

Kabir was a contemporary of Ravidas. He usually lived in Varanasi until the last year of his life when he shifted to Magahar near Gorakhpur where he died in 1495 AD. It is said that after his death there was a controversy between Hindus and Muslims regarding the disposal of his dead body.

KACHHA : *Kachha* or *kachh* is one of the five obligatory external symbols to be worn by the Khalsa brotherhood founded by Guru Gobind Singh in 1699 AD. It means drawers or knickers—two legged undergarment for the lower part of the body.

Though the primary significance of *kachha*, as of other *kakaars*, is as a mark of identity or belongingness to the Khalsa, the scholars have tried to look for deeper symbolism. According to Kapur Singh the injunction to wear *kachha* by the Khalsa has, among others, three most profound and far reaching symbolic meanings: (1) It is a badge and basis of civilization itself. (2) It is a repudiation of the ascetic ideal based on the *Sankhya* system of which *digambara* nudity is the primary characteristic and (3) It is an abandonment of the rituals of the Vedic religion and the practices of Brahamanism according to which sacrifices could be performed by only a person wearing a *dhoti* (Parasaraprasna) : Guru Nanak Dev univ, Amritsar pp 114-20).

KAHL GAON : Kahl Gaon is a village in Bihar about 25 km from Bhagalpur. A gurdwara here is dedicated to the visit of Guru Tegh Bahadur to the place.

KAHLOOR : Kahloor was a hill state with its capital at Bilaspur in the days of Guru Gobind Singh. Its ruler Bhim Chand was against the Guru and conspired with other hill chiefs to wage a movement to control him. As a result the Guru had to fight battles against the hill chiefs at Bhangani, Anandpur and other places.

KAHN SINGH : Kahn Singh was the son of Binod Singh, a devout follower of Guru Gobind Singh. Both father and the son were with the Guru at Nanded during his last days and were among the five Sikhs chosen to accompany Banda Singh Bahadur to Punjab in 1708 AD when he set out on his expedition to punish the evil forces at the behest of Guru Gobind Singh. After the capture of Sirhind in 1710 AD Kahn Singh was made deputy to his father who was given charge of the border district of Karnal. Later, he developed differences with Banda Singh Bahadur during the siege at Gurdas Nangal because of which he left the camp. He was captured and taken to Delhi along with other Sikh prisoners of execution in 1716 AD.

KAIRON : A village in Amritsar district. It has a historical shrine Gurdwara Jhar Sahib dedicated to Guru Arjan. The shrine marks the spot where the Guru had halted during one of his journeys through the Majha region. The Guru's horse was tethered to a *jhar* tree; hence the name.

KAITHAL : A district town in Haryana Guru Tegh Bahadur had visited. Two gurdwaras are dedicated to him. Gurdwara Nim Sahib which marks the site of the tree under which the Guru had sat and preached and Gurdwara Manji Sahib where the Guru had stayed at the house of a devout Sikh Roda Badhi.

KAKAAR : *Kakaar* in Punjabi is the same as *kakka*, the name representing of the phonetic sound of the letter in the Gurmukhi alphabet corresponding to 'K'. The five external symbols of the Khalsa Panth : *Kesh, Kangha, Kirpan, Kara, Kachha* whose wearing was made obligatory for the members of the Khalsa by Guru Gobind Singh in 1699 AD, all begin with 'K' are therefore, collectively referred to as five K's, *kakaars* or *Panj Kakke*. See respective entries for meaning attached to the wearing of these symbols.

KALA KHAN : Kala Khan was the *faujdar* of Peshawar during the days of Guru Hargobind. On the orders of Emperor Shahjahan he came to Kartarpur (Jalandhar) along with Painde Khan and other generals in 1634 AD to capture the Guru. In the ensuing battle, he died at the hands of the Guru.

KALH, BHATT : Kalh was the most prominent *Bhatt.* 53 of his *Sawayyas* in praise of the first five Gurus are included in the Adi Granth. In his verses on Guru Nanak, he calls him the Supreme Guru of both the temporal and spiritual worlds. According to him, Guru Angad dispelled the darkness of ignorance from the world. Guru Amardas became Guru by virtue of *Nam simran*. He likens Guru Ramdas to a fount of nectar from whence flowed many a life-giving streams. Guru Arjan's time has been characterized as *Janak Raiya*. Kalsahar says that Guru Arjan remained calm and unperturbed even in moments of greatest turbulations.

KALIYUGA : See Yugas.

KALLAH RAI : Kallah Rai was the chief of Raikot in Ludhiana district. His father Rai Ahmad had founded the town of Raikot in 1648 AD. Kallah Rai was a devoted disciple of Guru Gobind Singh. The Guru came to Raikot from Machhiwara in the guise of a *pir* after the battle at Chamkaur. Kallah Rai was at his service. He sent his employee Nuru to Sirhind who brought the news of martyrdom of younger *sahibzadas* to the Guru. The Guru gave Kallah Rai a sword as a momento. It is now kept in Gurdwara Saropa Sahib in Nabha.

KALMOT : Kalmot is a village about 15 km from Anandpur in Ropar district. Pilgrims used to pass through it while going to Anandpur from Hoshiarpur region. Once the residents of the village plundered the pilgrims. Guru Gobind Singh moved against them and punished them. A gurdwara dedicated to the Guru exists here. At some distance from the village is Gurdwara Gurplah which marks the tree under which the Guru had halted.

KALU, BABA : Baba Kalu whom chroniclers also called Kalyan Chand, Kalyan Rai, Kalu Chand and Kalu Rai was the father of Guru Nanak. He was a *Khatri* of the Bedi subgroup and was a revenue official in the Muslim-owned village of Talwandi now known as

Nankana Sahib which is in Pakistan. He was born in 1440 AD and died at Kartarpur (Pakistan) in 1522 AD. According to some chroniclers he died at Talwandi.

KALYAN : An Indian classical *raag* usually sung within three hours (one *pahar*) after sunset. It is twenty-ninth of the thirty-one *raags* used in the organisation of hymns in the Guru Granth Sahib covering pages 1319-1326. It has many variations. The pure *kalyan* follows the following sequence of basic notes :

   Arohi : *sa, re, ga, pa, dha, sa,..........*
   Avrohi : *sa, ne, dha, pa, ma, ga, re, sa,..........*

KALYANA, BHAI : Bhai Kalyana was a devoted disciple of Guru Arjan. During the construction of the Golden Temple he went to the hills to collect money and wooden fuel. The Raja of Mandi put him in prison for not observing fast at the time of Janam Ashtami. But when Bhai Kalyana explained his background, the Raja not only forgave him but accompanied him to Amritsar to meet Guru Arjan whose devotee he became.

KAM : See Lust.

KAMALPUR : There are two villages of the same name in Punjab having historical shrines. One is near Sunam and has a gurdwara dedicated to Guru Nanak and Guru Hargobind, both of whom are believed to have visited the place. The gurdwara was constructed by Maharaja Karam Singh of Patiala.

The other Kamalpur is near Jagraon in Ludhiana district. It has a gurdwara dedicated to Guru Gobind Singh who had come to the village from Hehran.

KAMLAH GARH : Kamlah Garh is a village in Himachal Pradesh about 40 km from Mandi which had an old fort of the same name. Guru Gobind Singh had stayed here for some time. The Raja of Mandi constructed a new fort and named it Gobindgarh in honour of the Guru. Maharaja Ranjit Singh made special efforts to capture it in 1830 AD.

KANDH SAHIB, GURDWARA : *Kandh Sahib* is situated in Batala, a small town about 40 km from Amritsar. It is a gurdwara associated with the marriage of Guru Nanak.

According to the Sikh tradition Guru Nanak insisted on simple marriage rites but his father-in-law was chary of breaking old traditions. He asked Guru Nanak to convince the priests for which purpose he sat near a mud-wall (*kandh*) which still stands encased in glass. An impressive gurdwara has been constructed at the site. Every year there is a big gathering at Kandh Sahib on the marriage anniversary of the Guru.

KANECH : A village about 20 km from Ludhiana. It has a historical gurdwara called Manji Sahib built in honour of Guru Gobind Singh's visit to the village in December 1705 AD after leaving Machhiwara. He was still disguised as Pir of Uchch. According to the local tradition, a farmer Fatta, hesitated to lend him his best horse and instead offered a gaunt mare. The horse later died of a snake bite.

KANGAR : Kangar is the part of village Dialpur Bhai ka where Gurdwara Zafarnama Sahib is situated. For details about Dialpur Bhai ka, see the relevant entry.

KANGHA : *Kangha* means comb and is one of the five *kakaars* wearing of which was made obligatory by Guru Gobind Singh at the time of setting up of the Khalsa brotherhood in 1699 AD. The Guru had desired the Sikhs to comb their hair twice every day and therefore made the possession of a *kangha* in the head hair compulsory by way of forbidding keeping the hair in a matted condition as was the practice among ascetics which was disapproved by Sikhism. Thus while *jata* (matted hair) symbolizes renunciation of social citizenship in Hinduism, *kangha* symbolizes orderliness and discipline among the Sikhs as active and useful citizens. Indeed, *kesh* and *kangha* constitute a pair of complementary symbols.

KANGMAI : Kangmai is a village near Hoshiarpur. Bhai Tiratha who was a devotee of Guru Arjan and was appointed as a missionary for the Doaba region by the Guru belonged to this village. The Guru came here in 1594 AD. A gurdwara commemorates the visit of the Guru.

KANHA : Kanha was a well-known *bhagat* of Lahore and was a contemporary of Guru Arjan. When the Guru was compiling the Adi Granth, he came to Amritsar with three other *bhagats* : Shah Hussain, Chhajju and Peelo to request the Guru that their compositions should be included in the Adi Granth. They recited them to the Guru but he did not find them upto the mark. According to the Sikh tradition, Kanha did not like the rejection and cursed the Guru that he would die at the hands of his enemies. But he himself died while returning to Lahore after a fall from the horse.

KANHAIYA, BHAI : Kanhaiya also written as Ghaneeya was a disciple of Guru Tegh Bahadur who later on served Guru Gobind Singh. In the battle at Anandpur in 1705 AD, he would offer water to the wounded irrespective of whether they were from the enemy camp as a part of service. The Guru had overlooked the complaint made against him on this issue.

KANHAIYA MISL : Kanhaiya *misl* was one of the *misls* that came up in the turbulent days following the martyrdom of Banda Singh Bahadur. Its chief Jai Singh had taken part in the expedition of the Dal Khalsa in 1763 AD to capture Sirhind. His grand daughter Mahtab Kaur was later married to Maharaja Ranjit Singh.

KANJHLA : A village about 18 km from Sangrur which has a historical gurdwara, Jhira Sahib. According to the local tradition three Sikh Gurus had visited the village in their times *viz* Guru Nanak, Guru Hargobind and Guru Tegh Bahadur. The gurdwara is situated where there used to be large coppice (*Jhira* in Punjabi) in which the Gurus used to put up their camps.

KANRA : An Indian classical *raag* usually sung within three hours (one *pahar*) before mid-night. It is twenty-eighth of the thirty-one *raags*, used in the organisation of hymns in the Guru Granth Sahib covering pages 1294-1318. *Kanra* has many variations. *Darbari Kanra* uses the following sequence of basic notes :
   Arohi : ne, sa, re, ma, pa, dha, ne, sa,..........
   Avrohi : sa, dha, ne, pa, ga, ma, re, sa,..........

KAONKE : A village about 7 km from Jagraon in Ludhiana district. It has a historical gurdwara called Gurusar commemorating the visit of Guru Hargobind to the place in 1631-32 AD.

KAPAL MOCHAN : An ancient pilgrimage centre of the Hindus, about 20 km from Jagadhari. Guru Gobind Singh stayed here for 52 days in 1688 AD while returning from Paonta to Anandpur. A gurdwara complex was raised after the partition of India in 1947 AD to commemorate the Guru's stay.

KAPURA, CHAUDHRY : Chaudhry Kapura was a Jat chief of Faridkot who had taken over after the death of his uncle Chaudhry Bhallan in 1643 AD. He was born in 1628 AD. He was a devotee of the Sikh Gurus and used to send donations to Guru Gobind Singh at Anandpur. He founded the town of Kotkapura in 1661 AD.

When Guru Gobind Singh came to the Malwa region in 1703-4 AD he administered *amrit* to Chaudhry Kapura and named him Kapur Singh.

In December 1705 AD, when Guru Gobind Singh was being chased by the Mughal forces, he came to Kotkapura area. He was, not however, sure whether Chaudhry Kapura will be able to ward off the Mughal army. So the Guru left Kotkapura and went to the nearby village Dhilwan Kalan. When the imperial forces caught up with him at Muktsar, Chaudhry Kapura was with them. A fierce battle took place at Muktsar after which Chaudhry Kapura persuaded the commanders to give up the case and withdraw from the area because of shortage of water.

Chaudhry Kapura was captured and killed

by a neighbouring chief Sardar Isakhan in 1708 AD.

(See also Jandu Singha.)

KAPUR SINGH, NAWAB : Nawab Kapur Singh was a noted Sikh hero of the post-Guru Gobind Singh era who played a prominent role in the consolidation of the Khalsa. He groomed Jassa Singh Ahluwalia and gave him the command of the newly formed Dal Khalsa in 1748 AD which was divided into eleven *misls*. (The twelfth *misl* was not a part of Dal Khalsa and sometimes acted against the interests of the community.) The former division into Buddha Dal (Veterans) and Taruna Dal (Verdants) was retained. Kapur Singh was born of a Virk family of Jats in 1697 AD. His native village was Kalo-ke, now in Shiekhpura district of Pakistan. Later, when he seized the village of Faizullapur, near Amritsar, he renamed it Singhpura and started living there. That is why he is also known as Kapur Singh Faizullpuria or Singhpuria. He was eleven years old at the time of Guru Gobind Singh's death and nineteen at the time of the massacre in Delhi. He was baptized on the occasion of Baisakhi of 1721 AD.

Kapur Singh became Nawab in 1733 AD when Zakariya Khan governor of Lahore sent a delegation to make peace with the Sikhs. He sent a *khilat* (present) with a letter granting *jagir* and he wanted the leader of the Sikhs to have the title of Nawab. The congregation decided that it should be given to Kapur Singh.

Kapur Singh died in 1759 AD at Amritsar and was cremated near Baba Atal.

KARA : *Kara*, a steel bangle, is one of the five *kakaars*, the wearing of which was made obligatory by Guru Gobind Singh for members of the Khalsa brotherhood set up by him in 1699 AD. Primarily it is a mark of identity and belongingness to the brotherhood, but scholars interpret the injunction regarding wearing it in terms of deeper symbolism.

Kapur Singh relates a *kara* to *dharamchakkar* of Hindu and Buddhism symbolism. He further derives meaning from the figure and the substance of *kara*. Circle is a perfect figure without a beginning or an end and therefore stands for perfect divinity which a Sikh must aim at. (*Parasaraprasna*; Guru Nanak Dev university, pp. 113-14). There is symbolism attached to iron or steel of which *kara* is made of. Steel is symbolic of strength, yet resilient under stress. In the same way, human soul must become as strong and unbreakable as steel. Gold *karas* worn by certain Sikhs do not, therefore, strictly satisfy the symbolic meaning.

KARAH PARSAD : *Karah Parsad* is the standing dish for all religious ceremonies and congregations and has the status of the sacrament which is distributed among the *sangat* after the *ardaas*. It is prepared in an iron pan called *karaha* in Punjabi. Hence the name. *Karah* was also offered among the ancient Aryans to the deities and idols as *lapasi*. Muslims, who call it *halwa*, prepare it in large quantities on the occasion of Eid.

Karah Parsad is very easy to prepare. It needs equal proportions of flour (or semolina), sugar and *ghee* (butter oil) with a double proportion of water. The dish is placed in the presence of the Guru Granth Sahib and is sanctified by crossing the *kirpan* through it towards the end of the recitation of the *ardaas*. It is partaken by equally by everyone in the congregation as a mark of receiving divine grace. It is believed that the practice was started by Guru Arjan.

KARAM CHAND : Karam Chand was the son of Chandu. He bore enmity towards Guru Hargobind because of his father's death at the hands of the Sikhs. He fought against the Guru in the battle at Hargobindpur and was killed at the hands of the Guru in 1621 AD.

KARHA : Karha is a village in Haryana about 25 km from Kurushetra. Guru Nanak and Guru Hargobind had visited the place. It was also sanctified by a visit by Guru Tegh Bahadur. According to the local tradition, even Guru Gobind Singh passed through the village. He did not, however, dismount from his horse and gave his sermon to the local residents from the horse-back. A gurdwara complex commemorates these events.

KARHALI : A village about 20 km from Patiala. It has a historical gurdwara called Karhali Sahib commemorating the stay here of Guru Tegh Bahadur during one of his travels through the Malwa region. Guru Hargobind is also believed to have visited it earlier while on his way to Kurukshetra.

KARMA, LAW OF : The law of *Karma* states that man, in his present life, is the product of his actions in the past life; he reaps what he sows. The doctrine is the counterpart of the physical law of casualty in the moral realm. Every event is considered to have its cause and every event leads to a certain result. Guru Nanak states that man receives the due reward of the good and the bad that he does. Thus the Law of *Karma* of Sikhism is very similar to that of Hinduism.

Apparently the Law of *Karma* seems to contradict *Hukam*, the cosmic order of the Will of God. If the law of *Karma* is considered inexorable, there is no place for *Hukam* in its working. *Karma* becomes a blind, unconscious and mechanical principle governing the whole universe. God is reduced simply to the status of a clerk which Sikhism does not accept. That is why the Law of *Karma* does operate in Sikhism but it is not inexorable—it is subservient to *Hukam*. The reward or punishment of any action of man is given by God's order according to merit—he may give it or withhold it. He had kept the implementation in his hands. It gives supremacy to God. The difference between the Law of *Karma* and the Will of God is that the former is an instrument of fear and the latter that of love.

KHERI : See Gangu.

KARMO : Karmo was the wife of Baba Pirthi Chand, elder brother of Guru Arjan. She conspired to kill Guru Hargobind when he was a child by poisoning his curd but did not succeed. Baba Pirthi Chand has planned that by removing Guru Hargobind from the line of succession, he might reopen it for himself.

KARNAL : Karnal is a district town, in Haryana and is situated on G.T. Road between Delhi and Ambala. Guru Nanak had stayed here on his way to Delhi in 1515 AD. A gurdwara commemorates the Guru's visit. Guru Tegh Bahadur is also believed to have visited the place in 1670 AD during his journey from Delhi to Lakhnaur. Banda Singh Bahadur had captured Karnal and the surrounding areas in 1709 AD.

KAR SEVA : *Kar* means work and *Seva* means service. *Kar Seva*, therefore, means work or service organized for religious purposes especially for the construction of gurdwaras. Since it involves voluntary service by the community, this is the most respected method of constructing historical gurdwaras. Most of the Gurus resorted to *Kar Seva* as a method of organizing labour for a common cause.

The sentimental value of getting the important gurdwaras constructed through *Kar Seva* dates back to the days of Guru Hargobind. When the Guru was busy with *Kar Seva* for the construction of Akal Takht, Mughal emperor Jahangir visited Amritsar. He wanted to make a handsome contribution for accelerating the construction work. Politely yet persuasively, the Guru prevailed upon Jahangir not to insist. "Let this Akal Takht be constructed by the followers of the faith with their own hands. Let this dream be accomplished into reality as a true symbol of Sikh spirit of service, selflessness and sacrifice. Please permit this monument to permeate a spirit of self-confidence among the people through a process of participation of *Kar Seva*, rather than accomplish this historic monument with royal court's generosity." had pleaded the Guru.

KARTARPUR (JALANDHAR) : Kartarpur (Jalandhar) is a flourishing town near Jalandhar on G.T. Road. It is an important Sikh religious centre besides being known for its wooden furniture. It was founded by Guru

Arjan in 1596 AD. Guru Hargobind used to stay here off and on. In 1634 AD he fought a battle here against Kale Khan, Painde Khan and other generals. Guru Tegh Bahadur was married here to Mata Gujri in 1632 AD. It was destroyed by Ahmad Shah Abdali in 1756 AD.

Kartarpur is dotted with a number of historical shrines important ones being Shish Mahal, Gangsar and Thamb Sahib. (See respective entries.)

In the controversies regarding succession to Guru Hargobind, his grandson Baba Dhirmal who was born at Kartarpur and was son of Baba Gurditta made Kartarpur his headquarters with the original copy of the Adi Granth in his possession. This original copy is still at Kartarpur. His plans did not succeed but his descendants continued to exercise control over Kartarpur.

KARTARPUR (PAKISTAN) : This is the name of the place where Guru Nanak had settled after his missionary travels. Guru Nanak had set up an ideal Sikh community here in 1504 AD and put his teachings into actual practice. He lived here with his family for eighteen years till his death in 1522 AD.

The place is now in Sialkot district of Pakistan on the other bank of the river Ravi opposite to Dera Baba Nanak in India which is on its left bank. Bhai Doda and Duni Chand had helped Guru Nanak set up this habitation. Guru Angad had met the Guru here for the first time and it was here that he was anointed as the successor to Guru Nanak.

Some years after the death of Guru Nanak, the habitation of Kartarpur became a victim of the changing course of the river Ravi. The sons of Guru Nanak : Baba Sri Chand and Lakhmi Das shifted the urn containing the ashes of Guru Nanak to the other side of the river where the historic town of Dera Baba Nanak has come up. (See Dera Baba Nanak). A three-storeyed gurdwara at Kartarpur can still be seen from a high embankment at Dera Baba Nanak.

KASHI : See Varanasi.

KATHA : *Katha* which means an exposition of the teachings of Sikhism generally based on the hymns of the Adi Granth or the Dasam Granth is one of the two approved modes of congregational worship, the other being *kirtan*. According to Guru Arjan, listening to *katha* purifies one's mind.

Katha sunat mal sagli khovai (AG, p. 104)

KATTU : Kattu is a village about 12 km from Barnala in the Malwa region. According to Sikh tradition, Guru Tegh Bahadur visited the village during his travels in the area and recited his *shabad*: *kahe re ban khojan ja-ee* in a congregation in the village. A gurdwara called Gurusar has been dedicated to the Guru's visit.

Kattu has produced the well-known Sikh preacher Dhyan Singh. He produced a new recension of the Dasam Granth by replacing *Charitr* with *Sarbloh* but it did not become popular.

KATTU SHAH : Kattu Shah was a Kashmiri Muslim who became a devoted disciple of Guru Hargobind. He did considerable work in preaching Sikhism in Kashmir.

KAUDA : In the folklore of the Gond tribe of central India, Kauda is the name of the demon who made the ancestor of the Gonds, Lingo his prisoner. Lingo escaped with the help of the demon's daughters.

There is a mention about Kauda in the *Janam Sakhis* of Guru Nanak as the head of a clan of cannibals. Mardana had fallen into the hands of Kauda and was saved by Guru Nanak.

KAULAN : See Kaulsar.

KAULSAR : The tank Kaulsar was got excavated by Guru Hargobind for the convenience of Kaulan. It was rain-fed and remained neglected until it was desilted, cleaned and renovated in 1872 AD and connected to the water channel bringing waters of the River Ravi to Amritsar *sarovars* in 1884 AD. On one edge of Kaulsar is situated Gurdwara Mai Kaulan da Asthan.

Kaulan was the daughter of Rustum Khan of a suburb of Lahore. She had a religious bent of mind and became a devotee of Guru Hargobind. Her father did not quite approve of it and subjected her to a cruel treatment. She ultimately left her father and sought refuge with Guru Hargobind at Amritsar. Gurdwara Mai Kaulan da Asthan marks the place where she used to live in Amritsar. After a few years she shifted to Kartarpur (Jalandhar) where she died in 1629 AD.

KAUR : *Kaur* is a derivative of the word *kawre* which comes from *kunwre* meaning woman or damsel. It is now an essential ending for the name of a female Sikh particularly one who has undergone baptism. It corresponds to Singh in male names.

KEDARA : An Indian classical *raag* usually sung within three hours (one *pahar*) before mid-night. It is twenty-third of the thirty-one *raags* used in the organisation of hymns in the Guru Granth Sahib covering pages 1118-1124. The sequence of basic notes in it as follows :
Arohi : ne, sa, ma; ga, pa; ma, pa, dha, ne, dha, pa;
Avrohi : sa, ne, dha, pa; ma, pa, dha, pa, ma; re, sa.

KESH : *Kesh* which means hair is one of the five *kakaars* of the Khalsa brotherhood. One of the injunctions imposed by Guru Gobind Singh at the time of setting up of Khalsa brotherhood in 1699 AD was to forbid shaving or trimming of hair on any part of the body. As such, the long uncut hair and a natural unspoilt beard in case of men are the most visible features of a Sikh. The practice is one of the most distinctive and cherished symbols of Sikhism. According to the Sikh tradition, the first *hukamnama* that Guru Gobind Singh issued to his followers, carried *inter alia*, the stipulation : "In future the Sikhs should come into my presence wearing long hair. Once a Sikh is baptised, he should never trim his hair or shave them," Disregarding the Guru's injunction is a *kurahit* which results in automatic suspension from the Khalsa brotherhood.

Kapur Singh derives the symbolism of *kesh* from the beauty of the cosmic man who is an embodiment of the beautiful and the holy. According to the Adi Granth, the cosmic man has "beautiful nose and long uncut hair"
Sohane nak jin lammare wala (AG, p. 567)
At another point this First Man is said to have "unshaved untrimmed body with a turban on head" "...*sabat soorat dastar sira* (AG, p. 1084). This injunction of not shaving or trimming the hair is also a reaction to Hindu observance of tonsure. [*Parasaraprasna*: Guru Nanak Dev University, pp. 75 ff]

Sikh aesthetics even disapprove of the dyeing of hair which makes a person look different from what he or she is.

KESHADHARI : *Keshadhari* means a Sikh man or woman who observes the prohibition against cutting the hair. It is not synonymous with *amritdhari* who is a Sikh who has undergone formal baptism. In other words, a *keshadhari* may not be an *amritdhari* but it is obligatory for an *amritdhari* to be a *keshadhari*.

KESHGARH SAHIB : Keshgarh Sahib is regarded as one of the five Takhats. It is the most important Sikh shrine at Anandpur. It is rightly the birthplace of the Khalsa. It marks the spot where on a day before the Baisakhi day of 1699 AD *Panj Piaras* offered themselves for sacrifice. It is here that next day they were baptized and a new Khalsa Order was initiated by Guru Gobind Singh.

The present building of the gurdwara came up in the forties of this century. It stands on a hillock. Some of the weapons of Guru Gobind Singh are displayed in the shrine. The most important of these is the *khanda* (double-edged broad sword) which was used by Guru Gobind Singh when he prepared *amrit* (baptismal water, nectar) at the time of inauguration of the Khalsa.

KEVAL : A village in Sirsa district of Haryana about 15 km from Talwandi Sabo. Guru Gobind Singh while going to the Deccan from Talwandi made his first overnight halt here in October 1706 AD. A gurdwara has been dedicated to the Guru's visit.

KHADUR SAHIB : Khadur Sahib has been an important religious centre of the Sikhs. It is an old village about 20 km from Tarn Taran and is sacred to the first three Sikh Gurus. Guru Nanak is said to have visited Khadur to meet his disciple Bhai Jodha. Guru Angad's father had settled here and the Guru made Khadur as his headquarters. It was here that Guru Amardas served Guru Angad and in turn was anointed Guru. Guru Angad spent the major part of his life at Khadur where he finally breathed his last. It has a number of gurdwaras commemorating the holy Gurus : Gurdwara Tapiana Sahib, Gurdwara Angitha Sahib, Gurdwara Tap Asthan, Gurdwara Mal Akhara, Gurdwara Thara Sahib etc.

KHAHRA : See Baoli Sahib

KHAIRABAD : Khairabad is a village about 5 km from Amritsar. Two gurdwaras here are dedicated to Guru Hargobind. Gurdwara Gurplah marks the tree under which the Guru used to rest during his hunting expeditions. Gurdwara Kalapbrichh marks the spot where a group of devotees from Kabul were looted by the dacoits who were punished by the Guru.

KHALSA : *Khalsa* which is derived from *Khalis* literally means pure. In Sikh thought, however, it refers to a distinct brotherhood, entirely different from Hindus or Muslims in outward form, conception of God and Gurus, language and script of scriptures, religious rites, mode of worship, social customs and in its attitude towards caste and creed. It was founded by Guru Gobind Singh on the Baisakhi day of 1699 AD when he prescribed the code of conduct for it including the wearing of five *kakaars*. In a way it was a complete transformation of the Sikh community as set up by Guru Nanak and consolidated by other Gurus.

A member of the *Khalsa* brotherhood—also called a *Khalsa* is conceived as an ideal Sikh. A sovereign person, the *Khalsa*, fit to provide true leadership and meaningful service to society, must be a person of deep religious faith and humility and must be in possession of the power of arms to maintain his own integrity and to function truly in relation to the society. "All the virtues of heart and excellence of mind—these are the natural qualities of the *Khalsa*. This is to be a new and unique type of man, who bears arms and constantly lives in the presence of God and who strives and fights against evil with his gaze rivetted to the stars. Such is the goal to achieve for which the *Khalsa* has been ordained. And lo, it is a well-armed and well-integrated man." (*Gurpartapsurya; ain*1, *ansu* 36)

Guru Gobind Singh had created the *Khalsa* in his own image and the concept was very dear to him.

"Khalsa mero roop hai khas
Khalse meh hau karau niwas
Khalsa mero pind pran
Khalsa meri jan ki jan"
(*Sarbloh Granth*)

Whether the creation of the *Khalsa* brotherhood had any political overtones is a debatable issue. According to Kapur Singh : "Such a party and such a *sangha* (brotherhood), in the very nature of things, must be a group of persons dedicated to the cause which includes political activity and it is in this context that the litany (*Raj karega khalsa*) which is repeated in every Sikh congregation, throughout the world, is to be understood and appreciated. The order of the *Khalsa*, as divorced from political activity and not dedicated to the achievement of political ends, aiming at eventual establishment of universal equalitarian global fraternity, has no intelligible connotation." (*Parasaraprasana*; p.40). It is a historical fact that the creation of the Khalsa generated considerable fear and animosity among the hill chiefs. They conspired with the Mughal forces to subdue the *Khalsa*.

KHAN CHHAPRI : A village about 8 km from Goindwal. It was originally known as Khanpur. Some villagers just call it Chhapri. The village was visited successively by Guru Angad, Guru Amardas, Guru Arjan and Guru Hargobind. It has a historical gurdwara Chhapri Sahib at the site of the hut (*chhapri*) of

Bhai Hema where Guru Arjan and his retinue had taken shelter when caught in rain and storm.

KHANDA : *Khanda* is the emblem of the Khalsa. It consists of a two-edged sword (which itself is known by the name khanda), circled by a *chakar* (quoit) and the two being flanked by two swords.

The two-edged sword at the centre of the *khanda* symbolizes disintegration of false pride and vanity and demolition of the barriers of caste and other inequalities. The *amrit* which is used at the time of Baptism is stirred with the *khanda* (two-edged sword). The original *khanda* with which Guru Gobind Singh stirred the baptismal waters on March 30, AD 1699 is now preserved at Anandpur.

The *chakar* being a circle without a beginning or an end exhorts the Sikhs to make the whole creation as the object of their compassion and activities.

The two *kirpans* (swords) flanking the quoit represent the two swords of Guru Hargobind signifying the spiritual and temporal leadership of Gurus. Apart from giving it symmetry, the two *kirpans* impart a conceptual balance to the *khanda* like the yin and yang of ancient Chinese philosophy.

KHANDOOR (KHANDUR) : Khandoor is a village about 25km from Ludhiana. It has a gurdwara dedicated to Guru Hargobind called Manji Sahib.

KHANWAL : Khanwal was a village in Amritsar district. The religious centre of Tarn Taran was set up by Guru Arjan in a portion of the land of this village purchased by the Guru. (See Tarn Taran.)

KHARAK BHOORA : Kharak Bhoora is a village near Narwana. Guru Tegh Bahadur had passed through it on his way to Delhi. A gurdwara near the village marks the spot where the Guru had halted.

KHARAK SINGH : Kharak Singh was the eldest son of Maharaja Ranjit Singh. He was born to Maharani Datar Kaur in 1803 AD. After the death of Maharaja Ranjit Singh in 1839 AD, he ascended the throne at Lahore. His reign did not last long. He became a victim of a court conspiracy hatched by crafty Dhian Singh Dogra who had him replaced by his son Naunihal Singh. Kharak Singh remained sick there-after and passed away in 1840 AD.

KHARI BIR : See Banno, Bhai

KHATKAR : Khatkar is a village near Narwana. Guru Tegh Bahadur had visited it during his travels. According to the Sikh tradition some thieves stole and took away the Guru's horses when he was camping here. As a consequence the thieves lost their eye-sight. They felt repentant and returned the horses. Since the water in the village wells was brackish, the Guru is believed to have helped the villagers in locating the spot where they could dig for sweet potable water. A gurdwara in the village commemorates the Guru's visit.

KHATRI-SIKHS : Khatri-Sikhs constitute a major group in the Sikh community. They were converted to Sikhism from among the Hindu mercantile classes. Incidentally all the Sikh Gurus were *Khatris*.

Khatri-Sikhs, by and large, live in towns and cities and are engaged in business and commerce. They are famous for their undiluted devotion to Sikhism.

KHEM KARAN : A small border town in Amritsar district. It has two historical shrines: Gurdwara Thamm Sahib which is sacred to Guru Amardas, the relic of the long pillar (*thamm*) given by him to Bhai Kheda having been destroyed in the Indo-Pakistan war in 1965 AD and Gurdwara Gurusar Sahib which marks the site where Guru Tegh Bahadur had stayed.

KHERI : See Gangu.

KHIALA : Khiala is a group of three villages

about 8 km from Mansa. Guru Tegh Bahadur had halted outside the villages at a spot where he got a well dug and also planted a *ber* tree which exists upto now.

The group of villages has three gurdwaras commemorating the Guru's visit.

KHIDRABAD : Khidrabad is a town near Kharar which has a gurdwara dedicated to Guru Gobind Singh. The Guru had halted here on his way to Anandpur. Bhai Santokh Singh in his *Gurpartap Surya* mentions about a battle fought by the Guru near here.

KHIDRANA : See Muktsar.

KHIVA KALAN : A village in Mansa district. Guru Tegh Bahadur passed through it during his travels in the region. A gurdwara marks the site where the Guru had camped.

KHIVI, MATA : Mata Khivi was the wife of Guru Angad. She was the daughter of Devi Chand, a Marwaha Khatri belonging to village Sanghar near Khadur Sahib. She was married to the Guru in 1519 AD and gave birth to four children—two sons, Dasu and Datu and two daughters, Amro and Anokhi. Some chroniclers, however, mention only three children, leaving out Anokhi. Mata Khivi passed away in 1582 AD at Khadur Sahib.

KHUSRAU : Prince Khusrau was the son of Jahangir and grandson of Akbar the Great. After the death of Akbar in October 1605 AD, the throne was contested by Khusrau who was just 13 at that time. He did not succeed and was captured. But he managed to escape from Agra fort on April 6, 1606 AD and made for Punjab. The prince knew Guru Arjan whom he had met earlier in the company of Akbar. So he sought benediction of the Guru at Tarn Taran where he was then staying. The Guru received him warmly and applied saffron *tilak* on his forehead. According to Macauliffe (The Sikh Religion IV, p 271), the Guru gave a few thousand rupees to the prince. Beni Parsad (*History of Jahangir*, p. 130) puts this amount at Rs 5000. Khusrau was ultimately arrested and partially blinded by Jahangir. His meeting with Guru Arjan also became a sore point with him against the Guru.

KHWAJA ANWAR : Khwaja Anwar was one of the generals of Shah Jahan who along with Kale Khan and Painde Khan took part in the Kartarpur (Jalandhar) operation against Guru Hargobind. Before the actual battle he came to spy on the Guru's forces. He died in the battle at the hands of Bidhi Chand.

KIARA SAHIB : Kiara Sahib marks the historical spot in Nankana Sahib where the cattle tended by Guru Nanak in his childhood had eaten a field of crop (*kiara*). According to the Sikh tradition when the complaint was enquired into, the field was found in tact.

KILA RAIPUR : A small town in Ludhiana district. It is believed that Guru Hargobind halted here during his journey from Dehlon to Gujjarwal in 1631 AD. A gurdwara called Damdama Sahib commemorates the Guru's visit.

KIRAT : *Kirat* in Punjabi means work or labour inspired by the spirit of holiness—it is toiling for one's bread, for goodness, for love for man and for God in the spirit of devotion. Such a toil never goes unrewarded.

Jio goad tio tum sukh pawo, kirat na maitya ja-ae (AG, p. 1171)

According to the Sikh tradition when Guru Nanak started practising Sikhism by setting up an ideal Sikh community at Kartarpur (Pakistan) during the last eighteen years of his life, he gave three commandments to his followers: *Kirat karo; Wand chakko;* and *Nam japo* which mean: Do honest labour; share the fruits of your labour with others; and worship the Name of God. Since then *kirat* has become a part of Sikh ethics. It knits the Sikhs with the whole humanity of labourers by teaching them the dignity of labour.

The pride of place given to *kirat* in Sikh ethics has its natural corollaries. Anything earned without *kirat* is less than virtuous. Not to speak of stealing or robbing which are universally accepted as crimes, Sikhism disapproves of even begging as a means of making both ends meet. That is why one does not find beggars among the Sikhs. Because of the importance of *kirat*, Sikhism also puts its weight against gambling which otherwise contradicts Hukam (God's will) also.

KIRAT BHATT : *Bhatt* Kirat has contributed eight *swayyas* to the Adi Granth, four each in praise of Guru Amardas and Guru Ramdas. According to modern research Kirat was the son of Bhikha. He enlisted in the army of Guru Hargobind and was killed in the first battle that the Guru fought against the Mughals.

KIRATPUR : Kiratpur, on the banks of Sutlej, near Anandpur, has a long association with the Sikh Gurus. Guru Nanak visited the place when it was little more than a wilderness. Guru Hargobind founded the village and spent the last few years of his life there. Guru Har Rai and Guru Harkrishan were anointed in Kiratpur. Guru Hargobind and Guru Har Rai died in Kiratpur and the ashes of Guru Harkrishan were also immersed there in the Sutlej. The ninth and tenth Gurus were also connected with the place. Kiratpur has several small but important historical gurdwaras: Charan Kamal Sahib (reminiscent of Guru Nanak's visit), Shish Mahal (where Guru Har Rai and Guru Harkrishan were born), Kot Sahib (where Guru Har Rai and Guru Harkrishan were anointed), Babban Garh (where Guru Gobind Singh took charge of the head of Guru Tegh Bahadur after his martyrdom at Delhi), Patal Puri(where Guru Hargobind and Guru Har Rai and the ashes of Guru Harkrishan were immersed in the Sutlej), Harmandir Sahib, Damdama Sahib etc.

KIRPAL CHAND : Kirpal Chand was the brother of Mata Gujri—maternal uncle of Guru Gobind Singh. He was a brave man who showed exemplary valour in the battle at Bhangani, a mention about which has been made by Guru Gobind Singh in his *Bachitra Natak*. Kirpal Chand outlived Guru Gobind Singh and after him undertook the responsibility of managing the holy shrines at Amritsar. The date of his death is not known.

KIRPAL DAS : Kirpal Das was an *Udasi mahant* and a warrior. He fought for Guru Gobind Singh in the battle at Bhangani and is known for killing Hyat Khan who had betrayed the Guru. Guru Gobind Singh had presented him with a *saropa* for his bravery.

Kirpal Das had his headquarters at village Heharan in Ludhiana district. After the battle at Chamkaur in December 1705 AD, Guru Gobind Singh changed over to the blue attire of a *pir* for a disguise at Machhiwara and reached Heharan. Here Kirpal Das looked after the Guru well and at the time of his departure, he helped in carrying the Guru on a cot on his shoulders for a few kilometres. A gurdwara at Heharan is dedicated to Guru Gobind Singh and Guru Hargobind. The latter is also believed to have visited the village earlier.

KIRPAN : *Kirpan* which means sword is one of the five *kakaars*—external symbols with their names beginning with 'K'— the wearing of which was made obligatory for the Khalsa brotherhood set up by Guru Gobind Singh in 1699 AD. Basically it is a mark of identity and belonginess to the Panth. Scholars also interpret the wearing of *kirpan* in terms of deeper symbolism.

According to Kapur Singh, *kirpan* is a symbolic weapon which cuts at the very roots of *avidya*, nescience, that separates the transient individual self from the immortal universal self. Unlike the dagger, *kirpan* is associated with open combat and is therefore symbolic of the Sikh way of life representing an intelligent aggressive and useful citizenship of the world. More importantly wearing a *kirpan* is symbolic of Khalsa's freedom and sovereignty (*Parasaraprasna*): Guru Nanak Dev Uni, Amritsar ; pp. 107-8)

The *kirpan* has a chequered history. Although Sikhism required its followers to wear *kirpans*, the law of the country stood in their way. The Sikhs had to struggle for it. It was in June 1914 AD that the possessing and wearing of *kirpan* was allowed by law in Punjab. Other provinces took a little longer. It was in May 1917 AD that it was allowed throughout India. But the prosecutions still continued. In March 1922 AD, the government and the Shiromani Gurdwara Committee came to an understanding about the *kirpan*. It was agreed that the government would not interfere with the Sikhs for wearing *kirpans* as long as they ordinarily wear them by the side and do not unsheath them except for purely religious purposes.

Keeping in view this history, the Indian Constitution adopted after independence, while granting the fundamental right to freedom of religion, explained that "the wearing and carrying of *kirpans* shall be deemed to be included in the profession of Sikh religion." In spite of this, sometimes there is a controversy regarding the length of the *kirpan* particularly in the context of carrying it on air-flights where weapons are not allowed.

KIRTAN : *Kirtan* or *Shabad Kirtan* is the expression used for the singing of the hymns of the Guru Granth Sahib according to the prescribed classical *raags*. The singing of the hymns from the Dasam Granth and the compositions of Bhai Gurdas is also called *kirtan*. In Sikh tradition it is the most approved mode of congregational worship. It creates an aura of spirituality. It enables the individual to attend and participate in the congregation and to take advantage of the spiritual environment leading to temporal and social understanding and happiness. It helps to elevate the mind to full spiritual heights and attempts to bring peace and repose to it. "Wherever the saints congregate, they sing the Lord's praise with the accompaniment of music and poetry".

Jah sadh santan hovai ekrat, tah har jas gavai nad kavit (AG, P. 676)

Guru Arjan has summarized the importance of *kirtan* when he says :

Jaiso Gur updaisia main taiso keha pukar;
Nanak kahai sun re mana, kar kirtan ho-ai udhar (AG, p.214).

This means "I am giving you the message of the Guru. Nanak says; O mind if you indulge in *kirtan*, you liberate yourself." It is further elaborated : "Some sing, some listen and others reflect. Similarly some sermonize while others enshrine the wisdom. But all are liberated."
Koee gawai ko sunai, koee karai bichaar; ko updaisai ko drirai tis ka hoae udhar (AG, p. 300)

Sikhism, therefore, advises : "Do what shall keep you free from impurity so that your mind awakens to *kirtan*".

So kichh kar jit mail na lagai;
Hari kirtan meh aiho man jagai
(AG, p. 199)

In conclusion we may add the oft repeated expression of Guru Arjan about *kirtan* : "Kirtan is a priceless jewel. Its deep merits give us Divine Bliss".

Kirtan nirmolak hira
Anand gunni gahira
(AG, p. 893)

KNOWLEDGE : Knowledge (Gian) has been given its appropriate place in Sikh thought. The ultimate aim of human existence is the pursuit of Truth and truthful living. But knowledge is taken as a means towards that end as it shows the way by removing ignorance. "As with the appearance of the sun, the moon disappears, so with the attainment of knowledge , ignorance is dispelled." (AG, p. 791). In the hierarchy of cognitive domain called *Gian, dhian, simran jugti* (i.e. knowledge, concentration, understanding and thinking), knowledge is the starting point and man is supposed to go much above that. The Sikhism's view about knowledge is best described by Guru Arjan :

Gian, dhian, kichh karam na jana, nahin nirmal karmi; Sadh sangat kai anchal lawo bikham nadi jaye tarni (AG, p. 702)

"Knowledge and concentration may not lead to the path of *dharma*. Man's activities are not always pure. It is the company of saints which leads him across this world."

KOT BHAI : Kot Bhai is a well known village about 8 km from Giddarbaha. It is sacred because of its association with Guru Gobind Singh. Two gurdwaras in the village have been dedicated to the Guru. One commemorates the Guru's partaking his meals with his devotees who were originally *banias*. The other marks the site where the Guru has stayed on his way from Guptsar.

KOT DHARMU : See Soolisar.

KOTHA GURU KA : Kotha Guru ka is a village in Malwa about 25 km from Jaito. It was established by Baba Pirthi Chand, the elder brother of Guru Arjan, in 1596 AD. According to the Sikh tradition, Solhi Khan, who was an official of Jahangir and was very friendly with Baba Pirthi Chand, was roasted alive when he fell into the hot brick oven at Kotha Guru ka during his visit there.

KOTHA MALUKA : Kotha Maluka sometimes known as just Maluka is a village in Malwa about 20 km from Jaito. A gurdwara has been dedicated here to Guru Gobind Singh who had visited the place. According to the Sikh tradition, when the Guru was resting in his camp, a crazy *Sadhu* came and insisted on meeting him. He was wounded in the skirmish with the bodyguards of the Guru. In the meantime the Guru woke up and called him in but he died soon after meeting the Guru.

KOTHARI SAHIB, GURDWARA : Kothari Sahib is one of the historical gurdwaras at Sultanpur Lodhi. While Guru Nanak was serving the Nawab as *modi* (Storekeeper) in his *modikhana*, a complaint was made to the Nawab that he was mismanaging the stores and squandering state wealth. The Guru was kept under arrest while the accounts were being checked. The lock-up is virtually a tiny dungeon where Gurdwara Kothari Sahib stands today.

KOTHA SAHIB : Kotha Sahib is a gurdwara in village Udoke about 8 km from Batala. Guru Nanak had visited the village on his way to Batala.

KOT KALYANI, MATA : Mata Kot Kalyani was one of the wives of Guru Har Rai. See also Krishan Kaur, Mata.

KOTKAPURA : See Kapura, Chaudhry.

KOT MIRZA JAN : Kot Mirza Jan is a village between Batala and Kalanaur. Banda Singh Bahadur had started the construction of a fortress here. But the attack from the imperial forces came too soon and he had to abandon it and take shelter in the *ihata* of Bhai Duni Chand in Gurdas-Nangal near Gurdaspur where he was ultimately captured after a long siege in December 1715 AD.

KOT SAMHIR : Kot Samhir is a village near Bhatinda. Guru Gobind Singh had come here from Talwandi Sabo (Damdama Sahib). A gurdwara commemorates the visit.

KRISHAN AVTAR : A composition by Guru Gobind Singh included in the Dasam Granth. It was composed in 1688 AD at Paonta, a little before the battle of Bhangani. In ten verses, the Guru describes heroic and parental sentiments.

KRISHAN KAUR, MATA : Mata Krishan Kaur was the wife of Guru Har Rai and mother of Guru Harkrishan. Her sister Kot Kalyani was also married to Guru Har Rai and was the mother of Ram Rai who was elder to Guru Harkrishan. Mata Krishan Kaur and Mata Kot Kalyani were the daughters of Daya Ram, a resident of Anupshahar in Uttar Pradesh and were married to Guru Har Rai in 1640 AD.

KRISHAN LAL : Krishan Lal was one of the court poets of Guru Gobind Singh. He translated the Mahabharata into Hindi poetry. Gobind Gita which he attributed to Guru Gobind Singh was in all probability written by him. It contains 18 chapters of the Bhagvat Gita in the poetic style of Krishan Lal and not of the Guru.

KRODH : See Wrath.

KUBB : See Tahla Sahib.

KUKAS : See Namdharis.

KURAHTS : *Kuraht* in Punjabi means prohibition. In Sikh tradition, *kurahts* refer to the vows of abstenance that a Sikh has to take at the time of his initiation into the Khalsa. These are :
1. Not to trim or shave hair of the body;
2. Not to eat kosher meat or that obtained by similar semitic methods ;
3. Not to have unnatural sex gratification or sexual relationship outside the marital bond ;
4. Not to use tobacco.

Breach of any of these vows results in automatic suspension from the Khalsa brotherhood and re-initiation ceremony of *amrit* administration in full is then necessary, after penance, for restoration of the original status. One who infringes the above code is known as a *patit* (apostate).

KURUKSHETRA : The holy town of Kurukshetra, the scene of the battle of Mahabharata, was visited by several Sikh Gurus. It has a number of shrines connected with them.

The foremost among them is Gurdwara Sidh Bati Sahib which is located near the sacred tank. Guru Nanak came here at the time of solar eclipse when the place attracts a large number of pilgrims.

Adjoining the town of Thanesar, and towards the west of Mohalla Khakrob, is a gurdwara associated with Guru Amardas and Guru Har Rai. Close to the Senayat tank is a gurdwara at a place graced by Guru Hargobind.

Kurukshetra has atleast four more historical gurdwaras that remind us of Guru Tegh Bahadur and Guru Gobind Singh.

KUVRESH : Kuvresh was one of the court poets of Guru Gobind Singh. Besides other compositions, he is known for the translation of a part of the Mahabharata into Hindi poetry.

L

LABOUR : See Kirat.

LACHHAMI, MATA : Mata Lachhami whom chroniclers also refer to as Bakhat Kaur, Bhup Kaur or Rup Kaur was the mother of Guru Amardas and wife of Baba Tej Bhan, a Bhalla Khatri of village Baserke in Amritsar district. Bibi Amro, daughter of Guru Angad was married to one of her grandsons.

LADDHA, BHAI : A widely respected Sikh who lived in Lahore during the time of Guru Arjan. According to some chroniclers *Bhatts* Satta and Balwand had been punished by Guru Arjan for their arrogance by banishing them from his presence. He had also declared that anyone pleading pardon for them would face punishment of riding through the town astride a donkey. Bhai Laddha came to their rescue when they were penitent even at the risk of the Guru's displeasure. He came to the Guru's presence riding a donkey leaving the *Bhatts* at the gate. On this the Guru pardoned Satta and Balwand and readmitted them to the *sangat*.

LAHA : Laha is a village in the foothills of Shivalik whose residents had stolen a camel belonging to Guru Gobind Singh. According to the Sikh tradition, on hearing the news, the Guru had remarked that this is not *laha* (profit) but *tota* (loss). Since then the village is also known as Tota. The Guru camped here for twelve days after the battle of Bhangani. It has a gurdwara named Tota Sahib dedicated to the Guru.

LAHAURA SINGH : Lahaura Singh was an attendant for the sons of Guru Gobind Singh at Anandpur. According to the Sikh tradition he had borrowed money from one Bhai Mala Singh and refused to return it inspite of repeated requests and instead quoted scriptures : Lekha koee na puchhai jaan Harbakhsanda (where Guru forgives, don't ask for accounts). Since he was very close to the Guru's residence, he overheard it and in reply loudly recited : Haq parayea Nanaka us soor, us gaa-ai (To usurp the right of others is pork for the Muslims and beef for the Hindus). On hearing this Lahaura Singh paid back his debt.

LAHILI KALAN : A village 15 km from Hoshiarpur. It has a historical gurdwara Jand Sahib raised in honour of Guru Har Rai who visited it during one of his journeys from Kiratpur to Kartarpur (Jalandhar). The *jand* tree believed to have existed since the time of the Guru's visit and lending its name to the gurdwara is about 30 metres from the main building.

LAHORE : Lahore which is now the second largest city of Pakistan has been a prominent city of north India since medieval times. It was the capital of the Sikh kingdom set up by Maharaja Ranjit Singh. It is also associated with a number of Sikh Gurus. It was visited by Guru Nanak. Guru Ramdas was born here in Chuna Mandi. Guru Arjan was martyred here. Guru Hargobind had encamped here for some time. Bhai Mani Singh and Bhai Taru Singh were martyred here. As such a number of gurdwaras and memorials to Sikh heroes exist here and they are visited by Sikh *jathas* that are allowed to go to Pakistan at the time of religious festivals or gurpurbs.

LAICHI BER, GURDWARA : It is a small domed structure near the gateway to the Golden Temple. It is named after the *ber* (jujube) tree by its side which yields cardamom (laichi) sized berries. According to tradition Guru Arjan used to sit under the tree to supervise the digging of the holy tank. Mahtab Singh and Sukha Singh when they avenged the desecration of the Golden Temple by Masa Ranghar by killing him on the spot had fastened their horses to this *ber* tree.

LAIL KALAN : Lail Kalan is a village near Sunam in the Malwa region. Guru Tegh Bahadur had camped here. It has a gurdwara dedicated to him.

LAKHAMI CHAND : Lakhami Chand was the younger son of Guru Nanak and Mata Sulakhani. He was born to Mata Sulakhani at Sultanpur Lodhi in 1496 AD. He died at Kartarpur (Pakistan) in 1555 AD. Some chroniclers call him Lakhami Das. His descendants are called Bedi *Sahibzade*.

LAKHAN MAJRA : See Manji Sahib.

LAKHA SINGH : One of the attendants of Guru Gobind Singh at Nanded. He killed one of the Pathans who had conspired to assassinate the Guru in 1708 AD. The other Pathan who actually stabbed the Guru had been done to death by the Guru himself.

LAKHNAUR : The ancestral village of Mata Gujri near Ambala cantonment. Guru Gobind Singh accompanied by Mata Gujri had stayed here for a few months when they were shifting from Patna to Anandpur. A gurdwara managed by the SGPC marks the spot, where they had camped. A well dug under the instructions of Mata Gujri still exists. The cots used by Mata Gujri and Guru Gobind Singh are kept as relics.

LAKHPAT RAI : See Jaspat Rai.

LAL CHAND : Lal Chand was the father-in-law of Guru Tegh Bahadur and father of Mata Gujri. He was a Subhikhia Khatri of village Lakhnaur near Ambala Cantonment but had settled down at Kartarpur (Jalandhar).

LALL : See Gurusar.

LALLA BEG : Lalla Beg was a commander of Shahjahan who took part in the operation against Guru Hargobind at Mehraj. He died in that operation at the hands of the Guru.

LALO, BHAI : Bhai Lalo was a resident of Eminabad (Syyadpur) in Pakistan belonging to backward classes. He was a devotee of Guru Nanak whose contemporary he was. The Guru stayed with him for a number of days. According to Sikh tradition, the Guru recited the hymn: *Jaisi mai aawe khasam ki bani, taisara kari gian wai Lalo* (AG, Raag Tilang). Bhai Lalo's proximity to the Guru raised jealousy in the mind of Khatri administrator of Eminabad Malik Bhago.

LALU, BABA : Baba Lalu was the younger brother of Baba Kalu, father of Guru Nanak. He was born in 1444 AD and passed away in 1542 AD.

LAMBE : A village 6 km from Chandigarh. It has a gurdwara called Amb Sahib commemorating the visit of Guru Har Rai who came and stayed here in a mango grove belonging to a devotee Bhai Kakru. The mango tree under which the Guru sat still exists.

LAMBHWALI : Lambhwali is a village 10 km from Jaito in Faridkot district. The shrines in Dod have sometimes been treated as belonging to Lambhwali. For details see Dod.

LAMMAN (OR LAMME) : See Jatpura.

LANGAH, BHAI : Bhai Langah was a Dhillon jat of the Patti area in Amritsar district. He was a devotee of Guru Arjan and did lot of service at the time of the construction of Amritsar. He was also imprisoned and tortured along with Guru Arjan. Mai Bhago was the grand daughter of one of his cousins.

LANGAR : *Langar* is the name given to the institution of free community kitchen which has become an essential part of every gurdwara. Puran Singh calls it the 'temple of bread.' Consistent with the principle of *Wand Chhakna*—Sharing one's food with others—*Langar* is open to all devotees and pilgrims. Every devout Sikh is expected to contribute to it either by donating food stuffs or by participating in the cooking and serving of food.

Guru Nanak set up the first *langar* at Kartarpur (Pakistan) where people brought corn and fuel and worked for preparing and serving of common meals. Guru Angad extended it further and used to serve meals personally. Guru Amardas turned it into an institution and ordained that all visitors to him must first participate in the *langar*. *Pehlay pangat, peechhay sangat*—first common meals, then congregation. Even Emperor Akbar and Raja of Haripur who came to see him had to sit with the common people for *langar*. The scope of *langar* was further widened by Guru Ramdas who ordained that water and meals be served to travellers and squatters. Guru Arjan and his wife used to serve water personally. They even massaged the weary travellers and fanned them to sleep. Over time, *langar* has been institutionalized.

LAWAN : *Lawan* refers to the four stanzas of the nuptial hymn composed by Guru Ramdas in *Raag Suhi*. They appear on pages 773 and 774 of the Adi Granth.

Recitation of *lawan* is an essential part of *Anand Karaj* (Sikh wedding). See Marriage. The couple, generally, do circumambulation of the Guru Granth Sahib when each stanza is being recited.

The first round is the Divine consent for commencing the householder's life through *Anand Karaj*. Through the second round, it is stated that the union of the couple has been brought about by God Himself. Through the third round the couple is described as the most fortunate as they have sung the praises of the immaculate Lord in the company of saints. Through the fourth round the feeling of the couple that they have obtained their heart's desire and are being congratulated is described.

LEHNA : Lehna was the original name of Guru Angad. It was changed to Angad by Guru Nanak.

LIFE : The mysteries of life have been no less important to Sikhism than to other religions. Sikhism takes the view that life is a union of the body and the soul brought about by God. "On six round pillars is our body erected in which is placed the unique object (soul). Breath is its key and lock. In an instant has the Creator made it."

Khat nem kar kothari bandhi bastu anoop bich paa-ee, Kunji kulf pran kar raakhe karte bar na laa-ee (AG, p. 339)

Sikhism also subscribes to the Hindu doctrine of birth-rebirth in accordance with the Law of *Karma* but tempered with the God's Grace. The soul goes on changing the body as one would change old garments. An idea which clearly comes out of Sikh thinking on the topic is that human existence is the acme of the transmigration of soul and is achieved with great difficulty and hard work. It is like the ripe fruit which once fallen from the branch cannot be put back. This has been well described by Kabir :

"*Kabir manas janam dulambh hai,
hoe na barai bar
Jeo ban phal pake bhoe girhe,
bahure na laage dar*"
(AG, p. 1366)

Coupled with this theme is the idea that human existence is short "Brief like the spark of lightning off is our sojourn in the world."

"*Damani chamatkar teo wartara jag khe*"
(AG, p. 319)

Being a pragmatic religion, Sikhism draws an immediate corollary that one must follow the path of righteousness in the short spell given to one on this earth. "If you spend 12 hours in loitering about and the rest of 12 hours in sleep, what possible account can you give to the Lord regarding your achievement".

"*Farida char gwayea handh ke
char gwayea samm,
Lekha rabb mangesia,
toon aaho kaireh kamm*"
(AG, p. 1379)

As such Sikhism adores religious and virtuous life—a God-centred existence bereft of egoism. "Accursed is the life which does not achieve the love of God".

Dhrig ewahia jeewna jit Hari preet na paa-ee
(AG, p. 490)

Sikhism gives its best appraisal of the quality of life when it asserts : "Those that live caught in egoism are verily dead; those whose egoism is dead are truly alive."

Jiwat mo-ai, mo-ai se jeewai   (AG, p. 374)

LIKHANSAR : Likhansar is a holy tank in Damdama Sahib (Talwandi Sabo). Guru Gobind Singh used to throw reed pens in it with the explanation that the place would produce good scholars in Punjabi.

LITTAR : Littar is a village near Raikot in Ludhiana district. Guru Hargobind had visited the village during his travels through the Malwa region. A Gurdwara called Manji Sahib commemorates the visit.

LOBH : See Greed.

LOHGARH : *Lohgarh* literally means abode made of steel and has been generally used as a popular name for a fortress. Some of the important *lohgarhs* in Sikh history are :

 1. **Lohgarh, Amritsar** : It is about 1 km from the Golden Temple in Amritsar. A fort of the same name was constructed by Guru Hargobind for the defence of Amritsar. The main battle of Amritsar between the Guru and an imperial force was fought here in May 1629 AD. The fort was razed by Ahmad Shah Abdali in the eighteenth century. A gurdwara has now been constructed at the site.

 2. **Loghgarh, Anandpur** : It was one of the five forts constructed by Guru Gobind Singh to protect Anandpur. It is about 1.5 km southwest of Takhat Keshgarh Sahib. The place has now been converted into a gurdwara. The present three-storeyed octagonal building was constructed in the late eighties of the twentieth century.

 3. **Lohgarh, Dina** : This is the place near village Dina in Faridkot district, where Guru Gobind Singh had stayed for a few days after the Battle of Chamkaur. It is from here that he dispatched his famous letter *Zafarnama* to Aurangzeb. The present building of the gurdwara was constructed during the eighties of the twentieth century.

 4. **Lohgarh, Gurdaspur** : This is the fort of Banda Singh Bahadur near Gurdaspur. It was constructed in 1712 AD.

 5. **Lohgarh, Sadhaura** : After the capture of Sirhind, Banda Singh Bahadur was the virtual master of territories between the Yamuna and the Sutlej. He made the old fort of Mukhlisgarh near Sadhaura his head-quarters and renamed it Lohgarh. Mughal forces with Emperor Bahadur Shah at their head moved against Banda Singh Bahadur and laid a cordon to Lohgarh in December 1710 AD, but could not capture Banda Singh Bahadur. Heavy fighting had also taken place here between the forces of Farrukhsiyar who had succeeded Bahadur Shah in 1713 AD and those of Banda Singh Bahadur who had recaptured Lohgarh after the death of Bahadur Shah.

LOHRI : *Lohri* is the fire festival which is celebrated by Sikhs along with the rest of north Indians. It is believed that the number of folk songs in Punjabi relating to *Lohri* are the largest proving thereby that it is one of the most popular festivals of Punjab.

Lohri is a secular festival. Its only relationship with Sikhism is that it always falls on the eve of Maghi which is celebrated in memory of the martyrdom of the *Chalis Mukte*.

LOPO : See Gurusar.

LUDHIANA : One of the major cities in Punjab. It has a historical shrine called Gurdwara Gau Ghat situated on the bank of the stream Buddha Nala. According to the local tradition Guru Nanak had visited the site in the course of his travels during the early sixteenth century.

LUST : Lust or *kam* in Punjabi is treated as one of the chief vices according to Sikhism. The concept of *kam* is, however, older than Sikhism.

The reference to *kam* is found in the utterances of all the Gurus but we find a detailed reference to it in the writings of Guru Arjan. In a passage of the Adi Granth he has this to say : *O kam*, you send men to hell and make them wander through myriad wombs. You cheat all minds; sway all the three worlds; and vanquish all one's austerities, meditation and culture. Your pleasures are illusory; you make us unsteady and weak; and punish the high and the low alike." (AG, p. 1358). Sikhism criticizes *kam* as a learnt sentiment and not wholly as a biological one. It does not treat normal sexual relationships as immoral. It is only the heightened passionate sensualism which may overpower all the activities of the self which is treated as a moral sickness and an evil.

M

MACHHIWARA : Machhiwara is a village about 40 km from Ludhiana and is associated with Guru Gobind Singh. The Guru had halted here in 1705 AD after the battle of Chamkaur. A beautiful gurdwara has been built on the outskirts of Machhiwara at a site where the Guru had rested in a garden. Here he composed his famous song : "Convey to my Beloved the plight of his humble servant.".

Mitr piare noo haal muridaan da kehna

MADDO-KE : Maddo-ke is a village near Moga. Guru Hargobind during his visit to the place is said to have reformed thieves here. A gurdwara has been dedicated to the Guru.

MADDOO : See Saddoo.

MADHO DAS : Original name of Banda Singh Bahadur.

MAEESAR KHANA : Maeesar Khana is a village in the Malwa region. Guru Tegh Bahadur had visited it during his travels in that area. A gurdwara has been dedicated to the Guru. Near it is a pond known as Titarsar where the Guru is said to have hunted a partridge (*titar*).

MAGHI : Maghi is an important festival of the Sikhs which is held on the first day of the month of Magh (BS) which falls on 14th January every year—a day following Lohri. It coincides with *Makar Sankranti* of the Hindus.

Maghi is celebrated in memory of the Martyrdom of the *Chalis Mukte* at Muktsar. The Sikhs visit gurdwaras and listen to *Shabad Kirtan*. The largest congregation is genrally at Muktsar where a big fair is also held on this day.

MAHADEV, BABA : Baba Mahadev was the middle son of Guru Ramdas and Bibi Bhani and therefore the elder brother of Guru Arjan. He was born in 1560 AD. He led a quiet spiritual life and passed away in 1605 AD at Goindwal.

MAHADEVI, MATA : Mata Mahadevi who is also referred to as Mata Marwahi by some chroniclers was one of the wives of Guru Hargobind (others being Mata Nanaki and Mata Damodari). She was the daughter of Daya Ram Marwaha, a Khatri of Mandawli. She was married to the Guru in 1615 AD. She passed away at Kiratpur in 1645 AD.

MAHALLA : The word *Mahalla* occurs very frequently in the Guru Granth Sahib as it has been used to indicate the authorship of compositions included in it by the Sikh Gurus rather than by their names. Thus *Mahalla*1 stands for Guru Nanak, *Mahalla* 2 for Guru Angad, and so on. Within the text of the composition, a common pseudonym Nanak has been used for all the Gurus. It serves a double purpose. It provides not only a unifying principle for the Guru Granth Sahib but also demonstrates the unity in the teachings of all the Gurus—all of them having the same *jyoti* which is now enshrined in the Guru Granth Sahib.

Mahalla may be taken to mean the ward in a town as also a woman or bride. Both these meanings have been advanced as the reason for its use in the Guru Granth Sahib.

Macauliffe in "The Sikh Religion" gives rather a simplistic explanation. "The hymns of the Gurus and saints are not arranged in the Granth Sahib according to their authors but according to the thirty-one *raags* or musical measures to which they were composed. The first nine Gurus adopted the name Nanak as their *nom de plume* and their compositions are distinguished by *Mahallas* or *quartiers*. The Granth Sahib is likened to a city and the hymns of each Guru to a ward or division of it." (introduction).

Many scholars go by the second interpretation

because of the popular imagery treating the Sikh Gurus as the brides of God. According to Bhai Kahn Singh the word *mahal* can also be considered to be derived from the word *halool* implying the inheritors of the teachings of Guru Nanak.

MAHANT : *Mahant* is a term used in Sikh speech and writings to refer to the men who administered or had the custody of gurdwaras prior to the passing of the Gurdwara Act 1925 AD. Like the institution of *masands* which was abolished by Guru Gobind Singh (See Manji), the institution of *mahants* also became highly corrupted and started working against the interests of the community. The Sikhs had to launch an agitation and make supreme sacrifices to get it abolished and replaced by a central organisation, the SGPG, democratically elected under the Gurdwara Act 1925 AD.

MAHA SINGH : Maha Singh was the *jathedar* of *Chalis Mukte* who along with his band of forty had deserted Guru Gobind Singh when he was besieged at Anandpur in 1705 AD after giving a written disclaimer. Nevertheless he, with his *jatha* fought for the Guru in his last battle at Muktsar in 1706 AD in which all of them were killed. He was fatally wounded but alive when the Guru came to the battle field to collect the dead bodies. According to the Sikh tradition, he asked for forgiveness of the Guru and requested that the disclaimer he had written at Anandpur may be torn off before he passed away. The Guru personally cremated Maha Singh and his followers.

MAHTAB KAUR : Mahtab Kaur was the daughter of Gurbaksh Singh and grand daughter of Jai Singh, chief of the Kanhya *misl*. She was married to Maharaja Ranjit Singh in 1795 AD and died in 1813 AD. Her mother Sada Kaur used to lend support of the Kanhya *misl* to Maharaja Ranjit Singh till 1821 AD when she developed differences with him and as a consequence lost her territory to him.

MAHTAB SINGH : Mahtab Singh was a resident of Miran Kot, a village in the vicinity of Amritsar. To avoid persecution which was rampant in the first half of the 18th century, he had taken up employment in Bikaner. Visitors from Punjab were always sure of a warm welcome in his house. Once a guest brought the news that Massa Ranghar, the *kotwal* of Amritsar had converted the Golden Temple into a dancing hall. This infuriated Mahtab Singh and he started with his friend Sukha Singh to avenge the descration of the Golden Temple. They entered disguised as revenue collectors and beheaded Massa Ranghar in the precincts of the Golden Temple. Mahtab Singh was arrested on information given by a Niranjania of Jandiala which he happened to visit. He was taken to Lahore where he was subjected to tortures on the wheel and crushed to death in 1740 AD.

MAINI SANGAT, GURDWARA : Gurdwara Maini Sangat is about half a kilometre from Harmandir Sahib in Patna. It is here that Guru Gobind Singh used to play in the evening. Maharaja Maini who lived there was very fond of him and used to feed him and his playmates with boiled gram. The *prasad* (sacred food) distributed at the place even now consists of boiled gram.

MAI THAN, GURDWARA : See Agra.

MAJH : An Indian classical *raag* usually sung in the evening before sunset. It is the second from the beginning of the thirty-one *raags* used in the organisation of hymns in the Guru Granth Sahib covering pages 94-150.

MAJHA : See Malwa.

MAJNU-KA-TILLA, GURDWARA : This is a famous historical gurdwara built on the banks of River Yamuna at a place in Delhi sanctified by visits by Guru Nanak, Guru Hargobind and several Muslim *faqirs* (mendicants) and Hindu *sanyasis*. Guru Nanak stayed here with a Muslim divine named Majnu; hence, the name Majnu-ka Tilla. When

Guru Hargobind came to Delhi for a meeting with Jahangir, he also stayed at this place. The Mughal emperor, however, got him arrested and sent him to Gwalior where he was imprisoned in the fort. On release from prison, and while returning to Punjab, Guru Hargobind spent some time again at Majnu-ka-Tilla.

MAKHO : Makho was a notorious dacoit during the times of Guru Tegh Bahadur operating from the Anandpur area. When the Guru founded Anandpur, he left that area. His village Makhowal was merged with Anandpur. For that reason some chroniclers treat Makhowal as the original name of Anandpur.

MAKKHAN SHAH : Makkhan Shah was a Sikh trader belonging to the Labana community from Jehlum district of Pakistan. On escaping a shipwreck he had vowed to offer five hundred gold *muhars* to the Guru. But when he reached Delhi Guru Harkrishan had just passed away saying "Baba Bakale". Accordingly Makkhan Shah with his retinue proceeded to Bakala. Where he found twenty-two claimants for succession to the position of the ninth Guru. He interviewed all of them and helped the followers in identifying Guru Tegh Bahadur who was living then in seclusion at Bakala as the ninth Guru in 1665 AD. He saw to it that Guru Tegh Bahadur was properly installed as the Guru by subduing Dhirmal and other *masands* who had even dared to fire unsuccessfully at the Guru.

MAKKHAN SINGH, BHAI : Bhai Makkhan Singh has been a prominent Head Priest of the Golden Temple. It was largely because of his efforts that Sir H. Lawrence, Resident of Lahore issued on March 24, 1847 AD a general order for the public to show due respect to the Golden Temple and other gurdwaras stating : "The priests of Amritsar having complained of annoyances, this is to make known to all concerned, that by order of the Governor General, British subjects are forbidden to enter the temple (called the Durbar) or its precincts at Amritsar, or, indeed any temple with their shoes on. Kine are not to be killed at Amritsar nor are Seikhs (Sic) to be molested, or in any way to be interfered with. Shoes are to be taken off at the Bhoonga (Sic) at the corner of the Tank and no person is to walk round the Tank with his shoes on."

MALERKOTLA : Malerkotla is an important town in the Malwa region of Punjab. According to the Sikh tradition, its Nawab Sher Muhammad had opposed the killing of the younger sons of Guru Gobind Singh in 1705 AD at the orders of the governor Wazir Khan of Sirhind saying that they could not be guilty of any crime. According to *Gurpartap Surya* Guru Gobind Singh had blessed the Nawab saying: "In Malerian ki jar hari." Since then the Sikh community treats the Muslims of Malerkotla with respect and honour.

Malerkotla was also the centre of Namdhari agitation against cow slaughter in 1812 AD when the Deputy Commissioner of Ludhiana got 49 Sikhs blown up with canon, the Commissioner had 30 of them hanged and Baba Ram Singh was deported to Rangoon.

MALHAR : An Indian classical *raag* usually sung at night and during rainy season. It is twenty-seventh of the thirty-one *raags* used in the organisation of hymns in the Guru Granth Sahib covering pages 1254-1293. The sequence of basic notes followed on it is :
Arohi : sa, re, ma, pa, dha, re, sa..........
Avrohi : sa, dha, pa, ma, sa..........

MALI GAURA : An Indian classical *raag* usually sung in the afternoon. It is twentieth of the thirty-one *raags* used in the organisation of hymns in the Guru Granth Sahib covering pages 984-988. It follows the following sequence of basic notes :
Arohi : sa, re, ga, ma, pa, dha, ne, sa..........
Avrohi : sa, ne, dha, pa, ma, ga, re, sa..........

MALTEKRI : See Hazur Sahib.

MALWA : The plains of Punjab fall into three

main natural divisions : Doaba, Majha and Malwa. Doaba is the region between Sutlej and Beas rivers. Majha is a high upland situated between Beas and Ravi rivers which now extends to some portion of Pakistan. The first six Sikh Gurus had long associations with this tract. Kartarpur (Pakistan), Khadur, Goindwal, Amritsar are all a part of this region. Malwa in local vocabulary is the tract below the river Sutlej-Beas extending upto Ghaggar covering some portions of Haryana. Greater part of this plain used to be sandy before canals came up. It now covers the area bounded by the districts of Ferozepur, Faridkot, Ludhiana, Patiala etc. This region became the home of Sikhs who followed a different line of action from that of their Majha brethren in the struggle for independence. The sandy desert provide them a secluded territory where they could quietly pursue their course of life. The Majha Sikhs often took refuge here when driven by the oppressors.

MANI KHAN : See Jani Khan.

MANI SINGH, BHAI : Bhai Mani Singh was an eminent theologian and a contemporary of Guru Tegh Bahadur and Guru Gobind Singh. At the instance of Guru Gobind Singh, he prepared the final rescension of the Adi Granth.

Bhai Mani Singh was born in a small village near Sunam in Punjab. When he was barely five, his father Kale offered him to Guru Tegh Bahadur. He later on served Guru Gobind Singh and Mata Sundri. In 1721 AD Mata Sundri sent him to Amritsar as the Head Priest of the Golden Temple in which capacity he produced many theological works—the most famous being *Bhagat Ratnavali*.

The celebration of Diwali at Amritsar had been banned by the Turks. Bhai Mani Singh took permission from Zakriya Khan, the governor of Lahore to celebrate Diwali on a payment of Rs. 5000 as tax. The tax could not be paid as the government did not allow the pilgrims to come to Amritsar. For this non-payment of tax, Bhai Mani Singh was executed at Lahore in 1737 AD.

MANJI : *Manji* which literally means a cot in Punjabi is generally used for the seat of the Guru, which meaning is used in the names of various gurdwaras called Manji Sahib. See Manji Sahib for more details. In Sikh writing *manji* is also the word used for the office of a Sikh missionary who is known as a *masand*— from the Persian word *massand* which is synonymous of *manji*. Guru Amardas introduced this office by setting up 22 *manjis* each under a *sangatia* (*masand*) responsible to him. Their main duties were to preach, make decisions on minor matters concerning the affairs of the community. Convey instructions from the Guru and to collect *daswandh*. During the later part of the seventeenth century *masands* grew in importance and the office became hereditary with all the accompanying evils. Guru Gobind Singh abolished the office at the time of the creation of the Khalsa in 1699 AD.

MANJI SAHIB : *Manji* is a Punjabi word for the cot. Manji Sahib is therefore the name given to a raised platform at a place where the Guru had sat. The important Manji Sahibs are :

1. **Manji Sahib, Alo Harakh :** See Alo Harakh.

1(a) **Manji Sahib, Amritsar :** This is situated adjacent to the eastern boundary of the Golden Temple Complex in the area which was formerly known as Guru ka Bagh. Guru Arjan used to hold the daily congregation sitting on a *manji* where a marbled platform has now been raised. Guru ka Bagh has been converted into a large *diwan* hall.

2. **Manji Sahib, Anandpur :** It is situated close to Takht Keshgarh at the place where the sons of Guru Gobind Singh used to play and receive education. It is a double storeyed gurdwara in the middle of a twenty metre square marbled compound.

3. **Manji Sahib, Baba Bakala :** It is a small gurdwara consisting of a glass covered domed pavilion raised over a marbled platform at Baba Bakala. It commemorates the spot where Guru Tegh Bahadur was fired at the behest of his nephew Dhirmal.

4. **Manji Sahib, Bhagrana :** It is situated in

village Bhagrana in Patiala district. Guru Tegh Bahadur had halted here in the course of one of his journeys through the region. The gurdwara was got constructed by Maharaja Karam Singh of Patiala and is now managed by the SGPC through a local committee.

5. Manji Sahib, Birk : It is situated in village Birk in Ludhiana district. Guru Hargobind had come here from Siddhvan Kalan in 1631 AD.

6. Manji Sahib, Budhmar : It is located in village Budhmar in Patiala district and is built to commemorate the visit of Guru Tegh Bahadur to the place during one of his journeys through the Malwa region. Originally constructed by Maharaja Karam Singh has now been replaced by a new building since 1980 AD.

7. Manji Sahib, Buria : It is about 4 km from Jagadhari and is built in honour of Guru Tegh Bahadur's visit to the town of Buria. The management is in the hands of the erstwhile chiefs of Buria.

8. Manji Sahib, Dhaleo : It is situated in village Dhaleo (or Dhalevan) in Bhatinda district. The gurdwara commemorates the visit of Guru Tegh Bahadur to the village and his holding a discourse with a *yogi* whose name was Tulsi Das.

9. Manji Sahib, Dhamtan : It is situated in the village Dhamtan in Jind district of Haryana. Guru Tegh Bahadur had visited the village more than once. The gurdwara constructed by Maharaja Karam Singh of Patiala, commemorates the Guru's visits.

10. Manji Sahib, Duddhi : It is situated in village Duddhi in Kurukshetra district and commemorates the visit of Guru Tegh Bahadur to the place.

11. Manji Sahib, Fatehpur Singhan : It is situated in village Fatehpur Singhan near Ropar and is dedicated to Guru Har Rai.

12. Manji Sahib, Gadial : This is in village Gadial about 20 km from Garh Shankar. Guru Gobind Singh had halted here for some time after his victory at Kheda Kalmot.

12(a) Manji Sahib Jatpura : See Jatpura.

13. Manji Sahib, Kaithal : See Kaithal.

14. Manji Sahib, Kanech : See Kanech.

15. Manji Sahib, Khandoor : See Khandoor.

16. Manji Sahib, Lakhan Majra : It is situated in village Lakhan Majra in Rohtak district of Haryana. Guru Tegh Bahadur had stayed here on his way to Delhi.

16(a) Manji Sahib, Littar : See Littar.

17. Manji Sahib, Mehma Shahanwala : See Mehma Shahanwala.

18. Manji Sahib, Maur : It is situated in village Maur in the Malwa region. Guru Tegh Bahadur had come here from Dhilwan where he was camping.

19. Manji Sahib, Nirmohgarh : See Nirmohgarh.

20. Manji Sahib, Phaguwala : It is situated in village Phaguwala near Sunam and is dedicated to Guru Tegh Bahadur. He had passed through the village during his travels in the Malwa region.

20(a) Manji Sahib, Rampur : It is the inner sanctum of Gurdwara Reru Sahib at Rampur in Ludhiana district. Guru Gobind Singh had halted here in December 1705 AD during his journey from Machhiwara to Malwa region.

20(b) Manji Sahib, Talwandi Sabo : There are two Manji Sahibs at Talwandi Sabo (Damdama Sahib) : (i) Manji Sahib Sri Guru Tegh Bahadur also called Darbar Sahib marks the site where Guru Tegh Bahadur is believed to have stayed and preached; (ii) Manji Sahib Patshahi IX & X where Guru Tegh Bahadur used to sit supervising the digging of the tank, Gurusar and Guru Gobind Singh sanctified it during his stay at Talwandi Sabo.

MANMUKH : *Manmukh* is an emotive and comprehensive word in Sikh literature generally standing as the opposite of *gurmukh*. While a *gurmukh* is a God-centred person, *manmukh* is devoted to self-interest and evil. Guru Nanak has given a fine description of a *manmukh* : "Day and night are the two seasons when he crops his land; lust and anger are his two fields. He waters them with greed, sows in them the seed of untruth, and his ploughman, worldly impulse, cultivates them. Evil thoughts are his plough, and evil the crop he reaps, for in accordance with the Divine Order, he cuts and eats." (AG. p. 955). Obviously for such a person there is no hope for salvation, he continues in the wheel of birth-rebirth.

MANSA DEVI, MATA : Mata Mansa Devi was the wife of Guru Amardas. She was the daughter of Devi Chand, a Bahil Khatri of village Sankhatra in Sialkot district now in Pakistan and was married to the Guru in 1502 AD. She gave birth to four children—two sons, Mohri and Mohan and two daughters, Dani and Bhani. She died at Goindwal in 1569 AD. Some chroniclers refer to her as Ram Kaur.

MANTRAS : See Incantations.

MARDANA, BHAI : Mardana was a *rabab* (rebeck) player who spent many years in the compnay of Guru Nanak and won his grace. Music has a special significance in Sikhism. The *Shabads* (hymns) are recited through *kirtan*. Mardana used to render the message of Guru Nanak in sweet and melodious notes.

Mardana was a Muslim of Nankana Sahib, belonging to the tribe of *dooms,* who are minstrels by heredity. He was the son of Bhai Badre and Mai Lakho. He accompanied Guru Nanak to all the places that he covered during his four long missionary travels. He died during the last journey in Afghanistan on the bank of the river Khuram, where a shrine honours his memory. Guru Nanak had performed the last rites of his companion with his own hands.

Mardana was not a mere musician but also a spiritually elevated soul. Three of his hymns are included in the Adi Granth under *Raag Bihagra*. These hymns denounce drink that engenders evil passions and upholds meditation of the Divine Name that creates a spiritual inebriation.

MARDON : Mardon is a village near Ambala Cantonment. It had been visited both by Guru Tegh Bahadur and Guru Gobind Singh. The latter had come here from the nearby village of Lakhnaur. The village has shrines dedicated to the two Gurus.

MARRIAGE : *Anand Karaj* is the name given to the religious wedding ceremony of the Sikhs. It is the only form of marriage recognized by the Sikh religion and was given a statutory recognition in 1909 AD under the Anand Marriage Act. The Sikh *Rahat Maryada* also enjoins upon all Sikhs to observe only this form of marriage.

Marriage is considered by the Sikhs to be a very sacred institution. It is a religious affair; it is neither a contract, nor a secular business; it is a spiritual union. It is, therefore, performed in the presence of Guru Granth Sahib (Adi Granth).

Anand Karaj can take place without previous betrothal and without waiting for an auspicious day. The wedding may be organized at any place where the Guru Granth Sahib is installed. At the time of wedding, the couple present themselves and occupy seats in front of the Guru Granth Sahib in the presence of relations and invitees with the bridegroom sitting to the right of the bride. The entire ceremony is very simple consisting of the following sequence : (i) Obtaining the consent of the parents and the congregation; (ii) Tying of the nuptial knot by the bride's father; (iii) Reading of the four hymns of marriage (*Lawan*) from the Adi Granth and going round it (which is not compulsory); (iv) General *ardaas;* (v) *wak;* and (vi) Distribution of *karah parsad*. The wedding ceremony must be performed in the morning before noon.

MARU : An Indian classcial *raag* usually sung in the afternoon, but more especially at the time of battles and funeral. It is twenty-first of the thirty-one *raags* used in the organisation of hymns in the Guru Granth Sahib covering pages 989-1106.

MASAND : See Manji.

MASSA RANGHAR : Massa Ranghar was the *kotwal* of Amritsar when Zakariya Khan was the governor of Lahore. The latter had introduced repressive measures against the Sikhs in the first half of the eighteenth century.

With his permission, Massa Ranghar occupied the Golden Temple and converted it into a dancing hall. This was avenged by Mahtab Singh Mirakotia and Sukha Singh in 1740 AD. They came in a disguise and beheaded Massa Ranghar in the premises of the Golden Temple.

MASTUANA : See Atar Singh, Sant.

MATA JITO, GURDWARA : Gurdwara Mata Jito is one of the shrines at Anandpur, situated outside Agampura village about 2 km from Anandpur. It marks the site where Mata Jito, wife of Guru Gobind Singh was cremated in December 1700 AD.

MATA SUNDRI, GURDWARA : Gurdwara Mata Sundri is situated in central Delhi and has been built in memory of the stay there of Mata Sundri and Mata Sahib Kaur, wives of Guru Gobind Singh. When the Guru was leaving for the south, he gave five of his weapons to Mata Sahib Kaur, who at the time of her demise, passed them on to Mata Sundri. The latter lived on till 1747 AD. Three of the weapons have since been lost and the remaining two are preserved in the basement of the shrine.

MATHURA, BHATT : In his 12 *swayyas* included in the Adi Granth, Bhatt Mathura pays tributes to Guru Ramdas and Guru Arjan. He says that the greatness of the Guru lies in his love of and meditation on the name of the Creator which symbolizes Truth. He is an ocean of God's Name and ever bathes in it like a playful child. Bhatt Mathura discerns the same spirit in all the Gurus from Nanak to Arjan. His *swayyas* on Guru Arjan are very popular.

MATI DAS, BHAI : Bhai Mati Das is a famous Sikh martyr. He was a *diwan* (minister) of Guru Tegh Bahadur. He had accompanied the Guru to Delhi along with four other devotees: Gurditta, Uda, Chima and Dayala. Aurangzeb had all of them arrested. For not agreeing to be converted to Islam, Bhai Mati Das was sawed alive in 1675 AD. This happened just before the martyrdom of Guru Tegh Bahadur.

MATTE DI SARAI : Matte di Sarai, now known as Sarai Nanga, is a village in Faridkot district and is about 16 km from Muktsar. The ancestral home of Guru Angad where he was born is located near the village and is now a gurdwara dedicated to the Guru. The village has another gurdwara dedicated to Guru Nanak.

MATTHO-MURARI : Prema, a Khatri of Lahore district was cured of his leprosy by Guru Amardas and was given the name Murari. With the Guru's blessings he was married to Mattho, daughter of another Khatri named Sihan. Both husband and wife were zealous preachers of Sikhism and the couple is remembered in Sikh history as Mattho-Murari and was offered a *manji* by the Guru.

MAU : See Ganga, Mata.

MAUR : See Manji Sahib.

MAUR KALAN : Maur Kalan is a village in the Malwa region near Mansa. It is about one kilometer from Maur. It has a gurdwara dedicated to Guru Tegh Bahadur.

MAYA : The doctrine of *maya* is basic to Hinduism and Buddhism. It is mentioned in the Hindu epics: the Ramayana and the Mahabharata. Various schools of thought in Hindusim have given varying interpretations to it.

According to the Ramayana, *maya* is indeed the whole world as seen through Space, Time and Causation. It is, therefore, unreal in the sense that the only reality is God. "I and thou, mine and thine, this is *maya*; which has all embodied beings under its control. Wherever sense and sense objects go, and as far as the mind can take you; know all that, O brother, to be *maya*." (Aranyakand 1.1, 2,3) The relationship between God, *Maya* and *Jiva* (embodied soul) has also been made clear. "The proud *jiva* is under the control of *maya*. And *maya*, the repository of all qualities, is controlled by God." (Uttarakand, 77.3).

In the Mahabharata, the term *maya* is taken for granted. But it comes out as illusion or a material veil. Everything that exists is sitauted in the *Brahmajyoti* but when the *jyoti* is covered with *maya*, it is called material. In other words, truth covered with *maya* is matter. Thus *maya* is the root cause of duality.

Saints of the Bhakti movement gave their own interpretation of the term *maya*. According to them, it is only *maya* which deflects us from realizing that the whole universe is pervaded by one God (Ishwara) and everything in the universe is his manifestation. So one has to transcend *maya* to understand this reality. The Muslim *sufis* in Punjab held the view that nothing is real except God and everything else is illusion.

In Sikhism *maya* is referred to at two levels : One as mammon and the other as illusion which is God's mystic power by which He created matter. The latter meaning is theologically more prevalent. Like ignorance and nescience *maya* does not have a positive existence.' "What is it that can be called *maya*? What activity can *maya* undertake? The human soul is subject to the pleasure and pain principle in its very nature as long as it operates on the individuated plane of consciousness."

Maya kis no akhi-ai, kia maya karam kamai,
Dukh sukh eh jio badh hai haumai karam kamai.
(AG. p. 67)

"What is *maya* except a befooling magic trick. Yea, a dry blade of grass afire; a passing shadow of summer cloud; a momentary flooding after a tropical rain, for him who is out of communion with God."

Maee maya chhal, trin ki agni, megh ki chhaya,
Gobind bhajan bin Har ka jal (AG. p. 717)

However it is clearly stated that :

"*Maya* is a wall of illusion, a strong perverse intoxicant; it wastes away your life."

Kamla bhram bhit, kamla bhram bhit hai tikhan,
mad biprit hai awadh akarth jat. (AG. p. 461)

Even when interpreted as pure illusion but more so as mammon, Sikhism preaches that *maya* has been created by God. "*Maya* came from the primal source only as a servant. But she has conquered the nine continents and all spaces. She has not spared the *yogis* and ascetics at river banks and holy spots. Even those studying simritis and expounding vedas are helpless."

Dhur ki bhaiji aa-ee, aamre nau khand jitai sabhi than thanantar. Tah tirath na chhode yog sanyas. Par thake Simriti Veda abhyas. (AG. p. 371)

Sikhism is very clear that "*Maya* works within His Will." *Agyakari kini maya* (AG. p. 294). "The Lord who has created *maya* has also created the craving for it."

Jin maya dini tin laa-ee trishna. (AG. p. 179)

Sikhism recognizes the importance of avoiding the illusion to find the way to the Lord. The solution is as simple as worshipping Nam "The whole world is gripped with false *maya*. It is the contemplation of God (Nam) that gives me joy."

Jhoothi maya sabh jag thapia, mai Ram ramat sukh paye-aa (AG. p. 482)

MAZHABI-SIKHS : With its respect for social equality and justice, Sikhism had a considerable attraction for the outcastes and the down trodden among the Hindus. Conversion to Sikhism provided them an immediate social ladder and they came in large numbers. These converts to Sikhism from the scheduled and backward classes of the Hindus came to be known as Mazhabi Sikhs—the Faithful ones. They are zealous protectors of the faith, starting with Bhai Jaita who when there was utter panic in Delhi after the martyrdom of Guru Tegh Bahadur dared to carry his head to Kiratpur for formal cremation.

Inspite of the fact that Sikhism does not approve of caste system the Indian constitution treats Mazhabi Sikhs at par with the scheduled castes among the Hindus according them the same facilities. This has made the Christian *dalits* to ask for a similar status.

MEAT : Sikhism has not taken a rigid dogmatic

stand about eating meat. The considered view is not to emphasize its importance. Sikh *Rahat Maryada* is silent about meat. Many devout Sikhs will not eat any form of meat, rejecting fish as well as eggs. The food offered in *langars* is always vegetarian. For some Sikhs, however cow is the only forbidden animal.

The practice of the Gurus is uncertain. Guru Nanak seems to have eaten venison or goat, depending upon different *Janam Sakhi* versions of meal which he cooked at Kurukshetra which evoked the criticism of Brahmins. Guru Amardas ate only rice and lentils but his abstemiousness cannot be regarded as evidence of vegetarianism, only of simple living. Guru Gobind Singh permitted the eating of meat but he prescribed that it should be *jhatka* meat and not *halal* meat that is jagged in the Muslim fashion.

Kabir, however, favoured a vegetarian diet. He says: "If you say that God resides in all, why do you kill a hen?" AG. p. 1350). "It is cruel to kill animals by force and call it sanctified food." (AG. p. 1375).

The conclusion is : "Men out of ignorance quarrel over this matter, not bother to know what is flesh and what is non-flesh, which food is sinful and which is not." (AG. p. 1289).

MEDANI PRAKASH : Medani Prakash was the raja of the hill state of Nahan (Sirmaur). He ascended the throne in 1678 AD and died in 1694 AD. He loved Guru Gobind Singh and invited him to spend some time in Nahan which he did in 1685 AD. The Guru brought about a reconciliation between Medani Prakash and Fateh Shah, the hill raja of Srinagar (Garhwal). On the land given by Medani Prakash, the Guru got a fort constructed at Paonta Sahib about 40 km from Nahan on the banks of the river Yamuna. See Paonta Sahib.

MEERI AND PEERI : The word *meeri* is a short form of *ameeri* which means riches and royalty and therefore stands for temporal authority. *Peeri* means old age and in religious terms it means holiness and therefore stands for spiritual authority. The first five Sikh Gurus were entirely holy persons but after the martyrdom of Guru Arjan, his son Guru Hargobind, the sixth Guru brought about a transformation in the concept of the Guru by synthesizing in himself *meeri* and *peeri* and the spiritual authorities. The Guru built forts and battlements, donned a royal aigrette in place of the traditional *seli* (the headgear of renunciation) and was known as *Sacha Patshah* (True King). This combination of *meeri* and *peeri* brought about a transformation in the Sikh community. No more did the Sikhs believe in self-denial alone; they grew increasingly aware of the need for assertion also. They reared horses, rode on them and racing and hunting became their pastimes.

According to the Sikh tradition, on the day of *tilak* ceremony of Guru Hargobind, Baba Buddha brought him *seli* but the Guru put it aside respectfully and asked for a sword instead. Baba Buddha who had never handled a sword brought one and put it on the wrong side. The Guru noticed it and asked for another. "I'll wear two swords", said the Guru, "a sword of *shakti* (power) and a sword of *bhakti* (meditation". This gave birth to the new concept of a saint-soldier. Later on he concretized it by constructing the Akal Takht at Amritsar opposite the Golden Temple. While the latter was the spiritual centre Akal Takht became the seat of temporal authority. In fact through *meeri* and *peeri*, Sikhism asserts that there is no such thing as sacred-secular distinction or in other words that politics is a part of religion.

MEHARBAN : Meharban was the son of Baba Pirthi Chand, elder brother of Guru Arjan. Like his father, he also worked against the interests of the Sikh community. He wrote a *Janam Sakhi* of Guru Nanak which contains wrong facts about the Guru, some of which are derogatory.

MEHMA PRAKASH : There are two works bearing this name but written by two different persons. They are: *Mehma Prakash Vartik* and *Mehma Prakash Kavita*. The first was written by Bawa Kirpal Singh Bhalla in 1739 AD. The second was composed in 1776 AD by Sarup Das Bhalla, a descendant of the third Guru, Amardas. The two accounts are basically the same, but the prose version is shorter. It contains 20 stories while the other account has 65 stories. *Mehma Prakash Kavita* is based on *Purtan Janam Sakhi*. It is also sometimes called *Vairowal Wali Janam Sakhi* as it was in possession of the *manji* holders of Vairowal.

MEHMA SHAHANWALA : It is a village near Kotkapura. Guru Gobind Singh had visited the village while passing through that area. Gurdwara Manji Sahib has been dedicated to the Guru.

MEHRA : Mehra was a Khatri resident of Bakala. According to the Sikh tradition when he constructed a new house at Bakala he vowed that he would not use it till it was blessed by the Guru's visit. It is said that Guru Hargobind along with his mother Mata Ganga lived in that house to fulfil Mehra's vow. Mata Ganga passed away in this house.

MEHRAJ : Mehraj is an important village in the Malwa region named after Mehraj, an ancestor of Baba Phul. It has two historical shrines both dedicated to Guru Hargobind. One marks the site where the Guru had stayed on the invitation of Chaudhry Mohan who was the grandfather of Baba Phul. The other one is known as Gurusar and is at about 3 km from the village. Guru Hargobind had fought a battle here. Guru Har Rai had also stayed here once.

MEHRON : See Gurusar.

MIAN MIR : Mian Mir was a nenowned Sufi saint of Lahore. Chroniclers trace his descent from Caliph Umar. He was born in 1550 AD at Sistan is Central Asia. His original name was Sheikh Muhammad. He became a disciple of Sheikh Khizr of the Qadiri order of Sufis and spent a major part of his life at Lahore. Guru Arjan invited him to Amritsar in 1589 AD to lay the foundation stone of the Golden Temple.

In 1606 AD when Guru Arjan was arrested at the orders of Jahangir and imprisoned in Lahore fort, Mian Mir came to see him in the prison and wanted to intercede with Emperor Jahangir on the Guru's behalf. But the Guru dissuaded him from doing so. Years later when Guru Hargobind was imprisoned in the Gwalior fort, chroniclers believe that he was released on Mian Mir's recommendations. Guru Tegh Bahadur had met him as a child.

Mian Mir was highly regarded by Hindus, Sikhs and Muslims. He passed away on August 11, 1635 AD and was buried at village Hashimpur.

MIHAN, BHAI : Bhai Mihan was a devotee of Guru Tegh Bahadur. His original name was Ram Dev and was changed to Mihan by the Guru. He used to store water for the *langar* and also looked after sprinkling of water. The Guru had appointed him as a *mahant*. He also served Guru Gobind Singh with dedication and was presented with a *saropa* by the Guru. His descendants who were *Udasi sadhus* are known as *Mianshahis*.

MINA : *Mina* in Punjabi literally means a person who camoufalges his feelings. In Sikh literature this is a title given by Bhai Gurdas to Baba Pirthi Chand, the elder brother of Guru Arjan. The followers of Pirthi Chand are called Minas. They produced spurious hymns attributed to Guru Nanak in support of their case and this was one of the reasons why Guru Arjan compiled the Adi Granth. The Minas no longer exist and knowledge of them is derived mainly from the writings of their opponents, but the memory of them is kept alive through the vow which Sikhs take to avoid their company at the time of baptism.

MIRA BAI : Mira Bai was the daughter of Raja Rattan Singh Rathod of Merta and was born in 1491 AD. She was married to Prince Bhoj Raj son of Maharaja Rana Sangha of Chittor in 1516 AD. She had a religious bent of mind and was a devotee of Lord Krishna. Her married life was not too happy and after the death of her husband she became a *sanyasin* and went to various pilgrimage centres and finally passed away in 1546 AD. She composed devotional poetry and Bhai Banno included one of her compositions in the Adi Granth without the permission of Guru Arjan. That version of the Adi Granth is called *Khari Bir* and is not in use.

MIR MAHNDI : A composition by Guru Gobind Singh included in the Dasam Granth. In ten verses which comprise it the Guru describes the incarnation of Mir Mahndi of the Shia sect of Muslims.

MIR MANNU : Mir Mannu was the governor of Lahore during the period 1748-53 AD. When he took over, under the utter confusion created by the first invasion of India by Ahmad Shah Abdali, Sikhs had organized themselves into a power force called Dal Khalsa. Although at times, he tried to reconcile with the Sikhs; yet on the whole indiscriminate killings and persecution of Sikhs continued during his reign. There was a folk saying among the Sikhs: "Manu is our sickle; we the fodder for him to mow.

The more he reaps, the more we grow."

(*Manu asadi datri, asi Manu de soe Jeon jeon Manu Wad-da, asi dune chaune hoe*)

During the third invasion of India by Ahmad Shah Abdali in December 1751 AD, Mir Mannu surrendered to him. But after Abdali's departure, he was upset to know that the Sikhs had spread out to Bari Doab, Jalandhar Doab and across Sutlej. He asked Adina Beg, the administrator of Jalandhar to pounce on Sikh pilgrims assembled at Anandpur on the occasion of Hola Mohalla in 1753 AD. Many Sikhs were killed in this operation. He also got the Ram Rauni fort at Amritsar blown up with the entire garrison of 900 people. This was rebuilt as Ramgarh Fort by Jassa Singh Ramgarhia.

Mir Mannu died in November 1753 AD.

MISL : In Sikh history, *misl* is the name given to an army unit. The term was first used by Guru Gobind Singh in the battle of Bhangani in 1688 AD when he organised his forces into eleven *misls*. Banda Singh Bahadur adopted the same organisation of eleven divisions in the battle of Sirhind in 1710 AD. In 1734 AD, Nawab Kapur Singh divided the Khalsa into Buddha Dal and Taruna Dal, both together comprising eleven groups. This division was permanently adopted at the time of the formation of Dal Khalsa under Jassa Singh Ahluwalia in 1748 AD.

Thus traditionally the Khalsa had been organised into eleven *misls*. Some historians tend to count Phulkian as the twelfth *misl*, a view which is not generally accepted. The eleven *misls* were :

1. Ahluwalia
2. Fyzullapuria or Singhpuria
3. Sukarchakia
4. Nishanwalia
5. Bhangi
6. Kanhaya
7. Nakkai
8. Dallewalia
9. Shaheed
10. Karorsinghia
11. Ramgarhia.

MOH : See Attachment.

MOHAN, BABA : Baba Mohan was the elder son of Guru Amardas and Mata Mansa Devi. He was born in 1537 AD. He was a saintly man and had retained with him the *pothis*, the collections of the compositions of the first three Gurus and of some saints and *sufis*. At the time of the compilation of the Adi Granth Guru Arjan persuaded Baba Mohan to lend him the *pothis* so that they could be made the nucleus of the Holy Book. According to the Sikh tradition Guru Arjan achieved his objective by personally visiting Baba Mohan and singing the *shabad : Mohan tere unche mandir mahal apara* below the first floor apartment of Goindwal where he was then residing. This place in Goindwal is known as Mohan ka Chaubara or Chaubara Sahib. Baba Mohan spent his entire life at Goindwal.

MOHAN, CHAUDHRY : Chaudhry Mohan

a Brar chief, was the grandfather of Baba Phul and father of Roop Chand. He was a devotee of Guru Hargobind and was helped by the Guru in his fight against Jaidprana, chief of Bhokhari. He founded Mehraj after the name of one of his ancestors.

MOHI : Mohi is a village in Ludhiana district. Guru Gobind Singh visited it and had his tight ring cut off by an ironsmith which was presented to the cutter. The ring continued to be with the descendants of the ironsmith in a neighbouring village. Mohi has a gurdwara dedicated to the Guru.

MOHRI, BABA : Baba Mohri was the younger son of Guru Amardas and Mata Mansa Devi. He was born in 1540 AD. He led a simple saintly life. According to the Sikh tradition, Guru Amardas has just finished the recording of his composition *Anand Sahib* (or *Anandu*) when he got the news that Baba Mohri had been blessed with a son. Accordingly the child was named Anand after the title of the composition he had just completed.

MOOLA : Moola was a trader of Sialkot who had become a devotee of Guru Nanak and also participated in his travels. According to the Sikh tradition, during his encounter with Hamza Gons of Sialkot, when Guru Nanak sent Bhai Mardana to the market saying : "Go there and buy Truth worth one Paisa and Falsehood worth one Paisa", it was Moola who accepted the bargain giving two chits—one carrying the message "Death is the Truth" and the other "Life is Falsefood." Moola's wife did not like his spending too much time with the Guru. Once when he hid himself in a dark place to avoid the Guru at the prompting of his wife, he was bitten to death by a snake.

MOOL CHAND, BABA : Baba Mool Chand was the father of Mata Sulakhani and father-in-law of Guru Nanak. He was a Chauna Khatri of village Pakkhoke near Batala.

MOONAK : See Tahli Sahib.

MORCHA : The original meaning of the term *morcha* is a trench where soldiers in the battlefield take a defensive position or make a concerted attack on the enemy. It got currency because of the style of agitation used in the Akali Movement since the twenties of the twentieth century. At present it is used to mean a persistent political agitation for a cause by a group or a party.

MORINDA : Morinda is a town near Ropar. Jani Khan and Mani Khan Ranghars belonged to this village. On the information given by Gangu, a Brahmin of the neighbouring village Kheri, they had caught Mata Gujri and two younger *sahibzadas* : Fateh Singh and Zorawar Singh and took them to the governor of Sirhind in 1705 AD. The town was ravaged by the Dal Khalsa in 1762 AD killing Jani Khan and Mani Khan and their supporters. A gurdwara has been constructed in memory of Mata Gujri and the two *sahibzadas*.

MOTI BAGH, GURDWARA : Guru Gobind Singh was proceeding to Deccan to meet Aurangzeb. While at Baghaur in Rajasthan, he heard of the emperor's death, changed his course and came to Delhi. Bahadur Shah sought the Guru's help in gaining the throne. It is believed that Guru Gobind Singh announced his arrival in Delhi by shooting an arrow into the Red Fort from a place called Mochi Bagh and belonging to a trader running a tannery there. This area in South Delhi is now called Moti Bagh and a gurdwara of the same name commemorates the Guru's visit.

MUHKAM SINGH, BHAI : Bhai Muhkam Singh whose orignial name was Muhkam Chand was one of the first *Panj Piare* who had offered their heads to Guru Gobind Singh on the Baisakhi day of 1699 AD at Anandpur and were thus the first to be initiated into the Khalsa brotherhood. There is no agreement about his biographical details. According to one version he was the son of Tirath Chand of Dwarka belonging to the *Chhimba* (tailors) caste. He was born in 1663 AD. After his initiation into the Khalsa he remained in devoted service of the Guru and was killed fighting in the battle at Chamkaur in December 1705 AD.

MUKHLIS GARH : See Lohgarh.

MUKHLIS KHAN : Mukhlis Khan was a military general of Shah Jahan. He attacked Guru Hargobind under the orders of Shah Jahan who wished to punish the Guru and his Sikhs for holding the royal hawk and beating the king's soldiers who had gone to retrieve it. Mukhlis Khan was killed at the hands of the Guru in this battle in 1628 AD. This was the first of a series of battles that Guru Hargobind had to fight against the forces of Shah Jahan.

MUKTE : See Chalis Mukte.

MUKTI : *Mukti* means salvation—the state of having been saved from sin or its consequences in semitic religions and from the cycle of birth-rebirth in oriental religions. Sohan Singh has summarized the views of different religious groups on the issue: "The eschatological speculations of the two religious streams of humanity are characteristically different. According to semitic beliefs, at death, soul passes into a kind of suspended animation, which lasts till the Day of Judgement. On that crucial day, the deeds of each soul in its earthly life will be evaluated and depending on these, he will be dispatched to heaven or hell—heaven for the righteous and hell for the unrighteous. In both Hinduism and Budhism, if a man has attained liberation (read salvation) nothing more is to be said about him. If he has failed to earn liberation, then in accordance with his deeds, he will be born again; good deeds will ensure him birth in a station in life where the achievement of liberation will be facilitated; bad deeds will give him station in life where the way to liberation will be longer and more tedious. Sikhism subscribes to both these approaches. Without espousing the doctrine of the Day of Judgement, it accepts the idea of a running balance sheet of good or bad deeds in a man's life. And, of course, springing as it does from the compelling culture of India, the belief in the rounds of births and deaths lies at the very core of its doctrine." (*Sikhism;* Punjabi University Patiala, pp. 148-49).

Mukti is obtained, according to Sikhism, through God's devotion by a mind which is free from egoism. "Not by expounding texts, nor by the study of tomes comes salvation. Nor is the purity of the self attained without loving devotion to the Lord."

Kathnai kahan na chhuti-ai na par pustask bhar Kayea soch na paa-ee-ai bin Hari bhagat pyar
(AG. p. 59)

Sikhism advises : "Make the body the soil; put therin the seed of good deeds with the Name Divine irrigate it. Let thy mind be cultivated and raise crop of God's devotion : Thus shalt thou obtain the state of *Nirvana.*"

Eh tan dharti beej karma karo, salle aapao sarang pani; Man kirsan Hari ride jamalai eh pawis pad Nirbani. (AG. p. 23)

See Also Life.

MUKTSAR : It is a town, 45 km from Faridkot, where Guru Gobind Singh fought his last battle. The place was then called Khidrana. It is here that the *Chalis Mukte* (hence the name Muktsar) laid down their lives for the Guru.

Muktsar has a number of important gurdwaras : Shahidganj, where the last rites of the *Chalis Mukte* were performed by the Guru himself; Tibbi Sahib from where the Guru used to shower arrows on Turkish army; Tambu Sahib where the Sikh army had camped and Wada Darbar where the Guru had stayed.

Muktsar is the venue of a big annual fair on the occasion of Maghi.

MUL MANTRA : *Mul Mantra* is the preamble to *Japji,* the well-known composition of Guru Nanak. It reads :

Ik Onkar, Sat-naam, Karta-purakh, Nirbahu, Nirvair, Akal-murat, Ajuni, Sai-bhang Gur-prasad.
meaning :

"God is one; Truth is His Name. He is the Creator; the Fearless, without Enmity, the

Immortal, the Unborn, Self-illuminated. And He is achieved by the Grace of the Guru." These are indeed the opening lines of the Adi Granth. In an abbreviated form it also stands at the head of each section of the Adi Granth based on a *raag*. Indeed it represents the essence of Sikh theology.

MULOWAL : Mulowal is a village near Dhuri in the Malwa region. Guru Tegh Bahadur had visited it during his travels through the area. According to the Sikh tradition the Guru's visit led to the finding of sweet potable water in the village which was generally brackish. A gurdwara has been dedicated to the Guru.

MUNDAWANI : *Mundawani* is the title of the closing composition of the Adi Granth (before Raag Mala) written by Guru Arjan. With this the Guru had put the seal indicating the end of the scripture saying that this is the spiritual food consisting of *Sat* (truth), *Santokh* (contentment) and *Vichar* (knowledge) offered to you on a platter which is the Adi Granth. This allegory occurs also in an earlier *shabad* called *Mundawani* on page 645 of the Adi Granth.

MURAD BEGUM : Murad Begum was the wife of Mir Mannu, governor of Lahore who after the death of her husband in November 1753 AD took over the reins of administration in the name of her minor son Amin-u-din. But soon she was replaced by Adina Beg, the administrator of Jalandhar at the orders of the Emperor of Delhi.

N

NABI KHAN : See Gani Khan.

NADAUN : Nadaun is situated in Kangra district of Himachal Pradesh about 30 km from Kangra. The place has been sanctified by Guru Gobind Singh's visit. A gurdwara has been built here which is visited by hundreds of devotees.

Guru Gobind Singh had helped some of the hill chieftains to win a battle against Alif Khan who had been sent by Mian Khan to collect the arrears of tribute from them. The battle was fought in 1690 AD and is mentioned in Bichitra Nantak.

NADHA SAHIB, GURDWARA : A small historical gurdwara in village Nadha near Chandigarh. Guru Gobind Singh had stayed here on his way from Paonta Sahib to Anandpur.

NAGARA : *Nagara* is a large kettledrum—a sort of percussion instrument. Since the days of Guru Hargobind it became a tradition to keep it in gurdwaras and to use its beating to signal the preparation of *langar* in place of the blowing of the conch shell. The *nagara* came to symbolize freedom combined with equality and readiness to share one's wealth with others. In those days *nagara* was also used by *rajas* to welcome guests and as a symbol of authority. Guru Gobind Singh got a huge kettle drum called Ranjit Nagara installed at the gate of his residence at Anandpur and used to beat it every morning and evening as a symbol of soverignty and it echoed for miles around. Raja Bhim Chand of Bilaspur in whose state Anandpur fell objected to this practice. He declared that use of a *nagara* was the privilege of the ruler alone but the young Guru paid no heed to it. This is cited by historians as one of the causes of the battles fought by Guru Gobind Singh at Anandpur in 1682 AD and 1685 AD.

NAGAR KIRTAN : *Nagar Kirtan* literally means the *kirtan* that goes round the town. Since traditionally almost all religious processions, as for example on the occasion of *gurpurbs*, are accompanied by various groups singing *shabads* the phrase has come to be used for the procession itself. This distinguishes it from the ordinary procession which is called *jaloos*.

NAHAN : See Medni Prakash.

NAINA DEVI : Naina Devi is a place near Anandpur and is the seat of Hindu goddess Durga . At the time of setting up of the Khalsa, Guru Gobind Singh wished to have the common people on his side in his mission by stimulating them in the name of Durga. The learned pandits in the service of the Guru advised him to perform the grand ceremony of *Hom*. At their suggestion he invited Pandit Kesho Das from Varanasi to conduct the ceremony on the hill of Naina Devi. The ceremony began on the Durga Ashtami Day in March 1698 AD and lasted for one full year. Bhai Santokh Singh in his *Suraj Prakash* says that the *havan* began on the full moon day of Baisakh in 1698 AD. Some chroniclers mention the duration of the *havan* as four years. It ended just before the Baisakhi day of 1699 AD when the Guru founded the Khalsa brotherhood at Anandpur. The entire audience at Naina Devi had converged to Anandpur.

NAINA SINGH : Naina Singh was the chief of the Shahid *misl* in the later part of the eighteenth century. His real name was Narain Singh. He is credited with the introduction of the Nihang type turban for his followers. He groomed the famous Sikh hero Akali Phula Singh and handed over the command of the Shahid *misl* to him.

NAJABAT KHAN : Najabat Khan was a

Pathan chief of hundred cavalary men belonging to Kunjpura near Karnal. He betrayed Guru Gobind Singh in the battle at Bhangani and joined the hill rajas. He was killed at the hands of Sango Shah.

NALH, BHATT : *Bhatt* Nalh is the author of 5 *swayyas* glorifying Guru Ramdas in the Adi Granth. They portray the history and personality of the Guru and also the Sikhs' unfaltering faith in the Gurus. Of all the *swayyas* in the Adi Granth, those of *Bhatt* Nalh are the most popular because they voice a true devotion to and faith in the Guru.

NAM : *Nam* is a pivotal concept in Sikh metaphysics and extremely difficult to understand for the non-metaphysically minded. It is based on the belief that the care of religious experience consists of non-moral holiness as a category of value which is quite distinct from the aesthetic and moral experiences. It is called *numina*—a spiritual experience of reality which is prominent feature of Sikhism. Etymologically the word *numina* is related to the Sanskrit word *naman* or the English word Name. In Sikh thought it is used as an antonym of phenomenon—that which appears as reality to the sensory motor apprehension of man and is the subject matter of physical sciences. *Nam* is the essence of all phenomena but is not discernible through sensory motor apprehension or even through speculative processes which are themselves grounded in the data of sensory motor apprehension. It is the treasure of all virtues. "Chastity, Truth and Continence are all contained in the *Nam*. Without the *Nam*, thou becomest not pure."
Jat, sat, sanjum Nam hai, bin Namai nirmal na hoe (AG. p. 33)
"I lean on the *Nam* which is the treasure of all virtues, gladness, beauty and flavour."
Sarb nidhan mangal ras roopa Hari ka Nam adhaaro (AG, p. 620)
Nam alone endures as the essence of the purified soul, as the divine light in the heart of man and as God of the Universe.

Sikhism accords the highest place to *Nam* among its theological concepts. According to it: "Lord's Name is the essence of all faiths."
Sagal matant kewal Hari Nam (AG. p. 296)
Guru Arjan elaborates it further. "I have searched many Shastras and Simritis. They do not equal the invaluable Name of the Lord."
Bahu sastar bahu simriti, pekhe sarb dhadhol, Poojasi nahi Hari Hare Nanak Nam amol.
(AG. p. 265)
In the same vein he says : "I tumbled through all the worlds but there is no place anywhere except in the *Nam*."
Tohe tahe buh bhawan bin Namai sukh nahi.
(AG. p. 225)
Nam in Sikhism is similar to the Christian concept of the Word used to guide practical religious life and the discipline of meditation. The word manifests itself in the being of the Guru as his inner personality and his gospel. Bhai Gurdas has summarized this aspect of the concept very well.

"In the Word is the Guru; and the Guru is in the Word." Guru's mystic word the *Nam* becomes symbol and substance of God's wisdom.

In a way, Sikhism is a religion of the *Nam*. The word *Nam* occurs 5999 times in the Adi Granth. Every time the *ardass* is said Sikhs beseach God that the religion of Nam preached by Guru Nanak may prevail and prosper."
Nanak Nam chardi kala tere bhane sarbat ka bhala.
See also God in Sikhism.

NAM-DAAN-ISNAN : *Nam-daan-isnan* is a popular triad of words like *degh-tegh-fateh* and *sat-santokh-vichar*. It expresses a whole lot of theo-ethical concepts in Sikhism. See the corresponding entries on each. *Nam*—the word—implies remembering God and submitting to His authority thereby avoiding unethical actions. *Daan*—charity implies helping the needy which presupposes that one by acquiring knowledge, art and skills would have reached a stage to do so and would not himself need charity. *Insan*—ablution—means keeping one's mind, body, behaviour, belongings, house etc. clean.

NAMDEV : Namdev who was born in 1270 AD was a celebrated saint whose name was a household word in Maharashtra. It is a historical fact that during his pilgrimage, he came to Punjab. The Sikhs and Punjabi followers of Namdev believe that he spent a number of years in village Ghuman in Gurdaspur where he died in the month of *Asso*. Every year a fair is held at his shrine as a mark of homage to his spirit. The Marathi chronicles show that Namdev died and was buried in Pandharpur in 1350 AD where his head moulded in brass on the lower step of the temple of Vishoba is now worshipped by the people.

Namdev was the son of Dam Seti, a tailor who resided at Narsi Bamni in the Satara district of Maharashtra. His mother was Gona Bai, daughter of a tailor of Kalyan in the same district. Both his father and mother possessed great devotional enthusiasm.

Namdev wrote in Marathi as well as in *Sant Bhasha*. Marathi *Abhangas* included in the *Nam Dev Gatha* are sung throughout Maharashtra. For the Maharashtrians they are evocative of the same spiritual ecstasy that the people of Uttar Pradesh find in the hymns of Surdas and Mira Bai. Sixty one of his hymns have been incorporated in the Adi Granth under different *raags*. The themes of these hymns are the varied spiritual experiences of Nam Dev.

NAMDHARIS : The *Namdhari* movement was started by Baba Balak Singh (1797-1861) and was sustained by his disciple Baba Ram Singh of Bhaini in Ludhiana district which is now the headquarters of *Namdharis*. There is another centre at Jiwan Nagar (Sirsa). Baba Ram Singh was succeeded by his brother Hari Singh who was in turn succeeded by his son Partap Singh.

Namdharis are a well-known community of farmers, artisans, contractors and businessmen spread to distant parts of the globe. They are also called *Kukas*.

The *Namdhari* movement was a puritan movement which came as a protest against the prevailing laxity of morals and sought to revive the old devotional spirit among the Sikhs. *Namdharis* lead austere lives, wear the simplest of white *Khadi* clothes, wear no ornaments save rosaries made of wool. They are strictly vegetarian and totally abstain from the use of alcohol and tobacco. Their wedding ceremony is very simple. They have an honoured place in the history of India's struggle for freedom. They were the first to evolve non-cooperations and the use of *swadeshi* as political weapons. They differ from other Sikhs in that they have a succession of living gurus.

NAMING : See Nam Karan.

NAM JAPNA : See Nam Simran.

NAM KARAN : *Nam Karan* or naming a new born is a religious ceremony among the devout Sikhs. No taboos of any kind are observed when a child is born. In due time at the discretion of parents, the child is presented before Guru Granth Sahib. This may be done in a gurdwara or in a social ceremony organized at some other place. The *granthi* (Sikh priest) prepares the *amrit* by mixing sugar with water and reading five stanzas of Japji. Then the general *ardaas* is offered. After reciting the prayers and thanks giving *amrit* is dropped into the child's lips. The mother is given to drink the rest. The name is selected from a number of names suggested by the *granthi*, all beginning with the first letter of the *Wak* (first hymn on the first page when the Adi Granth is opened at random). This is followed by the distribution of *Karah Parsad*.

The Sikh tradition requires that the name of a boy must end with *Singh* and that of a girl with *Kaur*.

NAM SIMRAN : *Nam Simran* also called *Nam Japna* is the most approved mode of individual meditation in Sikhism. It is not a formal exercise like the *yogas* which Sikhism does not approve of but is a technique of holding God constantly in mind. The basic ingredient of the technique is the mechanical repitition of the Name of God

(*Nam*). It should be accompanied by a constant and unceasing effort to empty the mind of all its content-conscious as well as subconscious. *Nitnem* (see the corresponding entry) prescribes the *banis* and their timings for the daily meditation. Since Sikhism recommends that religion must be lived and practised in the socio-political context, *Nam Simran* must be pursued while engaged in earning honest livelihood and living an ethically good life. Sikhism's credo is *Kirat karo, Wand chhako, Nam japo*.

Nam Simran performs three functions—it is purgative as it removes evils; it is illuminative as it gives us knowledge of Truth, Beauty and Goodness; and it is unitive as it brings one in tune with God. The remembrance of *Nam* is also three fold: with words, with mind and with actions.

In sum, *Nam Simran* is the key to salvation. "They who dwell on the Name, their toil is over."

Jini Nam dhiya-e-aa, gaye mashkkat ghaal
(AG. p. 8)

"Lord's Name is the panacea for all ills."
Sarb rog ka aukhad nam (AG. p. 274)

"The Name is the boat, the Name the raft which ferries one across (the sea of life).
Nanak Nao bera Nao tulhara, bhai jit lag par jan pae (AG. p. 603)

"Those who contemplate the Name, their bonds are loosened and they are rid of the vices of lust, wrath, selfhood and *maya*."
Nam nidhaan jin jan japeo tin ke bandhan kate Kam krodh maya bikh mamta eh biadhi te hate
(AG. p. 496)

NANAK, GURU : Guru Nanak, the founder of Sikhism, was born in April, 1469 AD at Nankana Sahib in Pakistan. (But his birth anniversary has, by custom, come to be celebrated in October-November). His father Baba Kalyan Chand, shortened by the biographers to Kalu, a *Khatri* by caste was the village *Patwari* (Accountant) who kept records. The name of Guru Nanak's mother was Mata Tripta.

Guru Nanak was sent for instruction in Hindi to Pandit Gopal in 1475 AD for Sanskrit to Pandit Brij Lal in 1478 AD and for Persian to Maulvi Kutubdin in 1481 AD. But the Guru was looking for much wider meaning in education rather than mere literacy.

As the Guru entered his eleventh year, he had attained the age when he must, according to prescribed usage, be given the *janeu* (sacred thread). As a boy, he used to take the cattle to pasture. But he was devoting his solitude to inward communion. His father wanted him to enter business but he preferred to spend the money on feeding the hungry *sadhus* (mendicants).

In 1484 AD Guru Nanak was sent to his sister Nanaki at Sultanpur Lodhi where he took up a job as storekeeper of Daulat Khan Lodhi. During his stay at Sultanpur, he was married in 1487 AD and was blessed with two sons Sri Chand and Lakhami Das. Here he continued his spiritual vocation along with his work as a storekeeper.

Once, while at Sultanpur, he did not return home after his morning ablutions in the *Bein* (rivulet) for three days. This was an interval of vivid mystical experience. On reappearance Guru Nanak uttered : "There is no *Hindu*, there is no *Musalman*." He was now ready to go forth into the wider world with the message he had to impart. Guru Nanak left Sultanpur in 1497 AD with Mardana on his first missionary travel covering Hardwar, Delhi, Varanasi, Guwahati, Jagannath Puri, Sri Lanka, Maharashtra, Gujarat, Ajmer, Mathura, Kurukshetra etc. He took three more travels taking him to all corners of India and the world. He visited Mecca (Saudi Arabia), Baluchistan, Afghanistan, Iran. Tibet and many places now in Pakistan. In his later years, Guru Nanak settled at Kartarpur (Pakistan) where he passed away in 1539 AD. He laid the foundation of Sikhism which was nurtured by nine other Gurus. 947 of his hymns in 19 *raags* are included in the Adi Granth. Some of his important compositions are :

Japji, Sidh Gosht, Sodar, Sohila, Asa di Var, Barah Maha etc.

NANAKI, BEBE : Bebe Nanaki was the elder

sister of Guru Nanak. She was born in 1464 AD. In 1475 she was married to Jai Ram who was an offcial working with Daulat Khan Lodhi governor of Jalandhar Doab with its headquarters at Sultanpur Lodhi, near Kapurthala. Bebe Nanaki had brought Guru Nanak to Sultanpur Lodhi and her husband Jai Ram had secured him employment as keeper of the Nawab's granaries and stores. According to Sikh tradition, Bebe Nanaki was the first disciple of Guru Nanak.

NANAKI, MATA : Mata Nanaki was the mother of Guru Tegh Bahadur and one of the wives of Guru Hargobind (others being Mata Mahadevi and Mata Damodari). She was the daughter of Hari Chand, a Khatri of Baba Bakala belonging to the Lamba sub-caste. She was married to Guru Hargobind at Amritsar in 1613 AD. She passed away at Kiratpur in 1678 AD.

NANAK JHIRA : See Bidar.

NANAKMATA : Nanakmata is about 50 km from Pilibhit in Uttar Pradesh. It was an important centre of *yogis* belonging to the Gorakhnath school of thought and was earlier known as Gorakhmata. Guru Nanak visited this place during his travels and preached to the *yogis*. Hence the name Nanakmata. Guru Hargobind is also believed to have visited this place.

NANAKPANTHIS : *Nanakpanthis* are the followers of the early Gurus who do not think it necessary to follow the ceremonial and social observances prescribed by Guru Gobind Singh. They are also called *Sahajdhari* Sikhs. Their characteristics are, therefore, mainly negative; they do not forbid smoking; they do not insist on long hair or other *kakaars*; they are not baptised; and they do not even in theory reject the authority of Brahmins. A *Nanakpanthi* is, in fact, a little more than a lax Hindu who has been influenced by the teachings of the Sikh Gurus and pays reverence to the Adi Granth.

NANAK PIAO, GURDWARA : Gurdwara Nanak Piao is situated on G.T. Road in Sabzi Mandi area of Delhi. Weary travellers used to quench their thirst from a well which still exists at this place. Guru Nanak visited Delhi around 1510 AD and halted at this place where he also served water to the people. That is why the shrine is named Nanak Piao.

NANAK PRAKASH : See Guru Nanak Prakash.

NANAKSAR : Nanaksar is the name given to a *sarovar* (tank) associated with Guru Nanak. It is often linked to a gurdwara. A number of such *sarovars* exist, some of which are :

1. Nanaksar, Damdama Sahib : This is the *sarovar* in Talwandi Sabo (Damdama Sahib). It has been so named in the belief that Guru Nanak had stayed on the edge of it during his visit to Talwandi Sabo.

2. Nanaksar, Hakimpur : Hakimpur is a village near Banga in Jalandhar district. Guru Har Rai had camped here for a few days on his way from Kartarpur (Jalandhar) to Kiratpur. A gurdwara built by Maharaja Ranjit Singh has been dedicated to the Guru. Nearby is a *sarovar* called *Nanaksar*. It is believed that Guru Nanak had visited the place.

3. Nanaksar, Nankana Sahib : This was the name given to the tank got dug by Rai Bular the Muslim chief of Talwandi in the name of Guru Nanak. Rai Bular was among the first disciples of the Guru.

4. Nanaksar, Takhtoopura : Takhtoopura is a village in the Malwa region about 25 km from Moga close to it is situated the gurdwara complex called Nanaksar comprising three main shrines associated with Guru Nanak (which has a *sarovar*), Guru Hargobind and Guru Gobind Singh.

5. Nanaksar, Verka : It is situated in village Verka in Amritsar district. Guru Nanak had visited it on his way from Nankana Sahib to Batala. A gurdwara with a *sarovar* commemorates the Guru's visit.

NANAKSHAHI : Nanakshahi is the name of

the rupee coin introduced in the name of Guru Nanak by the Dal Khalsa under the leadership of Jassa Singh Ahluwalia in 1765 AD at the Amritsar mint to commemorate the capture of Lahore in 1764 AD. It carried the Persian inscription :

Degh-o-tegh-o-fateh; nusrat-i-bedirang Yaft az Nanak-Guru Gobind Singh.

See also Degh Tegh Fateh. Maharaja Ranjit Singh who minted his own coins in 1800 AD continued the Nanakshahi with minor changes.

NANAK SHAHI, GURDWARA : Gurdwara Nanak Shahi commemorates the visit of Guru Nanak to Dacca and is located close to Dacca University. For some years in the recent past, the place had suffered neglect, and it was on January 2, 1972 AD after the liberation of Bangladesh that Guru Granth Sahib was installed again at the shrine.

NAND CHAND : Nand Chand was a *masand* of the Daroli region. Guru Gobind Singh took him in his service. He showed valour in the battle at Bhangani and the Guru has mentioned about it in his composition *Bichitar Natak*.

Once some *Udasi sadhus* who had prepared a hand-written copy of the Adi Granth came to Anandpur to get it initialled by Guru Gobind Singh. Nand Chand kept the copy with him and refused to hand it over to the *sadhus*. When they complained about it to the Guru, Nand Chand, out of fear, stealthily left Anandpur and went to Baba Dhirmal at Kartarpur (Jalandhar). Baba Dhirmal however took him to be a spy of Guru Gobind Singh and got him killed.

The copy of the Adi Granth which Nand Chand had kept with him is now at Daroli.

NANDED : See Hazur Sahib.

NANDLAL, BHAI : Bhai Nandlal was a very famous writer patronized by Guru Gobind Singh. He has left behind many important works, among them being *Rahatnama* and *Tankhanama* which are expositions of the Code of Conduct for the Sikhs as laid down by Guru Gobind Singh.

Bhai Nandlal was born in 1633 AD at Ghazni. His father Chhajjuram Khatri was chief secretary to the governor of Ghazni. At school Nandlal learnt Persian and Arabic and started writing poems in Persian. After his father's death in 1652 AD he migrated to Multan where he got a clerical job. Here he married a Sikh girl and purchased a house. As he could not find fulfilment here for his literary talents, he decided to shift to Delhi. While travelling from Multan to Delhi, he halted at Anandpur and bacame a disciple of Guru Gobind Singh. At Delhi, he got employment as a tutor to emperor Aurangzeb's son—Bahadur Shah. He did not stay there for long and returned to Anandpur in 1697 AD. After the Guru's death the retired to Multan where he died in 1715 AD. He had accompanied the Guru to the Deccan.

NANHERA : Nanhera is a small village near Ambala Cantonment. It has a gurdwara dedicated to Guru Gobind Singh who came here taking a walk during his stay at Lakhnaur.

NANHERI : Nanheri is a village in the Malwa region near Ghanaur about 5 km from Shambhu on the main railway line from Delhi to Amritsar. Guru Tegh Bahadur, impressed by the devotion of Masand Fateh Chand had spent a few days here. Guru Gobind Singh also passed through it on his way from Patna to Anandpur. A gurdwara has been dedicated to Guru Tegh Bahadur.

NANKANA SAHIB : Nankana Sahib is the Bethlehem of Sikhs. It is a small town in Pakistan situated at a distance of 60 km from Lahore. It was earlier known as Talwandi. Thousands of Sikhs go on a pilgrimage there every year particularly on important *Gurpurbs* associated with Guru Nanak as that is the place where he was born.

There are many important gurdwaras situated in Nankana Sahib, the most important of them being Janam Asthan (Birth place.) Nearby are other important gurdwaras : Bal

Lila, the place where Guru Nanak first played and subsequently spent most of his time in meditation; Maulvi Patti, where while under the charge of a *maulvi* (Persian teacher), he himself assumed the role of a teacher and composed an acrostic on the letters of the Persian alphabet; Kiara Sahib where he was accused of being careless in herding his father's cattle; Malji Sahib where a cobra is said to have protected the Guru from the sun by providing shade; Sacha Sauda Chuhrkana, where he distributed food to the *sadhus* out of the money given to him by his father for business; and Tamboo Sahib, where after the real bargain at Chuhrkana, the Guru when he returned to Talwandi, sat and was cuffed for disobedience.

The Sikhs had to start a vigorous campaign to free the places of worship from the clutches of *mahants* who were usurping the offerings made in the gurdwaras. During this campaign, Nankana Sahib became the scene of an outrage unparalleled for its barbarity in the history of mankind when hundreds of Sikhs were murdered. After a protracted struggle, the management of gurdwaras was entrusted to the Sikhs. It is an irony of fate that the places of worship which are so sacred to Sikhs and whose control was wrested by them after making many sacrifices, now lie in Pakistan and cannot be visited freely.

NANU : Nanu, a devout Sikh was the resident of Dilwali Gali of Delhi at the time of the martyrdom of Guru Tegh Bahadur in 1675 AD. The plan for the disposal of the martyred body of the Guru was prepared at his house where Jaita and Uda had joined him. Jaita carried the head of the Guru to Kiratpur and he was escorted by Nanu and Uda. See also Jaita, Bhai.

NASIHAT NAMA : *Nasihat Nama* is the name given to the *shabad* which begins with the line: *Keechai neknami je dewai khuda-ee* and is atributed to Guru Nanak. According to *Guru Nanak Prakash* by Bhai Santokh Singh this composition is aimed at the cruel king of Egypt. This is not, however, supported by historical research. Most probably it has been composed by a devoted Sikh.

NASIR ALI : Nasir Ali was a *faujdar* of Jalandhar. According to a noting in the blank pages of the copy of the orignial Adi Granth kept at Kartarpur (Jalandhar), the town had a big fire in 1757 AD. Gurdwara Thamb Sahib was damaged in this fire, Nasir Ali is regarded as responsible for this devastation at Kartarpur.

NATHA, BHAI : Bhai Natha who came from the *Udasi* order of *sadhus* was sent to Dhaka, now capital of Bangladesh, to preach Sikhism by Guru Har Rai. He also used to send for the Guru's use fine Dhaka muslin specially spun for him. When Guru Tegh Bahadur visited Dhaka he was there in attendance on him.

NATHANA SAHIB : Nathana Sahib is a gurdwara near village Maghauli in the Malwa region dedicated to Guru Tegh Bahadur. It is about 5 km from Shambhu railway station on the main line from Delhi to Amritsar.

NATI, MATA : See Ananti, Mata.

NAT NARAYAN : *Nat Narayan* is an Indian classical *raag* usually sung within three hours (one *pahar*) before sunset. It is nineteenth of the thirty-one *raags* used in the organisation of hymns in the Guru Granth Sahib covering pages 975-983. The sequence of basic notes ir it is as follows :
Arohi : sa, re, ma, pa, dha, sa..........
Avrohi : sa, ne, dha, pa, ma, re, sa..........

NAU DUAR : See Dasam Duar.

NAULAKHA : Naulakha is a prominent village near Sirhind which has a gurdwara dedicated to Guru Tegh Bahadur. According to the Sikh tradition, a tribal man had presented nine old rupees (takas) to the Guru here. While accepting them the Guru had remarked that they were like nine lakh gold *mohars*. Since then the village is known as Naulakha.

NAU NIDH · *Nau nidh* refers to nine special

treasures : *padam, mahapadam, shankh, makar, kachhap, mukand, kund, neel* and *warch* which are described in the *Markande Purana* in chapter 68. In Sikh literature *nau nidh* means all the possible treasures as is implied in its use in the *ardaas* and also in *Sukhmani : Prabh kai simran: ridhi, sidhi, nau nidhi*.

NAUNIHAL SINGH : Naunihal Singh was the gandson of Maharaja Ranjit Singh and son of Kharak Singh. He was born in February, 1820 AD at Lahore. He was married to the daughter of Sham Singh Attari in March 1837 AD.

After the death of Maharaja Ranjit Singh in June 1839 AD, Kharak Singh ascended the throne. In a conspiracy hatched by Raja Dhian Singh Dogra, Kharak Singh was put under house arrest, making Naunihal Singh the Maharaja in his place. Kharak Singh was later poisoned and he died on November 5, 1840 AD. On the same evening, when Naunihal Singh was returning after cremating his father, an archway of the north gate of the Hazuribagh was made to fall on him at the signal of Raja Dhian Singh. He was seriously wounded and died the same evening although his death was declared on November 8, 1840 AD.

NIHAL KAUR : See Ananti, Mata.

NIHANGS : *Nihangs* is a Persian word meaning crocodile. *Nihang* were suicide squads of the Mughal army and wore blue uniforms. The Sikhs took the name and the uniform from the Mughals.

Nihangs constitute an order of Sikhs who, abandoning the fear of death, are ever ready for martyrdom and remain unsullied by worldly possessions. A *Nihang* is one who has nothing and is free from anxiety. The order is said to have been founded by Guru Gobind Singh himself as a fighting body of the Khalsa. The *Nihangs* were also called *Akalis* (servitors of the Timeless God) which term has now become synonymous with the members of a political party in Punjab. (Most of them wear blue turbans).

Nihangs can be recognized from a distance as they wear dark blue robes with their legs bare below the knees and high blue and yellow turbans laced with steel discs. They usually carry spears, swords, daggers and shields.

They use a charming vocabulary of Braggadocio which has found its way into the Punjabi language.

NIM SAHIB, GURDWARA : See Akar.

NIRANJANIA : See Hindal.

NIRANKARIS : *Nirankaris* constitute a sect of the Sikhs which came as a result of a reform movement started by a Khatri of Peshawar named Bhai Dayal Das (1783-1855 AD). The word *Nirankar* means 'The Formless one.' The *Nirankaris* worship God as a spirit only, avoid the adoration of idols, make no offerings to Brahmins or to the dead, abstain strictly from flesh and wine and are said to pay strict attention to truth in all things. They believe that Baba Dayal Das was a successor to Guru Gobind Singh. This line of succession has been continued till today. They have developed their own scripture with alterations in the Adi Granth. This is objected to by the fundamentalists and is a source of tension between *Nirankaris* and the Sikhs.

NIRMALAS : Like *Nihangs*, the order of *Nirmalas* also started during the days of Guru Gobind Singh. It is said that the Guru sent thirteen of his followers to Varanasi to acquire knowledge of Sanskrit, and that, on their return, he blessed them as being the only learned men among the Sikhs and called them *Nirmalas*. They were allowed to take the *Pahul* and founded the order of *Nirmalas*. The fraternity had at first a great influence among the Sikhs, but their taste of Sanskrit literature led them to re-adopt many of the customs of the *Shastras*. The *Nirmalas* sometimes wear white robes but usually saffron or ochre-coloured ones like Hindu *sadhus*. However, they wear the long hair and symbols of the Sikhs and are classified as such.

It is generally believed that after the Khalsa

was created, Mani Singh and many other Nirmala Sikhs requested Guru Gobind Singh to initiate them into the new martial order of the Khalsa. By the command of the Guru in his life time, many *Nirmalas* went to different parts of India, especially of Punjab, preaching the spiritual message of the Gurus. It was due to this, that it became quite a custom amongst the Khatris of Punjab to dedicate one son to the Khalsa for the noble cause of the Guru. The custom has been followed till very recent times in some of the families.

NIRMOHGARH : Nirmohgarh is a village near Anandpur. The hill rajas were very much perturbed over the growing power of the Khalsa. In 1699 AD they made two attempts to dislodge Guru Gobind Singh from Anandpur but failed. After the second attempt, a strong contingent of the Mughal army was seen advancing towards Anandpur in 1700 AD. The Guru intercepted them at Nirmohgarh. Some hill rajas also joined the Mughals but the Guru's forces repulsed them. Gurdwara Manji Sahib at Nirmohgarh has been dedicated to the Guru.

NISHAN SAHIB : *Nishan Sahib* is the name given to the standard of the Khalsa. It has a *khanda* drawn on a triangular piece of ochre coloured cloth. The flag post is also generally covered with the same cloth. The flag post also has a *khanda* at the top.

The use of *Nishan Sahib* started during the days of Guru Hargobind. Ever since then, it has been used at all public gurdwaras.

NITHANA : Nithana is an important village in the Malwa region and has a gurdwara dedicated to Guru Hargobind. One *sadhu* named Kalu Nath who was a devotee of the Guru used to live here. He had helped the Guru at the time of the battle at Mehraj. After the victory in that battle he brought the Guru to Nithana, where he stayed for some time.

NITNEM : It is laid down in Sikh *Rahat Maryada* that every Sikh should daily recite *Gurbanis* (writings of the Gurus). This daily routine is called *Nitnem*. The *Gurbanis* included in the *Nitnem* are :

1. *Japji* by Guru Nanak to be recited at *Amrit Vela*.

2. *Japu Sahib* by Guru Gobind Singh for *Amrit Vela*.

3. *Rehras* which comprises hymns of Guru Nanak, Guru Amardas, Guru Ramdas and Guru Arjan to be recited at sunset.

4. *Sohila* by Guru Nanak which is recited at the time of retiring to bed.

NON-VEGETARIANISM : See Meat.

NURMAHAL : Nurmahal is a village near Phillaur in Jalandhar district. Impressed by the devotion of Sain Fateh Shah, a local saint, Guru Har Rai had visited the place. Two shrines in Nurmahal commemorate the Guru's visit.

O

OBED BEG : Obed Beg was the administrator of Gurdaspur area oppointed by the Mughal Emperor. In 1761 AD, Ahmad Shah Abdali, during his fifth invasion of India, had made him the governor of Lahore. After Abdali left, the Sikh *misl* chiefs attacked Obed Khan who had besieged the Sukkarchakia fortress at Gujranwala. Obed Khan fled in horror. The Sikhs attacked Lahore and victoriously entered the city on November 21, 1761 AD. Jassa Singh Ahluwalia was proclaimed *Sultan-e-Quam* (King of the Nation). Obed Khan locked himself up in the fort of Lahore.

OMENS : Sikhism's reaction of omens is best explained by Bhai Gurdas in his Vars. According to him paying attention to omens, the nine *grihs*, the twelve signs of Zodiac, incantations, magic, divination by lines and by the voice is all vanity. It is vain to draw conclusions from the cries of donkeys, dogs, cats, kites, malalis (black carnivorous bird) and jackals. Omens drawn from meeting a widow, a man with a bare head, from water, fire, sneezing, breaking wind, hiccups, lunar and weekdays, unlucky moments and conjunctions of planets are all superstition. If a woman who winks at every man try by deceit to inspire belief in her, how can her husband feel confidence? The holy who reject such superstitions obtain happiness and salvation (Var 5). People worship departed heroes, ancestors, *satis* deceased co-wives, tanks and pits but all this is of no avail. Those who enjoy not the company of saints and the Guru's instruction die and are born again and are rejected by God.

OMNIPOTENCE OF GOD : God manifested His omnipotence by calling the world into existence. His power is admired and glorified in Sikh scriptures through the wonders of His creation. The conception of omnipotence was made by Guru Nanak in Japji : "The Lord is great; His seat is high; higher still is his exalted Name. If anyone be as great as He is, only he shall know the Lord so High. How great He is, that is known to Him alone. Nanak, through His Grace we receive bounty."

Vada sahib oocha thaa-o
Ooche upar oocha naa-o
Evad oocha hovai ko-e
Tis ooche ko jaanai so-e
Jevad aap jaanai aap aap
Nanak nadri karmi daat
(AG. p. 5)

God is omnipotent because He has the power to invest the content of His Will with reality, and the whole realm of His existence is constantly sustained by His activity. Faith in God would be crippled in its assurance and fail to its fulness, if the object of its trust were a Being wrestling with difficulties which He could only partially overcome. Only the most powerful can be approached whenever and for whatever man might need. "The Lord Himself does all; then who else is there to go to; there is no one other than Him who can do a thing."

Aape kare kis aakhi-ai, hor
karna kichh na jae Ram
(AG. p. 570)

"As you are great, greatness flows from you."
Ja toon vada sabh vadiaye-aan
(AG. p. 145)

See also God in Sikhism.

OMNIPRESENCE OF GOD : One of the prominent attributes of God in Sikhism is His omnipresence. He is wholly free from spatial limitations. "God is here and God is there; without God there is no place in the world. So Namdev greets God in everything for He pervades and fills all."

Eebhai beethal oobhai beethal, beethal bin sansar nahi than thanatar Nama, pranwai poor rahio toon sarb mahi (AG. p. 485)

Further, "God exists on the earth and the sky and in the underworld; He fills the whole universe."

Dharni mahe akas peyal, sarb lok pooran pritipal
(AG. p. 293-94)

The attribute of omnipresence of God also expresses the truth that the Being of God is not separable from His activity. Another natural corollary is that one can search for God within oneself. "He for whom I searched the whole world. I found Him so near, within."

Ja karne jag dhoodhio nairio payeo tahe
(AG. p. 341)

See also God in Sikhism.

OMNISCIENCE OF GOD : According to Sikhism objects are not given to God from without to be known, but are the expression of His Will (*Hukam*) and remain dependent upon Him. "He who created the world, alone knows its state."

Jin siste saji so-ee jane   (AG. p. 129)

Omniscience always refers to and finds support in the conception of the omnipotent. The final purpose of life and creation is clear to Him because the whole creative process is conditioned by His Will "God resides in every living being and, therefore, knows everything."

Jia undar jio sabh kichh janla   (AG. p. 965)

Guru Gobind Singh has also echoed it in the Dasam Granth : "God knows the innermost thoughts of every soul; and feels the distress of good and evil men. He bestows his mercy on everyone—from a tiny ant to a huge elephant." (*Benti Chaupai, 14*).

See also God in Sikhism.

ONKAR : See Ik Onkar.

ORDER OF THE KHALSA : See Khalsa.

P

PAAP : See Sin.

PADA : *Pada* is a division of a hymn (shabad) in the Guru Granth Sahib. It may vary in length from one to four verses.

PADAL SAHIB, GURDWARA : Gurdwara Padal Sahib marks the spot near Mandi town in Himachal Pradesh where Guru Gobind Singh had camped while on a visit to Mandi at the invitation of its raja. The Guru had gone to the hills for a change.

PAHOA : Pahoa is a Hindu religious centre in the Kurukshetra area. Near the Saraswati temple, it has a gurdwara dedicated to Guru Nanak, Guru Tegh Bahadur and Guru Gobind Singh.

PAHUL : See Baptism.

PAINDA KHAN : Painda Khan was a Pathan belonging to village Alampur. He joined the services of Guru Hargobind and rose to the position of a *sardar* of his forces. Painda Khan, however, deserted the Guru at the instigation of his son-in-law Asman Khan. He attacked the Guru at Kartarpur (Jalandhar) along with Kala Khan in 1634 AD. He was killed at the hands of the Guru in the battle. The sword used by the Guru in killing is preserved as a relic at Kartarpur.

PAKHIAN CHARITRA : A composition by Guru Gobind Singh included in the Dasam Granth. It is a collection of 404 stories drawn from ancient literature on the character and qualities of women. It was written in 1696 AD at Anandpur. He wanted to warn his followers of the wiles of women as a preparation for *dharma yudh* which he was then contemplating.

PAKKA : Pakka is a village near Barnala. Guru Gobind Singh had camped near the village for three days on his way to Damdama Sahib (Talwandi Sabo). The tree with which the Guru's horse was tethered still exists. A gurdwara commemorates the Guru's visit.

PAKKA SAHIB, GURDWARA : Gurdwara Pakka Sahib is situated near village Madhe in the Malwa region. It is dedicated to Guru Gobind Singh who came here on his way to Dina from Takhtoopura. The Guru's thumb was sore (*pakka* in Punjabi) and he had changed the bandage here, hence the name.

PAKKHOKE : Pakkhoke is a village near Dera Baba Nanak on the other side of the river Ravi. Baba Moolchand, father-in-law of Guru Nanak was a resident of this village before settling down at Batala. Ajita Randhawa a devotee of Guru Nanak also lived here.

It has a shrine called Tahli Sahib. See under Tahli Sahib.

PAKKI SANGAT : Pakki Sangat is a gurdwara in Paryag (Allahabad) commemorating the visit of Guru Tegh Bahadur to the famous Hindu pilgrimage centre which is the confluence of the rivers Ganga and Yamuna (and the mythical Saraswati) situated in Uttar Pradesh. Guru Gobind Singh also passed through Paryag while going from Patna to Anandpur.

PALAHI : Palahi is a village near Phagwara. It has a gurdwara dedicated to Guru Har Rai.

PALKI : *Palki* is in general the Punjabi word for palaquin. However, in Sikh speech and writings it is specifically used for the structure in which the Guru Granth Sahib is ceremonially installed.

PANGAT : Literally *pangat* means the people sitting in a row for community dining. Since that is the practice followed in gurdwaras for *langar* the term has come to be used interchangeably with *langar* as in the saying : *Pehle pangat; peechai sangat*.

PANJ KAKKE : See Kakaars.

PANJOKHRA : Panjokhra is a small village near Ambala in Haryana. The place has been sanctified by the visit of Guru Harkrishan. The Guru stayed there while going to Delhi from Kiratpur. When he reached the village, the Guru made a boundary of sand and asked his followers not to go with him beyond that in his journey towards Delhi. A gurdwara has been built in this village.

PANJ PIARE : *Panj Piare* literally means the 'Five Loved Ones'. The term got into Sikh thought when it was used for the first five Sikhs to be admitted into the Khalsa Panth created by Guru Gobind Singh on the Baisakhi Day of 1699 AD at Anandpur. They were :
— Daya Ram, a *Khatri* from Lahore;
— Dharam Das, a *Jat* from Delhi;
— Muhkam Chand, a washerman from Dwarka;
— Sahib Chand, a barber from Bidar; and
— Himmat Rai, a water carrier from Puri.
See respective entries for more details.

On that eventful day of Baisakhi, the Guru administered the *amrit* of the *khanda* to the *Panj Piaras* and then himself took the *amrit* from them thus giving them the authority to admit even the Guru to the Khalsa Panth. This gave birth to the institution of *Panj Piare* who could exercise spiritual authority on behalf of the Khalsa Panth.

The term *Panj Piare* is now used for any five able-bodied devout Sikhs who have undergone baptism and collectively they are vested with the spiritual authority of the Khalsa. They, as such, lead the baptismal ceremony for admitting new members to the Khalsa brotherhood. They are also at the head of the *nagar kirtan* carrying *Nishan Sahibs* in their hands. Symbolically, at all religious ceremonies, *karah parsad* is first distributed to *Panj Piaras* before it is shared by the congregation.

PANTH : The word *panth* is of Sanskrit origin and literally refers to a path or way. However now-a-days it is used to describe a group of people who follow a particular teacher or doctrine. Among the Sikhs it is used to describe the whole Sikh community.

PANTH PRAKASH : *Panth Prakash* is the history of the Khalsa, written by Rattan Singh of Bhari. It is mentioned in the introduction : "The story of the Khalsa as told by Rattan Singh and written by captain Murray at Ludhiana in 1809 AD was reproduced in poetic form in 1841 AD for the benefit of Sikhs on the inspiration of Sir David Ochterlony." This was revised later by Gian Singh of Longowal in 1880 AD. It is used as a source book on Sikhism.

PAONTA SAHIB : Paonta Sahib, midway between Nahan (Himachal Pradesh) and Dehra Dun (Uttar Pradesh) was the abode of Guru Gobind Singh for a couple of years. Raja Medani Parkash of Nahan had sent a message to the Guru at Anandpur inviting him to spend some time in the Doon valley. This is the place where the Guru had a fort built in twelve days for the defence of Nahan. He also brought about reconciliation between Raja Medani Parkash and his rival Raja Fateh Shah of Srinagar which was a neighbouring hill state.

The majestic shrine of Paonta Sahib is situated on the bank of River Yamuna. Thousands of pilgrims visit the place on the occasion of Hola Mohalla.

PARKASH KARNA : *Parkash karna* literally means 'making manifest'. However, in Sikh speech and writing the expression is used for the early morning ceremony when the Guru Granth Sahib is formally opened at the beginning of the day's worship. The nature of the rituals varies according to the place where the Guru Granth Sahib has been kept for the night. If it has just been closed and wrapped with *rumalas* the *ardaas* is said, *rumalas* are removed and *Vak* is taken by opening the Scripture at random. If it has been kept at a separate resting place the *ardaas* is said there before bringing it reverentially on a Sikh's head to the throne (*palki*) in the gurdwara. The above mentioned opening ceremony will then commence. If the Guru Granth Sahib is taken out to preside over a ceremony, the same sequence of steps is used at the beginning of the ceremony. See also Sukh Asan.

PARMANAND BHAGAT : Not much is known about the life of Parmanand. It is believed that he was a resident of Barsi in Sholapur District of Maharashtra. He was a devotee of Krishna who later became a *Nirankari Bhakt*. Parmanand's writings are believed to excessively increase men's love for God. In his hymns he calls himself *Sarang* by which he means that he longs for God as the *Sarang* or *Chatrik* longs for the rain drops. One of his hymns has been included in the Adi Granth under *Raag* Sarang.

PARMANAND, BHATT : Parmanand is one of the seventeen *bhatts* whose compositions (5 sawayyas) are included in the Adi Granth. See also Bhatts.

PARO, BHAI : Bhai Paro was a Julka Khatri of village Dalla near Sultanpur Lodhi. He was a devout follower of Guru Angad. Later on through dedicated service he came very close to Guru Amardas who gave him the title of 'Paramhans' and appointed him a missionary as incharge of a *manji*. According to the Sikh tradition, he was instrumental in introducing the Baisakhi celebrations among the Sikhs.

PARYAG : See Pakki Sangat.

PATALPURI : Patalpuri marks the spot near Kiratpur on the banks of the river Sutlej where Guru Hargobind had passed away. Bhup Singh of Ropar got a memorial gurdwara constructed there. Guru Har Rai was also cremated here with a gurdwara dedicated to him. The ashes of Guru Harkrishan were brought here from Delhi where he had died and was cremated. It has now become customary among the devout Sikhs to immerse the ashes of their near and dear ones in the river Sutlej at Patalpuri.

PATHAR SAHIB, GURDWARA : Gurdwara Pathar Sahib is situated on the Srinagar Leh highway at a height of about 3700 m above see level. Its foundation stone was laid in May 1977 AD and at present is a very modest building. It commemorates the visit of Guru Nanak to this place while returning from Tibet and Mansarover. The Guru is believed to have subdued a demon here who had rolled down a huge rock (Pathar) towards him. The rock with the impression of the Guru's back still stands here.

PATHI : The word *pathi* is derived from *path*- reading of the Guru Granth Sahib. Therefore a person who specializes in the reading of the Guru Granth Sahib and undertakes it as a service or for remuneration is called a *pathi*.

PATIALA : Patiala is now one of the major towns of Punjab. It has been the capital of one of the Phulkian states of the same name. It was founded by Baba Ala Singh in 1753 AD and who gave a fillip to the growth of the town by constructing a fort in 1763 AD. The successors of Baba Ala Singh were zealous Sikhs and were responsible for the construction of a large number of historical gurdwaras in the state. The most important Sikh shrine in Patiala city is Gurdwara Dukh Niwaran which marks the spot where Guru Tegh Bahadur had rested for some time during his travels in the Malwa region in 1662-63 AD about hundred years before Patiala came up. See Dukh Niwaran, Gurdwara.

PATIT : *Patit* which literally means fallen refers to a Sikh who has failed to observe the *Rahat Maryada* (Code of Conduct) or after initiation has not lived up to the baptismal vows.

PATNA : Patna the capital of Bihar is a place of pilgrimage for the Sikhs. It was here that Guru Gobind Singh was born in 1666 AD and spent the first few years of his life before shifting to Anandpur. It has a number of important gurdwaras—the most important being Harmandir Sahib which is regarded as one of the five *Takhts*.

Besides the birth of Guru Gobind Singh, Patna has the unique distinction of being honoured by great prophets and religious teachers like Guru Nanak and Guru Tegh Bahadur.

PATTO : See Gurusar.

PAUDI : *Paudi* is a kind of poetry used in many compositions of both the Adi Granth and the Dasam Granth. It is generally a stanza of five verses which rhyme at the end. The verse is divided into two hemistiches by a calsura. *Paudi* generally follows a *salok*. It has usually 20 (10+12) *moras* like *salok*.

PAYEL : Payel is a village near Anandpur. Guru Hargobind had halted here while going to Kiratpur after the battle at Kartarpur (Jalandhar). Guru's personal horse that was wounded in the battle died here. The Guru also had a well dug in the village.

PEHAR : A unit for measuring time in the ancient Indian system. One *pehar* is equal to three hours.

PHAGUWALA : See Manji Sahib.

PHAGWARA : Phagwara is an old town on G.T. Road between Jalandhar and Ludhiana. It has two historical Sikh shrines. One is dedicated to Guru Har Rai who had halted here on his way to Kiratpur from Kartarpur (Jalandhar). The other one is Sukhchainiana which is dedicated to both Guru Hargobind and Guru Har Rai.

PHALAHI SAHIB, GURDWARA : See Duley.

PHARWAHI : Pharwahi is a village near Barnala. Guru Tegh Bahadur had spent a night here during his travels in the Malwa region. A gurdwara commemorates the Guru's stay.

PHERU, BABA : Baba Pheru or Pheru Mal was the father of Guru Angad. He was a Trehan Khatri and a trader of humble means belonging to the village Matte-di-Sarai, now known as Sarai Nanga, about 16 km from Muktsar. Very little is known about his life except that he became a cashier to the administrator of Ferozpur and died in 1526 AD.

PHERU, BHAI : Bhai Pheru whose original name was Sangat was born in Uppal Khatri family of village Ambmari in 1640 AD. He became a devotee of Guru Har Rai in 1656 AD who gave him the name Pheru (hawker) because he had met the Guru in the course of his hawking (*pheri*). Later on he was appointed as a *masand* by the Guru. Places associated with Bhai Pheru became a part of Pakistan after 1947 AD.

PHUL, BABA : Baba Phul was a devoted Sikh. He was the son of Roop Chand of Brar caste and was born in 1627 AD. He became a devotee of Guru Hargobind when he met the Guru first in his childhood in 1632 AD. Later on he remained a devoted disciple of Guru Har Rai. The association with the Gurus made the heirs of Baba Phul the chiefs of the Phulkian States. His grandson Baba Ala Singh had established the Phulkian *misl*.

Baba Phul died in 1690 AD at village Bahadurpur near Nabha.

PHULA SINGH, AKALI : A legendary Sikh hero who was a contemporary of Maharaja Ranjit Singh. Akali Phula Singh was born in about 1761 AD and was baptized by Baba Naina Singh, leader of the Shahid *misl*. In due course of time, he rose to become its most respected leader himself and the head priest of the Akal Takht, Amritsar. So powerful was he among the Sikhs that he was able to administer punishment to Maharaja Ranjit Singh for the sake of the Sikh Code of Conduct. He took considerable interest in the construction and improvement of gurdwaras at Anandpur, Damdama Sahib and other places. His headquarters were at Amritsar where a tower exists in his name (Burj Akali Phula Singh).

Akali Phula Singh was also a brave soldier and general. He helped Maharaja Ranjit Singh in winning many battles. He was killed in a battle in 1822 AD. He never married.

PHULKIAN STATES : Phulkian States is the popular name for the area under the control of the Phulkian *misl* which was set up by Baba Ala Singh, grandson of Baba Phul. It covered the area of Patiala, Nabha, Jind and some smaller states. Patiala state was the most powerful of all these and was directly controlled by Baba Ala Singh. The chiefs of other states were also the descendants of Baba Phul. They came under the British protection in 1809 AD.

PIARA RANDHAWA, BHAI : Bhai Piara Randhawa was a respectable devout Sikh when Guru Hargobind was sent to the prison in Gwalior Fort. Since Baba Buddha was the High Priest of the Golden Temple at that time he handed over the charge to Bhai Piara on leaving for Gwalior to meet the Guru.

PIPA, BHAGAT : Bhagat Pipa is one of the *bhagats* whose compositions are included in the Adi Granth. He was born in 1425 AD and was the king of a state called Gagraungarh. He was very spiritually inclined and took Ramanand as his spiritual guide. He travelled to Dwarka, Varanasi and other religious centres to progress towards spiritual perfections. A Marathi chronicler sums up the character of Pipa by saying that he was brave, liberal, learned, religious, self-restrained and watchful. One of his hymns is included in the Adi Granth under *Raag* Dhanasari. In it he emphasizes the internal worship as compared to the external worship.

PIRTHI CHAND, BABA : Baba Pirthi Chand was the eldest son of Guru Ramdas. He was born to Bibi Bhani in 1558 AD. When he was by passed by his younger brother Guru Arjan as a successor to Guru Ramdas he started working against the interests of the Sikh community. He conspired against Guru Arjan. When the Adi Granth was compiled, he seized the opportunity of complaining to Emperor Akbar through Chandu Shah that it contained derogatory references to Islam. Akbar summoned a copy for investigation when he was camping at Batala and was fully satisfied by the interpretations given by Bhai Gurdas.

Baba Pirthi Chand died in 1606 AD. His followers were called Minas. Although they are now extrict they might have survived until the end of the 17th century at least, as Guru Gobind Singh mentioned them as one of the five groups with whom the Khalsa shall have no dealings.

POLITICS AND RELIGION : See Meeri and Peeri.

PRABHATI : An Indian classical *raag* usually sung within about three hours (one *pehar*) before sunrise. It is thirtieth of the thirty-one *raags* used in the organisation of hymns in the Guru Granth Sahib covering pages 1327-1351. It has the following sequence of basic notes :
   Arohi : sa, re, ga, ma, pa, dha, ne, sa..........
   Avrohi : sa, ne, dha, pa, ma, ga, re, sa..........

PRIDE : According to Sikhism, pride (*Hankar* in Punjabi) is one of the five vices. Under its influence, man may treat even his friends as strangers; he may refuse to acknowledge his relationship or fulfil his social obligations. It blinds the individual to the underlying unity of mankind. Guru Arjan states in the Adi Granth : "O Pride, the cause of our coming and going in the world, O soul of sin, thou estrange friends, confirm enmities and make men spread out the net of illusion far and wide, and tire men by keeping ever on the round, and making them experience now pleasure, now pain. And men walk through the utter wilderness of doubt: thou affect men with incurable maladies." (AG p. 1358). Although this concept is similar to that of *Haumai*, it should not be confused with that. Pride comes from one's possession of beauty or power, or experience or competence while *haumai* conveys the sense of individuation.

PUNJABI : As the very name suggests, Punjabi is the language of Punjab as referring to the land of five rivers. Though the political boundaries of Punjab have changed from time to time, the linguistic boundaries for Punjabi have remained in tact since its origin. It is now one of the modern Indian languages recognised by the Indian Constitution. It is also one of the prominent languages of Pakistan. In India it is writtten in the Gurmukhi script while in Pakistan it is written in the Persian script. It has acquired a special significance for the Sikhs as most of their religious writings are written in it.

Punjabi belongs to the group of Indo-Aryan languages. The direction of evolution has been from Sanskrit to Prakrit; from Prakrit to Apabhramsha; and from Apabhramsha to Punjabi. It is natural, therefore to find characteristics of Sanskrit, Prakrit and Apabhramsha in Punjabi.

There are variations in Punjabi as spoken in different regions. This has led some scholars to make a distinction between Eastern Punjabi and Western Punjabi; the latter is referred to as Lehndi. However in both poetry and prose works of Punjabi literature, the standard literary medium is the dialect known as Majhi though the influence of other dialects is found here and there. Perso-Arabic influence on Punjabi is also quite perceptible because of the Muslim rule in Punjab.

Punjabi is a very rich language. Its oldest literature from 800-1500 AD was composed in the religious lore by *yogis* like Gorakhnath and *sufis* like Baba Farid. Modern Punjabi litera-ture may be deemed to have started in the Mughal period with romantic stories like 'Heer Ranjha', 'Mirza Sahiban', 'Sassi Punnu', 'Zusuf Zuleikhan' etc. The Sikh Gurus and other personages also made tremendous contribution to Punjabi literature in this period. Many modern writers have elevated its level in recent times.

PUNJAB KAUR : Punjab Kaur was the wife of Baba Ram Rai, the elder son of Guru Har Rai. After the death of Ram Rai and being fed-up with *masands*, she sought help from Guru Gobind Singh. The Guru went to Dehradun and set her house in order. She passed away at Dehradun in 1741 AD.

PUNJA SAHIB : Punja Sahib is a famous gurdwara associated with Guru Nanak. It is situated at Hassan Abdal, a place about 48 km from Rawalpindi. The site has been a sacred place since the Buddhist times. Hiuen Tsang provides evidence regarding the existence of a Buddhist monastery, the remains of which still exist.

During his travels, Guru Nanak encountered a proud and haughty Muslim *fakir* at this place. The latter is said to have hurled a big rock at the Guru which he stopped with the palm of his right hand. The rock carrying the impression of Guru Nanak's hand still stands there. Punja Sahib was got constructed by Hari Singh Nalwa, with a tank on the spot. Later on, the shrine was replaced by a two-storeyed building with beautiful frescoes in the interior of the building depicting scenes from the life of Guru Nanak and other Gurus. The Shiromani Gurdwara Prabandhak Committee which took it over in 1928 AD constructed a magnificent three-storeyed shrine in grey sandstone. The tank was also enlarged and rebuilt in marble.

PURANMASHI : See Amavas.

PURDAH : See Veil.

PUR HIRAN : See Jahira Jahoor, Gurdwara.

PUSHKAR : Pushkar, a small town at a distance of 13 km from Ajmer is a famous centre of pilgrimage for the Hindus. Guru Nanank visited it during one of his travels. Guru Gobind Singh paid a visit to Pushkar in October 1706 AD to energize the inert and deflated Rajput chiefs. To commemorate his visit, a part of the bank of the sacred tank of Pushkar has been named as Gobind Ghat. It is now proposed to build a memorial there.

Q

QATAL GARH SAHIB, GURDWARA : Gurdwara Qatalgarh Sahib also known as Shahid Ganj is the main shrine at Chamkaur. Situated very close to Garhi Sahib where Guru Gobind Singh and his party were staying and were besieged by the Mughal forces, Qatalgarh marks the site where the fiercest hand-to-hand fighting had taken place on December 7, 1705 AD between the Sikhs and the Mughal army. Two elder sons of Guru Gobind Singh : *Sahibzadas* Ajit Singh and Jujhar Singh and three of the original *Panj Piaras* fell fighting here. The complex comprises Manji Sahib, Akal Bunga, Baoli Sahib and Guru ka Langar.

QILA ANANDGARH, GURDWARA : Gurdwara Qila Anandgarh Sahib is situated on another spur and is about 800m from Takhat Sri Keshgarh Sahib in Anandpur. Although the old fort built by Guru Gobind Singh is still traceable, the present building of the gurdwara was constructed in 1970 AD. It has a *baoli* with 135 marbled steps.

QILA FATEHGARH, GURDWARA : Gurdwara Qila Fatehgarh Sahib is situated on the outskirts of Anandpur. This was originally one of the five fortresses built by Guru Gobind Singh at Anandpur, which has now been converted into a gurdwara. The present building was constructed in the late eighties of the twentieth century. In front of it is an old well which used to serve the needs of Fatehgarh Fort.

R

RAAG : In Indian classical music, *raag* is a technical term used for a sequence of basic notes employed in a prescribed order hearing which may arouse certain feelings. There are innumerable *raags*. However musicologists classify them into three broad categories :

Aurav — using five basic notes;

Chharav — using six basic notes; and

Sampooran — using all the seven basic notes.

Since the Adi Granth is set to music, all the hymns/compositions except Japji with which it begins are clubbed under thirty-one Indian classical *raags* and they are supposed to be sung in those *raags*. See Adi Granth : Organization and Raags.

Raagni, which literally means the female of a *raag*, is a term used by musicologists for some *raags* according to the combination of notes.

RAAGI : *Raagi* literally means a person who specializes in the Indian classical *raags*. Since the Guru Granth Sahib is set to *raags* and the hymns are supposed to be sung in the prescribed *raags*, the term *raagi* is now-a-days used for a musician who leads or accompanies the singing of hymns (*shabad kirtan*) of the Guru Granth Sahib in a gurdwara or a religious function.

RAAGNI : See Raag.

RADHASOAMIS : Radhasoamis constitute a distinct sect in India. They believe in tapping into the sound current the vibrations of the Supreme Creator, yogic meditation, a living Guru, householders way of life and bodily care through the rejection of drugs, alcohol and meat. The sect is also called *Santmat* and lays lot of emphasis on *satsang* (pious company).

The sect was started by Shiv Dyal — also called Shiv Dyal Singh by some—a resident of Agra. He was born in a Khatri family in 1818 AD and got his initial grounding in the teachings of the Adi Granth from Mahant Daya Singh of Gurdwara Mai Than in Agra although the sect has very little common with Sikhism. He spent 15 years in solitude before launching the sect. His book *Sarwachan* is read with devotion by Radhasoamis. Shiv Dyal died in 1878 AD and his cenotaph in Swami Bagh in Agra is a place of pilgrimage. Dyal bagh in Agra has become the headquarters of the sect.

In Punjab the main centre of the Radhasoami sect is located at Beas in Amritsar District.

RAHIRAS : *Rahiras* is the name of a *gurbani* which is recited by the Sikhs as divine service at sunset as a part of *Nitnem*. It consists of nine hymns—four by Guru Nanak, three by Guru Ramdas and the rest by Guru Arjan. They are to be found at the beginning of the Guru Granth Sahib, though each is also placed elsewhere in the scripture under the appropriate *raag*. There is also supplementary material: the *Benti Chaupai* of Guru Gobind Singh, six verses of the *Anand Sahib* by Guru Amardas and the *Mundavani* and a concluding couplet by Guru Arjan.

RAHIT/RAHIT MARYADA : See Code of Conduct.

RAHITNAMAS : *Rahitnama* stands for the Code of Conduct for Sikhs. A number of *Rahitnamas* are available. Their origin and validity is claimed on the basis of their having been dictated by Guru Gobind Singh himself. Bhai Kahn Singh has described three of them namely, *Tankhanama* and *Prashan-Uttar* of Bhai Nand Lal and *Rahitnama* of Bhai Desa Singh based on their dialogues with the Guru. Among the other important *Rahitnamas* are those by Chaupa Singh and Perhlad Singh. All of these codes reflect in their contents the general spirit of the consolidation of Sikhism as was the need of the post-Gobind Singh era. They have a core which was inspired by the Guru.

Of all these, a conversation of Guru Gobind

Singh with Bhai Nand Lal is of utmost importance. It gives the gist of duties a true Sikh should perform :

"O friend, hear me, this is the way of life for a disciple of the Guru. Rise in the early hours of the morning, take bath, recite *Japji* and *Jap Sahib,* and meditate on the Name of God in the evening, join the *sangat* and hear the recitation of *Rahiras,* the praises of God, and the edifying sermons. Those who follow such a routine, always endure. Nand Lal, listen carefully to what I say. In these categories I subsist : the category of the attributes, the category of the Word of the Guru, that which the Guru teaches, men should hear and preach. Men should hear the Word of the Guru with love in their hearts and faith in their minds. This, the Form of the Guru, the men should behold, day in and day out. Men should serve each other, without pride and selfishness. Those who serve humanity, their service do I acknowledge as the service of my person. Listen, O Nand Lal, thus humanity shall be freed and attain everlasting bliss."

Rahitnamas go even into minor details.

RAI BALWAND : See Balwand, Bhai.

RAI BULAR : Rai Bular was the son of Rai Bhoee, a Bhatti Muslim landlord of Nankana Sahib (Talwandi) and neighbouring villages. He came under the influence of Guru Nanak's teachings and is counted among the first few disciples of the Guru.

RAIKOT : See Kallah Rai.

RAJA YOGA : See Yoga.

RAJGARH : Rajgarh is a village in the Malwa region which was originally known as Burj Manawala. Guru Gobind Singh had stayed here to preach to the local people. He came here from Dina. A gurdwara commemorates the Guru's visit.

RAJGIR : Rajgir is a famous town in Bihar associated with Hinduism and Buddhism about 20 km from Gaya. Guru Nanak had visited the town when he came to Gaya during his travels. A gurdwara called Sital Kund commemorates the Guru's visit.

RAJ KAREGA KHALSA : The full couplet reads as :

Raj karega khalsa, aki rahe na koe,
Khwar hoe sabh milenge bache saran jo hoe.

It means : "The Khalsa shall rule and no hostile refractories shall exist. Frustrated, they shall all submit; and those who come for shelter shall be saved." This couplet provides an ending to the general *ardaas* in religious congregations as a psychological uplift and an prophetic promise.

It appears that the couplet was composed in the beginning of the 18th century and was first sung by the Khalsa during the days of Banda Singh Bahadur when he was leading an expedition in Punjab in 1710-16 AD at the behest of Guru Gobind Singh. The reference in the couplet is to the later Mughal—Bahadur Shah I to Shah Alam II.

The couplet is a part of the *Tankhanama* written by Bhai Nand Lal.

RAKAB GANJ, GURDWARA : Gurdwara Rakab Ganj is located on a large plot of land opposite the Parliament House in New Delhi. This is the place where the headless body of Guru Tegh Bahadur was cremated after he was martyred at Sis Ganj. Lakhi Shah and his son had carried the body, concealed in a hay cart, to their house which they set on fire so that the cremation could go on without arousing suspicion. They used to live in a colony of stirrup-makers which also had a Mughal godown for keeping *rakabs* (stirrups); and hence the name of the shrine, Rakab Ganj.

The present building of the gurdwara is an impressive marble structure and has been completed only recently. The frontage on all four sides is alike with steps leading to the platform on which the building stands. Several domes, big and small, adorn the two-storeyed structure.

RAKABSAR, GURDWARA : Gurdwara

Rakabsar is situated in village Bahgabhaini near Mansa. It is dedicated to Guru Tegh Bahadur. According to the Sikh tradition, while the Guru was riding through the area, the lace of his stirrup (Rakab) snapped, when he reached the village he got it repaired there. Gurdwara Rakabsar marks the historical spot.

RAKBA : See Damdama Sahib.

RAMANAND : Ramanand was the son of Bhoor Karma and Sushila and was a Gaur Brahmin. He was born in 1359 AD at Mailkot, where Ramanuj had set up an idol of Vishnu and induced the Brahmins to renounce their devotion to Shiva. Very little is known of his life.

Ramanand is rightly regarded as an eminent pioneer of the *Bhakti* Movement in northern India and as a distinguished leader of the *Vairagi* Cult. He started preaching his gospel at Varanasi and imbued many devotees with the spirit of *Bhakti*. Kabir was the most renowned amongst his disciples. Ravidas, Sain, Dhanna and Pipa are believed to have been his followers even though all of them were not his contemporaries.

Ramanand was a learned pandit. Many of his books such as *Shri Vaishnava Matanbud Bhaskar, Shri Ramcharan Padhti* etc. are still available. One of his hymns has been included in the Adi Granth under *Raag* Basant.

RAM AVTAR : A composition by Guru Gobind Singh included in the Dasam Granth. It has 4360 verses and was written in 1698 AD on the banks of the Sutlej.

In contrast with Pakhian Charitra describing the wiles of women in Ram Avtar, the Guru offered his warriors of the *Dharam Yudh* celestial maidens. Every fairy selects her hero. She says : "Revered Sir, I have decided to marry you. I cannot find a warrior braver than you. I will serve you with heart and soul. I cling to your skirt, O Raja. As soon as you lay down your life in the *dharam yudh*, you will be in my arms, and I will take you to heaven." (DG. p. 607).

RAMDAS, GURU : Guru Ramdas, the fourth Guru of Sikhs, was born on September 24, 1534 AD in a simple God-fearing Sodhi family of Lahore. He was also known as *Jetha*, a word which in Punjabi means the eldest or first-born. His father's name was Haridas and mother's Daya Kaur. As he grew up, Guru Ramdas reached Goindwal and served Guru Amardas with such devotion that he could win the hand of his daughter Bibi Bhani to whom he was maried in 1553 AD.

From the day Guru Ramdas set foot in Goindwal he seemed marked out for the highest honour. Guru Amardas made several tests and being convinced he installed Guru Ramdas as the fourth Guru in 1574 AD.

Guru Ramdas had three sons : Pirthi Chand, Mahadev and Guru Arjan. He died in Goindwal in 1581 AD.

Guru Ramdas founded the city of Amritsar. He was a talented musicologist and has contributed 638 hymns and *saloks* in eleven *raags* to Guru Granth Sahib. Among his famous compositions is the routine of a Sikh given in a hymn on page 305 and the *Lawan*, the hymns recited at every *Anand Karaj*—wedding ceremony. He put missionary work on a sound footing and sent *masands* to different parts of north India to propagate the message of Sikhism. He himself was fond of serving his disciples. The Guru's mission spread quickly both among the poor and the rich classes. Some of the aristocrats visited Amritsar and became his followers. The Guru turned his friendship with Emperor Akbar to good account by persuading him to relieve distress and to remove the oppressive taxes on non-Muslims.

RAMDAS/RAMDASPUR : Ramdas is a well-known religious centre in Amritsar district. Baba Buddha had spent the major part of his life here. It was here that he died and his cenotaph is now a historical shrine. Outside Ramdas is the spot where Baba Buddha, as a child, had met Guru Nanak and was given the epithet of Buddha because of his sagacious talk.

RAMDASIA : *Ramdasia* is a term used in general for Sikhs whose ancestors belonged to backward classes. Originally it meant the descendants and followers of Ramdas who belonged to the weaver (*Julaha*) community and was a disciple of Lakhmir. See also Ravdasia Sant.

RAME-ANA : Rame-ana is a village about 10 km from Jaito in the Malwa region. It has a gurdwara dedicated to Guru Gobind Singh. According to the Sikh tradition, when the Guru reached this village he saw a farmer picking wild *delas* (berries used in making pickle) and asked him to throw them away. The farmer reluctantly agreed but still kept one-fourth part with him. To this the Guru remarked : "I wanted to get rid of the entire problem of poverty of this country but you have retained one-fourth of it."

RAMGARH : Ramgarh is a village about 5 km from Nabha. It has a gurdwara dedicated to Guru Tegh Bahadur.

RAMGARHIA SIKHS : Ramgarhia Sikhs is a distinct group in the Sikh community consisting mainly of carpenters but may include masons, blacksmiths or other artisans. It is generally believed that the term *Ramgarhia* became current in the 18th century. It was initially used as an epithet for Jassa Singh *Thoka* (carpenter) who came from the carpenter class but rose to become the chief of a *misl* which itself came to be known as Ramgarhia *misl*. After the Ram Rauni, a mud-fort near Amritsar, was destroyed, the responsibility of reconstructing and re-inforcing it was given to Jassa Singh *Thoka*. The new fort came to be known as Ramgarh Fort. Because of his association with it Jassa Singh *Thoka* came to be popularly called Jassa Singh Ramgarhia and his *misl* became Ramgarhia *misl*. Gradually the entire group of Sikhs who were carpenters, artisans etc. were termed as Ramgarhia Sikhs.

The artisan skills of Ramgarhia Sikhs brought them to the notice of the British who encouraged them to move to East Africa in the last decade of the nineteenth century for building the transport infrastructure there. With Africanization, many descendants of these emigrants have now moved to U.K., U.S. and Canada. Many of the urban Ramgarhia Sikhs are Namdharis.

RAMKALI : An Indian classical *raag* usually sung within three hours (one *pehar*) from sunrise. It is eighteenth of the thirty-one *raags* used in the organisation of hymns in the Guru Granth Sahib covering pages 875-974. The famous *Anand Sahib* by Guru Amardas falls in this section. The sequence of basic notes is :
Arohi : sa, re, ga, pa, dha, sa,..........
Avrohi : sa, ne, dha, pa, ma, ga, re, sa..........

RAM KAUR, MATA : See Mansa Devi, Mata.

RAMO : Ramo was the elder sister of Mata Damodari and therefore sister-in-law of Guru Hargobind. Daughter of Narain Das, a Khatri of village Dalla near Sultanpur Lodhi, she was married to Bhai Sain Das of village Daroli. Ramo and her husband were devout followers of the Guru who visited them at Daroli a few times.

RAMPUR : See Manji Sahib.

RAM RAI, BABA : Baba Ram Rai was the elder son of Guru Har Rai. He was born to Mata Kot Kalyani in 1646 AD at Kiratpur. When Aurangzeb summoned Guru Har Rai to Delhi, he thought it advisable to send Ram Rai as his ambassador. But he did not give a good account of himself in the court. When one day Aurangzeb asked him why the Sikh Scripture is derogatory to Islam in the *Salok* : "*Mitti Musalman ki*" he replied that there was a mistake in the transcript and the *Salok* should really read as "*Mitti Beiman ki.*" When the news of this incident reached Guru Har Rai at Anandpur he disowned him. Ram Rai settled at Dehradun on a *jagir* given by Aurangzeb where he died in 1687 AD.

RAM RAUNI : See Ramgarhia Sikhs.

RAMSAR : Ramsar is a tank (Sarovar) near Chativind Gate on the south-eastern side of the walled city of Amritsar. Guru Arjan had set up a quiet campus with salubrious surroundings for compiling the Adi Granth. The tank was got dug to keep the place cool and was named Ramsar after Guru Ramdas. Bhai Gurdas worked on the project during 1603-04 AD. Guru Arjan also composed his famous *Sukhmani*, the Psalm of Peace, here.

Gurdwara Ramsar stands on the bank of Ramsar *sarovar* and marks the site of the Guru's labours. It was built in 1855 AD.

RAM SINGH, BABA : Baba Ram Singh was a disciple of Baba Balak Singh, the founder of Namdhari Movement who played a very important role in its consolidation. He was born in 1815 AD in a family of carpenters of district Ludhiana. Initially he served in the army but left it in 1841 AD to spread the teachings of Baba Balak Singh. He set up his headquarters at Bhaini Sahib in district Ludhiana which continues to be the main centre for Namdharis.

Namdharis under Baba Ram Singh's leadership took an active part in the national freedom movement. Many of them were killed by the British by making them face the burst of guns or were hanged. Baba Ram Singh was exiled to Rangoon where he died in 1885 AD.

RANE MAJRA : Rane Majra is a village about 15 km from Ambala city. Guru Gobind Singh had come here from Lakhnaur on the request of the local people.

RANI KA RAIPUR : Rani ka Raipur is an old town in Haryana. According to the Sikh tradition, Guru Gobind Singh had visited the town. Raja Fateh Singh, who was the ruler at that time, being scared of the neighbouring Pathan chiefs, did not allow the Guru to enter the town. Consequently the Guru camped at Manaktabre. The queen, however, did not like this discourtesy on the part of her husband. She invited the Guru for meals who presented her with a *khanda*. Since the Guru called the town "Rani ka Raipur," it has since then been known by that name.

RANJIT NAGARA : See Nagara.

RANJIT SINGH, MAHARAJA : A famous Sikh leader who integrated the Sikh principalities into a soverign state of the Khalsa. Ranjit Singh was born in November, 1780 AD at Gujranwala now in Pakistan. His father Mahan Singh was the head of Sukkarchakia *misl*. Ranjit Singh was married at the age of five to Mehtab Kaur daughter of Sada Kaur and the grand daughter of the head of Kanhaya *misl*. His father died when he was only twelve. The conduct of the Sukkarchakia *misl* was, therefore, left to the care of his mother and *diwan* (Prime Minister) Lakhpat Rai. But soon, all the affairs passed into the hands of his mother-in-law who was the widow of the chief of the Kanahaya *misl*.

The *misls* through internecine quarrels had reduced each other to political impotence. Ranjit Singh was able to establish his suzerainty over them in a short period. He arranged a second marriage with a Nakkai princess. He subdued other *misldars* with force. When the Afghans invaded India, he consolidated the forces of various chieftains to push the invaders out. After that he never looked back. Ranjit Singh captured Lahore in 1799 AD and was coronated as the Maharaja on the occasion of Baisakhi in 1801 AD. This was the beginning of an astonishingly successful military career that led to the extinction of Afghan supremacy in Punjab and the building of a strong sovereign Sikh state.

The rapid successes of the Maharaja in the Trans-Sutlej area (between Sutlej and Indus rivers) made his intervention in the Cis-Sutlej area (between Sutlej and Yamuna rivers) inevitable. This alarmed the British who had an eye on the area. This led to the Amritsar Treaty signed in April 1809 AD restricting the activities of the Maharaja to the right side of the river Sutlej. Nevertheless, helped by capable generals like Hari Singh Nalwa and Akali Phula Singh he won many victories in that area.

After a successful career, Maharaja Ranjit Singh died of paralysis on June 27, 1839 AD. After his death the Sikh empire soon disintegrated and Punjab was finally annexed by the British in 1849 AD.

RATANPURA : Ratanpura is a village near Jagadhari in Haryana. It has a gurdwara which commemorates the visit of Guru Tegh Bahadur to the place on his way to Booriai.

RAVDASIA : *Ravdasia* is a term used for Sikhs whose ancestors got converted into Sikhism from the *chamar* (shudra) community. Since Bhagat Ravidas also belonged to that community they take pride in calling themselves as the descendants or followers of Ravidas. See also Ramdasia.

RAVIDAS, BHAGAT : Bhagat Ravidas is one of the saints whose hymns are included in the Adi Granth. The appearance of Ravidas on the spiritual scene in India in the 15th century represents the culmination of *Bhakti* Movement. He was a disciple of Ramanand and a contemporary of Kabir. The spiritual power of Ravidas was known far and wide. He inspired Meera Bai. The Queen of Chittor became his disciple. Ravidas was a resident of Kanshi and came from a cobbler's family. In spite of his low caste, he rose to a position of great honour and respect through a life of simplicity and piety. He is treated as the father of a sect among the Vaishnavas who are known as *Ravidasias*. See also Ramdasias.

REETHA SAHIB : Reetha Sahib is a famous spot in Nainital district in Uttar Pradesh associated with Guru Nanak. *Reetha* means soapnut tree whose fruit is bitter. During his travels Guru Nanak passed through this spot in a jungle. His constant companion Mardana felt hungry. When he was unable to bear the pangs of hunger, Guru Nanak asked him to pluck the fruit from the soapnut tree. It was sweet. The soapnuts from this branch are sweet even today. Pilgrims bring a soapnut or two back home as *Prasad*. Reetha Sahib is about 40 km from Nanakmata.

RERU SAHIB, GURDWARA : Gurdwara Reru Sahib dedicated to Guru Gobind Singh is situated on the outskirts of village Rampur about 3 km from Doraha in the Malwa region. Guru Gobind Singh had rested here under a *reru* tree after leaving Machhiwara.

RITUALS : Sikhism expresses itself clearly against rituals of Hinduism and Islam. Insistence on their careful observance results in formalism which keeps the worshipper preoccupied with the temporal to the neglect of the spiritual. The Guru Granth Sahib clearly advises: "Burn such rituals which take you away from the Lord."

Jalao aisi riti jit mai piara wisrai (AG. p. 590)

The futility of rituals is hinted again and again in the scripture. For example criticizing ritualistic bathing in rivers it says : "If by bathing alone one were to be emancipated, then the frog bathes continually and for ever."

Jal kai majni je gati hovai, nit nit maindak naweh
(AG. p. 484)

Men and women need only to meditate on the divine Name. All else is futile.

Sabh phokat nischan karam (AG. p. 470)

At the same time Sikhism has acquired its own rituals as a part of its evolution as a religion.

RIWALSAR : Riwalsar is a pilgrimage centre with a lake of the same name about 15 km from Mandi in Himachal Pradesh. Guru Gobind Singh had come here once on the Baisakhi fair to advise the hill *rajas*. A gurdwara marks the spot on the hill top where the Guru had camped.

ROHTA : Rohta is a village about 5 km from Nabha. Guru Tegh Bahadur had come here from Seembhro. A gurdwara near the village commemorates the visit.

ROHTAK : Rohtak is a district town in Haryana near Delhi. Guru Tegh Bahadur visited it on his way to Delhi. A gurdwara has been dedicated to the Guru.

ROOP CHAND, BHAI : Bhai Roop Chand was a devout disciple of Guru Hargobind. His parents belonging to village Vadaghar of Tarn Taran area had been his followers too. In fact Bhai Roop Chand was administered *charan amrit* by the Guru who also gave him the title of Bhai and founded the village Bhairoopa in 1631 AD after his name. His two sons Param Singh and Dharam Singh were administered *amrit* by Guru Gobind Singh whom they continued to serve till the end.

Bhai Roop Chand died in 1709 AD. A village called Bhai ki Samadh in the Malwa region has come up around his cenotaph.

ROPAR : Ropar is an important town in Punjab on the banks of the river Sutlej and is intimately linked with Sikh history. Guru Gobind Singh passed through it on his way to Kurukshetra. At one time it was the capital of one of the Sikh states. Maharaja Ranjit Singh had long parleys with Lord William Bentick here in October 1831 AD on the basis of which a treaty of alliance was renewed.

ROSARY : Rosary called *japmala* in Punjabi is a string of beads that is used for counting prayers by members of various religions. Although the number of beads differs from religion to religion, this counting aid is found in Hinduism, Jainism, Christianity and Islam.

Sikh meditation, however, does not need to be accompanied by counting. As such it does not require a physical rosary or *japmala* which should be a part of the mental concentration of the worshipper. There are some references to this in the Guru Granth Sahib. For example it says : "Remember the Name of the God with the rosary in your mind."

Gurmat Nam dhiya-ee-ai Har Har, man japi-ai Har japmala. (AG. p. 985)

In the same vein it further states : "One who meditates with *japmala* inside his mind is liberated from the cycle of birth-rebirth."

Harmala ur antardhare, janam maran ka dukh niware (AG, Asa, M. 5)

S

SABHRAI : Sabhrai was the sister of Baba Pheru father of Guru Angad. She was married to a resident of Khadur. Some chroniclers refer to her as Phirai as well.

SACHAN SACH : Sachan Sach was a Brahmin of village Mandir in Lahore district and was contemporary of Guru Amardas. He was a devout disciple of the Guru. He used to frequently utter the phrase "sachan sach", so the Guru gave him this name. The Guru also got him married to the former queen of Haripur whom he had cured of insanity. The couple became zealous missionaries and were awarded a *manji* by the Guru.

SACH KHAND : *Sach Khand* means the Realm of Truth—the fifth and final stage of spiritual ascent. In Japji, Guru Nanak describes it as the abode of the Formless one.
    Sach Khand wasai Nirankar (AG. p. 8)
    At the same place he makes it clear that : 'To describe it is as hard as steel.'
    Nanak Kathna Karara Sar (AG. p. 8)
    See also Heaven and Hell.
Sach Khand is also the name of the most important shrine at Hazur Sahib. See Hazur Sahib. The terminology is sometimes used for the Golden Temple as well.

SADA KAUR : Sada Kaur was the daughter of Chandu, a Khatri of Lahore who was a revenue official in the Mughal Court. Her hand was offered to Guru Hargobind but the offer was turned down by Guru Arjan. Because of this Chandu became inimical to Guru Arjan and started conspiring against him.

SADDHOO : Saddhoo, a resident of Lahore, was a devout Sikh of Guru Arjan. The Guru had stayed at his house from where he was picked up and sent to prison and later on tortured to death.

SADDOO : Saddoo and Maddoo were two brothers who were rebeck players and used to do *kirtan* in the court of Guru Gobind Singh at Anandpur.

SADHAR : See Gurusar.

SADHAURA : See Lohgarh.

SADHNA : Sadhna is one of the *bhagats* whose compositions (one *shabad* in his case) are included in the Guru Granth Sahib. His hymn is a prayer to the God to protect the honour of His devotees.
    Sadhna is believed to have been born in Sehwan in Sind and to have been a butcher by trade. He was a contemporary of Namdev. He embraced a religious life by listening to holy men. He became an object of persecution and it is believed that he was put to death by being built alive into a wall. His tomb exists at Sirhind.

SADH SANGAT : Literally *sadh sangat* means the company of saints. Since every Sikh is considered a saint-soldier, the term is a reverent synonym of the word *sangat*, meaning congregation or local community. *Satsang* which means holy company is another synonym of *sadh sangat*.

SAHAJ : See Equipoise.

SAHAJDHARI : *Sahajdhari* literally means a 'slow adopter.' In Sikh speech and writing the term is generally used for a person who has accepted the Sikh philosophy but does not follow the complete Sikh Code of Conduct as for example the *kakaars*. Since he has not received initiation into the Khalsa, the term is used in contrast to *amritdhari* or even *keshadhari*. Sometimes *sahajdharis* are also called *Nanakpanthis*.

SAHAJ PATH : See Path.

SAHERI : See Gangu.

SAHIB KAUR, MATA : Mata Sahib Kaur was one of the consorts of Guru Gobind Singh. She was the daughter of Ramu, a Khatri of Rohtas and was married to the Guru in 1700 AD. She had accompanied the Guru on his Deccan tour. The Guru returned her to Delhi with five weapons of Guru Hargobind. She spent her last years at Delhi with Mata Sundri.

Mata Sahib Kaur was cremated at Gurdwara Bala Sahib, in Delhi.

SAHIB SINGH, BHAI : Bhai Sahib Singh whose original name was Sahib Chand was one of the first *Panj Piare* who had offered their heads to Guru Gobind Singh on the Baisakhi day of 1699 AD at Anandpur and were thus the first to be initiated into the Khalsa brotherhood. Very little is known about his biographical details. According to one version he was the son of Chamna of Bidar belonging to the *Nai* (hair dresser) caste. He was born in 1662 AD. He was a devoted follower of Guru Gobind Singh. Even before his initiation into the Khalsa in 1699 AD he had fought for the Guru very valiantly in the battle at Bhangani. He was killed fighting in the battle at Chamkaur in December 1705 AD.

SAHIBZADE : *Sahibzade* literally means the son of a Guru and is the equivalent of *Rajkumar*. *Sahibzade* is the plural of *Sahibzada* but in Sikh speech and writing the term is specifically used for the four sons of Guru Gobind Singh : Ajit Singh, Jujhar Singh, Fateh Singh and Zorawar Singh. See respective entries for more details about them. They are remembered every time the *ardaas* is said because they sacrificed their lives for the cause of Sikhism.

SAIN, BHAGAT : There are two varying accounts of Bhagat Sain's life. Some people hold that he was an employee of the ruler of Bidar and faithful devotee of Saint Gyaneshwar. But according to the popular tradition, he was a barber at the court of Raja Ram, king of Rewa, then called Bandhvgarh.

He was a follower of Ramanand and Kabir and a forerunner of Ravidas.

Only one hymn of Bhagat Sain is incorporated in the Adi Granth under Dhanasari *Raag*.

SAIN DAS : Sain Das was a Khatri of village Daroli who was married to Ramo, the elder sister of Mata Damodari, wife of Guru Hargobind. He was a devout follower of the Guru who stayed at Daroli a number of times. See also Daroli and Ramo.

SAJJAN THUG : Sajjan was a *thug* belonging to the town of Tulambha in Multan district of Pakistan. He used to rob unwary travellers who would come to his inn in collaboration with his nephew Kajjan. Sajjan used to plan the robberies and subsequent murders so well that no one could discover them. In fact, those whom he spared used to praise him for the arrangements at his inn.

According to the Sikh tradition, Guru Nanak stayed at Sajjan's inn during his travels through that area. Sajjan had planned to rob the Guru but was so much influenced by the Guru's singing of hymns that he became a devout Sikh.

SAKHI : *Sakhi* literally means 'testimony' or an eyewitness account. Thus *Janam Sakhis* of the Gurus are a rich source of biographical material about them and also reflect the teachings of Sikhism. *Sakhi* is a part of the *Janam Sakhi* but sometimes is also used in a more general sense of a story or an anecdote. See also Janam Sakhis.

SALH, BHATT : Bhatt Salh is one of the 17 *Bhatts* whose compositions are included in the Adi Granth. He sings of the spiritual excellence of Guru Amardas in one *swayya* and that of Guru Ramdas in two *swayyas* in the Adi Granth. His main focus is on conquering passion, anger, greed and ego.

SALO, BHAI : Bhai Salo was a devout follower of Guru Arjan. He was the *kotwal* of Amritsar in whose construction he played an important role. A *dharmsala* has been dedicated to him in Amritsar. He died in 1628 AD and his last rites were personally performed by Guru Hargobind.

SALOK : *Salok* is a special kind of verse frequently used in the Guru Granth Sahib. It consists of one or more distiches which rhyme at the end. The verse contains 22 *moras* and there is a caesura generally after the twelfth *mora*.

SALOORI : Saloori is a village in the foothills of Shivalik. Guru Gobind Singh had stayed here while going to help the hill *rajas* in the battle at Nadaun in 1690 AD. A gurdwara on the hill top marks the spot since the times of Maharaja Ranjit Singh.

SALUTATION : The salutation used by the Sikhs has been undergoing a number of changes. During the days of Guru Nanak the accepted form of salutation was *pairi pauna* (I bow at your feet). Towards the last year of Guru Nanak when he had settled at Kartarpur (Pakistan), it appears that the accepted form of greeting among the Sikhs had changed to saying *Kartar Kartar;* the Guru in turn would say *Sat Kartar*. The name Kartarpur is also a pointer to this practice. But *pairi pauna* never lost currency and is still found in traditional families.

With the establishment of the Khalsa, Guru Gobind Singh wanted a complete transformation of the Sikh psyche. He gave a new salutation : *Waheguru ji ka Khalsa, Waheguru ji ki Fateh* (Khalsa belongs to the God and Victory belongs to Him). The Khalsa was supposed to win Victory and they were reminded that they owe them to the Almighty. It is laid down in Sikh *Rahit Maryada* that one Sikh (whether male or female) shall greet another with this salutation.

Nevertheless, the most common salutation among the Sikhs now is to greet each other with folded hands and to utter *Sat Sri Akal* (The Timeless is True). The origin of this greeting is perhaps the war cry : *Jo bole so nihal, Sat Sri Akal* (Whoever says that the Timeless is True is happy) in the post-Banda Bahadur period. It was perhaps used to hoodwink the enemy into a belief that there was roaming in the jungle not one but many Sikh warriors. Gradually this war cry got shortened into *Sat Sri Akal*. The devout still continue with *Waheguru ji ka Khalsa, Waheguru ji ki Fateh*.

SALVATION : See Mukti.

SAMVAT : See Bikarmi Samvat.

SANGAT : It is a Punjabi word which means congregation. *Sangat* has been institutionalized in Sikhism.

The origin of this institution can be traced to the days of Guru Nanak, who travelled extensively to preach the Name of God. Wherever he went, he left an assembly of men and women called *sangat* who were asked to build a shrine where they could meet and hold *diwans* and sing hymns together. This served a double purpose. First, it provided a meeting place for religious minded people. Second, it served as a centre for religious preachings.

After Guru Nanak, Guru Tegh Bahadur went to far off places and established *sangats*. With the passage of time, the Sikh *sangats* were sanctified until Guru Gobind Singh transferred the entire spiritual authority to them. With the creation of the Khalsa, the *sangat* assumed the personality of the Guru. "The good *sangat* is superior, in its company sins are washed" had ordained Guru Nanak.

Sangat must, however, be distinguished from Sarbat Khalsa which is the commonwealth of all Sikhs.

SANGAT SAHIB : See Hazur Sahib.

SANGAT TOLA, GURDWARA : Gurdwara Sangat Tola situated in Dacca is associated with Guru Tegh Bahadur. The Guru had stayed there on his way to Assam. The local followers received him with great affection and built the two-storeyed structure specially for his stay. Devotees visited him in hundreds every day and listened to the *kirtan* and holy discourses. It was here that the Guru learnt of the birth of his son Guru Gobind Singh at Patna. Some relics are preserved in the shrine.

SANGRANA SAHIB, GURDWARA : Sangrana Sahib is a gurdwara dedicated to Guru Hargobind. It is situated near village Chabba in Amritsar district. According to the Sikh tradition, a resident of the village Mai Sulakhani had asked for the boon of a son from the Guru during his visit. She gave birth to seven sons and now almost the entire village consists of her descendants.

SANGRAND : *Sangrand* is a Punjabi word for *Sankranti*, the day when the sun enters the new *Rashi* (zodiac sign). According to the Indian calendar it is the first day of the month. On this day special congregations are held in gurdwaras, in which the new month is announced with reading of the relevant portion of *Barahmaha*.

It may be mentioned that Sikhism discounts the notion of one day being better or worse than the other. "In the process of calculating and fixing auspicious days, we forget that God is above such considerations" (AG. p. 904). Nevertheless *sangrad* continues to be celebrated because of the strong tradition.

SANHARI MAL : Sanhari Mal was the elder brother of Guru Ramdas. He was a resident of Lahore. It was his son's wedding that Guru Arjan was deputed to attend on behalf of his father with the instruction not to return to Amritsar without being asked. According to the Sikh tradition, because of these instructions, Guru Arjan remained at Lahore for two years although always pining to meet his father. During this period he composed the hymn *"Mera man lochai Gurdarsan taee"* (I yearn to see the Guru) and sent it to Guru Ramdas. Sanhari Mal imbibed the teachings of Sikhism and became a follower of Guru Arjan.

SANH SAHIB : See Baserke.

SANKRANTI : See Sangrand.

SANMI : Sanmi which is also known as Samir is a village near Bhatinda. Guru Gobind Singh passed through it on his way from Bhatinda to Damdama Sahib (Talwandi Sabo) A gurdwara commemorates the Guru's visit.

SANT : *Sant* is a Punjabi version of the English word 'Saint'. It seems to have been derived from the Sanskrit word 'Shant' meaning peaceful and is now-a-days used for a highly religious person who has achieved a certain level of mental peace and equipoise.

Guru Arjan has summed up the characteristics of a *sant* in these words : "The saint realizes the presence of God at all hours; he regards the will of God as sweet; his only support is the Name. Yet he is humble to be the dust of all. He finds comfort in melodious *kirtan*. He regards friends and foes alike. He knows none as well as God." (AG. p. 392).

SANTOKH : See Contentment.

SANTOKHSAR : Santokhsar is one of the oldest *sarovars* (tanks) in Amritsar. This was dug for the first time by Bhai Jetha who later became Guru Ramdas in 1564 AD under the directions of Guru Amardas. The work, however, remained incomplete till it was completed by Guru Arjan in 1588 AD. It fell into neglect during the turbulent days of the eighteenth century and was cleaned and put to use in 1903 AD.

Santokhsar is situated close to the townhall and has Gurdwara Tahli Sahib attached to it. It is so named after a *tahli* tree under which Guru Ramdas and after him Guru Arjan used to stand while supervising the excavation of Santokhsar. Only a stump of the tree now remains at the site.

SANTOKH SINGH, BHAI : Bhai Santokh Singh was a renowned poet, author and theologian of the 19th century. He was born in 1788 AD at Amritsar where his father Bhai Deva Singh was having scholarly pursuits.

His contributions include : (i) Amarkosh, (ii) Guru Nanak Prakash, (iii) Exposition of Japji, (iv) Tanslation of Atam Puran (v) Translation of Balmiki Ramayan and (vi) Suraj Prakash.

Bhai Santokh Singh passed away in 1843 AD at Kaithal.

SANT SINGH : Sant Singh was a devout follower of Guru Gobind Singh. He belonged to the town of Patti in the Majha area. According to the Sikh tradition he was with the Guru at the time of the battle at Chamkaur in 1705 AD. While leaving Chamkaur the Guru had put *turra* and *kalghi* (aigrette) on his head. His son Hara Singh, who is also referred to as Bahadur Singh by some chroniclers, was favoured with a *hukamnama* which used to be in the custody of some residents of Peshawar before 1947 AD. Hara Singh had shifted to Peshawar from Patti.

SARALA : See Gurplah.

SARANG : An Indian classical *raag* usually sung at noon. It is twenty-sixth of the thirty-one *raags* used in the organisation of hymns in the Guru Granth Sahib covering pages 1197-1253. Its pure form has the following sequence of basic notes :-
   Arohi : sa, re, ma, pa, ne, sa..........
   Avrohi : sa, dha, ne, pa, ma, re, sa..........

SARAWAN : See Gurusar.

SARBAT KHALSA : *Sarbat* means whole. *Sarbat Khalsa* means collectivity of the Sikh people. It is a theo-political doctrine, by which the Sikhs assume powers and the status of the centralized conscience and will of the people.

Sarbat Khalsa was first used for the gathering of all Sikhs on the day of Diwali and Baisakhi at the Akal Takht. *Sarbat Khalsa* used to discuss the questions of Panthic interest at such gatherings and *Gurmatas* evolved out of the consensus of such meetings were passed. The *Sarbat Khalsa* made many important decisions which changed the history of Punjab as, for example, regarding accepting a *jagir* (1733 AD), building a fort at Amritsar (1747 AD), forming Dal Khalsa (1748 AD) attacking Lahore (1760 AD) etc.

The power and prestige of *Sarbat Khalsa* has been declining since the days of *misls* and Maharaja Ranjit Singh. However, a number of *Sarbat Khalsas* were held in recent years after the army action in the Golden Temple in 1984 AD. Some of them were very controversial.

SARBLOH : *Sarbloh* is the title of a composition whose authorship is disputable. It is also known as *Mangalcharan*. Although it is mentioned in it that it is a composition by Guru Gobind Singh, researchers generally do not accept it. According to the findings of Pandit Tara Singh it was written by Bhai Sukkha Singh who was a *granthi* at Patna.

Bhai Dhian Singh of Kattu developed a version of the Dasam Granth by replacing *Charitr* by *Sarbloh* but it did not get much currency.

SARBULAND KHAN : Sarbuland Khan was the maternal uncle and a famous general of Ahmad Shah Abdali. He spent all his life fighting against the Sikhs. For some time he was also the administrator of Jalandhar. In 1756 AD he was defeated near Jalandhar by Jassa Singh Ahluwalia. Charat Singh of Sukkarchakia *misl* imprisoned him in Rohtas Fort but later, after receiving compensation, released him and sent him to Afghanistan.

SARHEENA : Sarheena is a village near Moga in the Malwa region. It has a gurdwara dedicated to Guru Hargobind.

SARMAUR : Another name for Nahan. See Medni Parkash.

SAROPA : *Saropa* is a term for the robe of honour presented by the community to one of its own members or anyone else to whom it wishes to display formal respect. It often takes the form of a length of cloth for a turban or a broad scarf to be worn over the shoulders. Sometimes *kirpan* is also presented as a part of the *saropa*. The presentation takes place in a congregation where the Guru Granth Sahib is present.

SARSA : 1. A rivulet between Anandpur and Chamkaur. After leaving Anandpur when Guru Gobind Singh was crossing Sarsa many of his followers and armaments were swept in the floods in Sarsa.

2. Also the name of a small town in Hissar district in Haryana. There is a gurdwara commemorating the visit of Guru Nanak. Guru Gobind Singh also passed through Sarsa while going to the Deccan.

SAT/SATYA : See Truth.

SATI : *Sati* is the name of the practice among ancient Hindus according to which widows used to immolate themselves on their husband's pyres with the belief that by doing so they would obtain salvation. The widow who immolated herself was also called *sati*. Raja Ram Mohan Rai, the founder of the Brahmo Samaj raised his banner against the practice in modern times and got an Act passed against it in December 1829 AD through the then Governor General of India, William Bentick.

Sikhism expresses its disapproval of *sati* in very strong terms. This occurs at a number of places in the Guru Granth Sahib. For example it explains : "A woman cannot attain the Lord by burning herself as *sati*."

Jalai na pa-ee-ai Ram sanehi (AG., p. 185)

SATI DAS, BHAI : Bhai Mati Das and Bhai Sati Das were two brothers who came from a Brahmin family of village Kariala in Jehlum district now in Pakistan. They were devout disciples of Guru Tegh Bahadur and were arrested, chained and imprisoned by Aurangzeb along with the Guru in 1675 AD. After Bhai Mati Das and Bhai Dayala had been put to death, Aurangzeb's men took out Bhai Sati Das and on his refusal to accept Islam he was wrapped in cotton soaked with oil and burnt to death on November 11, 1675 AD. See also Mati Das, Bhai.

SAT BHIRAI : See Bhirai, Mai.

SATLANI : A place in Amritsar district with a historical gurdwara called Gurusar Satlani as its focal point within the revenue limits of Hoshiarnagar. The gurdwara marks the spot where Guru Hargobind travelling from Lahore to Amritsar made a night's halt near a pond, which has been properly lined and is now used as *sarovar*.

SAT NAM : *Sat Nam* is a popular chant in Sikhism. It may be translated as 'True *Nam*' or 'Truth is His Name' and basically stands for the Ultimate Reality or the Eternal Lord. Congregations often repeat this expression in the interregnum after the *Bhog* by way of remembering the Lord.

SAT SANG : See Sadh Sangat.

SAT SRI AKAL : See Salutation.

SATTA : Satta was a companion of Balwand. He was a rebeck-player who served Guru Angad, Guru Amardas, Guru Ramdas and Guru Arjan. Satta and Balwand jointly composed a *Var* (Ballad) which is included under Ramkali *Raag* in the Adi Granth. It is generally believed that the first five stanzas were composed by Balwand and the last three by Satta.

For more details see Balwand.

SATYUG : See Yugas.

SAU SAKHI : *Sau Sakhi* is a collection of one hundred *sakhis* (stories) attributed to Guru Gobind Singh. It is written in Punjabi prose with verses added at places. The authenticity of its authorship and the date of writing is not established without doubt. According to internal evidence it was written in 1724 AD by Sahib Singh as narrated to him by Gurbakhsh Singh, a close associate of Guru Gobind Singh. From its style of writing, it cannot be believed without doubt that it is the work of Guru Gobind Singh.

Sau Sakhi came into lime light with the popularity of *Kuka* movement as its rise is said to have been prophesied in this work. The mention about the rise of one Ram Singh was interpreted to refer to their leader. Since *Kukas* were at the forefront of the freedom movement, the British government evinced keen interest in this book. It was on this account that Attar Singh Rais of Bhadour translated this work into English. It was again much talked of after the damage to the Akal Takht in the army action in June 1984 AD.

The contents of *Sau Sakhi* can be a source of information about Sikhism. The doctrines of Sikhism, the *Rahit*, the Sikh institutions of *Langar*, *Manji* and *Masand* etc. have been discussed. It is the prophesies occuring here and there throughout the whole book and some anachronistic statements that mar the authenticity of the work.

SAWAN MAL, BABA : Baba Sawan Mal was the nephew of Guru Amardas. When the construction work was going on at Goindwal, he was sent to the hills near Haripur to bring timber for the same. He preached Sikhism in that area. As a result the Raja of Haripur came to see the Guru and got converted to Sikhism along with his family. The Guru appointed Baba Sawan Mal as a missionary and granted him a *manji*.

SAYYID BEG : Two Mughal commanders, Sayyid Beg and Alif Khan were going from Lahore to Delhi with a force of about five thousand soldiers. Raja Bhim Chand of Bilaspur who had not reconciled himslef to Guru Gobind Singh's presence at Anandpur persuaded the commanders to expel the Guru from his territory on a payment of one thousand rupees a day. Alif Khan had already fought in the Kangra hills and had a grievance against the Guru. They agreed and there were a few skirmishes in 1702 AD. Later on differences rose between the commanders with Sayyid Beg joining the Guru. Disheartened by it, Alif Khan retired.

SEEBHRO : Seebhro is a village near Patiala. It has a gurdwara dedicated to Guru Tegh Bahadur.

SEKHA : Sekha is a village in the Malwa region which has two gurdwaras sacred to Guru Tegh Bahadur. One marks the spot where the Guru had camped in the village during his travels. The other marks the place where the Guru took milk offered by an old woman.

SENAPATI : Senapati was a scholar in the court of Guru Gobind Singh. He is known for compiling the *Gurushobha* and the translation of Chankya policy.

SERVICE : *Seva* or service as an active help to the fellow beings occupies a central place in the social ethics of Sikhs. The spirit of service creates love and affection among others and tells them to live in humility. It makes man forget his social status so that he no longer thinks in terms of high or low, rich or poor. It helps man overcome his ego (*haumai*). *Seva* is a part and parcel of Sikhism and is a practical way of life for a Sikh. A real Sikh is one who, besides doing other duties, meditates in the name of God and performs service for the welfare of humanity.

Service could be of different types—serving the poor and needy, giving in charity, helping a person in distress or saving someone in danger, "Material, physical service, like providing food or giving rest to the bodies of others, or reading out the scriptures for their solace is far superior to the countless sacrificial fires and performances of ceremonies or mere meditation and worldly knowledge." (Bhai Gurdas, Vars, Stanza 5, *Var* 12). The service of others is enjoined by the Gurus. "All living beings are your own creatures, but none can obtain any reward without rendering service." (AG. p. 354). "We shall be rewarded according to the service we give" (AG. p. 468). But it is held by the Gurus that service, if it is to be worthwhile, ought to be done without any consideration of reward. In case any reward is solicited for rendition of service it can only be termed as bargain. "He who serves without desire for rewards, he alone attains to God" (AG. p. 286). Service is its own reward. "We get eternal bliss through the service of God and merge in the peace of poise" (AG., p. 216).

SEVA : See Service.

SEVAK, BHATT : *Bhatt* Sevak is one of the 17 *Bhatts* (Bards) whose compositions (4 *swayyas* in his case) have been included in the Adi Granth. See under *Bhatts*.

SEVA PANTHIS : The sect of *seva panthis* (social workers) has grown from among the Sikhs by almost exclusive emphasis on *seva* as a moral tenet of Sikh ethics. They believe that one ought to serve all persons because the Gurus are happy when the disciple serves humanity.

Seva panthis trace their origin from Bhai Kanhaya a Sikh contemporary of Guru Tegh Bahadur and Guru Gobind Singh. He is said to have served water to the wounded soldiers, both Sikhs as well as those of the opposing army. When someone complained to Guru Gobind Singh against it he is reported to have replied that he was doing so in the true spirit of Sikhism which requires not to distinguish between friend and foe. He was approbated and encouraged by the Guru who is believed to have given ointment to Bhai Kanhaya for application to the wounded without any discrimination.

SGPC : Abbreviation for the Shiromani Gurdwara Parbandhak Committee. See Akali Movement.

SHABAD : In Sikh thought the word *Shabad* or *Sabad* is used in two broad senses.

Theologically *Shabad* which is also called *Bani* means the primordial Sound and the Divine Wisdom which is contained in the Guru Granth Sahib. *Shabad* as eternal and self-existent sound is an Indo-Iranian concept also found in Hinduism and Zorastrianism. *Shabad* as Divine Wisdom—the Western idea of 'Logos' is closer to the Christian concept of the Word. One of the basic doctrines which is repeatedly laid down and reiterated is that *Shabad* (Bani) is the Guru and Guru is the *Shabad* for it contains the essence of everything. And whoever accepts *Shabad* as the Guru shall behold the Guru in himself."

Bani Guru Guru hai bani wich bani amrit sare
Guru bani kahe sevak jan manai Pritam Guru nistare (AG. p. 982)

Based on this concept, since the Divine Wisdom is contained in the Adi Granth. Guru Gobind Singh had declared it as the Eternal Guru—Guru Granth Sahib.

In common parlance the word *shabad* is used for a hymn taken from the Guru Granth Sahib, or the Dasam Granth or even from the compositions of Bhai Gurdas.

SHABAD HAZARE : See Hazare Shabad.

SHABAD KIRTAN : See Kirtan.

SHAHBAZ SINGH : Shahbaz Singh was the son of Subeg Singh who was tortured to death in Lahore along with his father in 1745 AD at the age of 18. He did not accept conversion to Islam and was known for his boldness of views.

SHAH HUSSAIN : Shah Hussain was a Sufi saint of Lahore. He was a contemporary of Guru Arjan. When the Adi Granth was being compiled, he came to Amritsar with other religious preachers to request the Guru to include his compositions in it as well. According to the Sikh tradition, the Guru heard him recite some of his compositions but did not find them upto the mark.

SHAHID BURJ, CHAMKAUR : Its full name is Gurdwara Shahid Burj Bhai Jiwan Singh. It used to be the gate of the *haveli* (*garhi*) used by Guru Gobind Singh as the bulwark of defence in the battle at Chamkaur on December 6-7, 1705 AD. This is a small shrine and has been named after Bhai Jiwan Singh who was originally Bhai Jaita who had brought Guru Tegh Bahadur's head from Delhi to Kiratpur in

1675 AD after the Guru's martyrdom. He was killed in a rearguard action on the bank of Sarsa.

SHAHID GANJ : In general the term Shahid Ganj is used for a memorial for a Sikh martyr. As such, Punjab is dotted with a number of spots called Shahid Ganj. Gurdwara Fatehgarh Sahib in Sirhind is a Shahid Ganj built in memory of the two younger sons of Guru Gobind Singh. There is a Shahid Ganj in memory of *Chalis Mukte* on the edge of the *sarovar* at Muktsar. We give below the details about Shahid Ganj, Baba Deep Singh and Shahid Ganj, Chamkaur. Needless to repeat that Sikh history has created innumerable such memorials which cannot be completely listed here.

1. Shahid Ganj, Baba Deep Singh : Gurdwara Shahid Ganj Baba Deep Singh is situated near the Chatiwind Gate of Amritsar. It commemorates the spot where Baba Deep Singh was fatally wounded fighting against the forces of the Amritsar administrator.

Ahmad Shah Abdali had blown up the Golden Temple in 1757 AD. Baba Deep Singh as chief of the Shahid *misl* marched from Damdama Sahib (Bhatinda) to Amritsar via Tarn Taran with the intention of freeing and rebuilding the Golden Temple. Baba Deep Singh was intercepted in Nov. 1757 AD at the place where Gurdwara Shahid Ganj has been constructed. He was severely wounded in the neck in the battle that ensued. According to Sikh tradition despite the fatal wound, Baba Deep Singh reached the precincts of the Golden Temple.

Jassa Singh Ramgarhia raised initially a memorial platform at the site which was developed into a gurdwara by Akali Phula Singh.

2. Shahid Ganj, Chamkaur : See Qatalgarh Sahib, Gurdwara.

SHAHJAHAN : Shahjahan took over from Jahangir after his death in 1628 AD as the fourth Mughal Emperor during the pontificate of Guru Hargobind. Initially the fanatical religious policy of Jahangir continued. There were small skirmishes between the imperial forces and the followers of the Guru upto 1635 AD. The Guru had to change his headquarters from Amritsar first to Chubhal, then to Hargobindpur, later to Kartarpur (Jalandhar), again to Phagwara and finally to Kiratpur. But these battles were rather local in nature. Shahjahan did not disturb the Guru during his stay at Kiratpur from 1935-44 AD. The same relationship of reconciliation continued even during the pontificate of Guru Har Rai. He is said to have written a letter to Guru Har Rai at Kiratpur on the lines : "... My son Dara Shikoh is very ill. His remedy is in thy hands. If thou give the myrobalan and the clove which are in thy store house, and add to them thy prayers, thou wilt confer an abiding favour on me." Dara Shikoh is also said to have visited the Guru at Goindwal when he was being chased by Aurangzeb's forces in 1658 AD in the war of succession. But finding the Prince in an indecisive mood and Aurangzeb in hot pursuit, the Guru did not extend any help to him. Nevertheless this became a sore point with Aurangzeb who summoned the Guru to Delhi when he assumed full command of the situation.

Shahjahan was imprisoned by Aurangzeb at Agra where he later died.

SHAHPUR : Shahpur is a village near Sunam in the Malwa region. It has a gurdwara dedicated to Guru Tegh Bahadur.

SHAKKAR GANJ : See Farid.

SHAM SINGH ATTARI : Sham Singh Attari was a brave Sikh general belonging to village Attari in Amritsar district. His daughter Nanaki was married to Naunihal Singh, the grandson of Maharaja Ranjit Singh in 1837 AD. He took active part in the first Anglo-Sikh War in 1845-46 AD and was killed in the battle at Sabraon on February 10, 1846 AD.

SHARING : See Vand Chhakna.

SHASTAR NAM MALA : A composition by

Guru Gobind Singh included in the Dasam Granth. It contains 1323 verses describing various weapons of war. Among the weapons the most important position is given to the sword.

Aus kirpan, khando, kharag, tupak tabar aur tir; Saif, sarohi, sehathi, yahi hamare pir. (DS. 717)

SHIKAR GHAT : See Hazur Sahib.

SHIROMANI AKALI DAL : See Akali Movement.

SHIROMANI GURDWARA PARBANDHAK COMMITTEE : See Akali Movement.

SHISH MAHAL : Shish Mahal is a general name for a gurdwara whose walls are studded with mirrors. Some of the important Shish Mahals are :

1. **Shish Mahal, Baba Bakala** : It is a gurdwara situated close to Bhora Sahib in Baba Bakala. It used to be the house where Mata Ganga, Guru Hargobind's mother and later Mata Nanaki, Guru Tegh Bahadur's mother, lived. It is a flat roofed room with glass panels on three sides.

2. **Shish Mahal, Kartarpur (Jalandhar)** : It was built by Guru Arjan and was further improved and decorated by Guru Hargobind. The original copy of the Adi Granth scribed by Bhai Gurdas is kept here along with many other relics.

3. **Shish Mahal, Kiratpur** : This marks the residential quarters where Guru Hargobind spent the last part of his life from 1634 AD onwards. Guru Har Rai and Guru Harkrishan were born here.

SHIV DAYAL (SINGH) : See Radhasoamis.

SHRI GOBINDPUR : Shri Gobindpur which is also called Hargobindpur is a town in Gurdaspur district. According to a note on the original copy of the Adi Granth now at Kartarpur (Jalandhar), it was founded by Guru Arjan in 1587 AD. Because of a conspiracy by Chandu it went to the possession of Bhagwan Das Gherar. According to *Gurpartap Surya*, the town was founded by Guru Hargobind. But it is a well established fact that Guru Hargobind visited it in 1630 AD and had to fight a battle against Abdulla, the Administrator of Jalandhar, Bhagwan Das and others.

The town has two gurdwaras Guru ke Mahal which was the residence of the Guru and Damdama Sahib where the Guru had addressed a congregation after the battle.

SIAHAR : Siahar is a village in Ludhiana district. It has a gurdwara dedicated to Guru Hargobind. According to the Sikh tradition, the Guru passed through Siahar while going from Rare to Jagere. His horse fell sick and died in this village. A memorial tomb for the horse at the spot where it was buried exists near the gurdwara.

SIAHI TIBBI : Siahi Tibbi is a spot near Anandpur. Two Muslim gunners sent by the hill rajas were trying to aim their shot at Guru Gobind Singh when he was addressing a congregation. The Guru spotted them and killed them with his arrows.

SIKHIA : *Sikhia* is a Punjabi term for the advice given to the bride and the bridegroom on how to conduct themselves after marriage. It is not a compulsory part of *Anand Karaj* but sometimes follows the *Lawan*.

SIKHISM : Sikhism is the latest world religion. It came into being during a period of religious revival led by Hindu Bhakti Movement and Muslim Sufism in India in the 15th and 16th centuries. It was originally founded by Guru Nanak (1469-1539) who emphasized the fundamental truth of all religions and whose mission was to put an end to religious conflict. He condemned the formalism both of Hinduism and Islam, preaching the gospel of universal brotherhood, and the unicity of God. His ideas were welcomed by the Mughal Emperor Akbar (1542-1605). Thus a succession of Gurus: Guru Angad (1504-52), Guru Amardas (1479-1574)

Guru Ramdas (1534-81) and Guru Arjan (1563-1606) were able to consolidate the religion. They established the great Sikh scripture, the Adi Granth and improved its organisation in general. Jahangir's (1569-1627) fanatical religious policy claimed the first Sikh martyr in Guru Arjan in 1606 AD. His successor Guru Hargobind (1595-1644) was forced to introduce a minor transformation in the Sikh community which continued during the pontificate of Guru Har Rai (1630-61), Guru Harkrishan (1656-64), and Guru Tegh Bahadur (1621-75). The Tenth Master Guru Gobind Singh (1666-1708) whose father Guru Tegh Bahadur was put to death by Emperor Aurangzeb for refusal to embrace Islam had to make himself a warrior and instil into the Sikhs a more aggressive spirit. In 1699 AD he founded the Khalsa brotherhood thereby completely transforming the community by instituting baptism and a Code of Conduct. After his death in 1708 AD Banda Singh Bahadur moved to Punjab to fight against the tyrancial forces and was able to set up the semblance of a Sikh state. He was captured and tortured to death in 1716 AD and a wide spread persecution of Sikhs followed. As a result they had to retire to the hills and forests. As the Mughal empire weakened under the onslaught of the incursions by Nadir Shah and Ahmad Shah Abdali in the first half of the 18th century Sikhs organised themselves into *misls* and leaders like Nawab Kapur Singh, Jassa Singh Ahluwalia and Akali Phula Singh provided them the right type of leadership. Maharaja Ranjit Singh (1780-1839) was able to consolidate the *misls* and set up a sovereign Sikh state whose influence was checked only by the British. After the death of Maharaja Ranjit Singh, two Anglo-Sikh wars followed in 1845-46 AD and 1848-49 AD which resulted in the British annexation of Punjab and the end of Sikh independence. Ever since then Sikhs have undergone many vicissitudes in history but Sikhism as a religion has always inspired its followers to be upbeat.

SIKHS : *Rahit Maryada* defines a Sikh as a person who believes in :
1. One Immortal God;
2. The Ten Gurus;
3. The Guru Granth Sahib;
4. The writings and teachings of the Gurus;
5. Tenth Guru's baptism; and does not believe in any other religion.

In practice, as in other religions, Sikhs constitute a range of persons who may slightly differ from each other. At the one end are *Amritdharis* who satisfy all the above conditions and have undergone the baptism. At the other end are *Sahajdharis* who do not believe in the Tenth Guru's baptism and some of his teachings. In between the two extremes are *Keshadharis* who are yet to undergo baptism Two prominent deviant sects of Sikhs have come up as outcomes of reform movements of the nineteenth century—Nirankaris who are the followers of Baba Dayal Das (1783-1855) and Namdharis who are the followers of Baba Balak Singh (1799-1861).

According to the 1991 census, there were 16.5 million Sikhs in India about 2% of its population. Majority of them live in villages and are engaged in agriculture. Some Sikhs have also settled in Malaysia, Singapore, East Africa, U.K., U.S.A. and Canada. The total population of the Sikh diaspora may be as many as one million.

SIN : Sin, the Punjabi equivalent for which is *paap*, is more an ethical concept than a theological one as in Christianity and Islam. It is mentioned at a number of places in the Guru Granth Sahib but generally in the sense of a vice. "Within the body abide virtue and sin— the twin brothers."

Kayea andar paap punn doe bhai (AG., p. 126)
"Many are our demerits, repeatedly done without count."
Hamre avgun bahut bahut hai bar bar har galat na aawe. (AG. p. 167)

According to Sikhism, sins are not destroyed by penances, since they cannot root out *avidya* which is the root cause of all sins. The best form of atonement is devotion to God. "You shed your sins by meditating on the Master."
Simrat swami kilwikh nase (AG. p. 194)
"Your sins will be washed off if you dwell on

the Lord even for a moment."

Mite paap japi-ai Hari bind   (AG. p. 281)

However the basic system of punishment for sins is the Law of Karma.

SINGH : The word *'Singh'* is derived from a Sanskrit word meaning 'lion'. Sikhism has made it a compulsory ending for the names of all male Sikhs. This ending was not created by Sikhism but was rather institutionalized by it during the days of Guru Gobind Singh. It was and still is being used by Rajputs, Thakurs and some other communities as a part of their male names. The Guru enjoined it on all Sikhs as a mode of their transformation into the Khalsa. Therefore, he instituted it as a part of Baptism by *amrit* to change his followers from Sikhs into *Singhs* or lions. Besides a change of name, the Guru wanted complete transformation. "They who accept *amrit* shall be changed from jackals into lions and shall obtain empire in this world and bliss hereafter."

SINGH SABHA : The courtly splendour of the days of Maharaja Ranjit Singh sowed the seeds of subversion of the Sikh way of life. The faith was weakened by the influx of large number of those who had adopted the Sikh form to gain worldly advantage, but whose allegiance to its principles and traditions was tentative. Then came the challenges of Christian proselytization with the advent of the British.

In the begining of 1873 AD four Sikh students of the Amritsar Mission School proclaimed their intention of renouncing their faith in favour of Christianity. This shocked Sikh feelings. A meeting of some prominent Sikhs was held under the presidentship of Sardar Thakur Singh, as a result of the deliberation of which an association called Sri Guru Singh Sabha came into being on October 1,1873 AD. The Singh Sabha undertook to (*i*) restore Sikhism to its pristine purity; (*ii*) edit and publish historical and religious books; (*iii*) propagate current knowledge, using Punjabi as the medium and to start magazines and newspapers in Punjabi; (*iv*) reform and bring back into the Sikh fold the apostates; and (*v*) interest the highly placed Englishmen in, and ensure their association with, the educational programme of the Sikhs.

The Singh Sabha proved the *elan vital* in the regeneration of Sikh society. It gained quick support of diverse sections of the community. Many Sikh scholars and leaders volunteered to join its ranks. A vigorous campaign was set afoot. Two of its major thrusts were the depreciation of non-Sikh customs and social evils and the encouragement of western education.

The reformist ideology spread quickly. Singh Sabhas sprang up in all parts of India and now we have them even in foreign countries. The momentum which the Singh Sabha gave to the Sikh renaissance still continues.

The problems of coordination led to the creation of Khalsa Diwans, the most important among them being the Chief Khalsa Diwan which played the part of the principal spokesman of the Sikh Community and the medium of channelizing its religious and cultural resurgence.

SIRHIND : During the Mughal period, Sirhind was a prosperous town and was the headquarters of a principality. Its governor Wazir Khan was the bitterest foe of Guru Gobind Singh. He was biting his lips in rage for his failure to capture the Guru at Anandpur. When Mata Gujri and the two younger *sahibzadas* : Fateh Singh and Zorawar Singh were handed over to him by Gangu after the evacuation of Anandpur, he got the children bricked alive. Mata Gujri died of shock on hearing the news. To avenge this dastardly crime Banda Singh Bahadur captured Sirhind and killed Wazir Khan in 1710 AD. It was captured again by the Khalsa Dal in 1763 AD after killing the ruler Jain Khan. They built the gurdwaras—the important ones among them are : Fatehgarh Sahib which marks the spot of martyrdom of the younger *sahibzadas*; Burj Mata Gujri where Mata Gujri and *sahibzadas* were imprisoned and Mata Gujri died of shock; Jyoti Saroop where they were cremated and a number of

Shahid Ganj in memory of martyrs who died in the battles at Sirhind.

SIS GANJ, ANANDPUR : This is the place where the *sis* (head) of Guru Tegh Bahadur was cremated when it was brought by Bhai Jaita from Delhi to Anandpur after the Guru's martyrdom.

SIS GANJ, DELHI : Gurdwara Sis Ganj is one of the nine historical gurdwaras in Delhi. It is built at a place where Guru Tegh Bahadur met his martyrdom in November, 1675 AD. The trunk of the tree under which the Guru was beheaded has been preserved at the shrine. The well from which he took his bath while in prison still exists.

After the martyrdom, a devotee Bhai Jaita, disguised as a sweeper carried the head to Anandpur for cremation. Lakhi Shah and his son carried the headless body and cremated it at a place where now stands Gurdwara Rakab Ganj. It was at that time a colony of stirrup-makers.

When Baghel Singh marched into Delhi at the head of a strong army in 1783 AD he took steps to build a gurdwara at Sis Ganj. During the later years, mosques and gurdwaras appeared alternately at that place. There was a prolonged litigation and ultimately the Privy Council gave its decision in favour of the Sikhs. The present building was constructed in 1930 AD.

Adjoining the gurdwara is the *Kotwali* (Police Station) where Guru Tegh Bahadur was kept in prison. The Government has recently passed on the *Kotwali* to the Delhi Sikh Gurdwara Management Committee.

SMADH BHAI : Smadh Bhai or Bhai ki Smadh is a village in the Malwa region which has grown around the cenotaph of Bhai Roop Chand. It has a gurdwara dedicated to Guru Hargobind. See also Roop Chand, Bhai.

SMOKING : See Tobacco.

SODAR : *Sodar* is a composition by Guru Nanak included in the Guru Granth Sahib. It also forms a part of the *Rahiras* which is recited by devout Sikhs daily at sunset. See also Nitnem. The title comes from the first two words of the composition which begins with :
So dar tera keha so ghar keha jit beh sarb samale
(AG. p. 8)
"What is that gate and what is that mansion where thou sittest and watchest all things."

SOHIANA SAHIB, GURDWARA : This is a holy shrine in village Dhaula near Barnala. It marks an old *dhab* (pond) where Guru Tegh Bahadur had made his ablutions when he was about to enter Dhaula from Hadiaya. The *dhab* has now been converted into a *sarovar*.

SOHILA : *Sohila* which is also called *Kirtan Sohila* or *Kirti Sohila* is a selection of hymns of Guru Nanak, Guru Ramdas and Guru Arjan taken from the Guru Granth Sahib. It is one of the *banis* of the *Nitnem* and is prescribed to be recited at the time of going to bed. It is also used at the time of funeral rites. The title is taken from the second line of the first composition included in it.
Tit ghar gawo Sohila siwreh sirjanharo.
(AG. p. 12)

SOMA, BHAI : Bhai Soma who belonged to the Jhang area now in Pakistan was a devout follower of Guru Arjan. He did considerable service at the time of the construction of Amritsar. According to the Sikh tradition he was one day sitting by the side of the Guru at Amritsar when a beggar came asking for alms. At that time the Guru did not have any offerings before him. So he asked those present whether they had anything. Bhai Soma offered two paise to the beggar on behalf of the Guru. On this the Guru remarked "Bhai Soma is our Shah (moneyed man)" It is said that Bhai Soma prospered in his trade. His descendants even now use the surname 'Shah'.

SOOHI : An Indian classical *raag* usually sung within about an hour (two *gharis*) from sunrise. It is fifteenth of the thirty-one *raags* used in the organisation of hymns in the Guru Granth Sahib covering pages 728-794. The *lawan* hymn recited at every Sikh wedding fall in this section. The basic notes occur in it in the following sequence.

Arohi : sa, re, ga, ma, pa, ne, sa.........
Avrohi : sa, ne, ma, pa, ga, re, sa..........

SOOLHAR : Soolhar is a village about 8 km from Ambala City. Guru Gobind Singh had visited it when he was camping at Lakhnaur. A gurdwara commemorates the visit.

SOOLISAR, GURDWARA : Gurdwara Soolisar is situated near village Kot Dharmu in the Mansa area and is dedicated to Guru Tegh Bahadur. According to the Sikh tradition, at this spot a thief, who had stolen the Guru's horse, committed suicide by thrusting a dry twig in his stomach as repentance. That is why it is called Sooli (hanging) sar.

SOPURAKH : *Sopurakh* is a composition of Guru Ramdas included in the Adi Granth. It is recited daily by the devout Sikhs as a part of *Rahiras*. See Rahiras. The title comes from the first two words of the composition :

So purakh niranjan har purakh niranjano, har agma agam appara (AG. p. 10)

SORATH : An Indian classical *raag* usually sung during the three hours (one *pahar*) before midnight. It is the ninth of the thirty-one *raags* used in the organisation of hymns in the Guru Granth Sahib covering pages 595-659. The sequence of basic notes followed is :

Arohi : sa, re, ma, pa, ne, sa..........
Avrohi : sa, ne, dha, pa, ma, ga, re, sa..........

SOUL : The word *atman* is used to denote the human soul. It has a peculiar relationship with the body. Soul is not born with the body, nor does it die with it. "When the body dies, where does the soul rest? It is released from the grip of three modes and merges with the unstruck melody of the Word." (Adi Granth, p. 327). "O my body the soul is all your sport. It is through the soul that I am joined to you. With it, you are sought after by all. Without it no one likes to look at you." (AG. p., 390)

"The body and the soul are immensely in love with each other; the male soul is detached like a *yogi*, while the body is like a beauteous woman. Lo, the soul enjoys a myriad joys but, then, he flies out; and while so doing consultth not his bride." (AG., Maru Mohalla 1). But the soul which leaves the body awaits a new dwelling, just as a person casts off worn out garments and puts on others that are new. During the unending cycle of births and deaths, the soul continues its upward march.

The soul is a part of God. "God resides in the soul; the soul is contained in God", (AG., Bhairo, Mohalla 1). It is deathless like Him. Before creation it lived with God. After creation it takes bodily forms according to His will. The soul is, however, nourished by virtue and meditation on the Nam. The transmigration of soul can come to an end by meditation and divine grace.

SRI CHAND, BABA : Baba Sri Chand was the elder son of Guru Nanak and Mata Sulakhani. He was born in 1495 AD at Sultanpur Lodhi. Right from childhood he had a mystic bent of mind and as he grew up he became an ascetic, never married and ultimately founded the ascetic order of Udasis.

Baba Sri Chand never reconciled to Guru Angad becoming the second Guru of Sikhs and a successor to his father. In fact, he kept on criticizing him. He never met Guru Amardas but the humility of Guru Ramdas attracted him to Amritsar (which was under construction) where he was received with due courtesies. Guru Hargobind went to see him at Kartarpur (Pakistan) where he was stationed. Baba Sri Chand was very old at that time but was immensely pleased by the Guru's visit and told him that he had nothing but his *fakiri* (ascetic order) to offer him. This meeting narrowed down the long standing rift between the Sikhs and the *Udasis*. It proved useful to the Sikhs in the post Guru Gobind Singh period when they were being persecuted by the Mughal rulers and had disappeared into the forests and hills, the *Udasis* took over the care of their holy shrines and the missionary work of *masands*.

Baba Sri Chand died in 1613 AD at the ripe old age of 118. According to the local tradition he vanished after crossing the river Ravi near Chamba and was never seen afterwards. The site is now a place of pilgrimage.

SRI RAAG : An Indian classical *raag* usually sung in the afternoon. It is the first of the thirty-one *raags* used in the organisation of hymns in the Guru Granth Sahib covering pages 14-93. Its sequence of basic notes is :
  Arohi : sa, re, ma, pa, ne, sa..........
  Avrohi : sa, ne, dha, pa, ma, ga, re, sa..........

SUBEG SINGH : Subeg Singh, a resident of village Jambar in district Lahore was a Persian scholar in the service of Zakariya Khan, the governor of Lahore who sent him to Amritsar as his ambassador with a title, documents for a *jagir* and other presents for the Khalsa which was holding its meeting on the occasion of Baisakhi in 1733 AD. *Sarbat Khalsa* declared Subeg Singh as a *Tankhaiya* and would not allow him to appear before it until he had undergone *tankha* (punishment) for helping the enemies of the Khalsa. Subeg Singh accepted the punishment with modesty. He could persuade Kapur Singh to accept the title of 'Nawab' on behalf of the Khalsa.

Subeg Singh was also the *kotwal* (administrator) of Lahore some time during which period he got built a number of gurdwaras. On a complaint by the *Qazis*, he was tortured to death along with his son Shahbaz Singh in 1745 AD in Lahore.

SUCHA NAND : Sucha Nand was a Brahmin official in the court of Wazir Khan, the governor of Sirhind. According to the Sikh tradition he had advised Wazir Khan to kill the two younger sons of Guru Gobind Singh with the remark that the young ones of a serpent do not deserve any mercy. That is why Sikhs call him 'Jootha Nand.' When Banda Singh Bahadur captured Sirhind, he killed Sucha Nand.

SUFISM : *Sufi* is derived from the word *suf* meaning wool. Thus *Sufi* came to mean a person wearing ordinary garments of wool which were treated as a sign of simplicity and a silent protest against the growing luxuries of the world. Sufism is a cult started by such people. Many regard it as a reaction of the Aryan mind against a semitic religion imposed upon it by force.

Sufism centres round two questions : 'How is man to realize God in himself?' and 'What is God in relation to the individual and the creation?' Sufism shows *tariquat* or path in answer to the first and imparts *marifat* or knowledge in answers to the second. The whole superstructure of Sufism is built upon two corner stones : (1) teacher, *pir*, or *murshid* (guru), and (2) love.

Sufism first of all took roots in Iran. The Muslim conquests of India brought in their wake a large number of Sufis. Originally, the Sufis in northern India came with the Muslim raiders and after the political conquest of a particular region preached Islam. Gradually Sindh and Multan region became centres of Sufism. It underwent a change in India towards the end of 17th century because of the ruthless religious policy of Aurangzeb. Bhakti Movement influenced the Sufis considerably in those days.

Guru Nanak's thought had been influenced by Sufism. Indeed in Sikhism we find a merger of Bhakti Movement of Hindus and Sufism of Islam.

SUHEWA : Suhewa is a village in the Bikaner area of Rajasthan where Guru Gobind Singh had stayed on his way to the Deccan. A gurdwara has been dedicated to the Guru. According to the Sikh tradition at the time of the Guru's visit to the village, it had a *Jand* tree with a small *Peepal* sapling growing on its trunk. On seeing this the Guru had remarked that the hardships of India would be over only when the *Peepal* sapling overpowers the *Jand* tree. By now the *Jand* tree has almost been swallowed. Near the tree one can see the footprints of a horse on a rock which are believed to be those of the Guru's horse.

SUKH ASAN : *Sukh Asan* literally means 'to sit comfortably'. However, in Sikh speech and writing the expression is used for the ceremony which takes place at the end of the day when the Guru Granth Sahib is formally closed for night. Before the Guru Granth Sahib is wrapped in *rumalas* (brocaded silk cloth) and reverentially taken to the resting place on a Sikh's head, the *ardaas* is said and *Vak* is taken by opening the Scripture at random. If the Guru Granth Sahib presides over a ceremony outside a gurdwara the same sequence is repeated at the close of the ceremony. See also Parkash Karna.

SUKHA SINGH : Sukha Singh is a famous Sikh martyr who along with Mahtab Singh killed Massa Ranghar, the *kotwal* of Amritsar in 1740 AD for desecrating the Golden Temple. He died fighting in a battle in 1753 AD near Lahore on the banks of the Ravi.

SUKHMANI : *Sukhmani* is one of the famous compositions of Guru Arjan included in the Adi Granth. The title literally means peace of mind.

The composition is divided into twenty four *ashtapadis*, which means eight *pads*, each *pad* containing ten lines. Each *ashtapadi*, therefore, contains eighty lines. It praises God and exhorts the devotees to seek salvation through *Nam*.

SULAKHANI, MATA : Mata Sulakhani was the wife of Guru Nanak. She was the daughter of Chona Khatri Mul Chand of village Pakkhoke in Gurdaspur district. For that reason some chroniclers call her Mata Choni. Since Mul Chand was residing at Batala as caretaker of the lands and property owned by an affluent landlord Ajita Randhawa, the wedding was solemnized on September 24, 1487 AD at Batala, Gurdwara Dehra Sahib also known as Viah Asthan marks the site. Close by is Gurdwara Kandh Sahib which marks the spot where the marriage party had stopped near Mul Chand's house waiting for formal reception by the host.

Mata Sulakhani gave birth to two sons, Baba Sri Chand and Baba Lakhmi Chand. She died at Kartarpur (Pakistan).

SULTANPUR LODHI : Sultanpur Lodhi is a small ancient town 25 km from Kapurthala situated on the left bank of the Bein (rivulet). It was founded by Sultan Khan Lodhi, a general of Mahmud Ghazni in the 11th century AD. For long, the town was a great centre of Muslim culture.

Guru Nanak went to Sultanpur in 1484 AD to earn his livelihood and spent 14 years here. Both of his sons were born at Sultanpur. It was at Sultanpur that the Guru received his divine call to renounce worldly ways and to travel to various lands to propagate the true religion. Several well-known gurdwaras, Ber Sahib, Hatt Sahib, Kothari Sahib etc. are situated here.

SUMANA : Sumana is an old town in the Malwa region. Its association with Sikhism is largely negative although it has been sanctified by a visit by Guru Tegh Bahadur. According to the Sikh tradition, Jalal-u-din, the hangman who beheaded Guru Tegh Bahadur at Delhi on the orders of Emperor Aurangzeb in 1675 AD belonged to Sumana. The *Sayyads* who pronounced the *fatwa* at Sirhind in 1705 AD for bricking alive the younger sons of Guru Gobind Singh also belonged to this place. Even the hangmen who actually did the bricking were residents of Sumana. For these reasons Banda Singh Bahadur captured the town in 1708 AD and punished the perpetrators.

SUMAYE : Sumaye or Sumha is a village near Mansa. It has a shrine dedicated to Guru Tegh Bahadur. According to the Sikh tradition, when the Guru was returning from Kheeva Kalan, he got the news here that followers from the Peshawar region had come to see him after their visit to Anandpur. The Guru immediately halted under a tree and addressed the congregation.

SUNAM : Sunam is an old town in the Malwa region. According to the Sikh tradition Guru

Nanak visited the town during his travels and camped outside it. But Lahra Khatris of Sunam brought the Guru to their house which is now a historical gurdwara.

SUNDER, BABA : Baba Sunder was the great grandson of Guru Amardas, he was the son of Anand and grandson of Mohri. At the request of Guru Arjan, Sunder wrote an account of the death of Guru Amardas. The composition is called *Sadd* (calling) and is included in the Adi Granth under *Raag* Ramkali. The hymn emphasizes the transitoriness of this world and the consequent futility of all human fears rising from a sense of death and despair. It presents the Sikh view of death according to which the Guru enjoins on the followers to recite *Kirtan* and *Bani*, which alone should constitute the last rites.

SUNDRI, MATA : Mata Sundri was one of the consorts of Guru Gobind Singh and mother of *sahibzada* Ajit Singh. She was the daughter of Ram Saran Kumrao, a *Khatri* of Lahore who had offered her in matrimony to the Guru. The wedding was solemnized in 1684 AD.

After the death of Guru Gobind Singh, Mata Sundri had full control of the Panth. She used to issue *Hukamnamas*. Bhai Mani Singh was sent by her as the head priest of the Golden Temple. Jassa Singh Ahluwalia spent his childhood with her. Mata Sundri spent the last years of her life at Delhi where she passed away in 1747 AD. At the place where she used to reside in Delhi, stands a historical gurdwara in her name. She was cremated at Gurdwara Bala Sahib in Delhi.

SURAJ MAL, BABA : Baba Suraj Mal was one of the sons of Guru Hargobind. His mother was Mata Mahadevi. He was born at Amritsar in 1618 AD.

Baba Suraj Mal was married to Khem Kaur daughter of Bhai Prem Chand, a Sili *Khatri* of Kartarpur (Jalandhar). His grandsons Gulab Singh and Shyam Singh were initiated into the Khalsa brotherhood by Guru Gobind Singh. According to the Sikh tradition the *khanda* used by Guru Gobind Singh for the preparation of *amrit* on the Baisakhi day of 1699 AD was handed over by the Guru to Shyam Singh whose heirs are settled at Anandpur.

SURAJ PARKASH : It is a poetic composition by well-known scholar and theologian Bhai Santokh Singh. It deals with the life and works of all the Gurus from Guru Angad to Guru Gobind Singh. It was completed in 1843 AD. It is also referred to as "*Gurpartap Surya.*"

SURDAS : Bhagat Surdas, one of whose hymns is found in the Adi Granth under *Raag Sarang*, must not be confused with Sur Das, a blind poet famous in Northern India as the author of *Sur Sagar*. (Sometimes this epithet is used for any blind person out of respect).

Bhagat Sur Das was a Brahmin born in 1529 AD. In addition to learning Sanskrit and Persian, he studied music and poetry. He was originally named Madan Mohan but later on came to be known as Sur Das. Emperor Akbar, who always respected and rewarded the virtuous and learned made him governor of Sandila. On a complaint by Todar Mal about squandering of funds, Sur Das was removed from governorship. He spent the later part of his life in meditation at Varanasi where a temple commemorates his memory.

SUTHRE SHAH : Suthre Shah was the son of a *Khatri* resident of Barampur near Baramula in Jammu and Kashmir. He was born in 1615 AD. Since he had teeth at birth he was disowned and thrown out thinking he might bring bad luck to the family. According to the Sikh tradition, Guru Hargobind was passing that way on his return from Kashmir. The Guru picked up the infant and brought him up under the name 'Suthra'. He became a devout follower of the Guru and even served Guru Har Rai. He managed to get permission from the emperor to collect money from the traders and shopkeepers of Delhi. His followers who have almost given up Sikh teachings are called *Suthreshahi*.

SWAYYAS : A prominent form of verse used in

the Adi Granth. It has a rhyme scheme consisting of four lines or phrases. Depending on the metre used, we get various variations in *swayyas*.

Guru Gobind Singh has written 33 *swayyas* which are included in the Dasam Granth under that heading. In them he dwells on the worship of the formless God. These *swayyas* are recited during the preparation of *amrit* to be administered at baptism of a Sikh.

SWORD : See Kirpan.

T

TAHELPURA : Tahelpura is a village near Sirhind. It has a gurdwara associated with Guru Tegh Bahadur. It marks the spot where the Guru sat under a *pipal* tree which still exists. There was no habitation there at the time of the Guru's visit. It came up in 1830 AD only.

TAHLA SAHIB : Tahla Sahib is a gurdwara in village Kubb near Mansa and is dedicated to both Guru Tegh Bahadur and Guru Gobind Singh. Guru Tegh Bahadur, while coming from Talwandi Sabo, had rested here under a *tahli* (*sheesham*) tree which does not exist now. Guru Gobind Singh had come here while hunting in the area during his stay at Talwandi Sabo.

TAHLIANA : Tahliana marks the spot near Raikot in Ludhiana district where Guru Gobind Singh had halted near a pond under a *tahli* (*sheesham*) tree after leaving Machhiwara in 1705 AD. Kallah Rai, chief of Raikot had met the Guru here and decided to send Noora to Sirhind to find out the position about the two younger *sahibzadas* : Fateh Singh and Zorawar Singh and Mata Gujri.

TAHLI SAHIB : *Tahli* is a Punjabi word for a *sheesham* which grows profusely in the Punjab climate. Any such tree which, because of its association with a Sikh Guru or personage, has become a shrine is called Tahli Sahib. Some of the important shrines of this name are :
 1. **Tahli Sahib, Amritsar** : It is situated near Santokhsar in Amritsar. Guru Ramdas used to sit under the *tahli* tree here, which still exists, to supervise the digging of Santokhsar.
 2. **Tahli Sahib, Daulatpur** : This is in village Daulatpur of Jalandhar district and is dedicated to Baba Sri Chand who had camped here under a *tahli* tree for three days while going towards Kiratpur.
 3. **Tahli Sahib, Ghakka Kotli** : This shrine is situated in village Ghakka Kotli of Gurdaspur district. It is dedicated to Guru Har Rai who stayed here for a few days under a *tahli* tree at the request of Bhai Fateh Chand. The original tree has dried up but a new one has come up in its place.
 4. **Talhi Sahib, Gondpur** : See Gondpur.
 5. **Tahli Sahib, Moonak** : This is a gurdwara in village Moonak near Tanda in Hoshiarpur district and is dedicated to Guru Hargobind. The Guru came here on a hunting expedition and his horse was tied to a *tahli* tree here.
 6. **Tahli Sahib, Pakkhoke** : This is situated in village Pakkoke in Dera Baba Nanak area. Baba Sri Chand used to camp under a *tahli* tree here. According to the Sikh tradition, Guru Hargobind came to meet with Baba Sri Chand here.

TAKHT : *Takht* is a Persian word signifying the imperial throne—a concept of total and all-pervasive focus of worldly temporal power such as was supposed to inherent in the emperor. This concept came into Sikhism through the doctrine of double sovereignty- *meeri* and *peeri* by which the Guru acquires both the spiritual and the temporal authority. To give it a concrete shape, Guru Hargobind constructed the Akal Takht as a complement to the Golden Temple. Which became the highest seat of temporal authority.

Besides the Akal Takht, there are four other gurdwaras which are designated as *Takhts* they are : Harmander Sahib, Patna; Keshgarh Sahib, Anandpur; Sach Khand, Hazur Sahib and Damdama Sahib, Talwandi Sabo. For more details see respective entries.

TAKHTOOPURA : See Nanaksar.

TAL, BHATT : *Bhatt* Tal is one of the seventeen *Bhatts* (Bards) whose compositions (one *swayya* in his case) have been included in the Adi Granth. See also Bhatts.

TALWANDI RAI BHOE KI : This is the

original name of Nankana Sahib. See Nankana Sahib.

TALWANDI SABO : Talwandi Sabo is a small town about 27 km from Bhatinda. According to Sikh tradition it was visited by Guru Nanak during one of his travels across the country. Guru Gobind Singh spent about a year here after his last battle at Muktsar in December 1705 AD. He was joined here by Bhai Mani Singh and his wives Mata Sundri and Mata Sahib Kaur. It was here that the Guru prepared with the help of Bhai Mani Singh the revised version of the Adi Granth which is now the eternal Guru of the Sikhs. In the earlier half of the eighteenth century it became for the Sikhs a cantonment as well as a centre of learning. It gained renown especially under Baba Deep Singh, chief of the Shahid *misl*. It has a number of gurdwaras the most famous of them being Damdama Sahib which was declared as the fifth Takht by the SGPC in November 1966 AD. Talwandi Sabo itself is generally now known as Damdama Sahib. Other well known gurdwaras are : Darbar Sahib, Manji Sahib, Tibbi Sahib, Thara Sahib, Nanaksar, Likhansar, Burj Baba Deep Singh etc.

TAMBU SAHIB : *Tambu* in Punjabi means tent. Some of the sites where the Sikh Gurus encamped during their journeys or expeditions have come up as historical shrines known as Tambu Sahibs. Some of the better known Tambu Sahibs are :

1. **Tambu Sahib, Dagru :** It is situated in village Dagru near Moga and is dedicated to Guru Har Rai who encamped here in the course of his journey through the Malwa region.

2. **Tambu Sahib, Muktsar :** This is the spot in Muktsar where the forces of Guru Gobind Singh encamped during his last encounter with the Mughal army. They had spread their clothes on the bushes to mislead the army about the number of tents and thus making them presume they were much larger in number than they actually were.

3. **Tambu Sahib, Nankana :** This is the place in Nankana Sahib, birth-place of Guru Nanak now in Pakistan, where the Guru sat after

Sachcha Sauda (the real deal in which he spent the money given for business on feeding the hungry *sadhus*) and was cuffed for disobedience.

TANKHAIYA : *Tankha* literally means salary. *Tankhaiya* would therefore literally means a person who receives salary and does not have independence of working or thinking. It is often used in a derogatory sense and in Sikh writings has come to mean a person who has committed a religious offence meriting punishment.

According to the Sikh *Rahit Maryada*, the following have been declared as *tankhaiyas* :

1. One who has social dealings with *masands*, Dhirmalias, Ramraiyas, or those who kill their daughters.

2. One who dines with those who have renounced Sikhism.

3. One who dyes his beard.

4. One who arranges the marriage of his children for money.

5. One who uses intoxicants and drugs (e.g. bhang, opium, alcohol etc.)

6. One who does anything against the traditions of Sikhism.

7. One who breaks the Code of Conduct for Sikhs in any manner.

Any person who has been declared a *tankhaiya* is supposed to present himself before the *sangat* to receive punishment and to ask for forgiveness.

TANKHA NAMA : *Tankha Nama* is a Punjabi composition consisting of questions and answers between Guru Gobind Singh and Bhai Nand Lal and serves as a Code of Discipline for the Khalsa. Some scholars believe Bhai Nand Lal to be its author which is disputed by others.

TANTRAS : See Incantations.

TARA CHAND : Tara Chand was a *masand* appointed by Guru Hargobind to preach Sikhism and to collect offerings in Afghanistan. During the pontificate of Guru Har Rai, he went to Delhi with Ram Rai.

TARAGARH : Taragarh is a gurdwara dedicated to Guru Gobind Singh and is situated at about 5 km from Anandpur. The Guru had initially built a fort here for the protection of Anandpur which does not exist now except for the foundations.

TARA SINGH, BHAI : Bhai Tara Singh is counted among the prominent Sikh martyrs of the 18th century. He was a devout Sikh *Zamindar* of Lahore district. Poor peasants of Naushera being harassed by its *lambardar* Sahib Rai took shelter with him. Sahib Rai accused them of stealing his horses and demanded that peasants be handed over to him. On his refusal, Sahib Rai persuaded Jafar Beg, the administrator of Patti, to send a force of 500 cavalry men to capture Tara Singh and the peasants. The force, however, suffered reverses. On this the governor of Lahore sent a larger contingent under Momen Khan in 1725 AD and in the ensuing battle Bhai Tara Singh was killed. The spot in village Khadim Garhi where he was cremated was converted into a Shahid Ganj.

TARI SAHIB, GURDWARA : It is a gurdwara in Chamkaur. Guru Gobind Singh left *Garhi* in disguise with three Sikhs going in different directions but agreeing to meet at a common place. This happened on the night of December 7, 1705 AD after the battle at Chamkaur. Since the Guru did not wish to go unannounced, he on reaching the mound where now stands the gurdwara gave a clap (*tari*) and shouted : "Here goes the *Pir* of Hind." The three Sikhs also raised shouts. Thus confusing the army, the Guru escaped the siege at Chamkaur.

TARN TARAN : Tarn Taran, which means a craft to take men across the world's oceans, is a small city 25 km from Amritsar. It has a beautiful gurdwara built by Guru Arjan in honour of Guru Ramdas. It resembles the Golden Temple at Amritsar in splendour and beauty. It is, however, not built at the centre of the tank but on one of its edges. The tank is much larger, about 300 m square and a dip in it is believed to cure leprosy. The tank was dug in 1590 AD. The final shape of the gurdwara, as we see it today, was given in 1830 AD. See also Khanwal.

TARU SINGH, BHAI : Bhai Taru Singh is one of the prominent Sikh martyrs of the 18th century. He was a resident of village Poolha in Lahore district. He was a devout Sikh engaged in agriculture at a time when Sikhs were being persecuted by the imperial forces. He is said to have incurred the wrath of the *Niranjania mahant* of his village who made a complaint to the governor of Lahore that Bhai Taru Singh was harbouring dacoits. The governor immediately ordered him to be arrested and brought before him. On his refusal to accept Islam, the governor ordered that his scalp be removed with a sharp knife in 1745 AD. A Shahid Ganj was raised as a memorial to him near the Lahore railway station.

TARUNA DAL : See Buddha Dal.

TAT KHALSA : After his initial victories, Banda Singh Bahadur introduced some new practices in Sikhism like the new salutation : *Fateh Darshan*. They were not liked by the orthodox Sikhs. These controversies led to a division of the Khalsa into two groups : *Tat Khalsa* who did not want any of the doctrines and practices laid down by Guru Gobind Singh to be changed and *Bandei Khalsa* who approved of the practices introduced by Banda Singh Bahadur. Overtime the distinction has died down as *Bandei Khalsa* became almost extinct.

TEGH BAHADUR, GURU : Guru Tegh Bahadur, the ninth Guru was the youngest son of Guru Hargobind from Mata Nanaki. He was born in 1621 AD at Amritsar. He was brought up in the most approved Sikh style. As a young boy, he was placed under the teachings of Baba Buddha and Bhai Gurdas. The former supervised his training in archery and horse-manship and the latter taught him the old classics. The Guru made rapid progress and showed early promise of mastery in both the fields.

Guru Tegh Bahadur was married in 1632 AD at Kartarpur (Jalandhar) to Mata Gujri. He had only one son Guru Gobind Singh. He travelled widely to far-off places in India like Bihar, Bengal and Assam. He spent considerable time at Baba Bakala where he was installed as the Guru in 1665 AD. He founded Anandpur by purchasing land from the hill chieftains.

Like his predecessors since the days of Guru Hargobind, Guru Tegh Bahadur maintained the marks of worldly dignity. But he lived austerely.

Aurangzeb was persecuting the Hindus. Some Kashmiri Pandits came to seek the Guru's advice at Anandpur. The Guru readily agreed to sacrifice himself for the sake of their faith. Accordingly a message was sent to the emperor that if Guru Tegh Bahadur accepted Islam, they would follow suit. Aurangzeb had the Guru arrested near Ropar and kept as prisoner at Bassi Pathana with his companions Bhai Mati Das, Bhai Sati Das and Bhai Dayala for nearly four months. He was then brought to Delhi and on his refusal to accept Islam was executed in 1675 AD at a place where now stands the famous Gurdwara Sis Ganj. Bhai Jaita a devout Sikh took the head to Anandpur. Lakhi Shah, a Lubana Sikh, helped by his son carried the headless body in their cart to their home and cremated it by setting fire to their house. At that place in Delhi now stands the famous Gurdwara Rakab Ganj at a stone's throw from the Rashtrapati Bhawan and the Parliament House. The martyrdom was no small happening. It was something of immense magnitude and of immense consequence. A most sensitive and comprehensive genius of the age had undertaken to answer the time with all his moral strength.

Guru Tegh Bahadur was a prolific writer. 115 of his hymns are included in the Adi Granth.

TEJ BHAN, BABA : Baba Tej Bhan or Tejo in short was the father of Guru Amardas. He belonged to a Bhalla Khatri family of village Baserke in Amritsar district. Bibi Amro, daughter of Guru Angad was married to one of his grandsons.

TEJ SINGH : After the death of Maharaja Ranjit Singh in 1839 AD, the Sikh empire quickly disintegrated largely because of the palace conspiracies and the role played by Dogra-Brahmins occupying high positions in the court. One of these Dogra-Brahmins was Tej Singh son of Nidhe Misr who had risen to the post of the Commander-in-Chief of the Sikh forces. The first Anglo-Sikh War in 1845-46 AD was lost among other things because Tej Singh deliberately directed the Sikh forces to advance towards those targets where they could easily fall into the enemy's trap. According to J.D. Cunningham, he was in league with the British. Tej Singh died in 1862 AD.

THAMM SAHIB : *Thamm* is a Punjabi term for a column. So Thamm Sahib is a column which has become a shrine because of its association with a Guru. Some of the important Thamm Sahibs are :

  1. Thamm Sahib, Dumeli : See Dumeli.

  2. Thamm Sahib, Goindwal : It is a part of Haveli Sahib in Goindwal, the residential quarters of Guru Amardas. It is a wooden column near the place used by Bibi Bhani as a kitchen (chulha). According to the Sikh tradition, Guru Arjan, as an infant, learnt to stand up with the support of this *thamm*.

  3. Thamm Sahib, Kartarpur (Jalandhar) : This is an imposing shrine. Originally it was constructed as a congregation hall by Guru Arjan using a larger wooden column of *Tahli* (i.e. *Sheesham*) in place of a concrete or brick column at the centre. So the place came to be known as Thamm Sahib.

  4. Thamm Sahib, Khemkaran : See Khemkaran

  5. Thamm Sahib, Udoke : Situated in village Udoke in Amritsar district, it is dedicated to Guru Nanak. During his travels the Guru spent nine days here at the residence of a disciple. During his stay, the Guru used to sit against a wooden *thamm*. Hence the name.

THANESAR : See Kurukshetra.

THARA SAHIB : *Thara* is a Punjabi word for

a platform. Some platforms sanctified by the Sikh Gurus have been converted into gurdwaras. Important ones are :

1. Thara Sahib, Amritsar : It is a gurdwara close to the Golden Temple built to commemorate the visit of Guru Tegh Bahadur to Amritsar from Bakala after assuming the office of the Guru. He wanted to pay homage at the Golden Temple but the *Mina Mahant* who had control over it closed the doors of the holy shrine. The Guru sat praying for some time at the place which is now Gurdwara Thara Sahib.

2. Thara Sahib, Anandpur : It is a 5 metre square raised marble platform in the open space in front of Damdama Sahib, Anandpur. It is here that Guru Tegh Bahadur had received a group of Kashmiri Pandits in 1675 AD and had asked them to tell the authorities that they would accept Islam if he were to accept it first. Because of this the Guru was arrested and publicly beheaded in Delhi the same year.

3. Thara Sahib, Dera Baba Nanak : See Darbar Sahib, Dera Baba Nanak.

4. Thara Sahib, Talwandi Sabo : This is situated close to Burj Baba Deep Singh in Talwandi Sabo (Damdama Sahib). It marks the spot where two Ranghreta Sikhs : Bir Singh and Dhir Singh had offered themselves as targets for Guru Gobind Singh to test a muzzle loading gun presented to him by a disciple.

TIBBI SAHIB : *Tibbi* in Punjabi stands for an earthen or sand mound. Some of the mounds associated with the Sikh Gurus have been converted into gurdwaras known as Tibbi Sahibs. Important among them are :

1. Tibbi Sahib, Jaito : This is situated about 4 km from Jaito. Guru Gobind Singh used to hold *Rahiras Diwan* in the evenings at the spot.

2. Tibbi Sahib, Kotkapura : It is situated near village Behbal close to Kotkapura. Guru Gobind Singh had stayed here.

3. Tibbi Sahib, Muktsar : This is situated on the outskirts of Muktsar. During the battle at Muktsar, Guru Gobind Singh had taken position on the mound and had showered arrows on the imperial forces.

4. Tibbi Sahib, Talwandi Sabo : It is an open space close to a pond known as Mahalsar in Talwandi Sabo (Damdama Sahib). Guru Gobind Singh used to train his followers in mock battles here during his stay at Talwandi Sabo.

TILANG : An Indian classical *raag* usually sung in the afternoon. It is fourteenth of the thirty-one *raags* used in the organisation of hymns in the Guru Granth Sahib covering pages 721-727. The sequence of basic notes followed in it is:
   Arohi : *sa, ga, ma, pa, ne, sa*..........
   Avrohi : *sa, ne, pa, ma, ga, sa*..........

TILOKHARI : Tilokhari is the old name of the spot in South Delhi which used to be on the bank of the river Yamuna where Guru Harkrishan was cremated in 1664 AD. A beautiful shrine has been built at the spot called Gurdwara Bala Sahib. See also Bala Sahib, Gurdwara.

TIRATHA BHAI : See Kangmai.

TOBACCO : Tabacco is the name given to the leaves of several species of the Nicotiana plant employed for use as a narcotic. It is used in smoking, chewing and snuff taking, but smoking is the most widely prevalent habit of the modern man. The ill effects of smoking are now being widely recognized throughout the world. All the Sikh Gurus were against smoking, but Guru Gobind Singh came out with a draconian injunction to refrain from it at the time of creating the Khalsa brotherhood in 1699 AD. It is now one of the four *kurahits* (prohibitions) in the Sikh *Rahit Maryada*. See also Intoxicants.

TODI : An Indian classical *raag* usually sung within three hours (one *pahar*) before noon. It is twelfth of the thirty-one *raags* used in the organisation of hymns in the Guru Granth Sahib covering pages 711-718. The sequence of basic notes is :
   Arohi : *sa, re, ga, ma, pa, dha, ne, sa*..........
   Avrohi : *sa, ne, dha, pa, ma, ga, re, sa*..........

TOTA SAHIB : See Laha.

TRAVELS OF GURU NANAK : The *Puratan Janamsakhi*, one of the oldest accounts available regarding Guru Nanak mentions five journeys or *Udasis* undertaken by him. The important identified places given in each *Udasi* are as follows :

First Udasi : Sultanpur, Tulamba (Modern Makhdumpur, District Multan), Panipat, Delhi, Varanasi, Nanakmata (District Nainital), Tanda Vanjara (District Rampur), Kamrup (Assam), Asa Desh (Assam) Pakpattan (District Montgomery), Kirian Pathanan (District Gurdaspur), Saidpur (modern Eminabad, Pakistan), Pasrur (Pakistan), Sialkot (Pakistan).

Second Udasi : Dhanasri Valley, Sea and Singladip (Sri Lanka).

Third Udasi : Kashmir, Sumer Parbat and several other Parbats difficult of identification, Achal Vatala etc.

Fourth Udasi : Mecca.

Fifth Udasi : (within Punjab). Goarkhatri (Peshawari).

At the end of these *Udasis*, Guru Nanak settled at Kartarpur (Pakistan) which was founded by him.

TRETA YUG : See Yugas.

TRILOCHAN : Trilochan, a name which literally means three-eyed, that is seer of the present, past and future was a celebrated saint of the Vaish caste. Four of his hymns are included in the Adi Granth. In these he condemns superficial rituals and pretentious renunciation and stresses the holiness of the heart.

There is no unanimity regarding the place of birth of Trilochan. Some historians give this honour to the Barsi village near Sholapur (Maharashtra). Other hold that, though born and brought up in Uttar Pradesh, he spent most of his time in Maharashtra. The fact that two *saloks* of Kabir constitute a dialogue between Namdev and Trilochan shows that these two saints were contemporaries.

TRIPTA, MATA : Mata Tripta was the mother of Guru Nanak and wife of Baba Kalyan Chand (Kalu), a Bedi Khatri of Talwandi, now known as Nankana Sahib in Pakistan. Not much is known about her early life. She died in 1523 AD at Kartarpur (Pakistan) where Guru Nanak had settled down in the last about 20 years of his life. Some chroniclers, however, take Talwandi as the place of her death.

TRUTH : See God in Sikhism.

TUKHARI : An Indian classical *raag* usually sung within about two hours (four *gharis*) after sunrise. It is twenty-second of the thirty-one *raags* used in the organisation of hymns in the Guru Granth Sahib covering pages 1107-1117. The basic notes in *Tukhari* follow the sequence:
sa, re, ga, ga, ma, ma, pa, dha, ne, sa..........

TURBAN : Turban is not just confined to the Sikhs. It is a popular male head gear for diverse communities in all parts of Indo-Pakistan subcontinent. There are references to it in the Adi Granth. For example : "The head that you deck with a turban will be pecked at by crows when it falls" (p. 330) and "How beauteous is your turban and how sweet your tongue". (p. 727).

The Sikhs have, however, institutionalised turban. It has become an identification mark for them. Its purpose is more symbolic than functional. It is laid down in Sikh *Rahit Maryada* that "For a Sikh there is no restriction on dress except that he must wear a *kachha* (drawers) and *dastar* (turban). A Sikh woman may or may not use turban." According to the *Tankha Nama*, Guru Gobind Singh told Bhai Nand Lal that a Sikh should comb his hair twice and wrap his turban properly folded.

The turban as worn by the Sikhs at present grew out of the style used by the princes at the court of Maharaja Ranjit Singh. One can notice distinct styles of turban in various regions. Namdhari turban is always white and flat at the forehead.

U

UBAID KHAN : See Obed Khan.

UCHCH KA PIR : Uchch is a holy place of Muslims near Panjnad, confluence of the rivers Sutlej, Beas, Ravi, Chanab and Jhehlum in Pakistan. *Uchch* in Punjabi means high. Thus Uchch ka Pir has a double meaning : *Pir* belonging to Uchch and high level *Pir*.

After the battle at Chamkaur Guru Gobind Singh reached Machhiwara where Gani Khan and Nabi Khan two Pathan brothers who had earlier worked with the Guru helped him escape under disguise. The Guru put on blue clothes, spread his hair loose on shoulders and assumed the appearance of a Sufi saint. He was also identified by Gani Khan and Nabi Khan to the Muslim forces by the double meaning title of Uchch ka Pir by which the forces took him to be a Muslim saint. The Guru also sat on a cot carried by four persons during the journey from Machhiwara as was the custom of the *Pirs*.

UDAI SINGH : Udai Singh was one of the five sons of a Rajput of Multan area named Mani Ram who had offered all of them to Guru Gobind Singh. They were initiated into the Khalsa on the Baisakhi day of 1699 AD by the Guru himself and were known for their bravery.

Udai Singh once killed a tiger and offered its skin to Guru Gobind Singh. In the battle at Anandpur in 1703 AD he killed Raja Kesari Chand and brought his head on a spear to the Guru. He accompanied the Guru when he evacuated Anandpur in December 1705 AD and died fighting in the battle at Chamkaur.

UDASI SECT : *Udasi* sect is an order of *sadhus* which was founded by the elder son of Guru Nanak, Baba Sri Chand. They generally wear a red *chola* with a black scarf (*seli*) and a tall cap and carry a *toomba* (a stringed instrument) in their hands. *Udasis* consider themselves the followers of Guru Nanak. Guru Angad had, however, declared them non-Sikhs. They again tried to join Sikhism but Guru Amardas emphatically declared that there was no room for *Udasis* in Sikhism and this prevented disintegration of the religion. Baba Sri Chand had called on Guru Ramdas at Amritsar and was impressed by his humility. Guru Hargobind brought *Udasis* closer to Sikhism by visiting Baba Sri Chand at Kartarpur (Pakistan). According to the chroniclers Baba Gurditta, son of Guru Hargobind, became the first disciple of Baba Sri Chand from among the close relations of the Sikh Gurus. After this, Guru Hargobind sent the *Udasis* into the hills to spread Sikhism. They also offered their services to Guru Gobind Singh and were permitted to take part in the battle at Bhangani in 1688 AD.

In the post Guru Gobind Singh period, when Sikhs were being persecuted they became custodians of gurdwaras and could preserve Sikhism as its zealous preachers since they were spared of persecution as they did not wear the symbols of Sikhs. "It may be said to their credit that in the darkest days of Sikh history....... these selfless monks kept the torch of Sikhism burning."

UDASIS OF GURU NANAK : See Travels of Guru Nanak.

UDEKE : See Kotha Sahib.

UGAUNI : Ugauni is a village near Rajpura. It has two shrines in the same enclosure—one dedicated to Guru Tegh Bahadur and the other to Guru Gobind Singh. Maharaja Karam Singh of Patiala had got them constructed.

UNA : See Damdama Sahib.

USMAN KHAN : Usman Khan was the Darogha of Sadhaura in the beginning of the eighteenth century. Pir Budhu Shah, a Muslim saint of Sadhaura had helped Guru Gobind Singh against the hill *rajas* at the cost of personal sacrifices. In 1705 AD, on the Guru's escape from Chamkaur every attempt was made by Wazir Khan, the governor of Sirhind to capture him alive or dead. Having failed in his attempts, the governor's wrath fell on Buddhu Shah. Accordingly he ordered Usman Khan to destroy the Pir and his family which he did in cold blood on March 21, 1706 AD.

VADALI : See Wadali.

VADBHAG SINGH : Vadbhag Singh was a descendant of Baba Dhirmal and chief of the Sodhi clan at Kartarpur (Jalandhar). He avenged the burning of the Thambh Sahib at Kartarpur by Nasir Ali, the Faujdar of Jalandhar, in 1757 AD by digging out his grave and burning his remains. Vadbhag Singh died in 1762 AD.

VALLA : Valla or Valla Sahib is a village near Amritsar. It has a gurdwara dedicated to Guru Tegh Bahadur. When the Guru came from Baba Bakala to Amritsar to visit the Golden Temple he was not allowed to enter it by the *masands*. The Guru saw the Golden Temple from a distance and went to Valla where he camped under a *pipal* tree, where a shrine exists now. It has another gurdwara called Kotha Sahib which commemorates the visit by the Guru to the house of Mai Harian. It was here that ladies from Amritsar pleaded with the Guru to forgive the *masands* which he did.

VAND CHHAKNA : *Vand Chhakna* which means the sharing of one's honest labour with others in an ethical value complementary to *kirat karni*. According to the Sikh tradition, Guru Nanak had laid down the commandments for an ideal Sikh as : *Nam Japo* (Practise Name), *Kirat Karo* (Earn your livelihood through honest labour) and *Vand Chhako* (share your possessions in the spirit of love and service). In practical terms, Sikhism has suggested *Daswandh* as a means of sharing one's labours. See Daswandh.

VAR : *Var* is a Punjabi term for a ballad. It is very commonly used in the Adi Granth and takes the form of hymn in praise of the spiritual exploits of God. The most famous is *Asa di Var* on pages 462-75 of the Adi Granth. It is sung daily in major gurdwaras early in the morning. See under *Asa di Var*.

Var has also been extensively used in the Dasam Granth. The first part of the *ardaas* is an extract from *Var Sri Bhagauti Ji Ki* in it.

Bhai Gurdas composed 39 *Vars*. They constitute the most authentic source material about Guru Nanak. See Vars of Bhai Gurdas.

VARANASI : Varanasi is an old holy city of Hindus. It is situated in Uttar Pradesh on the left bank of the river Ganges. In religious writings it is referred to as Kashi. It was visited by Guru Nanak during his travels. Gurdwara Guru ka Bagh marks the site where the Guru had halted and had given a sermon to Gopal Panda. Guru Tegh Bahadur had spent over seven months at Varanasi in 1665 AD. The site where he lived in seclusion is now Gurdwara Waddi Sangat. Guru Gobind Singh also came here on his way to Anandpur from Patna in his childhood. The gurdwara was constructed by Maharaja Narinder Singh of Patiala.

VARS OF BHAI GURDAS : Bhai Gurdas was a nephew of the third Guru, Amardas. He wrote the Adi Granth at the dictation of Guru Arjan. He also composed thirty-nine *Vars* or ballads and 556 *Kavits* or couplets. In *var* 1, stanzas 23-45 and *var* 11 stanzas 13-14, he gives a short account of Guru Nanak. Bhai Gurdas dealt with only the religious aspect of Guru Nanak's life. He collected information about Guru Nanak from his contemporaries, then living one of them was Baba Buddha. These *Vars* were written during the first two decades of the seventeenth century. As such they are as good as an original source. They can safely be called as a sort of *Janam Sakhi*.

VEGETARIANISM : See Meat.

VEIL : Sikhism has expressed its disapproval

for the practice among women to veil their faces, as it is thought to be inconsistent with the egalitarian spirit of the religion. Kabir while advising his daughter-in-law says: "Stay, stay my daughter-in-law, veil not thy face; at the last moment it will not avail thee the eighth of a paisa."

Rahu rahu ri bahuriya, ghunghat jin kadhe,
Ant ki bar lahaigi na aadhe (AG. p. 484)

According to the Sikh tradition, when the queen of King Sur Sen who was a disciple of Bhagat Pipa came to remonstrate against separation from her husband, Pipa had told her that it was unnecessary for women to veil themselves in the presence of holy men. According to Macauliffe this was "probably the first effort in modern times in India to abolish the tyranny of *purdah*." *Rahit Maryada* now lays down. "It is contrary to Sikh belief for women to veil their faces." As a result of these stipulations the use of *purdah* among Sikh women even in rural areas has been progressively on the decline. But *purdah* is different from covering the head as a part of modesty in general and as a mark of respect when in the presence of elders in particular.

VERKA : See Nanaksar.

VIAH SAHIB, GURDWARA : This is a shrine in Batala about 40 km from Amritsar where the wedding of Guru Nanak was solemnized. It is situated close to Kandh Sahib where the Guru had sat to convince the priest about the simplicity of rites.

VICES : According to Sikhism, the five chief vices are : *Kam* (Lust), *Krodh* (Wrath), *Lobh* (Greed), *Moh* (Attachement) and *Ahankar* (Pride). These propensities are considered evil not only because of their consequences of indiscrimination and praxis leading to socially undesirable results but they are criticised also because they stand in the way of concentration by the self on the supreme value of the union with the Spiritual Absolute. See respective entries.

VICHITAR NATAK : See Bichitar Natak.

VICHITAR SINGH : Vichitar Singh was one of the sons of a Rajput named Mani Ram and brother of Udai Singh. See also Udai Singh. In 1701 AD the hill *rajas* besieged Anandpur and let a drugged elephant to break open the gate of Lohgarh fort. According to the Sikh tradition it was Vichitar Singh who fighting for the Guru attacked the elephant with a lance and wounded it very badly. The elephant retreated and caused considerable loss to the enemy forces. It is said that Vichitar Singh used to change many dresses in a day. Guru Gobind Singh, therefore, used to address him as *'Bahroopia'*.

VIKRAMI SAMVAT : See Bikrami Samvat.

VIOLENCE : Sikhism's thesis on violence consists of two parts : one, non-violence or *ahimsa* as a natural corollary to its metaphysical doctrine of the unicity of God and two, a practical philosophy of violence as propounded by Guru Gobind Singh.

In purely metaphysical terms, *ahimsa* (non-violence) as not-killing, not-harming and not-injuring comes out naturally from the Sikh doctrine of the unicity of God. According to Sikhism, all created beings in this phenomenal world are God's manifestation and therefore intrinsically one with Him. This idea of the inherent unity of beings with the Supreme Being debars man from using violence (*himsa*) against another being because that would amount to hurting the Divine. But Sikhism does not allow this interpretation to go as far as offering the other cheek when the first is hit.

Guru Gobind Singh enunciated a practical philosophy of violence. At the time of creating the Khalsa Brotherhood in 1699 AD, he made it compulsory for every Sikh to wear *kirpan* (sword) as a part of the five *kakaars*. The symbol of *kirpan* may give an impression to the uninformed mind that arms bearing and soldiering became the essence of Sikhism. This is far from truth. *Kirpan* was introduced as a symbol of intelligent, aggressive and useful citizenship of the world as opposed to slavish, conformist and self-centred social existence. It rejected uninterrupted peace as a natural state of human existence and therefore did not conceive of *ahimsa* as a way of life without questioning its metaphysical aspect. It must be made clear that Sikhism does not advocate violence as a tool for solving problems. The basic stand of Sikhism on violence was stated by Guru Gobind Singh in his *Zafarnama* (A letter to Aurangzeb) : "When all peaceful means have been tried and do not succeed, it is then lawful to make use of the sword." A sense of preparedness any time to face a difficult situation has become the ethos of the Sikh community. "Those who would loosen their grip on the hilt of the sword may have to receive the sharp edge of the sword on their own soft boneless necks." (DG, p. 1247).

VIRAI, MATA : See Bhirai, Mata.

VIRTUES : To combat and overcome the vices, Sikhism had recommended a number of virtues which a person must acquire. The destruction of vices and the cultivation of virtues are essential for endearing the self to God. No minimum or maximum number for virtues has been laid down. However in the religious literature of Sikhism, we find a mention about quite a few of them like : truthful living, *kirat karni, vand chhakna, seva,* humility, contentment and equipoise. For details, see respective entries.

W

WADA GHAR : Wada Ghar is a village in the Malwa region. It has a gurdwara dedicated to Guru Hargobind. The Guru had come here from Daroli and spent five days in the village.

WADALI : Wadali or Wadali Sahib is an old village near Amritsar. Guru Hargobind was born here in 1595 AD. His father Guru Arjan had a long association with this village. Accordingly it has a number of historical shrines. Chheharta Sahib is a large well which can take six Persian Wheels for drawing water that was constructed by Guru Arjan. Now a township has grown around it. Manji Sahib marks the spot where the Guru used to rest, off and on, while supervising the crops grown there for the *langar* at Amritsar. Janam Asthan is the place where his son Guru Hargobind was born. Damdama Sahib is the shrine at the spot where Guru Hargobind had rested after pig hunting.

WADHANS : An Indian classical *raag* sung at noon and late night. It is the eighth *raag* from the beginning out of thirty-one *raags* used in the organisation of hymns in the Guru Granth Sahib covering pages 557-594.

WAHEGURU : *Waheguru* which may be translated as the Wonderous Teacher is the term used for God in Sikh devotion. Scholars have tried to explain a complex etymology of the term which is not being discussed here.

The word *Waheguru* does not occur in the compositions of Guru Nanak but is found in the *Janam Sakhis* being used in *Nam Simran* as it is still. The word occurs in the Guru Granth Sahib in the compositions of *bhatts* on pages 1402 and 1404. "Our praise worthy *Waheguru, Waheguru, Waheguru* you are eternally just and true, the abode of excellence, the Primal Person."

Sat saach sri niwas ad purakh sada tuhi Waheguru, Waheguru, Waheguru, Wah Jio (AG. p. 1402)

"O Wonderous Lord, all the world is Your play and Your creation."
Kia khel bud mail tamasa, Waheguru teri sabh rachna (AG. p. 1404)

WAHEGURU JI KI FATEH : *Waheguru ji ka Khalsa : Waheguru ji ki Fateh* which means : "The Khalsa is of the Wonderous Lord; and His is the Victory" is the Sikh salutation introduced by Guru Gobind Singh at the time of setting up the Khalsa order in 1699 AD. Bhai Mani Singh had explained the Guru's instructions in the matter as :

"A person who greets the Sikhs by saying *Waheguru ji ka Khalsa*.......... while facing them will have my face towards him; one who does so loudly from the back will have my right shoulder towards him; one who only whispers it from the back will have my left shoulder towards him and one who does not greet the Sikhs at all will have my back towards him." (*Bhagat Ratnawali*) See also Salutation.

WAJIB-ALARAZ : *Wajib-Alaraz* is an extract from Bhai Mani Singh's *Bhagat Ratnawali* in which Guru Gobind Singh gives replies to ten important questions raised by *Sahajdhari* Sikhs after the setting up of the Khalsa order. According to some scholars, as for example Bhai Kahn Singh, this does not seem to be the writing of Bhai Mani Singh, nor did Guru Gobind Singh give instructions as claimed in *Wajib-Alaraz*.

WALLA : See Valla.

WEDDING : See Marriage.

WAZIR KHAN : Wazir Khan who belonged to Kunjpura (Karnal) is notorious for his atrocities against the Sikhs as governor of Sirhind. He assumed command of the forces against Guru Gobind Singh in 1700 AD and was finally able to besiege the Guru at

Anandpur in 1705 AD. He had plans to capture the Guru dead or alive and send him to Emperor Aurangzeb to win his pleasure and goodwill. To that end he even began negotiations with the Guru promising safe evacuation. The Guru did not accept capitulation but reluctantly evacuated Anandpur in December 1705 AD but was chased by Wazir Khan. Two elder sons of the Guru died fighting in the battle at Chamkaur. Mata Gujri and two younger sons were captured by Wazir Khan because of betrayal by Gangu. The younger sons were bricked alive by him at Sirhind in 1705 AD and Mata Gujri died of shock on hearing the news. Banda Singh Bahadur avenged these atrocities by capturing Sirhind and killing Wazir Khan in 1710 AD.

WIDOW REMARRIAGE : As a practical aspect of social justice, Sikhism took a number of steps to ameliorate the lot of women—one among them being permission for widow remarriage which is not allowed in Hinduism.

WINE : See Intoxicants.

WOMEN, STATUS OF : One of the most notable social improvements introduced by Sikhism is the emancipation of women. Guru Nanak asserts : "From the woman is our birth; in the woman's womb are we shaped. To the woman are we engaged: to the woman are we wedded. The woman is our friend and from woman is the family. If one woman dies, we seek another; by woman's help is man kept in restraint. Why call woman evil who gives birth to kings? From the woman is the woman, without the woman there is none". (AG. p. 473). This shows unequivocally the high esteem in which a woman is required to be held in Sikhism. It also took practical steps for the socio-religious equality of man and woman. In the various moral codes of the Sikhs a large number of injunctions deal with the rejection of female infanticide, *Sati* (immolation of the widow with the deceased husband) and *purdah* (wearing of veils by women). The Sikhs also permitted widow remarriage whereby the widow could be rehabilitated, if she so desired. See also Sati and Veil.

WRATH : Wrath (*Krodh*) is treated as one of the five chief vices according to Sikhism. It is not only biologically hurting but is socially destructive, destroys brutally as it does so many social relations which become difficult to redeem. Paralyzing reason and reasonableness, it follows its own dialectic of destruction. Guru Arjan clarifies in the Adi Granth : "O *Krodh*, O father of strife, you know no compassion. You have powerful sway over vicious men who dance to your tunes as does the monkey and then have to face punishment at the hands of couriers of death in whose company human beings turn into devils". (AG. p. 1538). It is clear, therefore, that Sikhism does not consider *krodh* as a mere situation—inspired and that too subjectively—inspired. It is taken as a complex motive from which arise actions causing social conflict and strife.

Y

YAHYA KHAN : Yahya Khan was the son of Zakriya Khan and became the governor of Punjab after his father's death on July 1, 1745 AD. He continued the persecution of Sikhs who were reorganizing themselves under Nawab Kapur Singh, Jassa Singh Ahluwalia, Hari Singh Bhangi, Naudh Singh and others. In one of the skirmishes between the Khalsa and the state constabulary, Jaspat Rai, *faujdar* of Eminabad and brother of Lakhpat Rai, one of the ministers of Yahya Khan was killed. On this Lakhpat Rai vowed to finish the Khalsa. He rounded up all the Sikhs living in Lahore and beheaded them at Shahid Ganj. He collected all the known copies of the Guru Granth Sahib and burnt them. He along with Yahya Khan marched towards the north of Lahore to the banks of the River Ravi where there was a large concentration of Sikh families. The Sikhs retreated further northwards and some 7000 of them who could not escape to the mountains of Mandi and Kulu were ambushed near the marshes of Kanuwan and mercilessly killed by Yahya Khan's forces helped by the forces of hill *rajas* on June 1, 1746 AD. This was the first large scale massacre of Sikhs and is referred to as *Chhota Ghalughara* (small holocaust).

Shah Nawaz, the brother of Yahya Khan revolted against him and put him in prison in 1747 AD after capturing Lahore. Yahya Khan escaped from prison and went to his father-in-law at Delhi.

YOGA : *Yoga* is a Hindu discipline which teaches a technique for freeing the mind from attachment to the senses, so that once freed the soul may become fused with the universal spirit, which is its natural goal. It is very old and when the sage Patanjali (C. 300 B.C.) composed the famous book containing instructions the *Yoga Sutras*, he probably compiled many ancient traditions. Depending on slight variations in the technique we have different kinds of Yogas : *Jnana yoga*, *Bhakti yoga*, *Karam yoga* and *Raja yoga*. *Raja yoga* is perhaps the most important and has been explained by Patanjali in his book. It consists of eight disciplines : (1) *Yama* which involves the extinction of desire and egotism and their replacement by charity and unselfishness; (2) *Niyama*, during which certain rules of conduct must be adopted such as cleanliness, the pursuit of devotional studies and the carrying out of rituals of purification; (3) *Asana* or the attainment of correct posture and the reduction to a minimum of all bodily movement; (4) *Pranayama*, the right control of the life-force or breath in which there are two stages at which the practitioner hopes to arrive, the first being complete absorption in the act of breathing which implies the mind of any other thought, the second being the ability almost to cease to breathe which allegedly enables him to achieve marvellous feats of endurance; (5) *Pratyahara* or abstraction which means the mind's complete withdrawal from the world of sense; (6) *Dharama* in which an attempt is made to think of one thing only which finally becomes a repitition of the sacred syllable OM; (7) *Dhyana*, meditation which finally leads to (8) *Samadhi*, the trance state which is a sign of the complete unity of soul with reality.

During the times of Guru Nanak, the *Nath* cult was prevalent in North India. The *Naths* practised a special type of *yoga* called *Hatha-yoga* which demands an austere bodily discipline. Its literal meaning is the *yoga* of force because of the physically demanding nature of the processes and postures used in realizing it. It is a form of *tantric yoga* the origins of which may lie in Mahayan Buddhism. Guru Nanak and other Gurus have made many references to *Yogis* and *Naths* in their compositions. They have disapproved the practice of *yoga* and *hatha yoga*. "Should one die of practising *hatha* (yoga), it would be of no account to the Lord."

Hatha kar mare, na lekhe pawe (AG. p. 226)

According to Sikhism: "Lord's Name is the true joy and true *yoga*."

Har ka Nam jan kau bhog jog (AG. p. 265)

Rejecting the rigorous drill of *yoga*, Sikhism's concept of a *yogi* is very simple. "The *yogi* is one who thinks of the way to slay the Five Demons and to enshrine the Truth within."

Aisa jogi jugat bichare, panch mar sach urdhare (AG. p. 223)

"The *yogi* is one who serves the True Guru."

Satgur saiwe so yogi ho-ai (Ibid). "One united to the Lord for ever is a Yogi."

Baba jugta jee-o jug-h-jug yogi (AG. p. 360)

He alone is a *yogi* who knows the way and by the Guru's grace knows Him, the One alone."

So yogi jo jugat pachhanai, Gurparsadi eko janai (AG. p. 662)

Sikhism's view on *yoga* can best be summarized : "One attains the true state of *yoga* if one remains detached in the midst of attachments".

Anjan mah niranjan rahi-ai, jog jugat iw payee-ai (AG. p. 730)

YUG/YUGA : *Yugas* or the ages of the world is a Hindu mythological concept related to the *avtar* theory. The *yugas* are four in number. In the first *yuga* called *kritya* (or *satya*) whose duration is computed to be 4800 years of gods (each year of gods being equal to 360 years of men) there is perfect and eternal righteousness and *dharma* represented by a majestic bull who is said to be standing firm on its four legs. In the next three *yugas* viz *treta*, *dvapara* and *kali* consisting respectively of 3600, 2400 and 1200 years of gods, *dharma* loses its one leg in each *yuga* or in other words gradually decreases by one-fourth, remaining to the extent of only one-fourth in the *kaliyuga*. These four *yugas* together make a *mahayuga* and 2000 each such *mahayugas* make a *kalpa*. This concept occurs prominently in the *Puranas*.

Sikhism does not accept the mythological background of the concept of *yugas* but finds the vocabulary connected with it useful in communicating its own theological concepts. "In *Satyug* Truth reigned supreme; in *Treta* charity and in *Dvapara*, worship in piety. In the three *yugas*, men held fast to these acts; but in the *Kalyug* one's only mainstay is the Name".

Satyug sat treta jagi dwapari pooja chaar,
Teeno yug teeno dire kali kewal nam adhaar.
(AG. p. 346)

Guru Nanak has used concept of *Yugas* to convey the philosophy of Sikhism in a manner which is unsurpassable in the following words: "Nanak : for the valued bead of the self is provided a chariot and a charioteer. As the wise know they go on changing age after age. In *Satyug* contentment is the chariot and religion the charioteer. In *Tretayug* continence is the chariot and power the charioteer. In *Dvaparayuga*, austerity is the chariot and charity the charioteer. In *Kalyug*, passion is the chariot and falsehood the charioteer." (AG. p. 470)

According to Manu, the rulers are the main cause of *Yugas*. This is stated in the Mahabharata as well.

Z

ZAFARNAMA : The *Zafarnama* is one of the important compositions of Guru Gobind Singh included in the Dasam Granth. It is a letter in Persian addressed to Emperor Aurangzeb. After a short description about the qualities of God, the Guru tells the Emperor that he went back on his solemn promise and deceived him. It is in the *Zafarnama* that the Guru lays down the criteria for the use of force. "...When all peaceful means have been tried and do not succeed, it becomes lawful to make use of the sword."

The *Zafarnama* was composed by the Guru during his stay at Dina after his escape in the battle at Chamkaur. According to the Sikh tradition the Guru had retired for a day to a grove around a pool of water in the neighbouring village of Dialpur Bhai ka where he composed the letter. A gurdwara Zafarnama Sahib commemorates the event. The letter was sent from Dina through his emissary Bhai Daya Singh accompanied by Bhai Dharam Singh to Ahmadnagar where Aurangzeb was then camping.

ZAFARNAMA SAHIB : See Dialpur Bhai ka.

ZAIN KHAN : Zain Khan was appointed governor of Sirhind by Ahmad Shah Abdali in 1761 AD. Khalsa Dal with the chiefs of Phulkian states led an expedition against him and killed him in a battle at Pirjain about 10 km from Sirhind in 1763 AD. After this victory, major portion of Sirhind became a part of Patiala state with some villages going over to Nabha and Jind states.

ZAKRIYA KHAN : Zakriya Khan was the son of Abdus Samad Khan who as governor of Lahore had besieged and captured Banda Singh Bahadur in 1715 AD. When Abdus Samad Khan was transferred to Multan in 1726 AD, Zakriya Khan took over from him as governor. In fact, the son proved more cruel to the Sikhs than his father. He not only revived repressive measures but also insisted on their ruthless implementation to annihilate the Sikhs. He announced a reward for every head of a Sikh. As a result, the Sikhs suffered inhuman persecution during his reign. Nevethelss they became well organized under the leadership of Nawab Kapur Singh to face and fight this repression.

In 1733 AD, Zakriya Khan thought of a machiavellian plan to reconcile with the Sikhs by offering a *jagir* for the Panth and the title of Nawab for Kapur Singh. In 1735 AD he withdrew the *jagir* and became more ruthless than before. In 1738 AD, he got Bhai Mani Singh who was then the High Priest of the Golden Temple arrested and brutally killed on a flimsy excuse.

When Nadir Shah invaded India in 1739 AD, he allowed him to proceed towards Delhi on the advice of some Mughal noblemen. After Nadir Shah left India leaving Delhi completely plundered and ravaged, Zakriya Khan continued his repression of Sikhs with redoubled zeal, perhaps on Nadir Shah's advice. With his approval, Massa Ranghar, the *kotwal* of Amritsar occupied the Golden Temple and even converted it into a dancing hall. This was avenged by Mahtab Singh and Sukha Singh who came in disguise from Bikaner and killed Massa Ranghar in the Golden Temple in 1740 AD.

Zakriya Khan died in 1745 AD when his son Yahya Khan took over as the governor of Lahore.

ZORAWAR SINGH, SAHIBZADA : *Sahibzada* Zorawar Singh was the third son of Guru Gobind Singh. He was born to Mata Jito in 1696 AD. He was arrested along with *Sahibzada* Fateh Singh and Mata Gujri by Wazir Khan, governor of Sirhind. The latter got him bricked alive along with *Sahibzada* Fateh Singh at Fatehgarh in 1705 AD. A historical gurdwara exists at Fatehgarh.